Administering Education in Namibia: the colonial period to the present

Administering Education in Namibia: the colonial period to the present

Cynthia Cohen

Namibia Scientific Society
Windhoek

First published in 1994 by the
Namibia Scientific Society
P.O. Box 67 Windhoek Namibia

© Cynthia Cohen, 1994

Book and Cover design by Linda Rademeyer
Typeset by Mixed Media, Observatory, Cape Town
Printed by Creda Press, Cape Town

ISBN: 99916 702 1 1

To the memory of my grandfather, Sam Cohen,
and my father, Jacky Cohen,
both of whom always had Namibia at heart.
And also to the memory
of my brother, Stephen Cohen.

CONTENTS

ACKNOWLEDGEMENTS

The completion of this book owes a great deal to the contributions of others, whether by suggestion, technical assistance or words of encouragement.

I am especially grateful to Dr Trevor Coombe who, throughout the course of my research, was an outstanding supervisor and mentor with his enthusiasm, constant guidance, meticulous editing and sensitive and valuable criticism.

Thanks are due to Sandie Vahl who has always been available with her helpful suggestions and assistance and who put me on the trail of a team of superwomen. Josie Egan, a busy mother and career woman, has been a thorough and extremely supportive editor. Jo-Anne Goodwill, despite the rigours of work and demands on the home front, has given generously of her time and expertise. Linda Rademeyer, to whom credit for the cover design is due, has unfailingly given much of her time notwithstanding an immensely busy work schedule. I am indebted to my friends Ruth Coetzee and Alisa Reich for all their comments and, above all, for the many hours spent poring over the manuscript, and to Rhona Amoils for her assistance. Karla Holberg not only taught me the Old German script but also transcribed one of the manuscripts for me.

My appreciation is also extended to the staff of the many libraries I have used. In particular, I would like to thank Francoise du Pouget and Elizabeth Grunow of UNESCO's International Institute for Educational Planning, who always gave me a warm welcome in their library and were ever willing to chase down material. Noah Akiki of the UNESCO Documentation Centre for Education was always most helpful and forthcoming in making documents available to me. Barbara Faulenbach of the Vereinigte Evangelische Mission in Wuppertal, Germany, did much to ease my journey through the archives. The efforts of Rosamund Campbell, librarian at St. Antony's College, Oxford, enabled me to consult many an obscure German manuscript. Strike Mkandla of the former

UNIN was a meticulous communicator and source of information, as were Sarah Hillier and Cynthia Holme of Universities Statistical Record, United Kingdom.

During my studies at Oxford, Richard Moorsom drew my attention to many an important document, while David Simon furnished me with recent sources from Namibia. My appreciation is also extended to the many people I have interviewed in various countries for giving generously of their time and providing invaluable information and insights.

Katrin Köhler and Boris and Joan Friedman have been more than wonderful to me on my trips to Windhoek. Other friends have given support and assistance. I have not listed names individually; the friends know who they are and how much they have done.

Finally, I am deeply appreciative of the encouragement, understanding and assistance given to me by my husband and family, without which this task would have been that much more difficult to complete.

Cynthia Cohen

FOREWORD

This book is about the administration of a national education system from its beginnings until the present. That makes it unusual because few authors in this field have attempted to cover the entire history of an education system. However, two things make this work particularly distinctive. One is the country, Namibia, and the other is the author's method or approach.

Namibia's modern educational development represents in extreme form many of the characteristics of colonial education systems in the countries of white settlement in Africa, with the added twist that the colonial power for most of the century has been South Africa. Colonies of white settlement applied the rule that education for white children was an entitlement and a political necessity, whereas education for black children was a problem that required special handling, including extreme caution, and a theory to justify it. In Namibia's case, the theory was formalised in the fifties in the shape of South Africa's Bantu Education doctrine. In the late colonial period, as the South African administration tried to keep the lid on, crude Bantu Education gave way to the neo-apartheid theories of cultural autonomy, administered by 'second tier' 'own affairs' ethnic departments. The first tier, which controlled policy and resources, was occupied by the colonial administration.

Educational administration in colonial Namibia was therefore strictly segmented. One part dealt with the management of privilege, on an increasingly opulent scale, on behalf of the white minority. The other parts managed scarcity, and thus a system of ethnic grading and rationing, through which the largest of the black communities inevitably received the least provision. Not surprisingly, educational deprivation was one of the earliest grievances levelled against the colonial system and it continued to provide fuel to the liberation fire until independence was won.

It follows that educational administration has a bad name in Namibia and, like many other institutions inherited from the colonial state, it needs to be rehabilitated.

This brings me to the author, Cynthia Cohen, a Namibian who had the foresight to realise that the management of the education system after independence could make or break a democratically elected government's attempts to overhaul and expand educational provision. In her words, 'the success of educational reform is dependent upon effective management as much as on popular consent' (p. 4). Hence this study. It started as a proposal for a doctoral thesis at a time when Namibia's future was still an item on the Cold War agenda. Dr Cohen was convinced that good management would make the difference to Namibia's educational future and she feared that no one was taking this seriously.

The design and method of the study reflect the author's initial training as a historian and her postgraduate work in public administration. The book does not set out to contribute to the theory of educational administration. It is, rather, a record of how modern Namibian education has been organised and administered since its missionary beginnings and by whom. It is also an inventory of the possible stock of candidates for recruitment into educational administration. In part it is a narrative history of Namibian education. In part it is a record, based on a meticulous but, in the end, frustrating investigation of the provision for educational management training both within the country and among Namibians in exile. Finally, anticipating that the reconstruction of educational administration would require not just well-prepared people but a strategy for dealing with the inherited bureaucracy, the author undertook an extended case study of Zimbabwe's experience at the point of transition to democratic rule and in the early years of independence.

This is not just the first book ever on Namibian educational administration. It also makes a contribution to the history of Namibian education and of the liberation struggle (in particular, the somewhat confused role of external assistance programmes in developing Namibian expertise). As a bonus, it offers a valuable comparative perspective on the process of bureaucratic transition which accompanies the shift from minority to majority rule.

Educational administration is not a subject which makes many pulses race. As a field of study it has attracted little of the glamour of its somewhat distant relative, business administration, with its flagship business schools, the world-wide mystique of the MBA degree and its aura of energy, competition, and high stakes.

As a field of practical service, however, the management of an education system like Namibia's, which is being radically restructured and equipped with a democratic vision, should attract the sharpest minds, the most energetic activists, the most determined reformers and the most creative innovators. The challenge has been well put in Namibia's new charter for educational reconstruction:

> Just as education in Namibia is in transition, so are the systems we use to manage and administer them. We must learn how to operate them effectively and efficiently even as we reform them. We will surely find that some patterns that seemed appropriate when the task was to educate an elite are not suitable to education for all and learner-centred instruction. Just as we shall have to re-evaluate and discard some older ideas about teaching and learning, so must we rethink how we manage and administer the education system, both nationally and locally. For both learning and its management the benchmarks are our major goals — *access, equity, quality,* and *democracy.*

As Namibians define their educational vision for the era of one nation and democracy, and construct an educational management system committed to both efficient delivery and reform, their neighbours to the south are setting their hands to the same tasks. The message of Cynthia Cohen's book is as valid for them as it is for her compatriots.

Trevor Coombe
Director, Centre for Education Policy Development
Johannesburg, December 1993

ACRONYMS AND ABBREVIATIONS

AAI	African-American Institute
ACHSR	Advisory Committee for Human Sciences Research
AET	Africa Educational Trust
AG	Administrator-General
AGN	Advieskomitee vir Geesteswetenskaplike Navorsing
ANC	African National Congress
APEID	Asian Programme of Educational Innovation for Development
BA	Bachelor of Arts
BC	British Council
B Ed	Bachelor of Education
BETD	Basic Education Teachers' Diploma
BOLL	Bureau of Literacy and Literature
B Prim Ed	Bachelor of Primary Education
BREDA	Regional Office for Education in Africa (translation from French)
CCN	Council of Churches in Namibia
CDM	Consolidated Diamond Mines
CFTC	Commonnwealth Fund for Technical Co-operation
CIDMAA	Centre d'Information sur le Mozambique et l'Afrique Australe
CIIR	Catholic Institute for International Relations
COST	College for Out of School Training
CPI	Central Personnel Institution
CPST	Centre for Public Service Training
DAAD	German Academic Exchange Service (translation from German)
DHRMD	Directorate of Human Resources Management and Development
DNE	Department of National Education
DSE	German Foundation for International Development (translation from German)

DSRE	Diploma in Special and Remedial Education
DTA	Democratic Turnhalle Alliance
ECP	Education Certificate Primary
ED Prim	Education Diploma Primary
ED Prim (Academy)	Education Diploma Primary (Academy)
ELPN	English Language Programme for Namibians
EMT	Executive Management Team
ESAMI	Eastern and Southern African Management Institute
FINNIDA	Finnish International Development Agency
GSSA	Government Service Staff Association
HED	Higher Education Diploma
HED (Prim)	Higher Education Diploma (Primary)
HED (Sec)	Higher Education Diploma (Secondary)
HED (Tech)	Higher Education Diploma (Technical)
HPEC	Higher Primary Education Certificate
ICJ	International Court of Justice
ICPE	International Centre for Public Enterprises for Developing Countries
IDAFSA	International Defence and Aid Fund for Southern Africa
IIEP	International Institute for Educational Planning
ITTP	Integrated Teacher Training Programme
INSET	In-Service Training
IUEF	International University Exchange Fund
JMB	Joint Matriculation Board
JSTC	Junior Secondary Teachers' Certificate
LPTC	Lower Primary Teachers' Certificate
M Ed	Master of Education
MOEC	Ministry of Education and Culture
MECYS	Ministry of Education, Culture, Youth and Sport
MPC	Multi-Party Conference
M Phil	Master of Philosophy
MPLA	Movimento Popular de Libertacao de Angola

NANSO	Namibian National Students' Organisation
NEU	Namibian Extension Unit
NIED	National Institute for Educational Development
NIEPA	National Institute of Educational Planning and Administration
ODA	Overseas Development Administration
OPC	Ovamboland People's Congress
OPO	Ovamboland People's Organisation
PD	Presidential Directive
PLAN	People's Liberation Army of Namibia
PPTD	Pre-Primary Teachers' Diploma
PSF	Phelps-Stokes Fund
PST	Public Service Training
PTC	Primary Teachers' Certificate
ROSTA	Regional Office for Science and Technology in Africa
RRR	Repatriation Resettlement and Reconstruction
SA	South Africa
SADF	South African Defence Force
SAIRR	South African Institute of Race Relations
SEC	Secondary Education Certificate
SIDA	Swedish International Development Authority
STC	Secondary Teachers' Certificate
Std.	Standard
Sub	Sub-Standard
SWA	South West Africa
SWABC	South West African Broadcasting Corporation
SWANU	South West Africa National Union
SWAPO	South West Africa People's Organisation
TCTP	Technical Co-operation and Training Programme
TEFL	Teaching English as a Foreign Language
TESL	Teaching English as a Second Language
TGNU	Transitional Government of National Unity

TMB	Training and Management Bureau
TUCSIN	The University Centre for Studies in Namibia
UK	United Kingdom
UN	United Nations
UNAM	University of Namibia
UNESCO	United Nations Educational, Scientific and Cultural Organisation
UNETPSA	United Nations Educational and Training Program for Southern Africa
UNHCR	United Nations High Commissioner for Refugees
UNIN	United Nations Institute for Namibia
UNISA	University of South Africa
UNTAG	United Nations Transitional Assistance Group
WUS	World University Service
ZANU	Zimbabwe African National Union
ZAPU	Zimbabwe African People's Union
ZINTEC	Zimbabwe Integrated Teacher Education Course
ZIPAM	Zimbabwe Institute of Public Administration and Management
ZOV	Public Administration Promotion Centre (translation from German)

TABLES

MAPS

NOMENCLATURE

SOUTH WEST AFRICA/NAMIBIA, RHODESIA/ZIMBABWE

In the discussions dealing with the period of colonial rule, we have referred to Namibia throughout as South West Africa or, in Chapter 4, as German South West Africa when dealing with the German period of occupation of 1884–1915. South West Africa was the country's official name until the 1968 United Nations decision to refer to it as Namibia. Discussions of events following that year therefore refer to the country as Namibia. The same rule applies to the use of the name Rhodesia for Zimbabwe's colonial period which terminated in April 1980.

REFERENCES TO ETHNIC GROUPS

Throughout most of the text, use is made of the apartheid terminology of 'black', 'coloured', and 'white' when referring to either Namibia's or Zimbabwe's population groups. This in no way implies personal approval of such terminology. The labelling of groups by the South African regime was done primarily on the basis of colour. In Namibia people so labelled came from at least eleven differentiated ethnic groups. 'Blacks' was the umbrella term for the largest grouping. Bushmen, Damaras, Caprivians, Hereros, Kavangos, Ovambos, and Tswanas all came under this heading. 'Coloureds' originally referred to offspring of white settlers and soldiers and the indigenous peoples. In Namibia, however, the Nama population, presumably due to their fairer colouring, were also categorised under this heading along with the coloureds and Rehoboth Basters (who were a migrant community originating south of the Orange River). Whites were the descendants of Europeans who comprised different linguistic and cultural groups such as Afrikaners, Germans, British, and Portuguese. The term 'African' in Chapter 4 refers to the indigenous peoples of Zimbabwe and Namibia at the time of the European arrival. However, in some contexts in the current period, all peoples born in Africa are called Africans.

Map 1 Namibia and Zimbabwe in Southern Africa

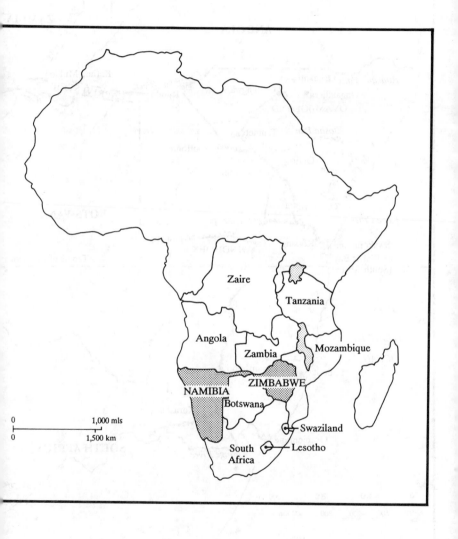

Map 2 Namibia: Major Towns and Transport Links

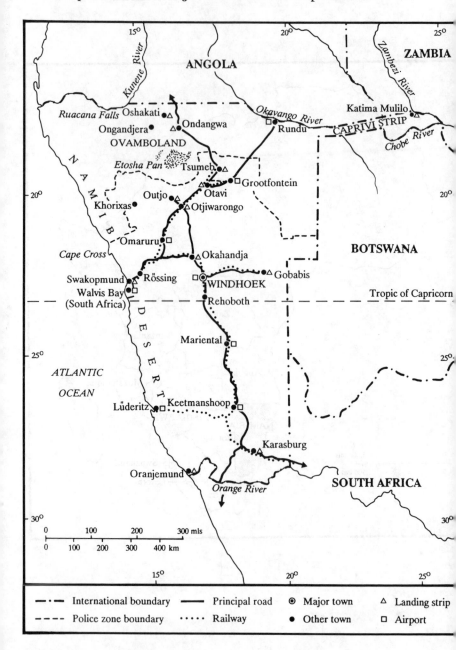

—·—·—	International boundary	——	Principal road	⊙	Major town	△	Landing strip
– – –	Police zone boundary	·····	Railway	●	Other town	▢	Airport

SECTION I

Contextualising the study

1
Introduction

We have for too long been the victims
of foreign domination. For too long we have had
no say in the management of our own
affairs or in deciding our own destinies. Now
times have changed, and today we are
the masters of our own fate.

K. NKRUMAH, 1958

GENERAL BACKGROUND

This book is based on a doctoral study which began in the mid-1980s in Oxford. At that time, although the South African government was in full control of Namibia's administration, there was little doubt that the country's accession to full, internationally sanctioned independence would only be a matter of time. The attainment of Zimbabwe's independence in 1980, the deteriorating political and economic situation in South Africa, the beginning of momentous changes in the Soviet Union and the increased international lobbying for Namibia's nationhood were important straws in the wind. Nevertheless, there was total uncertainty about the length of the interim period and the circumstances in which independence would finally be achieved.

The tendency for education to reflect and even reproduce the conditions prevailing in a society at large were never more evident than in Namibia.[1] The iniquities of the colonial education system and its concomitant effects on the country's supply of skilled human resources meant that, once a representative majority government finally came to power in Namibia, many changes would have to be introduced to redress past imbalances. However, among the practical consider-

3

ations in planning and implementing educational reforms and programmes are:

- □ full understanding of the operation of the colonial structures; and
- □ knowing whether there exists the expertise required to carry out, monitor and evaluate the innovations.

This is essential because the success of educational reform is dependent upon effective management as much as on popular consent. We decided to address the problematic nature of Namibia's fractured educational inheritance to ascertain whether existing administrators (both within Namibia and abroad) were equipped to take up the challenges that accompanied independence.

STATEMENT OF THE PROBLEM

The administrators who ran the Namibian education structure during the period of colonial rule were mostly white, many on secondment from South Africa. Although some among them may have questioned the injustices of the apartheid education system, these administrators were the very people responsible for its smooth operation and they did not obstruct its aims. Very few were trained in educational administration, most having been promoted from among the ranks of the teachers.

All were experienced only in the ethnically determined structures of the apartheid regime. The question was, when a majority-rule government came to power, could they be relied upon from an ideological standpoint and would they be professionally competent to carry out the innovations needed after independence?

There was another dimension to the problem. Very few blacks and coloureds occupied prominent posts within the colonial administrative structures. This was an outcome of the deliberate practice of job discrimination and more precisely because of the smaller relative number of blacks and coloureds who succeeded at school. Hence, if Namibia did experience a sudden white exodus after independence, this would spell the virtual collapse of the administrative structure. It was true that the country would have recourse to a supply of skilled Namibians training and living abroad, but were there sufficient trained and experienced educational administrators to overcome the shortages caused by a large exodus of skilled whites?

It appeared likely that the country would be faced with a severe shortage of trained and experienced educational administrators in the event of a massive white departure. It was also uncertain whether there were sufficient numbers of trained educational administrators among the majority communities either at home or in exile. Even if the anticipated white exodus did not occur, the commitment of the serving administrators appeared extremely doubtful, as did their former training and experience in relation to the task of bringing about the required structural reforms and pedagogical innovations that would surely follow independence.

STUDY OBJECTIVES AND RELEVANCE

Within this context, the work:

☐ documents the historical development of the education system independent Namibia inherited;

☐ analyses the organisational structure and personnel of the educational administrations created under South African rule;

☐ undertakes an audit of the Namibians who underwent training abroad in the educational and administrative fields during the period of resistance to South African rule so as to assess the scope and quality of the pool of educational administrators available to the independent government of Namibia;

☐ examines the problems of transition from colonial to independent government in the education sector by making a comparative study of the Zimbabwean experience; and

☐ assesses the challenge of educational management in independent Namibia and the need for qualified, competent educational administrators in the new system.

There are no studies of educational adminstration in Namibia and it is an undeveloped field of enquiry in African countries generally. Virtually all previous works on education in Namibia examined the differences in education provision between the country's various ethnic groups, thereby highlighting the iniquities of the system of segregated and inequitable educational provision and its disastrous effects on Namibia's skilled human resource supply.[2] None of these focused much attention on the actual structures and personnel involved in controlling and administering the education system beyond brief descriptions in some studies of how the system was administered. The vital role of the educational administrator in educational change has been overlooked. This research aims to fill the gap and in so doing has broken new ground. For the first time there is an attempt to focus on the educational administrative structures and more specifically on the staff employed within them. Moreover, the examination of externally trained potential educational administrators is the first of its kind. All the human resource studies on Namibia, conducted by the South African Department of Labour in the late 1960s and 1970s and by the South West Africa Department of Economic Affairs in the 1980s, as well as UNIN's two studies in 1978 and 1986 respectively, focused predominantly on the country's internal skills' supply. Here we attempt to review both the internal and external skills' supply of a specific sector.

Additionally, the work provides an overview of external support to Namibian education. No similar research has been done on this subject, other than Gerhart's 1983 study for the Ford Foundation. However, it dealt specifically with the various programmes of educational assistance available to Namibian refugees rather than examining the number of Namibians in training and their fields of study.

To complete the overall picture of the country's capacity to provide future educational administrators, this study analyses the quality of Namibia's teaching force (both internal and external) since the teaching force there, as elsewhere, has always been the traditional pool from which administrators have been drawn and will most likely continue to be so for the foreseeable future. Included in this analysis is a review of the education-specific training provision available to Namibians in the country and elsewhere, and the level of emphasis in such training on educational administration. More recent studies since independence have concentrated on teacher training provision within the country. Virtually none have focused attention on training for educational administrators. This lacuna was also strangely evident in the January 1991 joint Government of the Republic of Namibia/Commonwealth Secretariat Conference on the Organisation and Management of Ministries of Education.

METHODOLOGY AND SOURCES

The present study's approach is narrative description. This makes it possible to trace the way in which developments in education mirrored events in the local political arena and to explain why particular tendencies had emerged by the time of political transition in the late 1980s. A brief account is also given of educational development in Zimbabwe within the context of the case study.

The historical and descriptive sections of the book are based on the use of both primary and secondary sources pertaining to Namibia and Zimbabwe. The primary sources include missionary reports, governmental acts and proclamations, commission reports, governmental publications and extensive interview sessions. Most information on Namibia is gleaned from general histories of the country and the more specific works addressed directly to education. The wealth of literature on various aspects of educational administration provided useful insights into the organisational and managerial problems of colonial and post-independence Namibian education systems. Newspapers, predominantly from within Namibia and some from South Africa and the United Kingdom, were especially useful in keeping abreast of developments in education and the public service during the author's periods of absence from Namibia.

First-hand information and comment on Namibian and Zimbabwean educational development, Namibian students abroad, and the management demands of rapid political and educational change came from over 70 lengthy interviews. These were with middle- and top-level staff within the educational and various civil service structures in Namibia; the University of Namibia; the Zimbabwe Ministry of Education and Culture; the University of Zimbabwe; the Institute of Development Studies, Zimbabwe; staff situated in various international and non-governmental aid organisations assisting Namibians (predominantly in Germany and the United Kingdom); and various training institutions both in the United Kingdom and France.

LIMITATIONS OF THE STUDY

There were two major limiting factors in conducting this research, namely, the gathering of statistical data and political change.

THE STATISTICAL DATA

Throughout most of the period of occupation, South Africa did not publish separate statistics on Namibia. Statistics which were released were mainly for external consumption, and their accuracy was questionable because of South Africa's attempts to project a favourable image of her activities in the country. Until the end of the 1970s educational statistics were integrated with those of South Africa, appearing mainly in publications put out by the South African Department of Bantu Education. From 1985 the South West Africa Directorate of Development Co-ordination, which later on became the Department of Economic Affairs, began to publish detailed educational statistics by ethnic group. Complex as these data were, at no point was a breakdown provided of the age structure of the country's population, a feature that is vital to any development planning. Hence the data used in the discussion of the administrative structures are subject to question, since exact statistical information was not forthcoming. Additionally, the political sensitivities surrounding international assistance to the Namibian exiles made the gathering of that data extremely difficult.

POLITICAL CHANGE

Throughout a major part of the research, we were confronted by problems directly related to prevailing political events. The political unpredictability of the late 1980s meant that initially we were bound to write from a hypothetical stance since the sort of changes which would occur at independence in the structure and staffing patterns of educational administration were unknown. Late colonial and early independent Zimbabwe was therefore used as a case study in an attempt to illustrate what might occur in Namibia if it followed policies similar to those adopted in Zimbabwe.

By the late 1980s, however, we found that the situation had undergone a subtle change. During a visit to Namibia in 1988, although the question of independence was still veiled in uncertainty, most people seemed to believe that its arrival was closer than ever before. This belief was accompanied by fear that the whites would lose many of their privileges under a majority black government, as had occurred in most African countries after colonial rule. The conviction that they would soon lose all, and as a result there was no longer anything to protect or conceal, might well have contributed to the loquacity encountered during interviews with most white officials in Namibia.

In 1989, after a succession of favourable political and diplomatic developments, Namibia was suddenly under a United Nations transitional administration with the imminent prospects of full-franchise elections, a new constitution and independence. On 21 March 1990 Namibia became a sovereign republic and a new Ministry of Education was created (now the Ministry of Education and Culture). This sudden onset of independence and acceptance of Namibia into the international community posed yet another challenge to the research. The events about which we had conjectured for so long were taking their own shape. The focal point of the study, which was to have been a future Namibian independence, had now abruptly materialised and itself slipped into the stream of history, albeit very recent history. We had to switch from a predominantly hypothetical perspective to one based on rapidly evolving developments and trends. This meant changing to the role of an observer of real events.

Among the positive aspects of this change was that formerly unresolved questions, like the composition of the public service and the government's policies and orientations, were now clarified. Some things could never have been anticipated prior to independence, for example, the conciliatory tone of the country's constitution, the retention of former white administrators and the new government's encouragement of whites not to quit the country. Information from sources abroad also became more readily available. There was no longer the fear of South African reprisal and therefore the need for secrecy.

A period of rapidly changing political events is, however, difficult to research. Three years into Namibia's independence, moves are afoot to rationalise all ministerial structures following their unprecedented expansion after 1990. This growth was in part related to the application of the constitution's affirmative action principle. With the cutting back, it is not clear how the policy of affirmative action will be applied, nor is it clear whom among the serving staff will have to leave. Policies on training are still very embryonic.

However satisfying it is to be able to reflect on the actual conditions of post-independent Namibia and confirm previous assumptions or predictions, the research is being brought to a conclusion at a moment of change and volatility in the structures of education and public administration. For this reason we have attempted to adjust to the flow of events by taking into account the actual organisation of educational services and their staffing trends in independent Namibia, as these have evolved over the three years of independence up to August 1993, the date when this work closes.

Finally, in view of the onset of Namibia's independence, the study of Zimbabwe now provides a comparison with the pace at which Namibia is introducing changes. More importantly, it affords an insight into the suitability of adopting some of the more successful strategies used in Zimbabwe.

OUTLINE

This book comprises seven sections, each one made up of individual chapters.

Section I contextualises the entire study. Chapter 1 introduces the reader to the overall theme of the research: the examination of Namibia's educational administrator resource potential during its transition to independence and three years thereafter. Chapter 2 focuses on the role of educational administration in the educational reform process, providing the necessary basis for the analysis of the Namibian case study. The historical background appears in Chapter 3 which outlines the political developments from the onset of formal German occupation in 1884 until independence in 1990.

Section II describes the development of formal education in Namibia. Chapter 4 reveals that there was a nascent formation of separate administrative structures for the white and black population groups, as well as differences in educational provision and employment opportunities. Reference is also made to the contrasting educational and employment policies of the German Government in its East African colony during the same period. When South Africa took over Namibia (detailed in Chapter 5), it not only adopted the divided system of educational provision but also exacerbated the segregationist patterns. It did so by greatly weakening the missionary role in educating the indigenous peoples while gradually strengthening its own control over education. By

11

the late 1960s, the pattern of ethnically inequitable education was firmly entrenched. Education was administered directly from South Africa via separate black, coloured and white regional administrative offices in Windhoek.

Section III deals with the changes in educational policies during the 1970s and 1980s which reflected events in the political arena. During the 1970s (discussed in Chapter 6), educational administration began to devolve to some of the newly created 'homelands'. In reality, however, overall control remained firmly entrenched in South Africa's hands. Meanwhile, the effects of the inequitable educational system were beginning to manifest themselves on Namibia's skilled human resource potential. This was seen, for example, in the quality of the black teaching force — teachers being the traditional pool from which educational administrators are drawn. Chapter 7 examines the quality of the teaching force in the late 1980s, as well as the types of training available to them and the supply of teachers.

Section IV, Chapter 8, focuses on the organisational and staffing trends within Namibia's educational administrative structures shortly before independence and the training available to educational administrators. The findings reveal a shortage of trained educational professionals within the country.

Section V concentrates on the pre-independence training of Namibians outside the country in education-related or public administration fields. Chapter 9 covers those programmes offered by SWAPO and the various governmental and non-governmental organisations, while Chapter 10 examines the United Nations initiatives. The external training of Namibians shows a glaring lacuna in the provision of training in educational administration, teacher training having been more prominent.

Section VI reviews the Zimbabwean case study. Chapter 11, in focusing on the pre-independence period, alludes to the differences and similarities between Zimbabwe and Namibia regarding: educational provision for blacks and whites; quality of the teaching force; organisational, staffing and training patterns in the educational structures; and the internal and external skilled human resource supply. The outcome of the analysis reveals why the new government was able to embark upon a policy of rigorous affirmative action in the immediate post-independence period, as discussed in Chapter 12. This chapter also details the changes introduced to the administrative structures and examines the in-service training available to civil servants.

Section VII closes the study with an assessment of the research findings. Chapter 13 describes the changes which have occurred in Namibia in the first three years of independence in terms of staffing, structural changes, and training policies. Developments in educational administration since 1990 have served to substantiate the initial hypotheses, namely, that the few serving administrators are not all professionally equipped to face the challenges brought about by the need for innovations, while the number of trained and experienced professionals among former exiled Nambians is too small to close the skills gap. Suggestions have been made for further action to help overcome the shortage of trained educational administrators, thereby ensuring a greater measure of success in realising much-needed educational reforms.

NOTES

1. Weiler 1978:187.
2. Republic of South Africa 1964; Kennedy McGill 1967; Melber 1977; O'Callaghan 1977; Tjitendero 1977; Lachenmann 1979; Leu 1979; Katzao 1980; UNIN 1981 and 1984; Mbamba 1982; Kazapua 1984; Ellis 1984; Mukendwa 1985 and 1986; Mbuende 1987; Amakugo 1993.

2

Educational administration as a vehicle for educational reform

The educational administrator today
is the key person through whom many of the
education changes can occur.
J.C.S. MUSAAZI, 1982

INTRODUCTION

Namibia, like many other post-independent African countries, is currently engaged in educational reform. Among the most pressing tasks confronting the new government are:

□ the need to expand educational provision;
□ the design of a new curriculum that is more in line with the country's human resource requirements;
□ the restructuring and rationalising of the colonial educational administrative system into a unified common system of administration for all.

Similar attempts at reform in other countries have revealed that education systems were unable to respond effectively to such challenges without appropriately trained personnel. In short, the success of such reform was directly influenced by the competency of educational administrators at all levels of the system, while the lack of skilled administrators was identified as a typical barrier to innovation.[1]

In Africa, until late into this century, it was believed that anyone with a good general education could become an effective administrator. As a result, many officials working

15

within the educational bureaucracies were not trained in administrative and management techniques. These techniques are vital for the efficient functioning of educational bureaucracies faced with introducing major reforms.

Namibia's independence came at a time when there was increasing international attention being given to educational administration as a subject and to the issue of training in this field. In this chapter we discuss educational administration, focusing in particular on Africa, to provide a background for more detailed discussions of the Namibian situation. After defining educational administration, we attempt to explain the growing interest in this subject. We then analyse the important role played by educational administrators in the reform process, as well as examine how training can help to facilitate administrators to rise to the challenge of successful reform implementation.

EDUCATIONAL ADMINISTRATION AS A FIELD OF STUDY

Educational administration has a long past but a short history and its role, which had grassroot beginnings, came long before its conceptualisation as a field of study.[2] It is a relatively new discipline which draws from a wide range of basic disciplines like psychology, sociology, political science, economics and the cross-disciplinary study of organisations.[3] In the early years these borrowings were not well incorporated, adapted or tested in the educational setting. Instead, as one author described the field of educational administration:

> it lacks an organised body of subject matter of its own. It possesses no simple and elegant theoretical structure, it can present no series of well established empirical relations. In addition to the fragments appropriated from other fields of study, the content of the courses in educational administration has consisted of a description of practices, the cautious recommendation of promising techniques, and personal success stories and lively anecdotes, all surrounded with the aura of common sense, and often purveyed

with both lively good humour and appropriate sober-
ness.[4]

The United States was the forerunner in recognising and
sanctioning educational administration as a separate area of
study. Consequently, most major American universities had
established their own departments of educational administration by the middle of this century. By the 1970s interest in
educational administration had spread throughout the world
in universities, colleges of education and government departments of education. Amongst some of the first universities in
Africa to introduce educational administration as a subject
were the universities of Ibadan and Lagos in Nigeria. The
awakening of the educational administration movement in
Africa during the 1970s was a direct consequence of the
various administrative problems within the education systems
of many African countries.

WHAT IS EDUCATIONAL ADMINISTRATION?

Educational administration is essentially an applied field or,
as the following description reveals, an activity. In a broad
sense the term "applies to the full range of administrative
control in education ranging from classroom operation,
school management, administration of educational institutions and programmes in a locality to the control (and formulation) of educational policy of a nation as a whole". [5] The
educational administrator's profile is not defined in terms
related to teaching work. As such, this category of staff comprises all the technical or specialist and management personnel serving in educational administrations.[6] It is obvious that
educational administrators have a primary responsibility for
making educational systems function. Chinapah concluded
that successful educational administration depends more on
the quality of the administrative personnel than on the financial and material resources available to educational systems.[7]
However, the rapid pace of educational expansion and reform in most countries over the last few decades made heavy

demands on educational administrators for which many were
ill-prepared. What were these demands?

THE DEMANDS ON EDUCATIONAL
ADMINISTRATION IN DEVELOPING
COUNTRIES

A world-wide trend in education since the 1950s was the
unprecedented expansion of educational systems, especially
in developing countries. In Africa alone, the student population grew from less than ten million to over 53 million between 1950 and 1975.[8] To accommodate the swelling
enrolment, school systems grew quickly and chaotically into
gigantic organisations. In many countries education became
one of the biggest enterprises, both in respect of the number
of personnel employed and the size of the budgets. A direct
consequence of this expansion was the increased demand it
placed on administration. Large organisations are complex
by virtue of their size. As an organisation grows, the problems
encountered take on a new character and to tackle them
effectively requires more sophisticated technical and managerial methods. Expansion was accompanied by redefining the
aims and objectives of education. This was increasingly seen
as important for the overall economic and social development
and modernisation of a country, especially in supplying
skilled human resources.[9] Curriculum reforms of various
kinds have been undertaken in the hope of relating education
more effectively to economic needs, national language policy
or post-colonial nation building. Structural changes in the
education cycle and system of assessment have been installed.
In many countries there have been attempts to decentralise
educational control or public administration in general. In
brief, educational administration has been expected to
become pro-active in interpreting and implementing educational change and in supervising rapid expansion, with very
mixed results.[10] The skill, experience and level of prepared-
ness of educational administrators to tackle these new tasks
competently are a cause for concern; educational administra-

tion requires high-level administrative specialists in very
diverse fields.

There is a tendency to recruit educational administrators
predominantly from among the more experienced and successful teachers. This has been the time-honoured career
ladder for teachers: from teacher to head of department to
vice principal, principal, inspector or education officer and
so on, upward to the highest ranks of the education service.
No special administrative skill or aptitude was expected of the
promoted teachers other than those demonstrated in their
previous positions. Educational administration was seen as an
extension of teaching, a task requiring intimate 'chalk-face'
knowledge of the schools. The specialist skills of management
were regarded as being acquired essentially through learning
from others and on the job.

Such assumptions are not unreasonable in many administrative tasks, especially those performed close to the schools
and the teachers, and particularly in periods of stability or
consolidation. In an era of continuous change and growth,
however, many educational administrators have been found
wanting, as reports emanating from various conferences and
studies confirm. Already in 1967 at the International Conference on the World Crisis in Education, it was stated that:

> unless educational systems are well equipped with
> appropriately trained modern managers — who in
> turn are well-equipped with good information flows,
> modern tools of analysis, research and evaluation and
> supported by well trained teams of specialists — the
> transition of education from its semihandicraft state
> to a modern condition is not likely to happen. Instead,
> the educational crisis will grow steadily worse.[11]

At the UNESCO conference on major problem areas of
educational reforms in the 1970s and 1980s, the lack of
attention given to "the all-important role of the ... administrative staff" was listed as one of the reasons for the failure of
reform.[12]

Educational administrators as a group, like public servants,
are often considered to be conservative people who tend to

uphold the status quo rather than seeking to introduce change and innovation. However, this could be directly related to the nature of the organisations in which they serve. In stable social systems education usually functions to conserve and reproduce culture and social structure.[13] Schools inherit a pattern of fixed syllabuses, repetitive routines and rote learning. Not surprisingly, "educational institutions of all kinds are relatively conservative institutions and they do not thrive on an atmosphere of constant radical change".[14] El-boim-Dror concludes that "there are few organisations (that) are so much tradition-bound, passive and resisting change as the education system seems to be".[15]

Moreover, the tendency for educational systems to select their administrators mostly from among teachers results in a process of professional inbreeding. It tends to create a closed system of ideas and practices and may hamper creative leadership and innovation.[16] Reforming administrators, who are motivated by a strong sense of dissatisfaction with the status quo and who agitate persistently and pave the way for reforms, often find themselves at loggerheads with the more conservative elements and vested interests. As a result they could be blocked and frustrated by the powers that be.

Educational administrators need to be prepared for specific functions, if they are to overcome some of the shortcomings experienced in the management of formal education systems in developing countries. We will look at these in the next section.

THE ACTIVITIES OF EDUCATIONAL ADMINISTRATORS

As the scope of an organisation grows, so does the number of people whose activities must be carefully co-ordinated, while the variety of techniques employed increases as tasks became more complex and specialised. Consequently, the educational service tends to become more diversified and multi-disciplinary with more specialists from professions outside teaching.[17]

Yet educational administration has been one of the last sectors in public administration affected by the overall move towards modernisation. This is because it has been seen as being different because of its link with teaching, hence the knowledge and experience from other fields have not been applied. Moreover, any training or preparation for educational administration has occurred mostly in teacher training colleges. Here the emphasis has been more on the teaching profession and interests common to educators. Any improvements in administrative efficiency over the last fifty years has, however, been based on recognising how similar certain problems of administration in large organisations are.

WHO ARE THE ADMINISTRATORS?

Administrative personnel can be divided into two main categories: specialists or professionals, and managers. The professional staff, excluding teachers who constitute the largest group of employees in an educational system, are made up of educational specialists in teaching and learning. They include specialists in curriculum, educational materials and technology, assessment, supervision, teacher education, educational research and evaluation, as well as architects, psychologists, statisticians, computer experts, planners, economists, personnel management specialists and so forth.

Some of these professionals need generic skills with a high degree of application in educational needs or the requirements of educational system development and maintenance. Specialists in pedagogy, in particular, have knowledge vital for research, innovation and evaluation. They facilitate the setting of targets and programmes for quality improvement. These include new or revised curricula and methodology, evaluation of educational outcomes, the supply of teaching materials and professional support services to schools, and the preparation and implementation of in-service training programmes for teachers, for example.

Managers, by contrast, do not require a mastery of any one technical speciality. Their skill requirements differ depending on the size of the structure they are managing. For

21

example, in relatively uncomplex organisations or at the lower levels of management, managers must be familiar with the specific techniques of the group they employ. For instance, a principal must be familiar with teaching. The higher up in the hierarchy managers proceed, the more varied the number of professionals over whom they have control. Therefore, at the higher levels, it is essential for them to be familiar with more generalised administrative techniques which are applicable to most administrative situations. Managers must also be skilled in various aspects of management functions. These include being able to "obtain and summarise the appropriate information, formulate precise objectives, design and articulate projects of an interdisciplinary nature, encourage specialists to do their jobs, and prepare and make decisions".[18] Since skills of this sort can be applied right across a range of organisations, the very top levels of management can often be successfully interchanged between organisations.

WHAT SKILLS DO EDUCATIONAL ADMINISTRATORS NEED?

A high level of understanding and skill is necessary for managing the human and financial resources of education systems in order to establish and sustain cost-effective procedures in meeting educational objectives. This calls for sufficient knowledge of resource mobilisation, planning, budgeting, cost analysis, financial control and personnel management, all of which are highly specialised tasks.

There are normally at least two distinct levels of operation within educational systems when it comes to functions such as staffing, planning, organising, directing, co-ordinating, reporting, budgeting and so on. These are: the central level, comprising the ministry or department of education and its network of relationships; the local level, consisting of regional and district units with their respective networks including the educational institutions themselves. A sufficient supply of highly qualified staff is required at both central and regional offices. Without this, the educational systems cannot function efficiently. In a survey of 22 African countries whose education systems were judged to be performing poorly, it was found that in many of the countries "the local-level capacities in educational administration and management were ... the weakest links in the systems".[19] This was often because the best educated and most committed local educational administrators were promoted to central administration.

For educational changes to occur, educational administrators need to be convinced of the necessity for change and they have to be firmly committed to it. Otherwise, they could be obstacles to change. However, they also need the necessary skills to bring it about. These include up-to-date information on contemporary developments in education, both in national and international arenas; good general administrative skills; and a willingness to adapt creatively to changed circumstances. For example, the democratisation of education requires the involvement of parents, the general public, teachers, and pupils in the system's operation and, where appropriate, in formulating policy. This calls for new skills and approaches in the educational administrators' work in order to adjust to such changes. These, in turn, create new relationships, including the capacity to communicate, listen and persuade. Important new functions include the monitoring of reform in education, as well as assessing whether or not a reform programme requires modification, and whether it has achieved its objectives. All these functions highlight the need for adequate and up-to-date professional preparation of educational administrators.

A major World Bank report on education in Sub-Saharan Africa stressed that:

> although appropriate policy changes are necessary to improve education in Sub-Saharan Africa, they alone will not suffice. They must be coupled with measures to strengthen management if the benefits of the policy changes are to be realized.[20]

Management capacity in this region has remained insufficiently developed. As Chinapah's 1989 study of 22 African countries revealed, most countries in the region do not possess sufficient human resources to serve their expanding educational administrations. In fact, a familiar cry in Africa is still for trained personnel, while the lack of competent educational administrators is often said to be the major reason behind mismanagement of scarce resources, which developing countries can ill afford, and the poor performance of these countries' educational systems.

The situation has been compounded by the ineffective deployment of available trained staff — an inevitable consequence of chaotic and outdated personnel policies and practices in ministries of education. These persist largely because staff are insufficiently qualified. The long-term effects of employing under-qualified personnel can severely inhibit the effective deployment of new and possibly more competent professionals. Furthermore, failure to implement new educational policies has been attributed directly to "a general resistance to change from those not properly upgraded to meet the new challenges".[21]

HOW CAN TRAINING HELP IMPROVE EDUCATIONAL ADMINISTRATION?

Developing countries often emphasise higher-level training as a major feature of their development programmes. This is both a response to the need to replace the colonial or foreign expatriates as well as a long-term investment to build up local human resources and staff the various sectors of the national economy. Training educational administrators in developing countries as a means to overcome educational administration problems has been receiving increasing world-wide attention.[22]

According to Ogunniyi, training educational administrators is "the most important single factor in improving the effectiveness of educational systems", but training is frequently neglected in favour of attempts at structural change, often with disappointing results.[23] Yet one should not forget that administrative success in implementing reform is also de-

pendent on structural change; training alone cannot result
in the effective management of education systems.

If attempts are made to improve the performance of individuals without changing the structure of the organisation,
this could result in inefficiency. In Asia, for example, the
administrative machinery was old-fashioned and when large-
scale changes in education occurred, the archaic organisations were unable to cope because the organisational
structures were not flexible enough to meet the demands of
various development programmes. Most African countries'
administrative structures and procedures tend to be over-cen-
tralised and cumbersome. Such traditional methods and
structures do not provide an environment favourable to educational reform. What is needed is an organisational climate
which is both receptive to and supportive of innovative and
organisational skills and that enables the successful administration of reforms.

Miklos recommends that any attempt at improving administrators' performance should begin by looking at the structures within which they will function.[24] But structural changes
have only limited benefit if the personnel working within the
new structures are not equipped to respond to the new
demands and developments. Furthermore, although an administrative system consists both of people and structures, it
is the staff component of the structures which ultimately
determines structural patterns. "Better organization and
methods of work … are essential aids but they depend on the
quality and skills of those who man the organization".[25] The
issues of structural change and staff training are equally
important and should occur simultaneously.

Another important factor is the improvement of recruitment procedures. As Glatter pointed out, "in administration
… there will always be some whose mediocre personal skills
will defy transformation".[26] In most educational systems there
appears to be no clear policy governing the recruitment and
training of administrative personnel and many could benefit
from a comprehensive review of recruitment, selection and
placement policies. Training in educational administration

has frequently been considered a practice to be applied after the assumption of duties. As a result, the importance of appropriate pre-service training has been overlooked. Promotion criteria are also relevant to recruitment. Direct recruitment from outside an organisation rather than promotion from lower grades has often been found to be effective in filling management positions, especially for staff with specialised skills common to all administrative systems. To sum up: training policy must not be separated from revising the recruitment procedures.

HOW HAS TRAINING FAILED TO IMPROVE ADMINISTRATION?

Administrative training is not an unqualified good. Despite the expansion of training for educational administrators from the late 1970s, performance did not improve sufficiently, nor did it live up to expectations of being an agent of change. Chief among the explanations cited for its failure was the uncritical way Western ideas were embraced and the replication of Western models in developing country contexts. As Lungu pointed out, most theorising in administrative sciences was based on the experiences of European and North American organisations with little research in African settings, let alone African education organisations.[27] Majasan, writing in the early 1970s, stated that "although the art of administration is international, Africa has unique problems which require special analysis and unique treatment in order to facilitate her gaining enough confidence to train her own administrators".[28]

Notwithstanding, training programmes were not tailored to meet the needs of the developing countries. Instead, continued use was made of management concepts, theories and related training models from the West in third world contexts, with disappointing outcomes. Rodwell, in her study on training third world educational administrators in the late 1980s, noted that the theoretical content of educational administration courses would most likely remain essentially Western-oriented for the foreseeable future.[29]

The problem with this wholesale importation of programmes is that it makes no allowance for local conditions, perceptions and values. Nor is cognisance taken of each country's specific training needs and the techniques and skill levels applicable to the abilities of trainees. As a result, the imported programme might stress certain performance criteria and practices which are totally irrelevant to the context in which it is to be applied.

What then has happened with trained administrators in the past? After completing their training, candidates often experienced difficulties in applying their newly acquired skills and techniques once they returned to the work environment. Such candidates were often young with high expectations of being able to make rapid improvements to the existing system. Previously they may not have held very senior posts and therefore experienced difficulties in persuading their seniors to change methods that had been in use for years. The problem of older officials refusing to recognise or accept them was another drawback. Trainees also found it difficult to adapt the training they had received abroad to local conditions where rigid bureaucratic structures were not conducive to creativity and innovation. Also their training was not always appropriate to local conditions. Another problem for the returnees was that many were immediately moved or promoted to new administrative posts in the educational structure where their newly acquired skills may not have been of any use.

Another explanation for the failure of training is that the political and bureaucratic elites did not want the administrations to improve. Reilly discusses the existence of an elite skilled in managing the bureaucratic system to meet their own interests and to preserve the *status quo*.[30] This proposition refutes the external experts' interpretation of administrative inefficiency as being linked to 'poor management', claiming instead that absence of innovation is merely part of a well-designed strategy by the elite. The potential of an elite acting as an obstructive force intent on preserving their own interests calls for a careful examination of current staffing trends in top-level posts within education in Namibia. In general, the above factors are important to bear in mind when reviewing possible training strategies for Namibia.

PROPOSALS FOR TRAINING PROGRAMMES

Training is clearly not a panacea for all administration ills. It must be carried out in conjunction with structural reforms and the introduction of new recruitment policies within educational organisations. There are, however, other factors to bear in mind. Among the more important is that government should be convinced of the necessity to train educational administrators. Such training must occur within the context of the overall national objectives and reforms, human resource planning and personnel policies. Only a few governments have undertaken the formulation of coherent national policies for educational administrative improvement.

Prior to establishing training programmes, it is essential to clearly define the functions educational administrators must perform and also to analyse what kinds of specialists and managers are required for a modern education system to operate efficiently. It is important to staff the system with the kind of personnel that it really needs, namely, those who are capable of using appropriate technical and managerial methods.

Educational administration training needs its own unique curriculum, but it should also borrow from other fields of administration. For example, modern management techniques which have proved effective in industry and business could be adapted to the educational organisation. This calls for the establishment either of institutions capable of offering specialised pre-service and in-service or short-term courses, workshops, seminars and conferences, or the reform of existing institutions to enable them to offer such specific training. Such institutions should not necessarily be limited to universities or teacher training colleges. Miklos suggests that professionals in positions more closely associated with the ministry of education and its functions should, for example, be trained within a certain branch of the ministry. Universities and teacher training colleges should be responsible for pre-service training for posts dealing with the classroom and teachers, while the ministry of education should be more directly involved in the in-service training of administrators.[31]

There is no universally applicable or valid training programme. It is therefore essential that:

□ the actual educational reform process in a particular country is studied before ascertaining what professional skills are necessary; and

□ the contents and methods of any training programme are relevant to national conditions and in accordance with each country's specifically identified administrative needs.

Such procedures require an in-depth analysis of specific national and local conditions and needs, prior to setting up training programmes. In his 1991 consultation report on higher education in Africa, Coombe calls for participatory diagnostic procedures. He states that not only should the local situation be studied but decisions should be worked out in dialogue with the African partners, namely, those responsible for the system. This, he asserts, will enable clearer identification of the areas where support is likely to be most acceptable and effective.[32]

Another factor to consider when devising training programmes is that different kinds of knowledge are essential for the various categories of personnel, namely, the different staff levels, especially in terms of upgrading technical capabilities. Guruge identifies at least five levels within an administrative organisation: the policy-making, executive, intermediate, operation-supervisory and operation levels.[33] These in turn fall into three tiers: top, middle and field level. Rodwell identifies the middle tier as principals, inspectors, subject advisers, curriculum developers, district and ministry education officers.[34]

Training must be geared towards the identified needs of each specific level and group of administrators, thereby taking into account the different roles performed by administrators in different sectors and at various levels of the educational bureaucracy. In this way training will prepare each group for the specific tasks that they will perform. This approach rules out the use of a uniform instructional package for all the different levels of administrative staff. At the 1982 Commonwealth Secretariat's meeting, it was suggested that greatest attention be paid to middle-tier management, namely, principals, inspectors, subject advisers and curriculum developers, district and ministry education officers. Administrators at this level were seen to be crucial to the introduction of new and more effective forms of management designed to achieve the objectives of national educational systems. Notwithstanding the important role played by this group of administrators, training programmes have tended to focus on senior educational administrators. Training as an agent of change has mostly adopted a top-down strategy. It has been pointed out, however, that research has shown that innovations carried out in a system's lower echelons, namely, at grassroot levels, usually have a better survival record than top-down innovations.[35]

No matter what the process of recruiting educational administrators is, it is vital that the candidate is adequately prepared for the new duties. Only then will staff operate effectively. Administrators at all levels must be frequently updated on their professional knowledge so they can keep abreast of the latest developments and innovations. This will help to professionalise educational administration and hence facilitate the change and innovation process. There should also be continuous assessment of training programmes. This is necessary to gauge the effectiveness of training and to allow for its revision.

The extent to which educational administrators' training can or should be similar to that of public or business administrators is also important. If the administrative processes of various types of organisations have both common and unique characteristics, this must be noted when establishing training programmes. More generalised training should be offered to certain groups of educational administrators along with personnel from other sectors. Several training activities in developing countries have evolved a common approach whereby managers from education and industry attended the same workshops and seminars. In many third world countries, organisations outside the educational system were used, for example, institutes of public administration. In such situations it was rare that the relations between this training and the special needs of educational administrators were defined. This joint training of managers and educationists is more likely to occur among the higher administrator cadres. Despite the common pool of professional knowledge needed by all administrators, no matter in which sector they serve, it is important to remember that such training is not adequate professional training in the skills required for educational administration.

Finally, trainers within institutions preparing educational administrators must be competent to carry out their tasks of providing relevant and useful training and materials for the workplace. In developing countries, however, there is often a dearth of course organisers and people qualified to help with the professional development of educational administrators. This in turn stresses the need to establish schemes to train trainers, such as the 1990 UNESCO/SIDA Funds-in-Trust Project for the Training of Trainers in Educational Management in English-speaking African Countries.[36] A common problem with training is that professional trainers often lack familiarity with educational administration, while educational administrators are not *au fait* with training technology. This emphasises the need to balance the mix of practitioners and academics working together on a training team.

CONCLUSION

The preceding discussion traced the emergence of educational administration as a field of study in its own right. It highlighted the role of educational administration as a vehicle for educational changes, such as expansion and reform, two of the processes in which independent Namibia is currently deeply engaged. As a result of these two processes world-wide, educational administrators have been expected to undertake many new tasks for which they were not prepared. Training is not an easy solution to such complex problems of management in new and evolving systems of national education. Among the suggestions for improving the success rate of training in developing countries were:

☐ the need for participant diagnosis;
☐ culturally specific management theory;
☐ case material for locally based training;
☐ the rationalising of recruitment practices; and
☐ personnel development.

NOTES

1. Rodwell 1986:i; Murphy 1983:160; Malpica and Rassekh 1980:96.
2. Hatchard 1981:1; Watson 1974:9.
3. Glatter 1972:52; Campbell *et al.* 1983:2.
4. Lungu quoting Walton 1983:87.
5. Ayman 1974:220; Campbell *et al.* 1983:2.
   Some writings, for example, Coombs 1968 and Haag 1982, to name but a few, use the term educational management when referring to educational administration as defined here. This chapter, however, views management as a subsection of educational administration. It is an activity which focuses on decision-making, judgement and leadership and involves planning, guiding, integrating, motivating and supervising (UNESCO 1976:2; Guruge 1969:191).
6. Staff such as drivers and messengers, though they might be serving within some department within the administrative structure, merely make up part of the administrative staff; they are clearly not administrators (UNESCO, EPP/TM/05, 1987:20, 21).
7. Chinapah 1989:38.
8. World Bank 1980:53; UNESCO, EPP/TM/05, 1987:3.
9. Guruge 1969:265; World Bank 1980:14.
10. Development administration is essentially aimed at articulating and accomplishing national social and economic objectives. In this, it is more flexible and innovative in its orientation to better deal with the problems arising from rapid changes. The administrative provisions needed to develop and improve a system are different in crucial aspects from those necessary to maintain a system. This means that existing administrative functions and structures are inadequate to deal with needed innovation. If innovation or reform are to succeed, then the existing administrative functions and structures are unlikely to be adequate unless a system has made deliberate provision for the development and promulgation of change. This calls for structural and procedural modifications (Malpica and Rassekh 1983:62; Lungu 1983:89; Gant 1979:20; Guruge 1969:117).
11. Coombs 1968:168.
12. UNESCO 1979:13.
13. Weiler 1978:181.
14. Campbell *et al.* 1983:117.
15. Elboim-Dror 1971:201.
16. *ibid.*, 205.
    In many countries most administrators had undergone their teacher training many years prior to holding administrative posts and were therefore out of touch with current issues and thinking on educational development. Moreover, a typical university or college programme for teacher trainees did not provide adequate means for

developing an understanding of the administrative and managerial aspects of education (Musaazi 1982:1). This was typical of Namibian educational administrators whose situation was further exacerbated by the fact that the country was cut off from international developments in education, especially those pertaining to other African countries, due to the boycotts of South Africa.

17. There is apparently a direct correlation between the quantitative expansion of an educational system and the number of professionals who are not teachers (UNESCO, EPP/TM/05, 1987:21).

18. UNESCO, EPP/TM/05, 1987:36.

19. Chinapah 1989:31.
    The 22 African countries were: Angola, Benin, Burkina Faso, Burundi, Cape Verde, Comoros, Congo, Gabon, Gambia, Guinea, Guinea Bissau, Kenya, Mauritania, Niger, Central African Republic, Rwanda, Senegal, Sierra Leone, Tanzania, Chad, Togo and Zaire.

20. World Bank 1988:81.

21. Chinapah 1989:45.

22. International conferences and seminars have devoted themselves to the issue, while organisations like UNESCO (since 1962), the World Bank and the Commonwealth Secretariat, as well as bilateral agencies, sustain a broad range of studies and activities in this field (Commonwealth Secretariat 1980:24; Paul 1983; Rodwell 1986:iii, 1, 30, 31; Mbamba 1988 and 1990; Chinapah 1989:23, 49).

23. Ogunniyi 1974:39.

24. Miklos 1974b:110, 115.

25. Singh and Guruge 1977:123, 125.

26. Glatter 1972:41.

27. Lungu 1983:89.

28. Majasan 1974:31.

29. Rodwell 1986:57.

30. Reilly 1977:27.

31. Miklos 1974b:99.

32. Coombe 1991:8.

33. Guruge 1969:10.

34. Rodwell 1986:20.

35. *ibid.*, 19; Adams 1980:35.

36. Mbamba 1990.

3
The historical/political framework

Divide et Impera

INTRODUCTION

What were the historical and political events which helped shape German and South African policies in Namibia? In this chapter we will look briefly at these events. Such background knowledge is essential to understand why Namibia's educational system developed as it did. Furthermore, armed with the political and historical details, it is hoped that the reader will appreciate the extent to which trends in the educational system reflected the political tendencies of each decade of colonial rule and helped to underpin their goals. We begin with the German occupation in the late nineteenth century. This was the period when formal education for all ethnic groups began to develop in Namibia.[1]

THE FIRST COLONIAL PHASE: 1884 – 1915

GERMAN RULE

Late 1800s During the latter half of the nineteenth century, Africa was the arena for the give-and-take game played by the foreign offices of the leading European powers. The division of this continent in the 'great scramble' was a product of the new imperialism. This was characterised by the speeding up of colonial acquisition and an increase in the number of colonial powers in Africa. Before 1880 there were few colonial powers in Africa, but by 1900 the continent resembled a huge jigsaw puzzle with each piece controlled by a European country. Liberia, Morocco, Libya and Ethiopia were exceptions. Germany made its first bid for membership of the club of colonial powers between May 1884 and February 1885, when it announced its claims to the territory of South West Africa (SWA), Togoland, Cameroon and part of the East African coast.

Prior to this, European missionaries had been active in the territory of SWA as early as 1806, when the German brothers Abraham and Christian Albrecht and their companion Siedenfaden came to work there on behalf of the London Missionary Society. The Rhenish Mission, which arrived as late as 1842, was the first German missionary society in the region. From the late 1860s onwards, its requests for German protection against the indigenous inhabitants began to arouse Germany's interest in the territory. According to Goldblatt, the Rhenish Mission was one of the major moving forces which persuaded the German Government to intervene in the territory.[2] The British Government had repeatedly stated that it was not prepared to protect Europeans living beyond its annexed port of Walvis Bay (acquired by Britain in 1878) and a small portion of the surrounding country.

In May 1883 a German businessman, F.A.E. Lüderitz, purchased the Bay of Angra Pequena and some surrounding land from the Nama Kaptein (chief) of the Bethaniens, Josef Fredericks. In August that year, Lüderitz acquired more land from the same Nama Kaptein. This time the deal included the whole coastline from Angra Pequena (present-day Lüderitz) to the Orange River. Lüderitz's aim was not only to trade but also to have a port free of import duties, unlike Walvis Bay. From April 1884 Lüderitz's acquisitions were placed under the Reich's protection, and by the end of that year practically the whole territory had become a German Protectorate. In 1885 Lüderitz, unable to provide the funds for the exploitation of his colonial rights, sold his land to the *Kolonialgesellschaft Für Südwest Afrika*. Bismark had planned on leaving the running of the territory to this company, but this plan failed because the company lacked funds. As a result, the German Government decided to take over the governing of SWA itself. It appointed its first Imperial Commissioner, Dr H.E. Göring, in April 1885.

White settlement

Early 1900s
Windhoek became the first site of German administration, and white settlers and mineral prospectors were encouraged to move to the territory. However, it was only from 1900 that European settlement began to increase.[3] The Germans did not succeed in establishing control over the entire colony. Instead, they focused on the southern and central parts of the territory. Throughout the colonial period, this section of the country was referred to as the Police Zone. It was there that most Europeans settled. In time these settlers came to fully control the political and economic life of the colony.[4] Beyond the northern boundary of the Police Zone, namely, in the Caprivi, Ovamboland, Kaokoveld and Kavango, Germany maintained virtually no presence.

The Germans set in motion a process of gradual colonisation of the land and local inhabitants. They did this by exploiting the differences between the indigenous leaders who were frequently at loggerheads with one another over grazing rights. 'Protection' treaties were entered into with the Germans in return for large tracts of land. So successful were the Germans at this policy of *divide et impera*, that they managed to ally powerful groups like the Witbooi Namas. Ruthless trading practices also resulted in the locals losing both land and cattle.

The establishment of reserves

During this period when land was being appropriated, a system of reserves for the indigenous population began to emerge. The missionaries had encouraged the creation of reserves because they saw them as a means to guarantee future missionary work. Reserves also enabled them to maintain their Christian congregations more easily.[5] But the government wanted more land for the settlers. It began purchasing as much land as possible. What eventually remained for the indigenous peoples was poor quality land of no use to white settlers. The reserves were also so small that the indigenous peoples were restricted to the bare essentials of life.

Black resistance

Local resistance to the appropriation of the indigenous peoples' land and cattle was fierce. The period from around 1893 to 1907 was marked by unsuccessful risings and rebellions by various local inhabitants. The most notable resistance to colonial rule was made by the Bondelswart Hottentots (1903/1904), the Hereros (1904) and Namas (1904 – 1907). These campaigns, fought with great brutality on the side of the Germans and marked by severe defeat for the local inhabitants, resulted in the loss of nearly half the population of the country. An estimated 80 per cent of the Herero people died either while fighting or fleeing to the Omaheke desert from the German forces. At least three-quarters of the Nama population were killed.[6]

Drechsler described these uprisings as the most cataclysmic events in the history of SWA.[7] Many of the survivors were confined to labour camps where large numbers died. In accordance with directives issued by the colonial power during 1907, the indigenous peoples were barred from owning land and raising cattle. From the age of seven they were required to carry passes, and those unable to prove the source of their livelihood were liable to be prosecuted for vagrancy. This marked the culmination of the dispossession of the Hereros' and Namas' land. In order to survive, they were forced to seek employment from the white settlers, despite the draconian conditions under which they had to work. This period resulted in the extension of white control over most of the land and the indigenous population who became an exploited labour force.

The end of German rule

1915

German rule was short-lived. During World War I, the South African Forces, as part of the British Empire Forces, invaded the territory. They defeated the Germans in 1915. South African military rule was established and lasted until the end of the war in Europe. In 1919, with the signing of the Treaty of Versailles, it was declared that there would be no annexation of German territories. However, those territories which could not yet manage their own affairs were not to be granted independence. Instead, the German colonies were placed under appointed mandatories which were supervised by the Mandates Commission of the newly formed League of Nations.

THE SECOND COLONIAL PHASE: 1920 – 1990

CONSOLIDATION OF SOUTH AFRICAN RULE: 1920S AND 1930s

1920s On 7 May 1919 the League of Nations appointed the Union of South Africa as mandatory over SWA on behalf of Britain because of its geographical contiguity to the country. The ex-German colonies were differentiated into 'A', 'B' and 'C' mandates depending on the stage of development of their inhabitants and other factors such as economic conditions and geographical location. SWA was classified as a 'C' class mandate. This meant that South Africa could administer it as an integral part of its own territory. As mandatory, however, it was obliged "to promote to the utmost the material and moral well-being and the social progress of the inhabitants of the territory...."[8] The mandate system was intended eventually to lead the former colonies to independence. To enable the League to monitor progress towards this ideal, all mandatories had to submit annual reports to its Permanent Mandates Commission.

However, South Africa's plans for SWA differed from those envisaged by the League. Already at the Versailles peace conference, General Smuts requested that the former German territory become a fifth province of South Africa. This request was refused.

Early abuses of power

South Africa did not honour its duties as mandatory and continued to annex the indigenous inhabitants' land for the growing white settler population. It deliberately encouraged poor white South African farmers to settle in SWA with the help of generous incentive schemes. Large tracts of land were allotted to these settlers. The policy of setting aside reserves for the indigenous population, introduced by the German authorities, was perpetuated in the 1920s. Although blacks outnumbered whites, various black groups within the Police Zone were designated reserves much smaller than the land set aside for white farmers. This was done in accordance with the Native Administration Proclamation, No. 11 of 1922 which stipulated that the Administrator (who had been appointed in 1915 to run the country and exercise control over 'Native Affairs' and who was directly responsible to the Union of South Africa Government) had to establish specific reserves for the indigenous populations, not only in the Police Zones.[9] In 1929 Ovamboland and the East Caprivi were declared reserves and South Africa also expanded its influence over the Kaokoveld's inhabitants.

The South West Africa Constitution Act, No. 42 of 1925 resulted in the formation of a fully fledged system of local government for the country, namely, the South West Africa Administration. Henceforth, SWA was granted a large measure of autonomy and was to be separately administered from the Union of South Africa with the exception of matters such as customs, defence, immigration, police, railways and harbours, mining, currency and banking, and most coloured and black affairs. The Act provided for the four-yearly appointment of a white Administrator as chief executive and representative of the South African Government, a Legislative Assembly consisting of elected and appointed white members, an Executive Committee and an Advisory Council. Final authority still rested with the Government of the Union of South Africa. The Legislative Assembly enjoyed jurisdiction over education, health services, roads, and the construction of towns and dams.[10]

1930s   By 1939 seventeen reserves had been established for the country's different ethnic groups. The reserves were small sections of land scattered across the country and were neither economically nor politically viable. Restrictive and discriminatory laws, such as the vagrancy law, made it possible to punish blacks for leaving their reserves except when they were working for whites. This helped to ensure a supply of cheap labour for the settlers. There was hardly any economic development in the predominantly subsistence economies of the black reserves. These developments resulted in a situation whereby:

> class became directly linked to political and economic power. The whites constituted a ruling class, blacks a working class without real political and economic power or leverage.[11]

Any protest by the indigenous inhabitants against these policies was met with violent suppression as was evidenced in the handling of the rebellion led by King Mandume during the military rule period in 1917, the 1922 Bondelswart Rebellion, the 1924 Rehoboth Baster Rebellion, and the bombing of the Chief Ipumbu's village in Ovamboland in 1932.

INTENSIFICATION OF INCORPORATION: 1940 – 1969

The United Nations

1940s
1950s   Although the League was critical of South African administration, it had no power to enforce its strictures. Its general inability to take action against aggressor nations eventually resulted in the League's demise and its replacement after World War II by the United Nations (UN) in 1945. The period following the end of the War

42

was one characterised by the granting of independence to former European colonies. South Africa, however, refused even to place its mandate under the newly formed Trusteeship Committee of the UN which had replaced the League's system of mandates. In 1946 it again requested the incorporation of SWA. The UN rejected the request. At this point Chief Hosea Kutako of the Herero became a leading figure in the petitioning of the UN against incorporation with South Africa. Because South Africa refused passports to black Namibians, a British clergyman, the Reverend Michael Scott, became the intermediary and representative of the Herero and other Namibian communities. He presented the UN with petitions from these communities opposing incorporation and challenging South African rule in the country.

Outcome on South West Africa of the South African National Party victory

The National Party came to power in South Africa in 1948. It refused to recognise the UN's right as legal successor of the League to supervise South Africa's administration in SWA. As a result, from 1949 South Africa ceased sending annual reports on the country's administration to the United Nations Trusteeship Committee. That same year the Nationalists passed the South West Africa Affairs Amendment Act, No. 23, permitting whites from SWA to elect six representatives to the House of Assembly in Pretoria. By 1951 all the SWA members of the South African Parliament belonged to the South West Africa branch of South Africa's ruling National Party.

The new South African Government strongly opposed the social and economic integration of the different ethnic groups, viewing this as "a danger to our own Western civilization".[12] The National Party's dominant policy, better known as apartheid, was one of racial segregation and separate development of the different ethnic groups. South Africa's first step in realising this policy in SWA was to further strengthen its control over the affairs of that country's indigenous population. The South West Africa Native Affairs Administration Act, No. 56 of 1954, for example, transferred the SWA Administrator's powers over 'Native Affairs' to the South African Minister of Bantu Administration and Development.

Breaching the mandate

1960s Throughout the 1960s, South Africa systematically applied her policies of administrative apartheid in SWA. The principle underlying this policy was to allow different geo-political units, defined according to assumed cultural, political, socio-economic and ethnic differences, to develop separately.[13] This was one of the most blatant violations of South Africa's mandate. In 1962 the Commission of Enquiry into South West Africa Affairs, the Odendaal Commission, was appointed. Its task was to define the geographic, economic and political aspects of apartheid in the country. This Commission's recommendations formed the cornerstone of South Africa's policies in SWA.

The Odendaal Commission classified the country's population into twelve groups: Ovambos, Kavangos, Caprivians, Tswanas, Damaras, Hereros, Kaokovelders, Bushmen, coloureds, Rehoboth Basters, Namas and whites. Each group, with the exception of whites and coloureds, was to occupy its own 'homeland' (see page 46, Map 2). The implementation of these proposals entailed removing the small African reserves still in existence and the resettling of their inhabitants in the 'homelands'.

The 'homelands' constituted only 40 per cent of the country's land surface. They ranged from thinly populated desert areas to highly populated regions, most of which were not economically independent. The smaller white population, in contrast, occupied 44 per cent of the land which was also the richest in terms of mineral and agricultural resources. Consequently, the 'homelands' came to serve as pools from which cheap labour for the country's economy was drawn. The ultimate aim of the Odendaal Commission's recommendations was for the 'homelands' to become theoretically self-governing though economically dependent on the surrounding white area. The white area, in turn, was strongly tied to South Africa.

The implementation of the Odendaal Commission's recommendations commenced with the passage of the Development of Self-Government for Native Nations in South West Africa Act, No. 54 of 1968. This resulted in the establishment of six native 'nations', namely: Damaraland, Hereroland, Kaokoland, Okavangoland, East Caprivi and Ovamboland. Each was to have its own legislative council with nominal ordinance-making powers and an executive council with corresponding administrative powers. Matters that could be dealt with by the 'homeland' administrations included education, welfare services, business and trading undertakings of the local communities, roads, administration of justice, agriculture, labour, taxes and control of revenue funds, and so forth. The State President of South Africa retained the right to amend or repeal legislation, to make new laws for any black group by proclamation, and to replace the government

Map 3 Ethnic 'Homelands' according to the Odendaal Plan

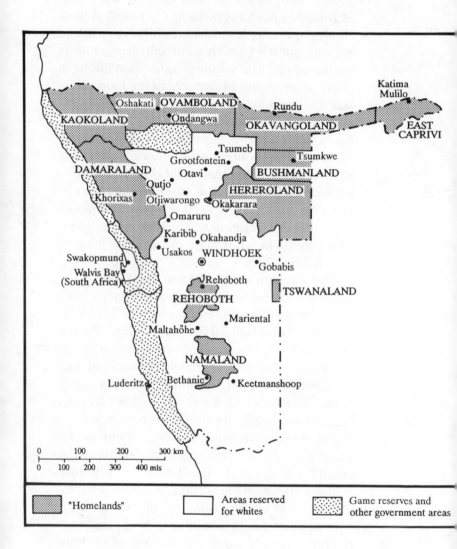

	Areas reserved for whites	Game reserves and other government areas

of any ethnic group or community. He could also establish other 'homelands' by proclamation.

Another defiant gesture of South Africa during the 1960s was the passing of the South West Africa Affairs Act, No. 25 of 1969. This gave South Africa total authority over the following branches of administration in the country: labour, black education, interior affairs, prisons, commerce, industries, justice, coloured affairs, agriculture, mines, cultural affairs, public works, posts and telegraphs, transport, social welfare and pensions, and water affairs. South Africa continued to enjoy control over the country's foreign affairs, defence, and police. SWA had now become a *de facto* fifth province of South Africa. But these incorporationist strategies and abuses did not go unopposed.

United Nations action

South Africa's blatant violation of its duties as mandatory began to arouse international indignation. The decades of the 1950s and 1960s were characterised by hearings brought to the International Court of Justice (ICJ) in the Hague. In October 1966 the UN General Assembly revoked South Africa's mandate and declared that henceforth the country was the direct responsibility of the UN. In 1967 the then eleven-member Council for South West Africa was established to administer the country until independence. In 1968 the General Assembly proclaimed that, in accordance with the desires of the country's people, the name South West Africa was to change to Namibia and the UN Council for South West Africa was likewise to be called the UN Council for Namibia. But UN action on Namibia failed to go beyond these moral assertions. South Africa did not con-

sider the UN resolutions as binding and flagrant-
ly continued to implement racist policies in SWA.

Further black resistance

In the meantime, the indigenous people of SWA
were also increasing their resistance to South
Africa's policies. During the post-war period protest was no longer led by traditional leaders. Instead, workers went on strikes and modern
political opposition parties were established.

Some of the Namibians who studied in South
Africa during the 1940s and 1950s had forged
links with the African National Congress (ANC)
of South Africa. On returning home they formed
the South West Africa National Union (SWANU)
in 1959. SWANU's base was predominantly
among the intelligentsia and the Herero Chiefs'
Council. Although it gained much support in the
early 1960s, it never developed into a national
movement, neither did it make the transition to
armed struggle.

Another political movement was formed in
1957 in Cape Town from among the Namibian
students and workers based there. Toivo ja Toivo,
a Namibian worker, founded the Ovamboland
People's Congress (OPC). In 1958 this changed
its name to the Ovamboland People's Organisation (OPO). The founding group was not exclusively Ovambo and, although the organisation's
immediate campaign focused on the system of
contract labour, "from the outset (it) had the
wider cause of national liberation in view".[14] In
1960 OPO changed its name to the South West
Africa People's Organisation (SWAPO) and
began broadening itself into a united national
front. Within twelve years, SWAPO grew into the
largest political organisation in the country (with
support from among the workers as well as those

outside the contract-labour force) based all over the country.

SWAPO became convinced that Namibia's independence would not come about without a military struggle. From 1961 onwards, many of its supporters quit the country to set up external offices of the movement and to establish military training facilities. In 1964/65 the first militants returned to set up rural bases to train local people. It was not until 26 August 1966, when SWAPO guerrillas engaged South African forces in military combat, that the armed struggle began. The decision to start battle then was prompted by the failure of the ICJ to deliver judgement against South Africa in its 1966 hearing. SWAPO realised that it could no longer rely solely on international legal and political efforts to achieve independence.

THE TRANSITIONAL PERIOD: 1970 – 1989

1970s The 1970s saw international pressure against South Africa's activities in Namibia moving beyond the confines of the UN. These developments and the independence of Angola were to have momentous effects on Namibia, resulting in the intensification of the armed struggle and the departure of thousands of Namibians. Discontent within South Africa erupted in massive school riots in 1976, which also spread to Namibia.

Concerted international action

The 1970s opened with the ICJ's advisory opinion which for the first time stated that South Africa's presence in Namibia was illegal, and as such it was under obligation to withdraw its administration there immediately. South Africa's defiance resulted in the UN Security Council in 1973 deciding unanimously to end all attempts at meaningful talks with South Africa over the future of Namibia. That year the General Assembly declared its recognition of the South West Africa People's Organisation (SWAPO) as "the authentic representative of the Namibian people" and in 1976 it was recognised as being the "sole and authentic representative of the Namibian people".[15] This recognition revealed the success of SWAPO's international campaign. Moreover, of all the opposition movements to South African rule in Namibia, SWAPO gave the greatest attention to training outside Namibia in the fields of health, education, and social welfare. In this way it played a vital role in helping to build up the country's human resource supply.

During 1974 the UN Council for Namibia enacted a decree which required its consent for any company to exploit Namibia's natural resources. Although the decree had no legal status, any party guilty of breaching this decree was to be held liable for damage by the future government of an independent Namibia. This decree was largely responsible for many of the more benevolent policies adopted by some of the larger multinationals operating in the country towards the end of the 1970s, as discussed in Chapters 6 and 7.

External influences on events

The overthrow in April 1974 of the Caetano Government in Portugal led to the demise of the Portuguese empire in Africa. This, in turn, opened a new chapter in the history of southern Africa. The actions which followed took on the dimensions of the Cold War. Marxist governments vied for power after the collapse of Portuguese rule in both Angola and Mozambique. South Africa, motivated by a strong anti-Marxist stance and supported by the United States, used

Namibia as a launching base for raids into Angola to destabilise that country. These activities, aimed at prolonging the full-scale civil war raging within Angola, served to intensify the Namibian armed struggle. In time time the Soviet-backed *Movimento Popular de Libertacao de Angola* (MPLA) was recognised as the legal government in Angola. The MPLA backed SWAPO whose military wing, PLAN (the People's Liberation Army of Namibia, so named since 1973), was able to establish bases within that country and expand its guerrilla activities against South Africa.

From 1972 South Africa's military presence in Namibia began to expand. This was the year the South African Defence Force (SADF) personnel arrived to help the South African Police quell a general strike by Namibian workers that had commenced in 1971. The forces were then increased over the years, reaching at least 100,000 early in 1981.[16] By 1989 Namibia was described as being "one of the most militarised countries in the world".[17]

Attempts at internal settlement

With increasing pressure from the UN to withdraw from the country by 1975 and the onset of independence in Angola that same year, South Africa set about seeking an internationally acceptable internal settlement. In 1975 it called a constitutional conference which took its name from the building in which it was held, the old German Turnhalle (drill hall) in Windhoek. The aim behind the Turnhalle Conference, whose delegates were selected on a tribal basis, was to form an interim government which would lead the country to independence by the 31 December 1978. However, its proceedings dragged on for the better part of the following two years.

The interim government proposed by the Turnhalle delegates excluded SWAPO and was based on a system of eleven ethnic governments, each responsible for education, housing, and health and each with its own bureaucracy. This was clearly an unacceptable solution. Meanwhile, the policy of creating self-governing ethnic 'homelands' was continued throughout the 1970s, although these areas were now given the trappings of self-government with a view to eventual independence.

The role of the Western Contact Group

In 1977 a Western Contact Group, comprising representatives from Britain, the United States, France, Germany, and Canada, was formed to mediate with South Africa over Namibia's independence and to persuade South Africa to comply with the UN resolutions. In accordance with these negotiations, the Turnhalle was to be disbanded and South African-sponsored elections held for a Constituent Assembly under UN supervision. The elections were to be based on universal adult franchise. That same year South Africa appointed an Administrator-General (AG) in Namibia, whose role was to rule over the country until a Constituent Assembly could be elected to achieve independence. The AG was to work closely with the UN Secretary-General to bring Namibia to independence.

The plan set forward by the Contact Group was adopted as Security Council Resolution 435 of 1978. It stipulated a cessation of hostilities, the withdrawal of South African troops, and the holding of free and early elections in Namibia, supervised by a military and civilian United Nations Transitional Assistance Group (UNTAG). South Africa defiantly announced it would pursue its own internal solution by holding elections in December 1978 for a Constituent Assembly. Needless to say, these were boycotted by SWAPO and contested by five internal parties. They were won, amidst allegations of widespread fraud and corruption, by the former Turnhalle representatives who had reformed to call themselves the Democratic Turnhalle Alliance (DTA).[18]

Removing apartheid laws

South Africa's tactics had failed to win over the international community and the DTA Government went unrecognised abroad. South Africa then tried to set about reassuring the world of the DTA's viability. This it did by repealing laws on influx control which, until October 1977, had required blacks to carry passes to live and work in white areas. That same year the Prohibition of Mixed Marriages Act, No.19 of 1953 and the Immorality Proclamation Act, No.19 of 1934 were abolished. In June 1979 the Abolishment of Racial Discrimination, Urban, Residential and Public Amenities Act was passed. This resulted in the *de jure* scrapping of apartheid, but the policy remained operative *de facto* as was evidenced, for example, by the continued existence of segregated schools and hospitals.

Attempts were made to foster a black elite in the country, one which would be opposed to the then 'scientific socialism' prescribed by the liberation movement SWAPO. The intention here was to create a group of Namibians with stakes in a neo-colonial political economy, who would resist the pressures for any radical transformation to the Namibian economy and thus serve as a dissident force after independence. Among the strategies used to realise this aim was increasing salaries for black teachers, nurses, and other professionals, a policy which was to continue throughout the 1980s. These changes were merely cosmetic, since the majority of the country's population was little affected by them.

Increased pressure on South Africa

1980 – 85   Nationalist feeling in Namibia was further fired by Zimbabwe attaining self-rule in April 1980. This also served to heighten South Africa's sense of encirclement. In 1981 compulsory military service in the South African armed forces was extended to black Namibians. This resulted in a further wave of refugees to neighbouring countries. Talks between South Africa and the Western Contact Group continued, and by 1982 a new element had crept into the negotiation process. In 1983 the so-called linkage policy was proposed by the United States. This stipulated that Cuban troops fighting in Angola on the side of the pro-Marxist MPLA be withdrawn before Namibian independence. This cudgel was then taken up by South Africa at all subsequent negotiations over Namibia's independence up to 1986, resulting in stalemate. The Angolan Government argued that Cuban military personnel were there at its own invitation for the purpose of countering perpetual South African aggression. It saw this issue and that of Namibia's independence as being entirely separate.

Events within Namibia were moving slowly. By 1983 the DTA administration was abolished by Pretoria, having been weakened by internal splits and defections and undermined by corruption and inefficiency. The South African-appointed AG assumed direct rule. South Africa's solution to replacing the DTA was to enter into discussions with a number of small parties in Namibia, including 'homeland' groups and political parties representing whites. Some of these then came together as the Multi-Party Conference (MPC) that was installed in June 1985 as the new administration in Windhoek, calling itself the Transitional Government of National Unity (TGNU). No elections were held for this new government and its members were appointed directly by Pretoria on a proportional basis from the seven groups participating in the MPC. Although the TGNU enjoyed greater powers than its DTA predecessor, the conduct of the war, foreign affairs, and overall economic control remained vested in Pretoria. This government too was spurned by the world despite its efforts, through the release of many SWAPO leaders, to gain credit for its attempt to prepare Namibia for independence.

EVENTS LEADING TO INDEPENDENCE

1985 – 89 The developments which subsequently turned the tide for Namibia's long-awaited independence were determined both within and beyond the region. These culminated by late 1988 in the signing of an accord between Angola and South Africa and the agreement of a time-table for the activation of Resolution 435.

During the late 1980s, international financial sanctions against South Africa were taking their toll on the economy, as was widespread internal opposition and conflict. The flagging South African economy, together with the rising challenge to white domination within South Africa, ensured that the South African regime would seek an early settlement of the Namibian problem. Namibia had become a liability to South Africa. By 1985 the military involvement in the country alone totalled around 4,274 million Rand a day and this amount was bound to have increased by the late

1980s.[19] It was, however, South Africa's severe military defeat at Cuito Cuanavale in southern Angola during 1988 that dispelled the myth of its invincibility and influenced the final decision to withdraw its forces from Namibia.

The international event which expedited Namibia's independence was the ending of the Cold War as a result of the rapprochement between the Soviet Union, under Mikhail Gorbachev, and the United States. The two superpowers determined to end the many regional conflicts where they had been supporting opposing sides. As a result, the Angola-South Africa stalemate was put on the agenda and with it Namibia's independence. Additionally, the retreat from Marxist-Leninist socialism in the Soviet Union due to *perestroika* placed socialism worldwide in a more vulnerable position. In Angola and Mozambique the wisdom of such a system was heavily challenged in the light of the economic collapse of both countries. For South Africa this meant that the 'communist threat', the sole justification for most of its destabilisation campaigns against neighbouring countries in the past, was no longer a justifiable excuse.

The time-table for Namibia's transition to independence was then enforced throughout 1989 under UNTAG auspices, though it was not without obstacles. SWAPO's failure to win a two-thirds majority in the November elections meant that it had to write a constitution with the participation of the more moderate opposition parties. The resulting document was a model for the continent with its principles of multi-party system, a bill of rights, free press, and a time limit on presidential tenure (a maximum of two five-year terms).

1990s   On the 21 March 1990 independence was finally achieved. Throughout that year the new government showed its determination to uphold its model constitution and set about pursuing a sincere policy of national conciliation. Previous SWAPO policies were moderated and, instead, plans were put forward for a mixed economy of public and private sector development in a bid to encourage local and foreign private investment. Namibia, so it appeared, was emerging as one of Africa's rare success stories and, as such, pointed the way to a post-apartheid South Africa.

CONCLUSION

This chapter set out to familiarise the reader with the historical and political background to the research. Such detail enables us to understand more clearly the evolution of the singular tendencies of Namibia's education system and in particular its educational administrative structures. Chapters that follow describe and analyse the educational administration system in its historical context. They provide the basis for an assessment of the country's educational administration needs in the post-independence period.

NOTES

1. 'Formal education' refers to the system of chronologically graded education, running from primary school to university level, and includes programmes for technical and professional training.
2. Goldblatt 1971:75.
3. The white settler population, which in 1894 numbered 1,343, had by 1913 reached 14,830 (Hoeflich 1961:114).
4. Bley 1971.
5. De Vries 1978:170.
6. United Kingdom, Parliament, 1918; Fraenkel and Murray 1985:6.
7. Drechsler 1980:231.
8. First 1963:96; Fraenkel and Murray 1985:7.
9. Du Pisani 1986:48.
10. *ibid.*, 70.
11. *ibid.*, 62.
12. O'Callaghan 1977:99.
13. Tötemeyer 1977:15.
14. SWAPO Department of Publicity and Information 1981:172, 176; Fraenkel and Murray 1985:11.
15. United Nations 1983:15, 20.
16. König 1983:9, 10.
17. IDAF 1989:69.
18. CIIR 1986:25; Spray 1988:723.
19. Legum ed. 1986:B698.

Formal education in Namibia: 1884 – 1969

4

Education during
the German occupation:
1884 – 1915

The Mission ought to collaborate in our
lofty purpose of educating the natives to work. The
natives must first become good workmen.
C. SCHLETTWEIN, 1910

INTRODUCTION

This chapter reviews the provision of formal education in
German South West Africa by the missionaries and the government, and the types of work available to the indigenous
people when they left school. The section on educational
provision is not detailed, since this has been extensively
covered by numerous other researchers and writers, most
notably in German.[1] There appears to be no study of the
similarities and differences in educational provision among
Germany's four African colonies (Cameroon, Togo, German
East Africa and German South West Africa) and the employment opportunities open to educated blacks within each
colony. We therefore attempt a brief comparison with German East Africa during the German occupation, revealing the
different attitudes which prevailed there, both in terms of the
government's role in African education and the types of
employment open to indigenous peoples. The intention of
this chapter is to help broaden the reader's perception of the
foundations of modern formal education in SWA and the
influence of the settler ideology on educational developments.

THE ROLE OF THE MISSIONS IN PROVIDING EDUCATION

Although formal education was introduced to SWA as early as 1805, when the London Missionary Society established a school at Warmbad in the south, this chapter concentrates on the period from 1884, the year Germany annexed SWA. After annexation European settlement in this region increased and a divergent pattern began to emerge in educational provision for the different ethnic groups.

The sole providers of education to the indigenous people were the various missionary societies operating in the region. Chief among these was the Rhenish Missionary Society whose activities in the area dated back to 1842, when it took over the work of the London and Wesleyan Missionary Societies. Rhenish missionaries then worked amongst the Namas and Herero living in the central, western, eastern and southern parts of the country. The Finnish Missionary Society began work amongst the Ovambo in the north in 1870, while Catholic missionaries arrived after the country's colonisation and started work among the Nama in 1888 and the Herero in 1896, extending their activities in 1910 to the Okavango in the north.

Initially, missionary education aimed to Christianise the indigenous people. The missionaries therefore emphasised literacy, necessary for reading the Bible, hymn books and other evangelical literature. The most promising pupils were selected and trained to aid the missionaries in spreading the Gospel. In addition to reading, writing and arithmetic ('the three R's'), music, singing, and handicraft formed part of the curriculum. Youths and men also received an 'industrial education' which included elementary training in agriculture, horticulture and trades, while women and girls were instructed in the domestic tasks of a 'Christian' household. This latter type of education was especially useful to the missionaries who of necessity were self-sufficient in food production and housing.

What were the settlers' attitudes to the local inhabitants? They are best expressed in the words of Carl Schlettwein, an independent farmer of high standing in the colonial community of South West Africa. In 1908 he said:

> The land at present available in our colony (excluding Ovamboland) is suitable for European settlement. We cannot carry out this settlement, however, without additional labour. This must be provided by the natives and we shall train them for it. Our policies will therefore be those of masters of the country. We shall make people realise that we Germans are the masters of the country, and the natives the servants whose welfare depends on the advantage of their masters.[2]

Because of the kind of education the missionaries gave the indigenous peoples attending their schools, they contributed to this settler ideal of cultivating black labour. The limited role played by the German Colonial Government in the indigenous peoples' formal education made the missionaries solely responsible for planning the curriculum and deciding on the teaching methods to be used. They also bore most of the costs of this education. In addition to religious and language education, the missionaries' emphasis on obedience, diligence, honesty, manual work and hygiene were all intended to mould their pupils into diligent labourers capable of understanding and communicating with their masters. Through their teaching the missionaries imbued their pupils with Western norms and values. The missionaries believed these to be superior to African values. In this way they severed local populations from their traditional African cultures, history and identity.[3] Education was one of the most important instruments of change within the old order, playing a crucial role in helping to create new social and economic structures.

MISSIONARY EDUCATION FOR BLACKS AND COLOUREDS

Each missionary society exercised full autonomy in educational matters as there was no central church or colonial government control of education. Nevertheless, the schools of the various denominations differed little in what they taught, with the exception of religious instruction, since most taught what they knew, namely, the elements of knowledge as featured in a German primary school curriculum.

The education of the black population

The Rhenish Mission

Of all the missionary societies operating in SWA, the Rhenish Mission was the oldest and most wide-spread in the country. By 1912 it had 35 schools consisting of a total of 1,585 black pupils.[4] At the Rhenish Mission's Herero Conference, held at Okahandja in 1910, the Mission formulated a set of school regulations. These represented the society's first attempt at organising its primary school activities into a system. Though the regulations' success was moderate, they did result in the establishment of a degree of uniform practice *vis-à-vis* schooling.

According to the 1910 regulations, primary schooling was to be conducted over four years if there was regular school attendance, or six years' if attendance was intermittent. Provision was made for an inspector to visit each mission school every three years and to submit a report to the mission deputation.

From 1910 onwards school was to take place five mornings a week for a total of fifteen hours. Religion, reading and writing in the mother tongue, and arithmetic were the main subjects. Table 4.1 indicates all the subjects taught and the number of hours allocated to each. Handwork instruction, although not featured in Table 4.1, was an important component of the Rhenish Mission's schooling activities and usually took place in the afternoon. The head of the Rhenish Nama Mission, Fenchel, recognised the importance of practically-oriented education. He said that education for practical service should, alongside an elementary knowledge, be the main aim of the missionaries — presumably after the teaching of religion — and that their task would be seen as being completed only once the pupils could be given into practical service.[5]

Table 4.1   The Weekly Number of Hours per Subject in
Rhenish Mission Schools for Blacks, 1910

Religion	5
Mother Tongue	4
Arithmetic	2
German	2
Singing	1
Nature Studies, Geography, Local Studies, History, Writing Practice	1
TOTAL	15

Source: Rhenish Mission, 1910:22

In addition to establishing schools, the Rhenish Mission founded an elementary teacher training institution, the Augustineum, at Otjimbingwe as early as 1866. The institution was then transferred to Okahandja in 1890 and evangelists were also trained there. In the 35 years of existence (it closed in 1901) it trained only 40 teachers.[6]

The Finnish Mission

The Finnish Mission also concentrated on elementary schooling in similar subjects to the Rhenish Mission, but all instruction was in the local languages and German was not taught at all. There was daily instruction for three to five hours except on Saturdays. The missionaries instructed the boys in handwork, while the women teachers or missionary wives taught the girls European-style domestic skills. By 1912 the Finns had enrolled 2,228 pupils at 39 schools.[7] From 1913 the Finns also undertook the elementary training of teachers at Oniipa in the north.

The Catholic Church

Although the Catholic Church's involvement in the education of the indigenous people began well after the activities of the other mission societies, by 1912 it had 26 schools of which twelve were elementary with 501 pupils.[8] Its aims, emphasis and the subjects taught were very similar to those of the other missionary societies operating in the country, the essential difference being that German alone was the medium of instruction. In addition to the elementary schools, the Catholics also ran evening classes where adults could learn reading and writing and German. Catechism schools trained boys aged between thirteen and sixteen to assist the missions with proselytisation, and girls were enrolled in domestic science schools to learn the Western mission style of housework.

At the Catholic handwork school for boys aged fourteen to eighteen, established in Windhoek in 1901, six fully trained brothers taught various trades and crafts. The training was three years long. For each pupil in training, the mission received 200 Marks from the colonial government to whose service the boys were assigned on completion of their training.[9] This was to the advantage of the government because it assured them of a flow of skilled artisans who were then in short supply. The official examination commission always expressed satisfaction with the quality of the boys' training, yet for its part the mission firmly believed that the indigenous people were better-suited as assistants to white masters than as independent or self-employed.[10]

The education of the coloured population

Coloured children were mainly the offspring of German fathers and indigenous mothers. Because of this white heritage, it appears that the missionaries often considered them to be superior to the blacks who had mothered them, although decidedly inferior to the Germans who had fathered them.[11] Coloureds too were said to regard themselves as superior to the purely indigenous people.[12]

Both the Catholic and Rhenish Missionaries established separate schools for this ethnic group. In 1890 the Rhenish Mission opened a school for coloureds in Okahandja and later on another at Keetmanshoop in the south. The Catholic missionaries also opened a school for pupils from this ethnic group in 1902. Their schooling resembled black schooling with the same subjects being taught in a rudimentary fashion. The emphasis in their education was on discipline, obedience and practical work rather than on academic subjects.[13]

Critique of missionary education for blacks and coloureds

Missionary education in SWA was elementary. Teaching was didactic and mechanistic with an emphasis on rote learning. In this it did not differ greatly from most elementary schooling in Europe where 'the three R's,' as well as some history, geography and needlework for girls and various handicraft skills for boys formed the basis of instruction.[14] Instilling the values of "obedience, order, punctuality, sobriety, honesty, diligence and moderation" was considered more important than academic learning.[15] It is no surprise therefore that advanced education for the majority of blacks and coloureds was virtually non-existent, only one institution for higher schooling run by the Catholics being listed in 1911, with a total of only twelve pupils.[16] There were few qualified teachers, most having progressed little beyond the stage of being able to read and write. Even though the Rhenish and Finnish Missions provided elementary teacher training, the number trained was very small. Schools were poorly equipped. Absenteeism was high because children were often kept back from school either by their parents, who needed them to work in the fields or with their animals, or by the white employers of their parents.

By the end of German rule there were about 115 mission schools with a total enrolment of 5,490 pupils in a country with an indigenous population of approximately 200,000.[17] The quality and provision of schooling in the colony was well behind that of Germany's other African territories, as we will see in the comparison with German East Africa. The mission schools of SWA for blacks and coloureds proselytised and attempted to mould their students into a semi-skilled and obedient labour force capable of attending to the needs of the colonial government system and the expanding settler population. This was clearly evidenced in the types of occupations which they were permitted to enter.

EMPLOYMENT OPPORTUNITIES FOR BLACKS AND COLOUREDS

As far as black pupils' ability to use the knowledge acquired at school was concerned, it was reported that "only the best found employment" and "only a small component (had) the opportunity to use the acquired knowledge".[18] Those who could read and write and had a knowledge of German could find jobs as clerks, messengers and servants with the government, the army, the post office, the police or businessmen and were, according to one source, very much in demand.[19] Many of the girls trained in domestic activities were able to take up employment as servants in white households or could work for the missionaries, while young men trained in handicrafts sought employment either with the missionaries or the settlers on farms or in towns. Some of the more adept men became teachers in mission schools. These so-called 'native helpers' were not involved in any decision-making processes and merely taught what the missionary stipulated.[20] Suitable converts also became evangelists or catechists.

On completion of their education, the coloured boys would search for jobs with the missions (in their workshops) or the post office, railways or businessmen. At the post office this entailed counter work or working as telegraphists or telephonists. Those trained in a specific trade undertook work like building, carpentry, saddlery, tailoring and shoemaking. Others worked at the mission press or went into farmwork. Some boys and men followed religious training, involving an additional three years of study with either the Catholic or Rhenish Missions. Like their black counterparts, they went on to serve the missionaries in the teaching and evangelical field. Most jobs occupied by the girls and women were in domestic service to the missionaries and the settlers, although a few of the better educated women were recruited as translators by the government. Generally the jobs available to coloureds were mostly restricted to artisan-type employment or lower-level administrative tasks for state structures. However, they had access to slightly better-placed jobs which would not have been as readily available to equally educated blacks.

In 1909 owing to a shortage of "diligent white tradesmen" in the colony, the government contributed 5,000 Marks to the Rhenish and Catholic mission schools to train coloured tradesmen and to provide handwork instruction to blacks.[21] It is interesting to note the differentiation made here between the two ethnic groups, in that coloureds were to receive better preparation than were blacks. The white settlers, however, were not happy with this action. They viewed the coloured and black tradesmen as competition and saw their training as ruining the opportunities for white settlers and tradesmen on the labour market.[22] As a result of their protestations, the government greatly reduced the sum of money earmarked to the missions for training. This reveals the extent to which the colonial authorities deferred to settler interests, a situation also clearly evidenced by the prominent role the government played in white education compared to its largely passive role where coloured and black education were concerned.

THE GOVERNMENT'S ROLE IN THE EDUCATION OF BLACKS AND COLOUREDS

From 1902 onwards, the colonial government involved itself in the education of blacks and coloureds largely by awarding grants to mission societies whose schools satisfactorily taught the German language. The first and apparently the only government school for blacks had been established in 1894 in Klein Windhoek, where nurse Marianne Bohler was paid by the government to teach young black boys and girls German, arithmetic and household work, in order to help overcome the great shortage of 'useful' servants for white housewives. By 1895, however, a pastor from the Rhenish Mission took over the running of the school for which he received annual financial assistance of 800 Marks from the government.[23]

The government reserved the right to inspect mission schools whether they received financial assistance from it or not. This was in accordance with the stipulations of a document entitled 'State Supervision and Regulation of Missionary Activities in Our Colonies' drawn up by the *Kolonialbund* (colonial federation) and submitted to the 1902 Colonial Congress in Berlin. The document stated that:

> All native schools established by missions or missionaries are subject to supervision by the government of the colony. The teaching activity of the missionaries has to agree with the intentions of the government, otherwise the governor is entitled to forbid any further teaching activity or act....[24]

This government supervision, however, was not exercised in German South West Africa and neither did the government there ever establish an effective system of controlling missionary education for the indigenous people. As a result, the education of blacks and coloureds remained predominantly a missionary domain, while most of the government's energy in the sphere of education was directed towards the whites.

WHITE EDUCATION

The white population enjoyed both missionary and keen government involvement in their education. The first school for settlers was established by the Rhenish Mission at Otjimbingwe in 1876 and remained in existence until 1901. The first government school for whites was opened in Windhoek in 1894 and henceforth educational facilities for this group expanded rapidly. Already by 1904 there were six state schools for whites alone throughout the country and by the end of German rule there were seventeen primary schools, two government secondary schools and one Catholic secondary school for girls.[25]

Whereas the education for blacks and coloureds focused mostly on conversion to Christianity and preparation for semi-skilled work, schools for whites served to reproduce the German schooling system. The building up of such a system of schools was considered by the colonial government as "the best protection against 'going native' ... (and) sinking to a more primitive level of civilisation...."[26] Primary schooling was divided into three phases: the lower primary school (two to three years), the middle primary school (two to three years) and the upper primary school (three to four years). Teaching occupied between 26 and 27 hours a week, much more than the fifteen hours or even less for blacks and coloureds (see Table 4.2).

Table 4.2   The Weekly Number of Hours per Subject in Government Schools for Whites, *circa* 1914

	Lower Primary	Middle Primary	Upper Primary
Religion	2	2	2
Arithmetic	4	4	4
History, Geography, Nature Studies	–	6	6
Physical Training	2	2	2
German	9	8	8
Drawing	–	1	1
Singing	2	2	2
Handwork	–	2	2
TOTAL	19	27	27

Source: Moritz, 1914:17

Secondary school was a six-year programme ranging from the sixth standard to the so-called *Unter Secunda.* By 1914 the curriculum resembled that of a Prussian *Realschule* (an academically and vocationally oriented high school) with subjects like religion, German, German history, French, English, geography (which was adapted to local conditions), arithmetic and mathematics, science, writing, and drawing.

The government spent much money on building schools and hostels and providing an adequate supply of qualified teachers. This was in marked contrast to the amount it gave towards black and coloured education. From 1909 onwards the German authorities set aside 9,000 Marks a year for blacks and coloureds, while in 1914 – 1915 alone it spent a total of 329,600 Marks on white education.[27] Although no figures are available for 1914 – 1915, we do know that in 1913 the total number of pupils was 775. Of these 405 were girls and 370 boys.[28] These figures are much smaller than the 5,490 black mission school pupils in 1915 (see page 67).

THE CONTROL OF WHITE SCHOOLS

Teachers in white schools came from various parts of Germany, all of which had different education systems. Therefore, they taught in the way they were accustomed. As a result, the first white schools had no uniform curriculum, no organised administration, subject inspection or advisory service. But with time a more definite structure began to appear, thereby enhancing the system's efficiency. On 20 October 1906 the government introduced compulsory schooling for white children aged six to fourteen living within a four-kilometre radius from a school. This requirement was extended in 1911 to include all white children. Hostel facilities were built at the schools to house children who lived far away. The compulsory schooling regulation, though difficult to enforce because of the widely dispersed white population, resulted in an increase in school attendance with numbers rising from 548 in January 1911 to 671 (22 per cent) in 1912.[29]

With the new school regulations came various prescriptions for the organisation of the school system as far as holidays, examinations, issuing of results, types of schools, curriculum, work projects, handwork for girls, and establishing school newsletters were concerned. There was now a need for heads of schools and an inspector. To encourage parental involvement in schooling, Governor von Lindequist as early as 1906 called a meeting in Windhoek to form a school committee for the election of a school board. A committee was duly formed which then drew up its own statutes. Various other school committees like the Windhoek one were formed in the following years and they adopted the Windhoek committee's statutes, making adjustments to suit local conditions.

In time the district administrations took over the managing of education in their respective areas and enjoyed full control over the appointment of teachers, payment of salaries and general running of schools, especially in the larger towns. In 1907 the government appointed a senior teacher in Windhoek to act as the official for educational affairs within a branch office of the territorial administration. His other function, when his workload allowed, was school inspector for the colony. Finally, in 1913 the government appointed Bernhard Voigts, an ex-teacher, as full-time inspector for the colony. By then an independent educational division had been formed within the territorial administration.

OVERVIEW OF WHITE EDUCATION

As we have seen, white education was far superior to that of blacks and coloureds in SWA by virtue of the larger number of facilities made available to whites, the greater role played by the government in their educational affairs, and its more generous financial contribution to their education. White education also enjoyed better organisation and control. Compulsory schooling for this group meant that they had an added advantage over the other population groups in terms of educational exposure. More hours a week were devoted to their schooling. Furthermore, white education tended to inculcate feelings of superiority. For example, at a government-subsidised farm school established for girls near Windhoek, the pupils were taught how to run farms, how to treat black servants and how to train them to be diligent workers.[30] White education helped entrench the roles of master and mistress, roles pupils were to play on leaving school.[31]

The government's keen involvement in white education, compared with that of coloureds and blacks, contrasted sharply with the situation in German East Africa. There the government's role in educating the indigenous people was much more active. We now examine the education system and job opportunities for the indigenous people of German East Africa to reveal why the German Government's educational policies there differed so widely from those in SWA.

Table 4.3   Schooling Provision for the Indigenous
Populations of South West Africa and
German East Africa, 1911

	South West Africa*	East Africa
PRIMARY SCHOOLS		
Rhenish Mission	30	512
Catholic Mission	18	363
TOTAL	48	875
Government Schools	—	78
SECONDARY SCHOOLS		
Rhenish Mission	—	18
Catholic Mission	1	11
TOTAL	1	29
Government Schools	—	2

* Statistics for the Finnish Mission schools are excluded.
Source: Adapted from Schlunk (a), 1914:360

EDUCATION AND JOB OPPORTUNITIES FOR THE INDIGENOUS PEOPLES IN GERMAN EAST AFRICA

Even though German East Africa was the largest of Germany's colonies in Africa and overall the most highly populated, there was less white settlement there than in SWA. A total of only 4,866 whites settled there in 1912 compared to 14,816 whites in SWA.[32] The reason for this discrepancy was that SWA's climate was considered more favourable to Europeans, unlike the other more tropical German colonies in Africa where settlers were far more susceptible to disease. They therefore never became settler colonies to the same extent. Furthermore, Bley maintains that the settlers in SWA enjoyed an economic and social supremacy lacking amongst the settlers of the other colonies where, although black resistance had been crushed by military force, economic initiative still remained in the hands of the indigenous peoples.[33] This in turn could have played a role in influencing government attitudes to the education and employment of the indigenous people of SWA, because a strong settler group there lobbied for protection from competition.

Missionary activity in what became German East Africa commenced in the latter half of the nineteenth century, preceding the advent of German Government rule there in 1891. Besides the mission schools in East Africa, there were also Koranic schools introduced by the Arabs which long pre-dated the arrival of the Christian missionaries. Once the colonial power was established, mission schools began to provide the local population with skills to suit both the commercial sector's requirement and those of the colonial administration. Previously the missionaries had looked to their own needs and the mission-educated Africans tended to remain in the missions' service as semi-skilled craftsmen, teachers, evangelists, catechists or as farm labourers. Others went to the plantations and the settlers. The essential difference in German East Africa was that, once the German Government arrived on the scene, education of the local people was not left entirely to the missionaries.

The reason for this difference was that Julius von Sodden, the first Governor of the region, realised the importance of a loyal and literate local staff in the vast colony devoid of many white settlers. Also, because the colony was short of funds, it would clearly be cheaper to use Africans in the lower ranks of the civil service rather than expatriates whose salaries were considerably superior.[34] But the Governor did not want to have to rely on recruiting local literate staff for his administration from amongst the mission school products. His experience as Governor of the Cameroons led him to believe that such reliance was dangerous because of the conflicting loyalties prevailing among recruits, depending on the nationalities of the missionaries who had trained them. Additionally, mission school graduates did not necessarily possess the skills required by the colonial administration.

Among the five rival missionary societies operating in East Africa prior to German rule, three were English and two French. This led Von Sodden to believe that he could be faced with similar problems to those of the Cameroons. From the start he therefore introduced a government school system in East Africa. This was geared towards training local male junior civil servants who would be loyal to the administration and possess the skills necessary to develop the colonial economy. An official education policy for the colony was laid down in 1895. It was called the 'Fundamental Principles for the Establishment and Direction of Schools in East Africa'.[35]

The system adopted was that of the German primary schools, somewhat modified to suit the requirements of administrative work. Swahili was the medium of instruction and was taught as a subject. The other conventional subjects were German, arithmetic, geography, natural history, drawing, singing, music and gymnastics. But the syllabus also included accounting, the drafting of official letters and forms, tax procedure, typing and similar subjects. Gardening, carpentry and other handwork did not feature highly in the curriculum of the government primary schools, unlike mission schools. Government schools providing education beyond the primary level offered the same subjects but in greater detail. The education provided by the government schools, therefore was functional and directly related to the jobs the pupils were expected to take up after having completed school.

Both government and mission schools emphasised usefulness, either to the mission or the administration, with a stress on obedience, punctuality, conscientiousness and a sense of duty. Another objective was to imbue the pupils with German culture and thereby enhance their appreciation and awe of that country. Education resulted in the formation of a class of Africans who served as a buffer between the colonisers and the rest of the indigenous population.[36] They also constituted a group of new leaders appointed by the Germans, especially in those areas where the traditional political system and the ruling groups had been totally destroyed. The governmental regulation of 1910, which made it compulsory for all chiefs and their children to learn to read and write, was a move to ensure the spread of German culture and loyalty amongst the traditional leaders and resulted in increased enrolments in mission schools. The state schools also recruited from amongst the sons of the local rulers and the nobility.

The government pressured the missionary societies, which had been operating independently of government control and direction, to adopt the official government syllabus. Despite the lure of government assistance to those who adopted it fully after 1898, this had little success. Eventually, some of the missionaries succumbed to the pressure, many conforming only partly to the official syllabus. By 1913 the government began to grant subsidies to mission schools which trained pupils specifically for government posts.

As a result of government activities in education, two separate but parallel education systems emerged: the government-controlled school system for indigenous people and the mission-operated school system. Some of the better missionary schools and seminaries offered an outstanding education to a few indigenous pupils, like St Andrew's College run by the Universities' Mission to Central Africa at Kiungani, Zanzibar, and the seminary of the Holy Ghost Fathers at Bagamoyo. Candidates from both these institutions were said to have had an education which was in no way inferior to that of their European counterparts.[37] Clearly there were no institutions of such high standing in SWA for educating the indigenous population. By 1911 in German East Africa, there were no fewer than 83 government schools, of which 78 were primary, two high and three handwork schools. Teacher training was also provided at one of the government schools.[38] SWA, by contrast, could boast only one short-lived government school during the entire German occupation.

The government's active role in educating the indigenous people of East Africa was directly related to its need for artisans such as blacksmiths, masons, leather workers, carpenters, printers, tailors, shoemakers, and skilled craftsmen to work in the workshops of the imperial navy and the railways. It also required white collar workers such as clerks, interpreters, customs officials, tax collectors, teachers, *akidas* (administrators of a district) and *jumbes* (village chiefs), all of whom it was willing to draw from among the educated indigenous population and include in the lower and middle ranks of its administrative structure. In fact, the Government of East Africa actively encouraged the indigenous population to take up such posts. In this respect it differed greatly from the colonial authorities in SWA. There, most work within the administration, both in the central government in Windhoek and in the administrative districts, was reserved for whites and many of the former district commanders of the German army who, on retirement, often entered the civil service. With access to a superior education, whites were better-prepared for such tasks.

The outcome of the education policy in German East Africa was that many black Africans throughout the country were able to read and write. So great was the impact of the educational efforts in that region that when the British took over as mandatory power at the end of World War I, they reported that "the degree of usefulness to the Administration of the natives of the Tanganyika territory is in advance of that which one has been accustomed to associate with British African Protectorates".[39] By contrast, a South African commission reported that under the Germans "the overwhelming majority of the population remained untouched, uneducated and illiterate...." [40]

CONCLUSION

At the end of German rule in 1915, there existed two separate systems of education in SWA: one for the indigenous people, run entirely by the missionaries and differentiating between coloureds and blacks, and one for whites that was predominantly government-run and which provided a superior education. The differing aims of each education system were further bolstered by the government's and settlers' desire that blacks and coloureds be a labour force within the colony serving white interests, rather than competing with the latter on the job market. This contrasted with the situation in East Africa where government and mission schools offered good quality education to the indigenous peoples. Some of the mission schools provided the local population with an extremely superior education, while the colonial government not only actively participated in and contributed towards developing formal education for the indigenous people but also greatly encouraged them to take up more responsible posts within its own administrative structures. By the time South Africa occupied SWA, the educational and occupational disadvantages of the territory's majority were well established and, as will be shown, this situation was to be exacerbated during the new coloniser's rule.

NOTES

1. Schlunk 1914; Schmidlin 1913; Moritz 1914; Noble 1977; Melber 1979.
2. Quoted in Bley 1971:228.
3. Melber 1979:241 n. 16.
4. Moritz 1914:187.
5. *ibid.*, 195.
6. Milk 1961:28.
7. Moritz 1914:201.
8. *ibid.*, 201, 203, 207.
   The two Catholic societies initially operating in SWA were the Oblate Brothers of the order of the Holy Untouched Virgin Mary, established in Fulda, Germany, and the Oblate Brothers of the order of the Holy Franz von Sales, established near Vienna, Austria.
9. Moritz 1914:204; Katholische Mission 1946:30.
   During the German occupation the Mark was the official currency. In SWA this was replaced by the South African Pound Sterling and, since 1961, the Rand (Simon 1983).
10. Moritz 1914:204.
11. Katholische Mission 1946:30.
    The Rhenish missionary Nowack noted that neither the government nor the white inhabitants of the colony were willing to take an interest in the coloureds. He claimed that the reasons for this was their belief that it was not good that an ethnic group who were partly indigenous should rise to the position of a special class. Another missionary report claimed that the children of mixed descent were not accepted by blacks or whites, but this did not deter their mothers from being proud of having half-white children (Nowack 29/12/1915).
12. Wellington 1967:155.
13. Moritz 1914:205; Katholische Mission 1946:30.
    The number of coloured pupils in the northern areas where the Finns ran schools must have been insignificant, especially since this was not an area settled by whites.
14. Gardner 1984:21; Hughes and Beanland 1902:405-449; Wittich 1837:145-171.
15. Hoeflich 1961:123.
16. Schlunk (a) 1914:134.
17. Republic of South Africa 1964:219; Melber 1979:244 n. 43.
18. Schlunk (a) 1914:125.
19. *ibid.*
20. Administration of South West Africa 1958.
    Black teachers were not always adequately qualified. Many were barely able to read or write, which accounts for their mechanical approach to teaching. Regarding the standard of black teachers in

general in Germany's African colonies, it was reported that prospective teachers were subjected to a standard German language examination but were not tested in any other area. Each school where these teachers were taught had its own standards. In consequence, some teachers were inadequately prepared, while others had a thorough knowledge of their subject areas (Mukendwa 1986:33; Katholische Mission 1946:33; Morgan 1964:49).

21. Katholische Mission 1946:30; Moritz 1914:185.
22. Katholische Mission 1946:31.
23. Moritz 1914:180.
24. De Vries 1978:114 n. 75.
25. Katzao 1980:27; O'Callaghan 1977:97; Schlunk (b) 1914:23.
    The seventeen primary schools were a combination of government and missionary schools. According to Moritz, in 1913 out of a total of 775 pupils at least 732 (94 per cent) were attending government schools. The establishment of private schools, especially those for Afrikaner children, was discouraged because the German Government looked upon Afrikaners as foreigners whom they wanted to assimilate. Already in 1892 Governor von Francois had insisted upon a German education for the country's white youth. Despite the attitude of the colonial government, some private Dutch/Afrikaner schools still existed, but their numbers were small (Moritz 1914:46).
26. Bley 1971:111.
27. O'Callaghan 1977:97.
28. Moritz 1914:46.
29. *ibid.*, 9.
30. Moritz 1914:178.
31. Those settlers wishing to obtain higher-level jobs within the colonial administration had to undergo further education in Germany (Moritz 1914:85).
32. Schmidlin 1913:86; Iliffe 1969:205; Moritz 1914:46.
33. Bley 1971.
34. Hornsby 1964:84.
35. *ibid.*, 85, 88; Lawuo 1978:52, 56, 60.
36. Hirji 1979:219.
37. Smith 1963:104.
38. Schlunk (a) 1914:246; Hirji 1979:209.
39. Great Britain Parliamentary Papers 1921:41.
40. Republic of South Africa 1964:219.

5

Education under South African rule: 1915 – 1969

Education must train and teach people
in accordance with their opportunities in life
according to the sphere in which they live. ...
Native education should be controlled in
such a way that it should be in accordance with
the policy of the State. ...
H.F. VERWOERD, 1953

Bantu Education is a component part
of the apartheid policy and ... it is designed to
foster and to inculcate a passive acceptance
of racial inferiority among the African people
while accommodating the myth of
white superiority.
G.H. GEINGOB, 1967

INTRODUCTION

On assuming control of SWA after the German defeat there in 1915, the South African Government inherited the educational arrangements of the former German colony. So well did that education system fit in with the aims and policies of the new colonial rulers that they not only maintained but gradually intensified the system of segregated education. This chapter focuses on three issues:

☐ the ways in which the South African Government strengthened its hold over the education of blacks and coloureds through various legislation over a period of roughly 40 years, starting in the 1920s;

□ developments in South Africa and changes the Nationalist Government introduced to education; and
□ the development of the educational administrative structure.

LEGISLATIVE DEVELOPMENTS IN EDUCATION: 1915 – 1926

FIRST MOVES TOWARDS GOVERNMENT CONTROL

The educational services in 1915 lacked any form of central control or co-ordination. Therefore, during the period of South African military rule in the country (1915 – 1919), the South African Government appointed an Organising Inspector of Education to SWA to build a school system based on that of the Cape Province. The first time that state management of all education in the country was mentioned was in the Treaty of Peace and South West Africa Mandate Act, No. 49 of 1919. According to this Act, South Africa assumed civil responsibilities and control over SWA. Almost immediately after becoming mandatory over the country in 1920, South Africa began to organise the educational system in order to place it under centralised control. Two education proclamations were issued in the 1920s which both tightened government control over education and confirmed educational segregation among the country's ethnic groups. These were: the Education Proclamation, No. 55 of 1921 and Education Proclamation, No. 16 of 1926.

The Education Proclamation of 1921

Government control of all the educational services for whites, coloureds and blacks came about with the first Education Act, Education Proclamation, No. 55 of 1921. This Act provided for the creation of a Department of Education with a Director of Education who was to supervise all education in SWA falling within the Police Zone. Ovamboland therefore did not come under the Department of Education.

The services of the missionaries were retained and mission schools remained in existence. They now received financial assistance from the state provided that they conformed to the government's regulations concerning the establishment, recognition, control and classification of schools, employment of staff, conditions of service, inspection, and syllabuses. A mission school for blacks would only be accepted by the government if, for example, it had an average of 20 pupils, an acceptable schoolroom and a teacher (not necessarily qualified). The management of mission schools, however, was left in mission hands. The Proclamation therefore did not much alter the situation regarding black and coloured education.

In contrast, the Proclamation of 1921 resulted in the state assuming direct responsibility over white education. It made education compulsory for all white children between the ages of seven and sixteen and called for the state to provide education from primary school until the end of secondary school. The South African Cape Province syllabus, fashioned on the British system with its emphasis on academic subjects, was to be applied in white schools. The medium of instruction in government schools was to be English or Afrikaans, while German was permitted in some private schools. The state therefore assumed direct responsibility over white education.

The 1923 Education Conference

The government made another important move with its first attempt at formulating a common syllabus for black mission schools, so as to attain some level of uniformity in black education, when it convened an Education Conference in Windhoek in 1923 for the various mission societies. Most missions attended, with the exception of the Finnish from Ovamboland. The major outcome of the Conference was the decision that the normal course of schooling for blacks would not be longer than four years, that is, up to Standard II. Any additional classes would need the approval of the Inspector of Schools of the Department of Education and would be subject to the number of pupils, availability of accommodation, and the teachers' ability. The medium of instruction was also discussed, with the Rhenish Mission opting for Afrikaans and the Catholics for English. The curriculum in most mission schools remained restricted to reading, writing, arithmetic, religion, biblical geography, and singing. The more remote bush schools were limited to religion, reading and singing. In Ovamboland the indigenous languages were used for instruction. The 1923 report of the Director of the Department of Education mentioned that the establishment of government schools for blacks had been contemplated, but owing to the government's satisfaction with the recent missionary conference on education, it had decided that the government's role in black education would be confined to the Director of the Department of Education having a say in the syllabus and the right of inspection in mission schools.

Prior to the passing of the next important educational legislation came the adoption of the South West Africa Constitution Act, No. 42 of 1925. The Act transferred executive power over education from the South African Government to the newly formed Administration of South West Africa, as far as the maintenance of schools and their subsidisation out of the country's own revenue were concerned. This was a financial and managerial arrangement, since final authority over education policy still rested with the South African Government.

The Education Proclamation of 1926

These changes (mentioned above) were embodied in the Education Proclamation, No. 16 of 1926 which, with the exception of certain provisions, repealed Proclamation, No. 55 of 1921. This was also not applicable outside the Police Zone. The new proclamation made Standard VI, the eighth year of school, the uppermost limit for missionary schools. Those schools wishing to proceed beyond this level had to obtain permission from the Director of Education, subject to the ability of the teacher, the number of pupils, and available accommodation. The new proclamation called for the classification of existing schools into separate schools for blacks and coloureds. This was the first legislation which confirmed educational segregation. The management and control of education continued to be vested in the Department of Education of the South West Africa Administration.[1]

Although authority over the control and management of educational services in the country lay with the Department of Education, the missionaries' services were retained for practical implementation. They enjoyed full direct control over local management and supervision of black and coloured schools in the country and retained sole responsibility for establishing schools for blacks as well as providing teacher and vocational training. These arrangements continued until 1949, when full legislative powers over education were transferred to the South West Africa Legislative Assembly under final authority of the South African Government. But the South African influence remained firmly entrenched in terms of educational policy.

EDUCATIONAL PROVISION: 1915 – 1940

BLACK EDUCATION

Despite state involvement in the provision of schools for blacks, there was still a shortage of schools, funds, equipment, books, and qualified teachers. Funds came predominantly from missionary contributions and direct taxation of blacks. The black community or the missions had to maintain the school facilities themselves. This placed a heavy burden both on the missions and on the unsophisticated, illiterate poor of the community. The Administration was willing, however, to pay two-thirds of the salaries of teachers teaching classes beyond Standard VI. But few black pupils reached the higher primary grades, and by 1949 there were no black pupils at school above Standard VI. Moreover, educational standards in the north were considered to be so low that two years of schooling there were equivalent to only one year in black schools in the Police Zone.[2]

The content of the black primary school curriculum was different from that for whites and coloureds and was generally rudimentary. It comprised biblical studies, ethics, hygiene, physical training, mother tongue, Afrikaans, English, arithmetic, history, geography, nature study, drawing, writing, singing, handicrafts (for boys), and domestic science (for girls). Only biblical history, ethics, and hygiene were examination subjects with an oral examination up to Standard II. Thereafter, examinations were written. The language of instruction up to Standard II was the mother tongue and thereafter it was substituted by Afrikaans.

Clearly the Administration stood aloof when it came to black education, stepping in only when the groundwork of establishing schools, teacher and vocational training institutions had been carried out by the missionaries. The government would help by paying salaries and providing certain equipment. In exchange for this state aid, the government was able to exert a measure of control over curricula, the school calendar, school hours, and departmental inspection.

Very little had changed since the period of German occupation in terms of the quality of black education and state provision of facilities. Black people were aware that their children were receiving an inferior education. At a meeting in Windhoek in September 1947 between certain Herero leaders and the Additional Native Commissioner, the leaders stated that schooling for blacks should be improved and made compulsory from age seven until Standard VI.[3]

COLOURED EDUCATION

Not only did the Proclamation of 1926 provide for earlier state participation in the provision of coloured schools, but it was easier for coloureds to study beyond Standard II. Provision was made for both primary and high school education by the state and the missionaries. However, enrolment in higher primary classes was very low and well-trained coloured teachers were hard to come by.[4] In 1935 the government also established an industrial school for coloureds, but this closed after a few years due to lack of pupils.

The syllabus used in coloured schools was similar to that used by coloured schools in the Cape Province, which was modelled after that of the whites in the Cape. In the primary school syllabus, the emphasis was predominantly on practical subjects and the local environment. The medium of instruction in the coloured schools was Afrikaans, mother tongue of most of this group. The state supported the mission educational services for coloureds by providing maintenance allowances for buildings, free furniture and equipment, and reduced prices on books and stationery to students. There were also free books for teachers.

WHITE EDUCATION

The government continued to bear full responsibility for white education with subsidised schooling, free textbooks and equipment for teachers and pupils. There were no mission schools for whites, although some privately run schools did exist. White schools were predominantly government-run and came under the direct control of the Department of Education. The syllabus in white schools was the same as that of the Cape Province of South Africa. Afrikaans and English were the languages of instruction in all the state schools and German was used in some private schools. Both primary and secondary schooling was available to whites in SWA. For university studies and teacher and vocational training, whites had to go to South Africa.

TEACHER AND TECHNICAL TRAINING

The Conference of 1923 had stressed the necessity of training black teachers. The Rhenish Mission's Augustineum at Okahandja had been closed since 1901, but it was reopened with state assistance in 1923. Courses there were determined in consultation with the Department of Education. Afrikaans was given special attention and predominated as the medium of instruction, though Herero and Nama were also used. The entry requirement to the Augustineum was Standard II (the fourth year of schooling). Upon qualifying, teachers were able to instruct pupils up to Standard IV (inclusive). All candidates were carefully screened. Those who did not meet the required standards were refused entry.

Two other mission training institutions for blacks included a Catholic institution at Dōbra, which had opened in 1925, and the Finnish establishment at Oniipa in the north.[5] Teachers graduating from the mission training institutions were not highly qualified. Entrance requirements were very low, most trainees having only attained Standard II.

By 1936 the Director of Education stated that black teachers trained in the country did not pass "an examination equivalent to even the lowest requirements ... in any of the provinces in the Union".[6] Nevertheless, the government erected no college of its own, its excuse being a lack of funds for buildings and no lecturers to train teachers.[7]

The state also played no role in providing technical education for blacks. Instead it encouraged the missionary societies to open vocational training schools to give the young an opportunity to train so as to be able "to do useful work in the workshops of the Europeans...."[8]

No teacher or vocational training institutions existed in the country for coloureds. They had to attend special institutions for their own ethnic group in the Cape. The minimum requirements for admission to a Coloured Teacher Training School was Standard VIII.[9] After the two-year course, students were awarded the Coloured Lower Primary Teachers' Certificate. At the Coloured Training Colleges, the entry requirement was Standard X (twelve years of schooling). Upon successful completion of the two- to three-year course, the trainees were awarded the coloured Higher Primary Teachers' Certificate. The South West Africa Department of Education set a minimum requirement of Standard VIII plus two years teacher training for coloured teachers, though it sometimes employed unqualified teachers. Although this group had to go to South Africa for almost all forms of training, no mention was made of financial assistance from the government for this purpose. Similarly, whites had to go to South Africa for any form of tertiary or vocational training. Unlike the coloureds, however, they received state financial assistance for this, in terms of the Proclamation of 1921.

Dismal though the educational situation appeared for SWA's majority, the casual attitude of the government did not greatly alter for many years. Furthermore, developments in

South Africa during the late 1940s and early 1950s were to have a profound, if somewhat delayed, effect on the education system in SWA. It is to these that we now turn.

EVENTS IN SOUTH AFRICA: THE LATE 1940s AND EARLY 1950s

Education was seen as a medium through which the recently elected South African National Party's apartheid policy could be implemented. It was to be "the primary method of inculcating (the Party's) racial scheme in the minds of the young of all racial groups".[10]

THE EISELEN COMMISSION OF 1949

As early as 1949, the new government appointed a Commission on Native Education in South Africa under Dr W.W.M. Eiselen, the South African Secretary for Native Affairs at that time. The Commission's mandate was to examine the formulation of a separate system of education for South Africa's indigenous peoples; one that would confine them to the role of subordinate workers. The Commission emphasised an increase in government control over black education as well as the alteration of the actual content of black education.

To this end, the Commission called for the establishment of a Division of Bantu Affairs with its own Department of Bantu Education. Control of black education was to pass from the missions to this new department. The Commission also recommended a reduction in central government aid towards black education in favour of greater contributions by local communities.

In terms of educational content, the Eiselen Commission proposed four years of primary education aimed at basic literacy in the mother tongue and a working knowledge of English and Afrikaans, in order to facilitate communication with whites. Education was to stress the values of tribal life and rural skills, religion, hygiene and separate communities, rather than academic subjects and was referred to as Bantu

Education. The explicit intention here was that "blacks should be confined to the lowest grades, with their ambitions restricted to the tribal context".[11]

THE BANTU EDUCATION ACT OF 1953

The Commission's recommendations formed the basis of the Bantu Education Act, No. 47 of 1953, which codified the policy of segregated education. The Act in no way improved black education; instead, it stressed a separate and inferior education. It was also designed to give the central government ultimate power to control and direct the development of the black population apart from the other ethnic groups. Henceforth, black education was to be solely determined by the government in its administration, management, control, content and finance. On 1 January 1954 the central government assumed control over black education through the Division of Bantu Education of the Department of Native Affairs. On 20 October 1958 a separate Department of Bantu Education was established. By the late 1950s moves were afoot to implement changes in SWA that would reinforce a strong centrally controlled segregationist system of education.

EDUCATION IN SOUTH WEST AFRICA: THE 1950s

THE ADMINISTRATION OF EDUCATION

By the early 1950s, the educational services of the whites, blacks and coloureds in the central and southern regions of the country were under a single controlling body, the Department of Education of the South West Africa Administration. Its headquarters were in Windhoek where there was a Director of Education assisted by a Deputy Director and professional and administrative staff who were all white. However, distinctions were drawn between the educational services for each ethnic group when it came to local control, courses of instruction, inspection, teacher training, subsidies, conditions of service, examinations, and promotions.

Black education

Because previous educational legislation was restricted to the Police Zone, two separate systems for blacks had come into existence: one operating in the northern areas of Ovamboland, Okavango and Kaokoveld and one in the southern regions. Each had different arrangements for administration, school control, management, content and finance. All education officials were white.

In the northern regions, all schools were mission owned and predominantly under Finnish or Catholic Mission control. They could apply for a subsidy from the Administration, which was not automatically granted, and they were subject to government supervision through an Organiser of Native Education authorised to inspect these schools and advise on staffing matters and cost estimates. An assistant Organiser was based in Grootfontein. The Organiser did not have to submit his inspection reports to the Department of Education but had a degree of independence and was able to use initiative when making decisions.

Syllabuses in schools beyond the Police Zone did not originate from the Department of Education. They differed from those used in the southern region and were drawn up by the individual missionaries. Examinations and promotions varied amongst the different mission schools, since each mission had its own rules and curricula. The Organiser of Native Education in the north exercised limited control in this sphere and inspectors played no role in the examinations. Only as late as 1952 was the Department able to impose a common syllabus on mission schools.

Generally, mission schools in the north were more independent. The only share that the Department of Education had in education beyond the Police Zone was in the granting of subsidies, leaving the Organiser to act freely in all other matters.

Within the Police Zone, there were three types of schools for blacks: government, mission and a few Church-run private schools. The latter were mostly junior schools not recognised by the Administration because they did not meet its minimum requirements for recognition. The Director of the Department of Education controlled the black government schools. As for the mission schools in the Police Zone, control rested with the missionaries or the Church who appointed a manager to run the schools. However, he had to be approved by the Director of Education.

The Director's tasks regarding government schools entailed appointing the Organiser for black education in the Police Zone to assist him in erecting and maintaining schools and training institutions, determining the lowest and highest levels of the classes in each school, the subjects and courses to be taught, pupil admissions, and staff matters. Unlike the north, it was the Director of the Department of Education who determined the courses of instruction for all government and recognised mission schools. The principals in the teacher training institutions in the south, the government-run Augustineum and the Catholic-run school at Dōbra, drew up the curriculum. This was then approved by the Department of Education. By contrast, the syllabuses of teacher training schools in the north were drawn up by the Organiser of Native Education in collaboration with the missions. This resulted in lack of uniformity in the syllabuses and in differing standards.

As for assistance to mission schools in the south, the government provided these schools with equipment and school requisites, teachers' salaries, books at reduced prices, and a maintenance allowance. Schools not recognised by the Administration received no financial assistance. The government also met all costs including board and lodging at the Augustineum, which in 1943 had become a government institution. Other recognised mission-training schools received grants in aid from the Administration. Usually no school fees were exacted from black students, but in at least two of the Herero reserves (Waterberg East and Aminuis) the local communities contributed to schooling by paying a monthly levy of one shilling per adult stock owner.[12] Clearly, mission schools in the south benefited far more from government assistance than schools in the north.

Coloured education

Schools for the coloured community were run either by the government or the missions. The control and management of the government schools rested with the Director of Education or with a manager appointed by him with the consent of the Administrator. To establish a government school, the coloured community concerned had to approach the Circuit Inspector, who then submitted the request to the Director of Education. Missionaries who wished to establish schools had to have the approval of the Director of Education; however, the control and management of their schools lay with the Church or mission which had established them. The appointment of managers to their mission schools was subject to the approval of the Director of Education. If a manager did not carry out his duties to the satisfaction of the Director, the Church, mission or even the person himself could be called upon to nominate another manager. This manager was also responsible for filling posts in mission schools with suitable candidates. All appointments had to be approved by the Director of Education.

Government schools were free, other than a subsidised book fee. In the mission sector, the mission had to construct the school with contributions from the local community, although the government paid building maintenance allowances. The Department of Education provided all furniture and equipment free of charge and reduced the prices on stationery and books, for which the mission (not the parents) had to pay.

White education

White education consisted mostly of fully maintained government schools directly run by the Department of Education, and their situation remained privileged as before.

School inspection

The white inspectors of the Department of Education had to visit black, coloured and white schools in the Police Zone. These all differed in character and standard of work. Often the inspectors did not carry out the annual visits to the black schools, and no black supervisors or organisers were appointed to assist with inspection. Moreover, inspectors from the Department of Education did not visit schools beyond the Police Zone; instead, this was left to the Organiser of Native Education and his assistant. Although both fell directly under the Department of Education's Chief Inspector, they enjoyed considerable freedom regarding control and even policy, but played no role in the examination process.[13]

Coloureds fared little better when it came to representation of subinspectors, because they were not permitted to fill posts higher than that of school principal. None of the white staff at the Department was assigned to coloured schools as a specific field.[14]

In summary, although the administration and control of education was theoretically vested in one department, it was still divided between the Department of Education and the missions. There was no effective control of black education outside the Police Zone, and as far as mission schools within it were concerned, they were not often supervised by the Department. Actual control remained firmly in mission hands with the Department's role reduced to handing out subsidies. All this amounted to a lack of effective control and co-ordination between the mission and government schools both within and beyond the Police Zone.

THE IMPLEMENTATION OF BANTU EDUCATION

The 1958 Commission of Enquiry into Non-European Education

In 1958 the South African Government appointed a commission under Dr H.J. van Zyl of the South African Education Department. The Van Zyl Commission was to investigate black and coloured education in SWA with a view to establishing separate systems of education for the two groups.[15] It was also to decide to what extent the South African system of Bantu Education should be applied to SWA.

The Commission's recommendations catered for:

☐ the establishment of a separate branch of black education within the South West Africa Department of Education, staffed by qualified white officers and including a Language Bureau headed by a white assisted by two competent black teachers;

☐ the conversion of mission schools into state and community schools;

☐ the introduction of an education levy for blacks;

☐ use of the South African Bantu Education syllabus in black schools in SWA.[16]

A separate branch for black education within the Department of Education would facilitate better control over this group's education and enhance the implementation of apartheid education policies. A Chief Inspector with his own staff was to be specially entrusted with the educational services of blacks.

By converting most black mission schools into so-called community schools under the control of 'native school committees', the missions' role in black education would be undermined. Such community schools were to include all primary schools and schools without white staff. The Commission stated categorically that "no European teacher should serve in any community school".[17]

According to the Commission's recommendations, the control of former mission schools was to be vested in black school boards and committees in order to put emphasis on local black participation in school management. School committees were to be appointed for every school and they would not necessarily consist of the parents of school-going children. Teacher training institutions, secondary and vocational schools with white staff were to be classified as government schools and to fall directly under the Department of Education.[18] This meant increased control over black education and made it easier to apply the Bantu Education syllabus.

At the time, some of the churches in SWA were beginning to speak out against the South African Government's apartheid policies and could therefore not be trusted to teach the Bantu syllabus. Those missions which refused to hand over their schools had to forfeit state aid. They could, however, register their schools as private institutions but would still be subject to official inspection and the use of the Department of Education's syllabus. The removal of state aid was a threat to the missions because many of them had only meagre resources which could not cover any planned expansion of education.[19]

The recommendation for an education levy on blacks meant the transfer of the major financial burden to black communities and a reduction of government spending on this group's education. The limited funds available to blacks meant that most of their school buildings remained primitive and there was a perpetual shortage of equipment and books. Although blacks now played a greater role in local school administration, they had no control over policy issues, which remained firmly in the government's hands.[20] The South West Africa Administration also passed regulations governing the control of schools, conditions of service of the teachers, syllabuses, medium of instruction, school funds, and so on.

The adoption of Bantu Education meant that the syllabus for black pupils remained as rudimentary as before. In addition to basic literacy in the mother tongue and a utilitarian knowledge of Afrikaans and English, it stressed crafts, manual training, tribal heritage, agriculture, religious instruction, elementary arithmetic, and hygiene. As a result, by the end of the proposed primary schooling, black pupils would be able to read and write in their mother tongue and make elementary calculations as well as have a basic knowledge of English and Afrikaans. As such, they would be equipped for only unskilled work.

Very little had changed in the 35 years since the Educational Conference of 1923, which had also limited the general level of schooling to four years and had done little to improve the syllabus for blacks. Additionally, for those blacks in the Police Zone who proceeded to the higher levels, the standard of education was often inferior to that in coloured and white schools, and separate Standard VI certificates were issued. In the north, exams and promotions varied between the schools since each mission had its own rules and curricula, the Organiser of Native Education exercising only limited control in this sphere.

COMPARISON OF BLACK, COLOURED AND WHITE EDUCATION

Black education

By 1958 at least 70 per cent of black children of school-going age were not at school.[21] The Commission aimed to increase the number of school-age blacks achieving four years of schooling to 80 per cent by 1988, thereby raising the number of blacks with literacy and numeracy skills necessary for the growing economy.

Only 20 per cent of blacks who completed four years of schooling were to continue on to higher primary school.[22] The Commission stipulated that each reserve was to have one central higher primary school. Though this was a positive move in terms of increasing provision to those living in the far-flung reserves, it was a stipulation in keeping with the government policy of ethnic differentiation. It called for only two junior secondary schools in the whole country for the majority black population: one in the Police Zone for the Nama and Herero, one in Ovamboland.[23] No provisions were made for senior secondary school. Instead, after 1958 any pupils who qualified for Standards IX and X had recourse only to the Augustineum Teacher Training school in the south; but this was reserved for Nama and Herero pupils. Although the Augustineum was the first institution in SWA to offer Standard VIII tuition to blacks, this occurred as late as 1953. By 1955 there were 32 blacks in Standard VIII. In 1958 the Augustineum was the pioneer yet again, providing classes up to Standards IX and X, and by 1959 three of its pupils had obtained a Standard X (matriculation pass).[24] Those in the north had to make use of the scarce missionary facilities there, until a proposed Ovamboland Training School came into existence. In all the schools in the Police Zone, there was not one black pupil in Standard X by 1958 and only five in Standard IX. In the north, the highest level of schooling beyond Standard II was the so-called Class III, which was equivalent to Standard V (the seventh year of school). Many schools, however, did not take pupils beyond Standard II.

Teaching, nursing, the police, the Church, public service, and local government were about the only fields open to blacks with schooling. The six teacher training institutes, which were predominantly mission-run, offered courses of two or three years' duration. Entry was after Standard VI. The black teachers' qualifications were lower than both those of the coloureds and whites, as were their salaries. The Commission also reported that the standards of teacher training in the areas beyond the Police Zone — Ovamboland, Kaokoveld and Okavango — were lower than those of the two training institutions in the Police Zone.[25]

Despite having pointed out that there were too few teacher recruits with the necessary preparatory training, that the training of teachers at secondary level was not satisfactory, and that there was generally a severe shortage of trained teachers in the country, the Van Zyl Commission was unwilling to suggest providing more institutions for teacher training other than the proposed Ovamboland Training School at Ondangwa. This was to have qualified white staff for its matriculation course. Nor was the Commission willing to recommend sending blacks to train in South Africa. Instead, it said: "Teacher training for South West African Natives cannot be satisfactorily carried out anywhere else than in South West Africa, and therefore it would have to be accepted as a local responsibility".[26]

Previously, the Administration had been willing to award bursaries to a few black teacher trainees who had attained the required levels for courses at black teacher training establishments in South Africa. On their return, they often worked for the Department of Education. But this was prior to the introduction of secondary school facilities at the Augustineum in 1958 and the Department of Education's resulting reluctance to grant bursaries. The number of applications for this kind of assistance was generally very small, totalling only two in 1952 with no further applications until the 1960s.[27]

The Commission raised the question of compulsory education but suggested that this initiative be decided by the school councils. It recommended financial assistance in the form of loans and bursaries to blacks with a 'matriculation exemption' to attend the proposed black university colleges in South Africa, on condition that they return to the country after completion of their studies. This was quite unrealistic in view of the lack of available facilities after primary level. Nevertheless, this route was followed by a few in later years.

The Commission also failed to recommend establishing vocational schools. This was, however, in keeping with the government's aim of restricting blacks to the level of unskilled workers. Although the Rhenish Mission had started vocational schools in the 1920s, these were closed in the 1940s due to lack of support. In 1956 the Augustineum became the only government institution for blacks offering (in addition to teacher training) vocational training in woodwork, bricklaying and tailoring.[28] Loans and bursaries were available from the Administration for vocational and technical training in South Africa, but no figures were provided as to how many blacks actually applied. One can assume that the numbers were very limited or non-existent. Vocational and technical teacher training were also offered at the Catholic Mission institution at Dōbra, near Windhoek, and two Finnish Mission-run establishments in the north at Ongwediva and Okahao.

The overall situation for the majority of blacks had not improved. Those who had managed to attain higher levels of education were severely restricted in the scope of career opportunities. They were either doomed to remain within their respective reserves, where certain levels of white collar work were available to them, or to seek work in the public and private sectors of the urban areas or the segregated amenities within the townships, where their positions were in no way a threat to white interests.

Coloured education

Among the Commission's most important recommendations was the call for a separate branch for coloured education within the South West Africa Department of Education.[29] This aimed to facilitate uniform and stringent control of their education and helped to bring it in line with the overall policies of apartheid. As with black mission schools, the coloured mission schools were required to convert to community schools which were to be run by school committees. In the case of the Rehoboth Gebied (area) and those districts where there were sufficient schools to justify it, there was also to be a school board. The functions of such boards were confined, as with the black school boards, to overseeing the smooth functioning of their schools. If the mission schools failed to convert, they had to forego state aid while their schools were still subject to government control in terms of syllabuses and inspection.

Concerning educational opportunity, the coloured school population did not fare very much better than the blacks. The Commission reported that of all school-going children the majority attended lower primary classes, with more than 50 per cent leaving school after only Standard I and more than 26 per cent after Standard II. Only 3.1 per cent of the school attenders in 1958 were in Standard VI.[30] As shown previously (see page 89, note 9), secondary education for this group was a relatively new phenomenon. By 1958 the provision of secondary education for coloureds was confined to one government school at Rehoboth, which had a total of 53 pupils, five in Standard IX and eight in Standard X.[31]

The Commission wished to expose more coloured children to education and emphasised this by recommending the extension of education for the six- to thirteen-year-old group. But it took no initiative to introduce compulsory schooling for them, maintaining that this should be left to the school boards.[32]

By 1958 there were still no institutions for vocational or post-Standard X training for coloureds, though a limited number (no figures available) could apply for financial aid for such training in South Africa. Those coloureds who were better educated became teachers, independent artisans and skilled tradesmen, while the large majority of the population were either farm and unskilled labourers, factory workers or domestic servants.

The Commission did not appear to want to alter this state of affairs, stating that as "most of the coloureds have to earn their living by manual labour, the development of their manual skills should be emphasized".[33] It recommended establishing an agricultural and vocational school in Rehoboth to provide training in farming, masonry, plaster work, cabinet-making and blacksmithing for males. An institution for females was also to be established in the same area, to train in needlework, cookery, laundering, domestic science, first aid, 'mothercare', and preparatory nursing courses.

There was no mention of establishing a coloured teacher training institution in the country because, the Commission said there were too few candidates. In 1958 there were only eleven teacher trainees studying in South Africa and the Commission stressed that the Department of Education should continue making loans and bursaries available for training there.[34] Although all the coloured teachers were trained in South Africa, according to the Commission, many teachers were poorly trained and incompetent. For example, the staff at the coloured government secondary school at Rehoboth had undergone only primary school teacher training. The principal was the only university graduate.[35]

Some coloured teachers were permitted to train at the Augustineum. But the Commission suggested that their certificates be considered equivalent to those of the South African teacher training colleges and that their salary scales be adjusted accordingly.[36] These recommendations revealed the discrepancies in the quality of training provided in the country. University-level training was still only available either through correspondence courses (with the University of South Africa in Pretoria) or at those South African Universities willing to accept coloureds, with financial assistance provided by the Department of Education.

Summary

By the late 1950s, the overall role played by the Department of Education in black and coloured education was restricted to paying salaries, supplying certain equipment, and the provision of inspection and curriculum services, as well as the establishment of a small number of schools for these two groups. The state's general neglect of black and coloured education was evidenced by how little it spent: black and coloured education made up about 1.1 per cent and 0.65 per cent respectively of the country's total estimated expenditure in 1958.[37] This clearly had an effect on the quality of their educational services. Generally, most energy and finance were directed towards white education.

White education

Whites, whose education under South African rule had been made compulsory since 1921, continued to have a better chance of entering secondary education than did coloureds, who in turn had a better chance than blacks. By 1955 there was a total of 71 white schools in the country. Of these, 55 were non-fee paying government-run and of this figure, nine were secondary schools. The remaining sixteen schools were private. The total school-going population was put at 12,088, making a ratio of 170.3 pupils per school. By comparison, the coloureds in 1955 had a total of 36 schools: three were government, 32 were mission-run and one was non-sectarian, for a total pupil population of 3,240, making a ratio of 90 pupils per school. For blacks in the north, there was a total of 161 schools, all mission-run, for 17,515 pupils, making a ratio of 109 pupils per school. In the south, there were 88 schools (eight were government and community) and 7,893 pupils, a ratio of 89.7 pupils per school.[38]

Teachers in white schools were better trained than those of the other two groups, the majority having post-matriculation training in South Africa. Most tertiary and vocational education was still only available in South Africa, but financial assistance from the state was available to white pupils on condition that the candidates, on completion of their training, worked for the Administration for the same number of years that they had received assistance. The only tertiary institution within the country for whites was the agricultural college at Neudamm, established in 1956 just outside Windhoek, where about 60 students a year with a Standard VIII or Standard X entry qualification could train for two years.

The white privileged position was therefore perpetuated. They had access to an education system which was centralised, relatively sophisticated and professionally run. The greater government financial backing they enjoyed meant high quality facilities, while the admittedly superior education they were exposed to inculcated leadership and elitist values and prepared them for dominant roles in the society.

THE ENTRENCHMENT OF BANTU EDUCATION: THE 1960s

THE EDUCATION ORDINANCE OF 1962

The Van Zyl Commission's recommendations were soon followed by Education Ordinance No. 27 of 1962. This dealt mainly with the management of black, coloured and white education in the country. The Ordinance was a major entrenchment of apartheid ideology with its different stipulations applying to each group. The Ordinance increased the control of the Department of Education, empowering it to draw up and apply syllabuses; compile, supervise and control the examination and certification of pupils, the training and certification of teachers; inspect educational institutions; and determine the staffing of schools and of the necessary facilities of the Department.

The Ordinance also strengthened the Administrator's role in black education: he could appoint an advisory board for black education or a Bureau of 'Native' Languages; create regional, local or domestic boards or bodies to control and manage black state and community schools or entrust such schools to reserve boards or tribal councils, all their powers being very limited. The Administrator could also establish and maintain state black schools or close such schools, hostels, and other institutions if he considered it necessary. It was also in his power to withdraw subsidies or assistance granted to any schools or make grants-in-aid to any black school. Concerning government black and community schools, the Department of Education could determine the curriculum and standards within the school and whether the school was to be co-educational or not.

The most important change introduced by the 1962 legislation was the drastic reduction of mission involvement in educational activities. Missions were no longer permitted to establish, continue or maintain schools for black pupils unless they registered such schools with the Department of Education.

Henceforth, all black schools not registered with the Administrator were required to pay a fine of R1,000 or their authorities would undergo a period of six months' imprisonment in default.[39] Qualifying for registration with the Department of Education meant adhering to all the stringent regulations laid down by the Administrator. Failing this, the establishment or continuation of black mission schools was to be prohibited. This amounted to much stricter control over the functions and duties of recognised mission schools. It also paved the way for the drastic reduction in the number of mission schools, as shown in Table 5.1.

Table 5.1   The Reduction in the Number of Mission
Schools, 1922 – 1976

Year	Schools
1922	211
1966	101
1973	36
1976	30

Source: Leu 1977:156; Murray, Morris, Dugard, Rubin 1974:171;
UNIN 1981:14

Coloured schools remained under the control of the Department of Education and had to register with this body. A positive feature for coloured education in the Ordinance was that it called for compulsory education for all children between the ages of seven and fourteen. A negative aspect here was the stipulation to strictly define a pupil's racial identity, a procedure which determined the quality of the child's education.

Provisions for whites were drastically different from those for blacks and coloureds. Unlike the latter, they had more say in educational matters. All white parents of school-going children, for example, were qualified to vote on their school committees. This contrasted with the situation of black and coloured school committees, where, although parents were represented, the numbers were limited and in some instances were not even drawn from the parents of the school-going children (see page 96). Moreover, black parental participation was often lacking, especially among rural communities where many were uneducated and lacked motivation and an awareness of their responsibilities. White school committees also enjoyed more power in the sense that the Department had to consult such committees when it came to making any changes to the schools. Additionally, the powers of the Administrator *vis-à-vis* white education were drastically reduced compared with the situation for black and coloured schools where the Administrator enjoyed great sway.[40]

THE ODENDAAL COMMISSION OF 1962 – 1963

The final phase of the entrenchment of the South African Bantu Education Act in SWA occurred with the realisation of the recommendations of the 1962 – 1963 Odendaal Commission. This aimed to extend the establishment of South Africa's policy of 'homelands' to SWA.

The Odendaal Commission endorsed the proposals of the 1958 Van Zyl Commission as well as the provisions of the 1962 Ordinance. In fact, at the time of the Odendaal Commission's investigations, many of the Van Zyl Commission's recommendations had been implemented or were in the process of being realised. For example, from the 1960s onwards, mission schools began converting into community schools. The following discussion focuses on the Odendaal Commission's proposals for the administration of education.

THE ADMINISTRATIVE STRUCTURE OF EDUCATION

At the time of the Odendaal Commission's investigations, the education of whites, coloureds and blacks was vested in the South West Africa Department of Education with its separate division for black education. This Department was responsible to the whites-only Legislative Assembly of SWA. The Department had a total of 26 professional and 44 administrative staff, seven of whom were professional and three administrative staff for black education. This change had come as a result of the Van Zyl Commission's proposals, after which special attention was given to the educational services of blacks by designating staff under a Chief Inspector who dealt solely with this group's education.[41]

Within the Department of Education, a distinction was drawn between the educational services of the professional staff for whites, coloureds and Basters on one hand and those of blacks on the other. The Odendaal Commission recommended that the white educational services remain as before, that is, within the Administration's Department of Education with its Director and specialist staff. Financing of white education was to remain the responsibility of the South West Africa Administration. The educational services of the coloureds, Basters and the Namas were to be integrated within the Department of Coloured Affairs of the Republic of South Africa, which was also to take on the financial responsibility for these groups. There was to be a Regional Director in SWA assisted by specialist staff. The black educational services were also to be integrated within the South African Department of Bantu Education, which would also bear financial responsibility for the SWA black educational services. There was also to be a Regional Director within SWA assisted by specialist staff.[42]

A key difference between the 1958 and the 1962 – 1963 Commissions' recommendations was that the earlier Commission sought change within the existing educational organisation in SWA, while the Odendaal Commission recommended management of black and coloured educational services by the relevant bureaucratic structures in South Africa. The Commission argued that the pertinent South African departments had the necessary machinery and experience to successfully administer black and coloured education in accordance with government policy. The outcome of the proposals was centralised control by South Africa over the direction of black and coloured education in SWA and a structure which was better suited to realise the apartheid ideology.

EDUCATIONAL ADVANTAGES BETWEEN THE ETHNIC GROUPS COMPARED

By 1962 illiteracy among the black population was about 68 per cent. Yet the Odendaal Commission felt that compulsory education could not "simply be imposed from above with any measure of success, unless the communities themselves take the initiative".[43] Of those fortunate enough to attend school, 90.7 per cent of the total number were in the lower primary classes (Sub-Standard A to Standard II); 8.9 per cent were in higher primary classes (Standard III – Standard IV); and only 0.3 per cent were in secondary school. That year, there were only three black matriculation pupils, compared with 326 whites and twelve coloureds.[44] The total number of black pupils with a matriculation certificate had risen to sixteen by 1964.[45] There were six black secondary schools with a total enrolment of 801 pupils. Whites, in contrast, had fourteen government secondary schools and coloureds still presumably had only one government secondary school (no precise figures are available). No data are available for the number of coloureds and whites in these secondary schools.[46]

Generally, the number of blacks gaining access to tertiary levels of training was insignificant. During 1962 there were merely three students with state bursaries studying at the

black University College of the North in the Transvaal.[47] By
1964 the number had risen to nine, three of whom were
studying in South Africa and six in the United States.[48] The
number of bursary candidates was five in 1966.[49]

In 1963 only six state bursaries were available to coloureds
to train as secondary school teachers in South Africa, while a
further eleven were available for primary teacher training.
There were still no local institutions for this group for post-
matriculation, technical or commercial training.[50] By 1966 a
total of 20 merit bursaries a year were available to them in
addition to loans (no figures given) specifically for teacher
training.[51] Similar arrangements existed for technical training
(no figures given). In contrast, there were 50 bursaries and
loans a year available to whites for training in South Africa.
In 1963, 39 of these 50 were studying teacher training.[52] There
were 136 whites on government loans and bursaries in 1966
pursuing teaching, engineering, medical studies, and so on,
in South Africa, while a further 209 were studying at technical
institutions there, with the assistance of the South West Africa
Administration.[53] Table 5.2 reveals the stratified levels of
inequality evidenced in government spending on coloured
and black education.

Table 5.2   Government Expenditure on Education
            in Rands, 1965/66

Ethnic Group	Enrolment*	Expenditure	Expenditure per Pupil
White	19,893	2,675,557	134
Coloured	9,402	680,000	72
Black	66,044	1,333,879**	20

* Figures for 1966.

** Figures for 1966/67.

Source: Adapted from South West Africa Survey, 1967:114 – 118.

Due to the lack of agricultural training facilities for blacks in the country (despite the Odendaal Commission's suggestions to introduce training in agriculture and animal husbandry), twelve students were sent to attend a special course for agricultural training officers at an agricultural college in South Africa in 1966. At that time, the Augustineum was still the only institution offering vocational training for blacks in tailoring, carpentry and masonry.[54] The Odendaal Commission therefore recommended establishing a technical training centre in Ovamboland for training blacks after Standard VI as well as short courses for adult employees. This was "to increase their efficiency in the practical performance of their duties, for instance courses in management and administration, commercial practice, mechanics, building, simple engineering, such as the construction and maintenance of ordinary roads, dams, etc.".[55]

The overall picture concerning black educational opportunities had not altered. Added to this, they were further disadvantaged, because by 1965 the Bantu Education syllabus had been introduced successfully into all black schools in the country with its different education and standards for this group.

Another familiar ongoing problem was a shortage of black teachers. This was compounded by the limited number of training institutions and the insufficient number of trainees. One reason for the low number of candidates, according to Kennedy McGill, was that teaching did not attract candidates.[56] The working environment was considered unattractive, especially in the remote rural areas. Moreover, poor conditions of service and a lack of incentives in the teaching profession were negative factors. An official report in the late 1960s justified black teachers' lower salaries, compared with those of coloureds and whites, on the basis that their salaries were determined so as to bear a reasonable relationship to the incomes of other members of their group. Lower teacher qualifications was another reason given. Meanwhile, from the late 1960s, more differentiated professional opportunities and employment options started becoming available to educated blacks and coloureds with the formation of the 'home-land' administrations. These new opportunities increased their demand for higher education.

There were only four teacher training establishments for blacks: the government-run Augustineum, the Catholic train-ing school at Dōbra, and the two Finnish training institutions at Ongwediva and Okahao, these last three specialising in technical and vocational teacher training (see page 100). In 1962 there was a total of 143 teachers in training at all four institutions. By 1966 the number rose by 78 per cent to 255.[57] Standard VI was the minimum entry requirement for three out of the four training institutions. Dōbra still allowed a lower entry requirement, possibly only Standard IV. This was much lower than the matriculation requirement for whites. As a result, very few black teachers obtained degrees. At some post-primary institutions, white staff were employed. How-ever, even at the Augustineum, white employees were de-scribed by one black commentator as being "semi-qualified rejects from white schools, even on the primary level".[58]

Table 5.3   Enrolment of Black Teacher Trainees, 1962

Training Institutions	Number of Pupils
The Augustineum	38
Dōbra	49
Finnish Establishments (2)	56
TOTAL	143

Source: Republic of South Africa, 1964:257

In recognition of the shortage of black teachers, the Oden-daal Commission called for the establishment of a govern-ment teacher training institution in central Ovamboland. This was to replace the two Finnish training schools there. Eventually, it was to transfer to the 'homeland' authority, once the latter was equipped to take it on. A special course for women teachers was to be introduced in Ovamboland as well, with only Standard IV as an admission requirement. Although this proposal recognised the poor performance of black girls in schools, at the same time it relegated women to the lower levels of the teaching profession.

ADMINISTRATIVE CHANGES IN EDUCATIONAL CONTROL

While the Odendaal Commission was carrying out its investigations, the control of coloured education was transferred to the Division of Education within the South African Department of Coloured Affairs according to the Education Act, No. 47 of 1963. Although a regional office for coloured, Rehoboth and Nama relations was established in Windhoek on 1 April 1969, ultimate control rested with the Department of Coloured Affairs at its headquarters in Cape Town, South Africa. As of 1 April 1969, the Nama ethnic group was classified together with coloureds and Basters. Prior to this, they had been classified as black.

The South West Africa Constitution Act, No. 39 of 1968 resulted in the South West Africa Administration relinquishing its control over black education to the Department of Bantu Education of South Africa in Pretoria as of January 1969. This was in accordance with the Van Zyl Commission's recommendation that the education of blacks in SWA be transferred to the South African Department of Native Affairs' Bantu Education Division.

The 1968 Act was also in line with the Odendaal Commission's recommendation that a wide range of powers be withdrawn from the South West Africa Administration and that these be vested in the South African Government instead. As a result, the South West Africa Legislative Assembly's jurisdiction in educational matters was limited to that of whites alone. The transfer of control over black and coloured education directly to South Africa facilitated South Africa's ability to regulate and manipulate these groups' education to its own political advantage. That year six 'homelands', namely, Damaraland, East Caprivi, Hereroland, Kaokoland, Okavangoland and Ovamboland were created in accordance with the Odendaal Commission's recommendations. This was to result in further changes to the administration of education during the next decade.

The Act of 1968 was a consolidation of the 1925 South West Africa Constitution Act in that the white legislative assembly of the South West Africa Administration continued to enjoy jurisdiction over educational matters for whites through the Department of Education. However, the Act of 1968 was amended by the South West Africa Affairs Act, No. 25 of 1969. This Act reduced the South West Africa Legislative Assembly's powers to that of a South African provincial council. It entitled the South African parliament to override territorial ordinances dealing with subjects which had remained within the competence of the Legislative Assembly, for example education. As such, it marked a wide-ranging derogation of power from the territorial legislature. After 1969, white education fell directly under the auspices of the South African Department of National Education in Pretoria, the policy maker and determining body of all white education in South Africa. From this time on, the Department of Education in Windhoek increasingly began to resemble a provincial education department.

CONCLUSION

This chapter has outlined the way in which the educational differentiations between the various ethnic groups in SWA were exacerbated during South African occupation, especially after 1948 when the National Party took power in South Africa. From that year onwards, there was a deliberate attempt by South Africa to use education to realise its apartheid policies. To this end it set about formulating ways to help attain its desired goals. Evidence of this can be seen in the disparities in the curricula, access to further schooling, teacher and tertiary training opportunities, salary scales of teachers, the annual government spending on education per student, and the attendance rates and laws concerning educational requirements for each of the country's ethnic groups. Moreover, by the end of the 1960s, there were separately administered education systems for whites, blacks, and coloureds, with different policies for all three ethnic groups determined in South Africa and then applied via regional branches in Namibia.

The decade that followed was characterised by the application of the recommendations of the Odendaal Commission to create ethnic 'homelands' for blacks. However, distinct variations from the apartheid theme began to emerge. As a result, the 1970s can also be seen as a transitional period from the old trends towards attempts at international legitimacy. Chapter 6 examines some of these trends and changes.

NOTES

1. The Proclamation of 1926 made provision for the establishment of government schools for coloureds, but not for blacks. It was only with the introduction of the Amendment Proclamation No. 10 of 1934 that provision was made for black government schools. The first school was established in 1935 in the Herero reserve of Aminuis and it used the Cape syllabus for black schools (Administration of South West Africa I 1958:48).
2. Harlech-Jones undated:6, 10, 14, 18, 21.
3. *ibid.*, 18.
4. Administration of South West Africa II 1958:12.
5. The Catholic Mission also opened a training school at Tses in 1927, but this closed down in 1937 due to lack of students. State aid was given to this institution on the proviso that its staff were trained (Republic of South Africa 1964:225; Administration of South West Africa I 1958:45).
6. Harlech-Jones undated:11.
7. Administration of South West Africa I 1958:48.
8. *ibid.*, 45.
9. Those pupils from SWA wishing to do teacher training probably went to South Africa to complete Standard VIII, since the first Standard VII class for coloureds in SWA only came into being as late as 1949 (Administration of South West Africa II 1958:60).
10. Kennedy McGill 1967:197.
11. Ellis 1984:25.
12. Administration of South West Africa I 1958:59.
13. *ibid.*, 75.
14. Administration of South West Africa II:1958:43.
15. In 1956 a similar Commission had investigated white education in SWA. Its recommendations merely served to reinforce this group's privileges (Administration of South West Africa undated; South West Africa Survey 1967:110).
16. Administration of South West Africa I 1958:111, 112, 122, 124.
17. *ibid.*, 123, 131.
18. *ibid.*, 123, 125, 126.
19. Ellis 1984:25.
20. Curriculum planning and development remained entirely in the hands of the Department of Bantu Education in Pretoria and its subsidiary, the white South West Africa Department of Education in Windhoek. Despite the Commission's recommendation that the local population be involved in the language bureau, school boards and committees, this was not implemented (Mukendwa 1986:47).
21. Administration of South West Africa I 1958:1.
22. *ibid.*, 101; Ellis 1984:25.

23. Administration of South West Africa I 1958:104.
24. Melber 1979:36, 37.
25. South West Africa Survey 1967:113, 225, 226; Administration of South West Africa I 1958:72.
26. Administration of South West Africa I 1958:84, 105.
27. Republic of South Africa 1964:241.
28. *ibid.*, 257.
29. Administration of South West Africa II 1958:75.
30. *ibid.*, 42, 65.
31. *ibid.*, 14, 21, 24; South West Africa Survey 1967:115.
32. Administration of South West Africa II 1958:63, 81.
33. *ibid.*, 63.
34. *ibid.*, 32, 83.
35. *ibid.*, 12, 38, 60.
36. *ibid.*, 81.
37. *ibid.*, 91; Administration of South West Africa I 1958:136.
38. South West Africa Survey 1967:114, 115, 117.
39. Authority of South West Africa 1962:913.
40. Mbamba 1982:72; O'Callaghan 1977:114.
41. Republic of South Africa 1964:241, 247, 261.
    Since 1951 the Caprivi was governed directly by the South African Department of Bantu Administration and Development in Pretoria (Du Pisani 1986:53).
42. At the time of the Odendaal Report, not all schools in the country had converted to community schools. About 57 per cent of all schools for blacks were still mission schools under the local control of the church authority or missionary body. In Ovamboland, however, the majority of schools were already community schools (Republic of South Africa 1964:223, 257, 261, 263).
43. *ibid.*, 251, 261.
44. *ibid.*, 255; Kennedy McGill 1967:205.
45. Melber 1979:192.
46. South West Africa Survey 1967:114, 116.
47. Republic of South Africa 1964:241.
48. Kennedy McGill 1967:207.
49. South West Africa Survey 1967:118.
    When it was announced in 1967 that a United Nations Educational and Training Program for Southern Africa (UNETPSA) was to be established, many Namibian teachers quit their professions and left the country to improve their qualifications abroad (Geingob 1967:221; Gerhart 1983:45).
50. Republic of South Africa 1964:257.
51. South West Africa Survey 1967:116.
52. Republic of South Africa 1964:233, 235, 237.
53. South West Africa Survey 1967:115.

54. *ibid.*, 116; Republic of South Africa 1964:259.
55. Republic of South Africa 1964:259.
56. Kennedy McGill 1967:204.
57. Republic of South Africa 1964:257; South West Africa Survey 1967:116.
58. Geingob 1967:215.

The road to independence: educational developments in the 1970s and 1980s

6
The 1970s

... the present character of the educational
system in Namibia is one of
'separate development' in its most negative way,
of a discriminating and oppressive
nature, and ... this is clearly the concrete
historical result emanating from
the South African colonial apartheid regime and
its policy in Namibia, which over the
past decades has been serving colonial interests
only, not taking into consideration the
demands and requirements of the majority of the
population under its rule.
H. MELBER, 1979

INTRODUCTION

Developments in education, especially from the mid-1970s until the 1980s, occurred against a background of rapidly evolving internal and international events, as discussed in Chapter 3. These were to have consequences for the education system, the most important of which were the quantitative expansion of educational provision, especially at secondary and tertiary levels for coloureds and blacks, and the growing role of private enterprise in education and training provision. In examining the events of the 1970s, a decade of change, this chapter focuses on:

☐ the educational administrative structure;

☐ educational provision;

☐ the effect of the education system on the country's skilled human resource output.

THE ADMINISTRATIVE STRUCTURE

During the 1970s, the system of separately administered educational systems for blacks, coloured and whites was continued. What had evolved was a situation whereby each system was independently administered by departments in South Africa via regional branches in Namibia (see Table 6.1). Moreover, there was no co-ordinating body between these various South African departments, each of which operated independently.

Table 6.1   Educational Administration in Namibia,
1970 – 1978

Ethnic Group	South African Administering Authority	Regional Administering Authority, Windhoek
Black	South African Department of Education and Training, Pretoria	Regional Office of the South African Department of Education and Training, since 1969
Coloured, Rehoboth Baster and Nama	Division of Education of the South African Department of Coloured Affairs, Cape Town	Regional Office for Coloured, Rehoboth Basters and Namas, since 1969
White	Department of National Education, Pretoria	Department of Education

Source: Adapted from UNIN, 1981:13; Mbamba,1984:112 – 114; Vos and Barnard, 1984:80

White Namibians' education continued to be fully integrated with that of whites in South Africa. Responsibility for the administration of both groups was jointly undertaken by the South African Department of National Education and the Department of Education of the South West Africa Administration in Windhoek. The latter body functioned much in the same way as the four South African provincial education departments. It enjoyed authority regarding pre-primary, primary and secondary education, the education of mentally retarded children and delinquents, and primary school teacher training at provincial teacher training colleges. The South African Department, among other tasks, carried out the compilation of examinations and the financing of higher education. Although the regional office enjoyed many administrative powers, any educational legislation had to have the approval of the South African Minister of Education. At local levels there were advisory school boards for the various school districts and individual school committees elected by the parents, while teacher recruitment remained the responsibility of the educational authorities. Whites still enjoyed far more autonomy over their education than did either coloureds or blacks.

Coloured education was directed from South Africa by the Department of Coloured Affairs' Division of Education with financial matters remaining the responsibility of the South African Minister of Coloured Affairs. There was a regional office in Windhoek. All coloured government schools had school boards and committees whose role was solely advisory. Parents were able to elect members to the school committees or boards, while the education authorities were also empowered to appoint members to the boards. Ultimate control rested with the Department of Coloured Affairs.

Black Namibians' education was administered by the South African Department of Education and Training, formerly the Department of Bantu Education. All the senior staff in this bureaucracy were whites (see Table 6.2). The regional office for Namibia was situated in Windhoek and headed by a white Regional Education Officer. This office controlled all institutions offering primary and secondary education, bar those

Table 6.2 The Administration of Black Education in
Namibia, 1976 and 1979

| Region | Office | Ethnicity of Officials | |
		1976	1979
East Caprivi-Head Office, Katima Mulilo	Secretary for Education	1 White	1 White
	Education Advisers	—	1 White
Kavango Head Office, Rundu	Secretary for Education	1 White	1 White
	Education Advisers	3 Whites	3 Whites
Owambo Head Office, Ondangwa	Secretary for Education	1 White	—
	Education Advisers	1 White	2 Whites
	Inspectors	2 Blacks 1 White	— —
Damara	Director of Education	—	1 White
	Education Advisers	—	1 White
Remaining Blacks' Head Office, Windhoek	Regional Director	1 White	—
	Education Planner	—	1 White
	Senior Education Planner	1 White	—
	Senior Assistant Education Planner	—	1 White
	Assistant Education Planner	—	1 White
	Inspectors	3 Whites	3 Whites
	Subject Inspectors	2 Whites	1 White
	Central Administrative Officer	—	1 White

Source: Adapted from UNIN, 1981:119

which were being delegated to certain black 'homeland' administrations during the 1970s.

The decade of the 1970s witnessed further changes to educational administration in Namibia. As mentioned in Chapter 3, the 1968 Development of Self-Government for Native Nations in South West Africa Act, No. 54 had provided for the establishment of ethnic 'homelands'. Each ethnic government was to consist of a legislative council with nominal ordinance-making powers and an executive council which was responsible for administration. The 'homeland' authorities enjoyed jurisdiction over matters such as education, welfare, roads, administration of justice, agriculture, taxes and labour bureaux, to name but a few. Issues such as defence, foreign affairs and police remained outside their domains. White civil servants were to be seconded to administrative posts within these 'homeland' governments.

By the early 1970s, legislative councils had been established in Ovamboland (1968), Okavangoland (1970) and East Caprivi (1972). Owambo and Kavango (the names changed in 1972) were then proclaimed self-governing territories in 1973 and East Caprivi in 1976.[1] In 1971 the Damara Advisory Council was established and its powers were expanded in 1977. The Coloured Advisory Council and the Nama Council were established in 1971 and 1976 respectively. The Rehoboth *Gebied* (area) became a self-governing territory through the Rehoboth Baster Self-Government Act, No. 56 of 1976. This 'homeland' act differed from those established for the various black ethnic groups in that it involved the formalisation in statutory form of the administration for Rehoboth through a *Kaptein* (captain), his Council and a legislative council with carefully defined, but very limited, powers. This constituted the so-called Rehoboth Government. Ultimate authority rested with the South African parliament, while the State President had the power to amend the Act and the institutions it created.

The existence of these 'homelands' resulted in a situation whereby the administration of education was no longer confined to three separate Windhoek-based administrative structures for whites, coloureds and blacks. Instead, South Africa intended that there was to be a devolution of responsibility to certain 'homeland' administrations, whose executive councils would be responsible for the control, administration and supervision of education, and related matters.[2] More specifically, these administrations:

> were to be responsible for the determination of educational policy, design of syllabuses, establishment and institutionalisation of school committees and boards, standards and subjects to study at school, inspection of educational institutions, establishment of teachers' training colleges and schools, and above all for deciding on the medium of instruction.[3]

In reality, however, a very different situation prevailed, as was demonstrated in Ovamboland where community schools were still in the majority. The Ovamboland Education Act, No. 11 of 1973 resulted in the abolition of the school board system, since the boards' functions were to be taken over by the Ovamboland Department of Education. The period 1977 – 1979 saw the abolition of all school boards, although school committees were retained so as to encourage popular involvement in educational matters. This is surprising, especially since school boards were said to function reasonably well, despite the allegation by Kazapua that many of the board members were illiterate, while the school committees "left much to be desired".[4] Committees were confined to administrative and advisory functions and were subject to the instructions and policies of the Ovamboland Department of Education. The latter also nominated members to the school committees, as did the local parents' associations, the traditional leaders, and the churches in the region. The Executive Councillor in charge of education was a local black. The first incumbent was reported to be illiterate, while the second only had a moderate knowledge of reading and writing. The third Executive Councillor, however, was reported to be well-educated.[5]

Generally, the education departments of the various 'homeland' administrations were fairly limited in their capacities to act independently. Decisions concerning educational policy, standards, the curriculum, examinations (especially the monitoring of school-leaving examinations), and so forth, continued to originate in Pretoria at the Department of Education and Training. They were then passed on to its regional office in Windhoek which, in turn, handed down the decisions for implementation to the administrators in the 'homelands' and the principals of schools. A corps of inspectors from the regional office in Windhoek ensured that policies were being correctly implemented and adhered to. The situation revealed the continuous ties with the South African system and its policies. In reality, the respective regional offices in Windhoek for the three main ethnic groups remained the highest levels of authority in the country regarding educational matters, with ultimate decisions emanating from South Africa.

Despite the move towards the transfer of responsibility, there was no great change. Many of the ethnic governments were unable to take responsibility for their own education and even those that did, retained a white education officer (see Table 6.2). By the late 1970s, all the executive and decision-making positions within the educational structures of the ethnic administrations of the East Caprivi, Kavango, Owambo and the Damaras were dominated by whites and the same pattern was evident in the central educational structure for the remaining black population. Moreover, the middle- and high-ranking posts were mostly staffed by seconded South Africans, as opposed to white Namibians, thereby enhancing administrative dependence on South Africa. To boost the South Africans' numbers, a further 32 South African government officers and employees were seconded to Namibia in 1979.[6]

Late in the decade, South Africa set in motion the process of creating Namibia's own governmental departments, ostensibly to shift control from Pretoria to Windhoek, in a bid to create an 'independent' government in Namibia. As a result, the Functions of Directorates Act, No. 4 of 1979 was passed and ten directorates were established in Windhoek, which were to take over the functions of 26 regional offices of the South African Public Service. However, the directorates remained under the auspices of the South African Prime Minister. In reality, they were merely South African regional offices with all personnel matters being dealt with by the relevant South African departments.

Among the ten directorates was the Directorate of National Education, which was established on the 1 October 1979 in Windhoek under the direction of a white official who was responsible to the Administrator-General. The Directorate was to take over the functions of the three Windhoek-based regional offices of the South African Department of Education and Training for blacks, the Department of National Education for whites, and the Department of Coloured Affairs. It also absorbed all the Windhoek-based officials previously involved in the administration of black education. These moves were clearly an attempt at unifying the three previously disparate educational administrations at central government level. However, the new body did not control the primary and secondary education of the 'homeland' administrations of the Ovambos, Kavangos, Caprivians, Damaras, whites and the Government of the Rehoboth Basters. The Directorate assumed responsibility for tertiary education, except the training of primary school teachers up to Standard IV level, which fell to the various representative authorities and the Government of Rehoboth. The Directorate only had a brief existence. By 1980 it was replaced by the Department of National Education (see Chapter 8).

EDUCATIONAL ISSUES

CHANGES TO THE SYSTEM: AN OVERVIEW

The changes to the educational system during the 1970s were the direct outcome of South Africa's attempts to create an internal solution to the constitutional question of its continued presence in Namibia. According to this 'solution', there would be a revised neo-colonial structure in Namibia. Melber claims that part of this plan was to create a middle class of blacks and coloureds. He argues that, because of its privileged status, this middle class would eventually have a stake in a neo-colonial political economy and, as such, resist attempts by any future SWAPO government to change existing institutions.[7] South Africa would then be more assured of having a stable buffer state as a neighbour. It was necessary, therefore, to adapt the education system in such a way that reflected the emerging priorities for limited social change.

Some of the changes introduced in this decade affected the structure and curriculum of schooling, improved black and coloured teachers' salaries, expanded enrolments considerably and, for the first time, admitted the principle of non-racial enrolment in certain schools.

Prior to 1975, whites and coloureds had a school system comprising twelve years of school compared to thirteen for blacks. The additional year of schooling, which had been the cause of much friction and criticism, was abolished.

From January 1978, the Bantu education curriculum in black schools was to be replaced by the Cape syllabus, previously applicable only to white and coloured schools. However, such changes were mainly cosmetic. Firstly, the Cape syllabus still promoted the principles of white domination and its emphasis was on South Africa rather than Namibia. Secondly, its application required the distribution of many new textbooks, training for teachers, and added administrative demands, most of which were not met. As a result, Bantu Education remained in force, especially in primary schools where the bulk of the black school-going population were concentrated. Most significant of all was the fact that the basic ethnic structure of the school system remained intact. It is doubtful, therefore, whether the curriculum changes had any significant impact on black education, which remained non-compulsory.

A further change during the late 1970s was the opening of church and other private schools to members of all population groups. However, this resulted in only a limited number of coloured and black pupils gaining access to such institutions where entry was subject to certain qualifications. More

Table 6.3 Statistics of the Namibian Education System, 1962 and 1979

	1962	1979
PRIMARY SCHOOL PUPILS		
Black	46,942	160,786
Coloured	6,054	24,408
White	14,262	12,883
TOTAL PRIMARY	67,258	198,077
SECONDARY SCHOOL PUPILS		
Black	147	11,609
Coloured	181	4,659
White	2,995	6,618
TOTAL SECONDARY	3,323	22,886
COMBINED TOTALS		
Black	47,089	172,395
Coloured	6,235	29,067
White	17,257	19,501
TEACHERS		
Black	1,238	4,596
Coloured	213	1,039
White	740	1,152
TOTAL TEACHERS	2,191	6,787
SCHOOLS		
Black	295	743
Coloured	50	103
White	69	74
TOTAL SCHOOLS	414	920
PUPIL/TEACHER RATIO		
Black	38:1	38:1
Coloured	29:1	28:1
White	23:1	17:1

Source: Adapted from Kennedy McGill, 1967:205; Republic of South Africa, 1967:119, 120; Leistner *et al*, 1980:57

coloureds than blacks successfully fulfilled the entry requirements. According to Melber, these pupils contributed towards the formation of a new intellectual elite in the country due to the better education offered at these institutions.[8]

In line with South Africa's perceived policy of fostering a black and coloured *bourgeoisie* was the raising of black and coloured teachers' salaries (in accordance with qualifications) to the levels of their white counterparts. As a result, after 1978 teachers' incomes and social situation were privileged in comparison to the majority of Namibians.

Another marked change during the 1970s was the rise in the number of black and coloured school enrolments compared to those of the 1960s. Between 1971 and 1981, the black and coloured primary school pupils' number rose 91 and 52 per cent respectively (see Table 6.4).[9]

Despite these increases, the general trend of an overwhelmingly bottom-heavy structure prevailed, with the majority of black school-age children concentrated at the lower primary levels. Furthermore, the old tendency of heavy drop-out in each successive school year, especially among black pupils, continued throughout the 1970s. According to both the 1971 and 1981 statistics, the highest number of drop-outs occurred between Sub-Standard A and B for blacks (see Table 6.4). Only 2.3 per cent of black Standard I pupils and 8.8 per cent of coloured Sub-Standard B pupils in 1971 reached Standard X in 1981 compared with 44.9 per cent of white 1971 Sub-Standard B pupils. The end result was that many black pupils left school before they were functionally literate.[10] Dropping out was a result of the long distances to reach school coupled with the lack of transport services, high school fees, irrelevant curriculum, lack of parental motivation, inadequate school facilities, poorly qualified teachers, and competitive exams for which pupils were ill-prepared.

By 1976 there were 24 secondary schools for blacks, ten of which offered classes to matriculation level.[11] This was a significant improvement over the situation in the 1960s. The number of senior secondary schools for blacks continued to rise throughout the 1970s totalling fifteen by 1980.[12] In con-

Table 6.4 The Three Main Ethnic Groups' Primary and
Secondary School Enrolments by Standard,
1971 – 1981

	1971			1981**		
Std.	Bl	Cl	Wh	Bl	Cl	Wh
Primary School						
Sub A	30,103	3,682	2,318	55,101	5,261	1,712
Sub B	18,281	3,228	2,206	35,078	4,507	1,693
Std. 1	14,742	2,981	2,249	29,603	4,195	1,714
Std. 2	11,284	2,518	2,177	21,259	3,609	1,837
Std. 3	9,063	2,171	2,247	17,227	3,695	1,665
Std. 4	5,788	1,871	2,163	12,390	3,154	1,669
Std. 5	4,021	1,489	2,053	14,294	2,936	1,622
Std. 6*	3,714	—	—	—	—	—
TOTAL	96,996	17,940	15,413	184,952	27,357	11,912
Secondary School						
Std. 6	938	1,241	1,796	5,176	2,684	1,486
Std. 7	654	579	1,729	3,107	1,457	1,422
Std. 8	368	255	1,518	3,047	952	1,206
Std. 9	106	106	1,035	905	581	1,155
Std. 10	44	53	778	346	284	990
TOTAL	2,110	2,234	6,856	12,581	5,958	6,259
GRAND TOTAL	99,106	20,174	22,269	197,533	33,315	18,171

* Black students had an additional year of primary school until 1975.
** Includes figures for the Department of National Education.
Source: Adapted from AGN 2, 1982:26, 65, 86

trast, whites had 24 secondary schools by 1976 and coloureds had nine in 1977. However, it is not possible to establish how many of these secondary schools offered only junior secondary schooling. Between 1971 and 1981, the coloured and black Standard X pupils increased fivefold and eightfold respectively. But the actual enrolment figures at this level were low (see Table 6.4). There were 971 white matriculation candidates in 1976; of these 877 passed and 352 gained distinctions. Only 29 coloureds gained university entrance that year. No figures are available for the number of blacks with university entrance passes that year, but in 1975 there were 39. By 1977 the number of black matriculation passes had risen to 57 out of a total of 63 candidates sitting the examinations. Between 1970 and 1979, no more than 300 blacks had gained university entrance qualifications.[13]

The inequalities between the ethnic groups are also revealed in government expenditure on each group's education.

Table 6.5   Government Expenditure on Education in Rands, 1974/75 and 1975/76

Ethnic Group	Fiscal Year		Expenditure per pupil 1975
	1974/75	1975/76	
White	12,351,000	14,451,000	614.94
Coloured	3,156,700	4,160,000	163.00
Black	7,374,000	9,135,000	68.38

Source: Thomas, 1978:202

Most black school leavers were clearly prevented from competing with whites for middle- and high-level employment in the private and public sectors where training in technical and professional skills at university-level was called for. But improved employment opportunities from the 1960s onwards resulted in more coloureds and blacks demanding higher education. By the 1970s, this led to a situation where an enormous demand for education co-existed with a widespread rejection of the type of education available in government schools.[14]

The decade of the 1970s saw mounting open dissatisfaction with the education system by teachers and pupils alike. In August 1973, 3,000 black school children (2,000 in Ovamboland alone) and a section of the Ovamboland teaching force went on strike.[15] Strikes were henceforth to become a common form of protest. In a 1974 study of Namibia, it was reported that "the state schools are frequently disrupted for extended periods by student strikes followed by mass expulsions".[16] Such boycotts were also symptomatic of the festering political unrest in the country. The strike of 1973, for example, was directly linked to the call for elections for legislative assemblies in Owambo and Kavango as laid down in the Self-Government for Native Nations in South West Africa Amendment Act, No. 20 of 1973.

Another outcome of the boycotts and political unrest of the 1970s was a decline in the number of black high school students at schools at this time. This decline was particularly apparent in the northern areas of Namibia, the main arena for the liberation war. There was a mass exodus with hundreds of pupils of all ages, as well as a sizeable number of teachers, fleeing to Zambia between June 1974 and early 1975. The main reason for this exodus, estimated at 6,000, was dissatisfaction with the apartheid system. Among those who left were the 'cream of the Ovambos', an educated and fairly westernised elite, many hoping either to further their education and training or to join the military wing of SWAPO. Church workers, nurses, civil servants, policemen and bank clerks joined those fleeing, with the number of those leaving increasing in the succeeding years.[17]

TEACHERS

There were differences between ethnic groups in the availability of teachers, their qualifications, provision of teacher training institutions, financial assistance for training, entry requirements for teacher training and salaries.

Table 6.6   Pupil/Teacher Ratios, 1978

Ethnic Group	Pupils	Teachers	Ratio
White	20,439	1,338	15:1
Coloured	30,375	1,054	29:1
Black	164,266	4,308	38:1

Source: Adapted from AGN 2, 1982:26, 39, 71, 92

Table 6.7   The Increase in Primary and Secondary
Teachers, 1971 – 1978

Ethnic Group	1971	1976	1978	Percentage Growth between 1971 and 1978
White	1,191	1,321	1,338	12
Coloured	711	968*	1,054	48
Black	2,249	3,311	4,308	92

* Whites teaching in coloured schools are included in this total.
Source: AGN 2, 1982:39, 71, 92; Melber, 1979:134, 170

Teacher availability

The availability of white teachers in 1974 and 1975 was said to be "in a very favourable position owing to a liberal award of bursaries to prospective teachers".[18] The white teachers' increase was the lowest compared to the other groups (see Table 6.7), but the white school population had actually dropped from 22,473 in 1971 to 20,439 by 1978.[19] In contrast, the coloured school population rose from 20,174 in 1971 to 30,375 (51 per cent) by 1978 and the number of black pupils for the same years increased from 99,846 to 164,266 (65 per cent).[20] The growing number of teachers, however, was insufficient to replace untrained teachers in the black and coloured schools. Bearing in mind that most coloureds and blacks were trained for lower-level teaching (see below), the increases amounted to a growth only in the number of teachers qualified to teach at the primary levels.

Therefore, the inadequate supply of coloured and black teachers, especially at the higher levels of schooling, still persisted. To solve this, once again the same solution of allowing white teachers to teach at both coloured and black schools was applied. About 20 per cent of the teachers in coloured schools were whites. In 1975, 125 white teachers were teaching in black secondary schools while there were only 91 black teachers.[21] White teachers, however, were not always sufficiently qualified to teach at the secondary level. Some did not possess teacher qualifications or they had been trained for primary level teaching.[22]

From the mid-1970s onwards, the war in the northern regions of Namibia resulted in many white civilians leaving. This could have affected the number of whites teaching at secondary schools. South African Defence Force conscript personnel were then posted to black schools to teach. Some of these soldiers were good teachers, according to one researcher involved with education in the Caprivi, and an official report noted that without such help "secondary education and teacher training in Caprivi would be hard put to meet the needs".[23] In 1979 there were 164 such teachers. The presence of soldiers in the schools, however, considering the tense political situation in the north, was also seen to be intimidatory, especially since they allegedly carried weapons to classes.[24] Throughout the 1970s, white teachers predominated in vocational teaching where coloured and black teachers were in short supply.

Teacher qualifications

Out of 1,273 teachers in white schools in 1975, only 38 (three per cent) did not possess any specific teacher training qualifications.[25] The situation for coloureds and blacks was not as favourable (see Table 6.8). The largest category of black teachers were those with a Standard VI and teacher qualification (37.4 per cent), followed by those with no matriculation and no other qualifications (27.2 per cent).

Table 6.8   Black and Coloured Teachers' Qualifications, 1977

Qualifications	Black	%	Coloured	%
Professional Qualifications with:				
University Degree	68	1.5	17	2.1
Matriculation or Equivalent	1,100	24.6	236	29.2
Junior Certificate or Equivalent	358	8.0	416	51.4
Standard VI	1,668	37.4	0	0
Other Qualifications (e.g. technical)	10	0.2	0	0
No Professional Qualifications but with:				
University Degree	10	0.2	38	4.7
Incomplete Degree	1	0.02	0	0
Matriculation or Equivalent	20	0.45	57	7.0
Technical or Other Vocational Qualifications	15	0.3	0	0
No Matriculation and No Other Qualifications	1,213	27.2	45	5.6
TOTAL	4,463	99.8	809	100.0

Source: Mbamba, 1982:105

For coloureds the picture was better, with the majority of teachers having at least eight years' schooling plus teacher training (51.4 per cent), followed by those with a matriculation or equivalent plus teacher training (29.2 per cent).

Teacher training provision

By the late 1970s, black teacher trainees had access to seven institutions within Namibia: the Augustineum in Windhoek, Cornelius Goreseb at Khorixas, Dōbra near Windhoek, Okakarara in Hereroland, Rundu in the Kavango, Ongwediwa in Ovamboland, and near Katima Mulilo in the Caprivi. These were virtually all secondary schools with teacher training 'wings'. The only courses available in the country were the two-year Lower Primary Teachers' Certificate (LPTC) and the Primary Teachers' Certificate (PTC). The LPTC was no longer offered in South Africa because of its very low standards. Mention was made in the late 1970s of phasing it out in Namibia and encouraging students to take the PTC instead, but most training institutions continued to offer the course in addition to providing the PTC course. By 1974 at least 70 per cent of black teacher trainees were still training for the lowest primary levels.[26] During 1976, 592 blacks took the LPTC and PTC qualifications, of whom 258 qualified.[27] Secondary school-level training was not offered to any of the three ethnic groups within Namibia.

In 1978, 687 blacks were training to be teachers within the country, not nearly enough to replace untrained teachers and overcome the unfavourable pupil/teacher ratios (see Table 6.6).[28] No figures are available for trainees undertaking secondary school training, but from 1977 black trainees could take the two-year Junior Secondary Teachers' Certificate (JSTC) at the Augustineum, this being the highest level of teacher training offered in the country. The introduction of the JSTC at the the Augustineum in 1977 marked the first time that such a course was on offer in Namibia.

No mention was made of the money provided for black teacher trainees in South Africa but, judging from the overall amount set aside for their education in general, this was probably less than that for coloureds. The lack of sufficient secondary school teacher training within the country and the financial difficulties of studying in South Africa, as well as the educational disadvantages of many blacks, resulted in teacher training being concentrated at the primary level.

There were no teacher training institutions for coloureds in Namibia until the 1978 opening of the Khomasdal Teacher Training College for primary school teachers. This had a capacity for 500 trainees.[29] Prior to its establishment, coloureds had to study in South Africa. Until the end of 1977, the Nama, who had been classified as coloureds only in 1969, were permitted to train in the country at the black teacher training institution, the Augustineum.

Between 1976 and 1977, at least 80 coloured bursary holders a year were admitted to South African training institutions at an average cost of R250 per student per annum. In 1976 the total number of coloured teacher trainees in South Africa was 164, 115 of whom were doing their training at South African colleges, while 49 were at the University of the Western Cape, the institution established for coloured students. With the opening of the training college at Khomasdal, bursaries for study in South Africa were limited to those wishing to do secondary school teacher training at university.[30]

White primary school teachers were trained in South Africa prior to the construction in 1979 of the Windhoek Teacher Training College. With a boarding capacity of almost 500 and an academic capacity reported to be over 2,000, it remained a showpiece strictly reserved for whites. When it opened in 1979, 110 students were enrolled.[31] Over 150 students continued to be trained as teachers in South Africa each year on full government bursaries of over R5,000 per student.[32]

Teacher salary differentials and entry requirements
A coloured teacher with a matriculation and four years' training received at least R900 less than a white colleague with the same qualifications in 1978, while a white principal could earn R16,800 a year and his coloured counterpart with the

same qualifications could receive only R13,800.[33] Black teachers were said to earn 46 per cent of the salaries paid to whites with similar qualifications employed in similar posts. There was much dissatisfaction because of these salary disparities, some of which resulted in school closures in 1976 due to strike action by Nama teachers demanding equal pay with whites.[34]

Black, coloured and white teachers trained for the same level of education had different entrance requirements and qualifications. Coloured trainees entered the three-year LPTC (upgraded in 1977 from two to three years with an optional fourth year) after Standard VIII. Black trainees required only Standard VI for the same qualification of two years' duration. To enter the three-year PTC course, coloureds required a Standard X, while the Secondary Teachers' Certificate (STC) course was available only at university-level after matriculation exemption. Blacks wishing to do the PTC required only a Standard VIII, while junior secondary training, which lasted two years, required a Standard X.

The lowest teacher training entry requirement for whites was Standard X. More courses were available to them, for example, the three-year Pre-Primary Teachers' Diploma (PPTD). Primary teacher training for this group lasted three years and there was a fourth specialisation year. Such courses were offered either at colleges or universities in South Africa or, from 1979, at the Teacher Training College in Windhoek. Secondary teacher training was offered only at universities. These discrepancies resulted in coloured and black teachers being poorly qualified in relation to their white counterparts. This, in turn, affected their ability to provide high quality teaching which, *ipso facto*, negatively affected the overall performance of black, and to a lesser extent coloured, pupils.

TECHNICAL AND VOCATIONAL TRAINING

Training for blacks in this sphere was concentrated mostly at the school level. It was generally very rudimentary and geared towards semi-skilled work. By the mid-1970s, seven black schools in the entire country were offering trade training:

Ongwediva, Rundu, Katima Mulilo, Cornelius Goreseb, Oka-karara, the Catholic school at Dōbra and the Augustineum in Windhoek.

These training institutions, which were predominantly concentrated in the poor 'homelands', were hopelessly few, with only a handful of blacks able to find places there. The number of students completing the one- to three-year courses at such institutions was low. In 1976 a total of only 261 black males undertook vocational training leading to artisan qualifications. Generally, the overall level of technical skills of blacks within the country was drastically inadequate. In 1975 there were estimated to be no more than twenty qualified Ovambo artisans, even though they were the single largest ethnic group in the country.[35] Those fortunate enough to be able to do technical training usually emerged as semi-skilled workers, while the majority of the black population had no exposure to formal skills' training. In short, there was no middle- or high-level technical training available to blacks in Namibia. Together with the other deficiencies in their training, their lack of exposure revealed a policy of deliberately keeping them at the level of unskilled labourers or, at most, semi-skilled workers.

White and coloured training was still provided in South Africa with government assistance. Coloured training concentrated on skilled manual or artisan work. In 1975 the number of coloured trainees was 169.[36] The number of whites undertaking technical studies was almost the same. Of these, less than one-third received state bursaries.[37] Because whites belonged to the higher income groups, it was easier for them to finance their training if government assistance was not forthcoming.

Since 1972, in addition to being able to apply for bursaries to study in South Africa, whites were able to attend a technical high school in Windhoek with a capacity for between 500 and 600 pupils to matriculation level. Also, from 1975 seven secondary schools began offering more practically oriented courses as part of the curriculum for less academically oriented pupils. This curriculum change also applied to coloured schools, though on a much more limited scale. By 1976, 396 white pupils were pursuing practical courses in nine secondary schools.[38] During that year, nine business-oriented subjects were offered in white secondary schools: typing, shorthand, book-keeping, business economics, business mathematics, general economics, administration, sales instruction, and business management. This technical training prepared whites for skilled and professional work and they usually occupied the middle- and high-level posts.

In addition to the possibility of a more varied education within the country, whites had access to Neudamm, the local agricultural college where, from its inception in 1956 until 1978, at least 447 students had been trained. These students either entered government service in management or stock inspection or worked on their fathers' or their own ranches. Two coloureds who were taking distance education courses in agriculture were permitted to do their practicals at Neudamm's experimental farm in 1978.[39] Blacks had recourse to only two agricultural schools in the north, one in Ovamboland and the other in the Kavango, despite the fact that the 'homeland' economies were based on agriculture and livestock. In 1974 only eighteen students were enrolled at the agricultural school in Ovamboland. No figures are available for the other agricultural school situated in Kavango, but Thomas claims that between them the two institutions had only a few dozen students by the late 1970s.[40]

THE ROLE OF THE MULTINATIONALS IN EDUCATION

Although the 1970s were not characterised by any radical changes, one of the more positive features of this decade was the new role attitude towards black education by the multinationals operating in Namibia. Initially, this was intended to project a favourable image in a bid to protect their operations after independence, especially in view of the international moves towards independence during the 1970s. Also, the establishment of new mines in Namibia had been illegal since the United Nations revoked South Africa's mandate in 1966. The development of the Rössing Uranium mine by the British multinational, Rio Tinto Zinc Corporation, which reached full production in 1979, was therefore a direct challenge to this ruling. But there were also other factors which prompted these moves.

Throughout southern Africa during this decade there was an acute shortage of artisans. Skilled white workers were both difficult and expensive to recruit. This was a direct outcome of the economic booms of 1968 – 1973 and 1978 – 1981. Namibia in particular had always suffered a shortage of skilled labour in all sectors.[41] This was exacerbated by the growing exodus of whites to South Africa and Germany, especially from the mid-1970s, due to the perpetual political insecurity regarding Namibia's future. Furthermore, continuing mechanisation meant that money could be saved in certain operations by replacing skilled workers with semi-skilled blacks. Consequently, Rössing Uranium, Tsumeb Corporation and Consolidated Diamond Mines (CDM), among the largest mining corporations in the country, began to train blacks for semi-skilled jobs previously reserved for whites. It was also in their interests to help develop a black elite which would at some future date possibly hold the reins of power and be well disposed towards them. These efforts were developed into full-scale upgrading courses. By the late 1970s the three companies admitted their first black apprentices. Prior to 1976 no blacks had been apprenticed.

All three companies offered scholarships for degree and diploma students, mostly in professions related to mining, in addition to running their own in-service training and upgrading schemes for their employees. Rössing's student programme, which commenced in 1978, was geared specifically towards providing the mine's future managers. By the 1980s, at least 30 students were enrolled in the programme.[42] The various training schemes offered by the mines raised the levels of the semi-skilled black workers considerably, but the number of skilled and professional blacks still remained very low. CDM in 1979 built the Valombola Technical Institute at Ongwediva in Ovamboland to provide trade training on both a full- and part-time basis. However, the training there was said by SWAPO "to go no more than to enable workers to understand and implement the instructions of their bosses".[43]

ADULT EDUCATION

Adult illiterates constituted 60 to 79 per cent of the black population. In 1962 the government had organised fourteen adult classes in languages, commercial subjects, and handicrafts for whites with a total enrolment of 399.[44] In contrast, it played no role in the provision of black adult education. Instead, this was left to the churches, mines, and some large farms that organised literacy programmes for the migrant contract labourers. There was also a community-sponsored programme in Katutura, the black township of Windhoek, and one evening school for adults in Ovamboland.

The Council of Churches in Namibia (CCN), of which most major Namibian churches are members, was one of the pioneers in adult education. Another body involved in this area was the Bureau of Literacy and Literature (BOLL). Previously a branch of the Adult Education section of the South African Institute of Race Relations, it had established its own executive committee comprising members of various churches since 1971. BOLL was a non-profit organisation that sought to promote adult education, provide educational materials, train literacy teachers and supervisors, and assist existing organisations in starting similar programmes. Essentially, its task was to respond to the demand for adult literacy by providing materials, teacher training, and advice.

By the late 1970s, 30 church literacy classes were operating in the entire country. Of the three mine-run literacy education programmes, one had 800 students in classes ranging from literacy training to matriculation with vocational and non-vocational emphasis.[45] These programmes assisted employees in securing promotion within the company. The lack of competent local supervision was a constant problem. Rössing Uranium, through the Rössing Foundation founded in 1978, established an adult education centre on the outskirts of the Windhoek business area in 1979. Its activities in this field really began having an effect only in the next decade.

On farms the overall outcome of literacy programmes was far from encouraging. In densely populated Katutura, there was merely one adult literacy class with a high drop-out rate and poor demand. The course was organised by the Katutura Community Centre, which maintained its independence from the churches, municipality, and local businesses. The overall critique of adult education in the country was that the situation needed much better organised and planned educational programmes, teacher training, and materials provision for such education to have any worthwhile impact. Furthermore, the courses were insufficient and the content of course materials was said to be unrelated to the learners' needs.[46]

UNIVERSITY TRAINING

Black, coloured, and white pupils who succeeded in qualifying for university had to study in South Africa as Namibia had no university of its own. The universities in South Africa, however, were almost all racially segregated and white universities were endowed with superior facilities and staff. Some of the more liberal white 'open' universities, like Cape Town, the Witwatersrand, Natal, and Rhodes, permitted other ethnic groups to attend if they could prove, as required by law, that the courses they wished to take were not offered at the black or coloured universities. This was an effort to overcome the Extension of University Education Act of 1959, which restricted ethnic groups other than whites to the specifically designed ethnic universities.

Black Namibians, for example, had access to the University of the North, at Turfloop near Pietersburg in the Transvaal; the University of Zululand, at Ngoye in Natal; and the University of Fort Hare, near Alice in the Eastern Cape. These universities were ostensibly reserved for Sothos, Zulus, and Xhosas respectively. Coloureds attended the University of the Western Cape, in Bellville (near Cape Town); Indians the University of Durban-Westville, while whites had access to ten universities, and all had access to the correspondence University of South Africa (UNISA) in Pretoria.

Table 6.9 Namibian Students at South African
Universities, 1971, 1974, and 1978

Ethnic Groups and Universities	Year		
	1971	1974	1978
WHITES at UNISA	503	574	818
WHITE TOTAL	1,564*	1,948*	2,268*
COLOURED			
White Universities	21	49	56
University of the Western Cape	23	58	101
TOTAL	44	86	157
BLACK			
White Universities	19	41	65
Black Universities	28	35	33
TOTAL	47	76	98
GRAND TOTAL	1,655	2,110	2,523

* These figures include all 'white' universities and the correspondence
University of South Africa. No data were available on the number of
blacks and coloureds at UNISA for the years listed. But in 1977 the number of black Namibians was said to be 63.
Source: Adapted from AGN 2, 1982:34, 108, 109, Melber, 1979:192

In 1974 it was estimated that there were only ten black
university graduates in Namibia, though this may well be low,
because the numbers attending universities in South Africa
between 1969 and 1974 totalled 168.[47] By that time, the
number of black graduates outside Namibia was increasing.
All three groups were eligible to apply for government loans
and bursaries to cover the high cost of university education.

Financial assistance was normally granted on a contractual basis by the state. For blacks and coloureds this meant returning to their respective 'homelands' on completion of their studies. Even though they were assured of jobs, especially with the 'homeland' governments, these contracts had a drawback in that they prohibited them from entering into middle- and high-level employment within the economically more viable white areas. Whites too were offered contractual assistance for their tertiary studies, but often they were able to pay back the loans and bursaries received and thereby escape the contract.

As Table 6.9 shows, the highest number of students at university in South Africa were white, followed by coloureds, while black students had the smallest number. Even at UNISA, the majority of students appeared to be white; figures are not available for blacks and coloureds. This situation was bound to affect the ability of blacks to challenge whites for any of the professional posts within Namibia.

HUMAN RESOURCE SUPPLY AND EMPLOYMENT TRENDS

The ethnically divided and inequitable education system had a direct impact on the country's skilled and professional human resource supply. This section examines its impact on skills' output, concentrating mostly on professional, managerial, executive, and administrative posts.

It has been estimated that by 1978 over 90 per cent of the economically active black population had not completed their primary education; for coloureds the figure was 35 per cent.[48] That same year only an estimated 0.2 per cent of blacks had university or equivalent tertiary training (the level required of professional and technical workers) and for coloureds it was 0.5 per cent.[49] As a result, the coloureds and particularly the blacks provided the overwhelming bulk of the unskilled and semi-skilled labour force in commercial and subsistence agriculture, mining, industry, domestic service, and the public sector. Within all sectors they occupied the least lucrative jobs.

As well as these imposed educational disadvantages, another factor militated against coloured and black occupational advancement. This was the practice of job reservation that resulted in the exclusion of blacks and coloureds from specific classes of employment, especially those involving skilled work. It was designed specifically to protect white workers from competition from other ethnic groups.[50] White unions insisted upon such job reservation, and as a result it was written into mining legislation and contracts. Even where formal agreements were lacking, "certain jobs (were) understood to be for whites only".[51]

As mentioned in Chapter 5, for many years coloured and black men who completed tertiary training and wished to take up professional careers generally had recourse to only teaching, school inspection, and the ministry, while women had an even more limited choice between nursing and teaching at the primary level. The official 1975 Human Resource Survey revealed that of 5,305 black and coloured professionals, at least 3,700 (70 per cent) had initially been trained as teachers. In 1977, of the 4,830 coloured and black professionals, semi-professionals and technical employees, 3,915 were involved in education (81 per cent of the overall total). The number of coloureds and blacks trained in nursing for both 1975 and 1977 was fewer than those trained as teachers, and the same applied to those in the ministry for both years.[52] Those who did not wish to choose or remain in these careers could enter the private sector as low-level administrative staff, small businessmen or taxi drivers. Needless to say, salaries in the private sector were better. At least one-third of qualified black teachers were said to be involved in fields outside of education by 1974, a reality which did not bode well for the educational situation, given the perennial shortage of black teachers.[53]

Coloureds were slightly better off than blacks when it came to job opportunities and training. For example, in 1971 there were more coloured than black artisans and apprentices, and on a percentage basis, they were better represented in the clerical, supervisory, skilled and semi-skilled jobs than were blacks. Whites, however, continued to make up the largest percentage of the skilled human resource force, especially in the professional, semi-professional, technical, managerial, executive and administrative occupations in both the public and private sectors, while blacks and coloureds were under-represented in all these (see Table 6.10). Such occupations constitute the middle- and high-level posts vital to a country's overall economic and social functioning. These realities reflected the gradation of opportunities on the basis of colour and were evident in the 1973 statistics.

Table 6.10 Employment of Blacks, Coloureds, and Whites in Namibia in Professional, Managerial and Administrative Occupations, 1973

Occupation	Black	%	Coloured	%	White	%	Total
Professional, Semi-Professional, Technical	3,659	39	271	2.9	5,447	58	9,377
Managerial, Executive, Administrative	29	1.3	8	0.4	2,180	98.3	2,217

Source: Thomas, 1978:196; Mbamba, 1982:203

It was from the late 1970s that coloureds and blacks began to enjoy increases in their share of professional and managerial jobs. A significant proportion of coloureds in particular began experiencing upward mobility as a direct consequence of the skilled human resource shortages during the economic boom periods and the large white exodus mentioned earlier (see page 143). These changes were also part of South Africa's strategy of encouraging occupational mobility among blacks and coloureds in professions previously barred to them. This was part of its policy of fostering a middle class resistant to any possible changes that a perceived future socialist SWAPO Government might introduce. But, because these were only recent trends, they did not make a difference to the large number of undereducated, unskilled workers. They remained occupationally immobile, while white predominance in professional and managerial posts continued. The increase in coloured and black professionals and managers was in part due to the severe shortages of skilled labour in all sectors which, together with the reasons stated above, sparked off more enlightened social policies among employers, especially on the mines.

There was, however, another factor at work. The greater variety of professional occupations available to blacks and coloureds during this decade was a direct outcome of the policy of separate development, which called for the establishment and broadening of regional ethnic administrative authorities in the 'homelands'(as recommended by the Odendaal Commission) and, as a result, the creation of more white-collar posts. But even within these 'homeland' administrations, whites dominated the policy-making, supervisory, and directive posts. The highest posts available to blacks in 'homeland' government structures were usually of an executive nature and generally occupied by traditional, conservative tribal elites who were not necessarily well-educated. The other white-collar jobs available to blacks were clerical. In Ovamboland, which had the highest population concentration, there was still a scarcity of suitably trained administrative staff by the late 1970s, resulting in continued subordination to white officials.

A similar pattern of occupational trends was reflected within each ethnic educational administrative structure: higher posts in the administration, especially those involving planning, organisation, and administration went predominantly to Afrikaans-speaking whites. The few posts within the coloured educational administration available to coloureds were limited to inspector of education, assistant or subject inspector, and school principal. The number of coloured inspectors, assistant inspectors, and subject inspectors was dismally low as shown below.

	1976	1977
Inspector of Education	1	1
Assistant or Subject Inspector	1	1
School Principal	32	36

(Melber, 1979:132)

Throughout the decade, it appears that blacks also had difficulty in rising above the post of school principal (Ovamboland was the exception here). As with the coloureds, there were very few black school inspectors, this being the highest post to which they could aspire within the educational administration (see Table 6.2). Possibly, the first time that a black was appointed to the post of inspector in Namibia occurred as late as 1966, when a black principal holding a university degree was made inspector of schools.[54] In 1972 there was only one black inspector of education for Ovamboland and by 1976 the number had risen to only two. By 1977 the total number of black inspectors was thirteen, compared to two coloured and nineteen white inspectors.[55] Whites dominated all the other ethnic administrations' middle- and high-level posts in education (see Table 6.2). These trends meant that coloureds and blacks lacked exposure to administrative functions at certain levels within the educational structure.

CONCLUSION

The overall picture of Namibia during the 1970s is one where, despite discriminatory job reservation against coloureds, and blacks in particular, the previously limited job opportunities were becoming broader. The major block to occupational mobility was the lack of education and training. This limited the quality and quantity of the majority's skilled members and kept them from competing with whites for professional jobs.

Since the human element "contributes substantially to the dynamism of development by providing the flexibility and manoeuvrability with which to effect structural change", the comprehensive lack of skilled human resources in Namibia did not bode well for its future development capabilities.[56] Firstly, there were not enough skilled coloured and black workers to overcome the gap that a possible exodus of white skilled workers at, or before, independence could create. Secondly, this was even more of a danger, regarding the white professional and managerial occupations in both public and private sectors. Even though the largest group of educated blacks was concentrated in the teaching force, the insufficient number of qualified black teachers, especially for secondary-level schooling, made this group an unlikely source for re-cruitment to other sectors. Additionally, drawing on black teachers at the primary level would mean both relying on resources which were scarce and on people who were poorly trained.

As the 1970s drew to a close and hopes for independence by 1978 were dashed, it became increasingly apparent that there was a severe shortage of skilled human resources in Namibia. There was a growing realisation that real political independence would come and, as in every other developing country, educational strategies and human resource develop-ment would be central issues in an independent Namibia, if it wished to sustain economic development. During the 1980s, these realisations were confronted to a certain degree by the government and private sector; but how did these responses relate to teacher output?

NOTES

1. Du Pisani 1986:185.
2. Tötemeyer 1978:62, 173.
   This was in accordance with a number of specific education acts, for example: the South West Africa Education Act, No. 63 of 1972 which dealt specifically with coloured education; the South West Africa Education Act, No. 86 of 1972 for the Namas; the Ovamboland Education Act, No. 11 of 1973; the Kavango Education Act, No. 3 of 1974 (Mukendwa 1986:55; Education Committee 1985:5; Thomas 1978:53; Rubin 1977:13; Department of Governmental Affairs 1988:44).
3. Mukendwa 1986:55.
4. Kazapua 1984:12; Tötemeyer 1978:173.
5. *ibid.*
6. UNIN 1981:119.
7. Melber 1984:3; Ellis 1984:29.
8. *ibid.*, 11.
9. It is difficult to gauge the actual impact of these increases in terms of the overall population, simply because no figures on the population's age structure were provided in any official documents. Increased enrolments resulted in larger classes in black schools. Classes there were three times larger in the lower primary level schools and twice as large at secondary level compared to white schools by the early 1980s (UNIN 1981:15; Mbamba 1982:44; UNIN 1986:512).
10. Functional literacy is the basic level of literacy attainable after four years of formal schooling. A person who has achieved functional literacy will lapse into illiteracy unless their reading and writing skills are constantly reinforced (Melber 1979:181; Doyle 1979:94).
11. UNIN 1984:11; SWAPO 1981:91.
12. Mukendwa 1985:81.
13. Melber 1979:93, 110, 128, 146, 188; AGN 2 1982:40, 77; Ellis 1984:8.
14. Private schools in Namibia, namely, the Martin Luther secondary school, at Okombahe, and the Gibeon and (more recent) Berseba secondary schools opted to teach the syllabus used in Botswana, Lesotho, and Swaziland.
15. Melber 1979:225.
16. Murray *et al* 1974:173.
17. A further 300 youths, said to be the cream of the 1976 students, were reported to have joined those leaving in 1977. They went to Angola, Zambia and Botswana (Melber 1979:155, 156, 225; Thomas 1978:199).
18. Melber 1979:96.
19. AGN 2 1982:35.

20. *ibid.*, 70,89.
21. Melber 1979:131, 170.
22. Tötemeyer 1978:174; UNIN 1981:30.
23. Mukendwa 1985:70; AGN 2 1982:54.
24. König 1983:33; Ellis 1984:39; Visser 1984:15.
25. Melber 1979:96, 97.
26. O'Callaghan 1977:153.

    Black female teachers predominated at the primary levels and the
    same applied to coloured and white women teachers. This meant that
    women were confined to the lowest levels of teaching and, for blacks,
    the worst-paid jobs in the educational sector. Even by 1981, it was
    reported in the Annual Report of the Coloured Representative
    Authority that only women could enter the Junior Primary Education
    Certificate course with a Standard VIII certificate. Men could enter
    teacher training only with a Standard X qualification. This ruling
    therefore actively encouraged women's confinement to the lower
    teaching rungs (Melber 1979:97, 135; O'Callaghan 1977:121;
    Coloured Representative Authority Annual Report 1980/81:9).
27. Melber 1979:193.
28. AGN 2 1982:74.
29. Melber 1979:150.
30. *ibid.*, 131, 148, 150.
31. Africa Contemporary Record volume 14 1981:B672; AGN 2 1982:40.
32. Melber 1979:115.
33. *ibid.*, 158, 159.
34. Rubin 1977:47.
35. Melber 1979:190 n.95; 191.
36. Mbamba 1982:110.
37. Melber 1979:113; AGN 2 1982:33.
38. Melber 1979:112, 147.
39. *ibid.*, 119.
40. Thomas 1978:203; Leu 1977:158.
41. Collett 1979:203.
42. Rössing 1985:17.
43. SWAPO 1981:91.

    This institution, which could accommodate 250 students, offered a
    two-year, full-time trade course to youths under eighteen with a
    Standard VI school-leaving certificate to train as bricklayers, plum-
    bers, carpenters, welders or motor mechanics. The ten week part-
    time training was available to industrial workers who had had little
    or no previous formal training (SWA Annual 1979:96).
44. Mbamba 1982:112, 399.
45. By 1979 there were thirteen mines in Namibia, yet only three em-
    barked upon adult education programmes (Doyle 1979:93, 94).
46. Doyle 1979:95, 96.

47. O'Callaghan 1977:154; Melber 1979:192; Doyle 1979:91.
48. UNIN 1978:12.
49. *ibid.*, 62.
50. In Namibia the 'job reservation' provisions of the South African Industrial Conciliation Act of 1956 were not reproduced in the relevant legislation applicable to Namibia because of the shortage of skilled labour in all sectors. But such practices nevertheless prevailed. For example, regulations issued in terms of the Mines, Works and Minerals Ordinance, No. 20 of 1968 were explicitly discriminatory in the appointment of personnel to certain positions on mines outside black areas. Specific jobs were said to be for whites only if the manager of the mine was white (Rubin 1977:48, 49; Collett 1980:203).
51. Rubin 1977:41, 48, 49.
52. Thomas 1978:196; South African Department of Labour 1977:3 – 5.
53. Melber 1979:218.
54. Republic of South Africa 1967:118.
55. South African Department of Labour 1977:5; UNIN 1981:119.
56. Collett 1980:219.

7

Trends in formal educational provision: the 1980s

New facades are in the process of being
created for the old system; the development of an
educational system appropriate to
neo-colonialism is starting to gain momentum.

H. MELBER, 1984

INTRODUCTION

This chapter reviews the continuing changes in educational provision in Namibia during the 1980s, especially those relating to the secondary level. The impact of these changes is then analysed in relation to the teaching force. To this end, we have posed, and attempted to answer, a number of specific questions in the discussion below so as to highlight the important issues concerning the country's teachers who not only staff the ever-expanding school system but also comprise the pool from which the nation's educational administrators will be drawn:

☐ What impact did governmental expansion of formal education for black Namibians have on the number and quality of teacher trainees?

☐ What was the availability and quality of the teaching force by the late 1980s?

☐ Was the provision and quality of training suitable to satisfy the requirement for trained teachers?

☐ Did the private sector's growing role in educational provision have a meaningful impact on the number of teacher trainees?

FORMAL EDUCATION PROVISION

DEVELOPMENTS IN PRIMARY AND SECONDARY EDUCATION

Not before time, the government began to make a serious effort to expand primary and secondary educational opportunities for the black population during the 1980s. According to an official report, of all pupils leaving school in 1981, at least 33 per cent were functionally illiterate, 45 per cent were unskilled or semi-skilled, with only 17 per cent fully schooled and therefore prepared adequately for further training as skilled workers. A mere 5 per cent were sufficiently educated to undertake middle- and high-level professional training.[1] A 1982 study of work-seekers in Windhoek found that very few whites had an education qualification lower than Standard VI (the eighth school year).[2] The most poorly qualified pupils came chiefly from the other two ethnic groups. It was also reported that among those undertaking technical training very few succeeded in gaining a recognised certificate or formal qualification due to poor performance in mathematics, science, and technical drawing.[3] Such statements confirmed the education system's continued inability to satisfy the country's requirements for skilled workers.

By 1988 enrolment figures had increased significantly, but the same trends were still very visible (see Table 7.1). The number of blacks in Standard X had risen from 346 in 1981 to 902 in 1988. For the first time, the number of blacks at this level did not differ too widely from that of whites and even outnumbered them, if the enrolments in Department of National Education (DNE) schools are included.

Of the 90 ordinary schools under the DNE, fifteen offered matriculation courses. One school in Windhoek even offered the post-matriculation German *Abitur* qualification. Standard X candidates totalled 353 with an additional 62 doing the

Table 7.1   Primary and Secondary School Enrolments by
Grade, 1988

Std.	DNE	White	Coloured	Black
Primary School				
Sub A	6,298	1,413	4,296	55,802
Sub B	5,512	1,264	4,091	41,130
Std. 1	5,088	1,224	4,049	35,360
Std. 2	5,059	1,250	4,005	35,990
Std. 3	4,843	1,196	4,017	28,464
Std. 4	4,994	1,252	3,773	26,466
Std. 5	2,877	1,266	3,100	17,566
TOTAL	34,671	8,865	27,331	240,778
Secondary School				
Std. 6	2,653	1,257	2,960	14,350
Std. 7	2,050	1,224	2,440	9,021
Std. 8	1,353	1,150	1,959	7,586
Std. 9	920	1,126	1,396	1,516
Std. 10	353	933	832	902
TOTAL	7,329	5,690	9,587	33,375
GRAND TOTAL	42,000	14,555	36,918	274,153
TOTAL SCHOOL ENROLMENT	367,626			
PERCENTAGE OF TOTAL	11	4	10	75

Notes: (1) These figures exclude those pupils in the bridging year, pre-
primary, special, auxiliary and practical classes and specialised education, special schools, and technical institutions.
(2) Figures for the DNE include students of all three ethnic
groups, but no breakdown by group is available.
Source: Adapted from the South West Africa Department of Economic
Affairs, 1988:19 – 28

Abitur.[4] Not surprisingly, the latter were predominantly whites from the German population group, since this qualification was meant to prepare students for further study in Germany.

Though the DNE's schools were open to all ethnic groups, at least thirteen of the fifteen high schools offering matriculation courses admitted mostly black or coloured pupils. Impressive though these developments may appear, the actual enrolments of coloured and especially black matriculants remained extremely small when one considers relative populations and the dire shortage of human skills in the country.[5] Moreover, education for blacks alone remained non-compulsory.

For Coloured students in Standard X in 1981 and 1988, the number increased from 284 to 832 respectively (see Tables 6.4 and 7.1). The total white school enrolment figure had dropped by 35 per cent between 1971 and 1988, reflecting the fall in the overall white population. It was reported in 1981 that at least 20,000 whites had left the country during the 1970s, roughly a 25 per cent decline.[6] In contrast, other population groups were growing rapidly by at least 3.6 per cent per year.[7]

However, the number of black students reaching Standard X was substantially less than it might have been. Young Namibians continued to flee to neighbouring countries. In February 1981 some 5,000 Namibians fled to Angola in direct response to the introduction of military conscription for all males between the ages of sixteen and 25 early in 1981.[8] But the perennial problem of poor educational facilities for blacks, which inhibited their potential to achieve, as well as the dismal employment prospects for them under the apartheid system, also added to the impetus to leave the country. Furthermore, the war in the north was disrupting schooling, and in June 1981 it was reported that nineteen of Ovamboland's 450 schools were closed.[9] School boycotts and closures, especially in northern Namibia, characterised 1988. According to annual reports of the DNE, these disruptions also affected the scholars' overall academic performance. The figures in Table 7.2 reflect the number of pupils enrolled in

159

schools in March of each academic year, not pupil performance. That the DNE avoided printing matriculation pass rates is in itself an indication that results must have been particularly poor.

Table 7.2   Standard X Enrolments, 1988 and 1989

Ethnic Group	1988	1989
White	933	992
Caprivian	210	225
Damara	180	169
Herero	37	33
Kavango	30	42
Coloured	385	378
Nama	210	119
Tswana	25	—
Ovambo	420	559
Rehoboth Baster	237	236
DNE	353	496
TOTAL	3,020	3,249

Source: Adapted from South West Africa Department of Economic Affairs, 1988:51 – 58; 1989:53 – 61

Many pupils registered in Standard X did not gain matriculation exemption. Within the DNE schools, where the pass rate was said to be higher than the average for the country, there were 462 and 426 matriculants in 1986 and 1987 respectively. Only 110 (24 per cent) obtained matriculation exemption in 1986 and 88 (21 per cent) the following year, the pass rate having dropped consistently since 1984.[10]

By 1988, despite the overall expansion in formal educational provision, the disparities between black, coloured and white education persisted. Moreover, there were additional disruptions: political protest, war, and exile. As such, the expansion in formal education provision fell short of overcoming the country's skilled human resource requirements. However, one cannot ignore the fact that the increase in the number of primary and secondary coloured and black pupils was significant compared to earlier decades.

The number of senior secondary students remained small. This was exacerbated by the fact that not all of these pupils actually gained matriculation exemption. However, a greater number than before were entering higher formal education and they had the potential to become skilled professionals capable of participating in the previously all-white power structures. They were the 'new' middle class in the making, upon which, as Melber predicted, "a modified (South African-backed) neo-colonial minority regime could rely".[11] But senior secondary student numbers remained small compared with the number of whites already occupying positions of power and influence. The situation in general was still characterised by a scarcity of skills and a surplus unskilled labour pool made up of coloureds and blacks.

THE ROLE OF THE PRIVATE SECTOR

The private sector's role in education helped towards fostering the growth of a potential black and coloured bourgeoisie in Namibia. In 1983 Consolidated Diamond Mines (CDM) in co-operation with the DNE established the English-medium, multi-racial, fee-paying Concordia College in Windhoek for gifted pupils. This institution offered secondary education from Standard V to Standard X. Like most schools in Namibia, Concordia followed the Cape Education Department's syllabus. The DNE controlled Concordia and the government paid staff salaries and running costs. Hostel and tuition fees were subsidised by CDM, which enabled talented pupils of all ethnic groups to attend the school, regardless of their financial situation.

Initial enrolment at Concordia was 500 and the figure was expected to rise considerably in the years following its establishment to at least 1,800.[12] This institution was academically biased and aimed at "providing a corps of potential teachers

161

with university entrance qualifications; increasing the number of matriculants interested in careers other than teaching; producing matriculants with the necessary skills and leadership abilities so urgently required by both public and private sectors...."[13]

The emphasis at this school was on mathematics, physical and biological sciences, and commercial subjects, as well as on the two official languages, English and Afrikaans. This orientation precluded most black pupils from gaining entry because mathematics, general science, and English were poorly taught in black schools. Concordia had a 100 per cent pass rate among its Standard X students in 1987; 71 per cent obtained matriculation exemption (university-entrance qualifications).[14]

The Rössing Foundation's scholarship scheme was another programme aimed at encouraging the formation of an elite in Namibia. The programme sent two to three, mostly black and coloured, pre-matriculation candidates to the United World College of the Atlantic, in South Wales, each year. There they would take the international *baccalaureate*. Upon completion, the candidates were not committed to work either for Rössing Uranium or its Foundation, but they were required to return to Namibia where it was hoped they would make their way into decision-making positions in the Namibian community. The pass rate of this programme has been between 65 and 70 per cent. Most candidates at this level have either gone on to do further studies in South Africa or remained in the United Kingdom to pursue further studies with assistance from either the United Nations or church organisations.[15]

THE TEACHING FORCE

TEACHER AVAILABILITY

In 1981 the number of teachers in Namibia totalled 8,139, a 20 per cent increase over the 1979 figure.[16] Pupil teacher ratios for blacks remained unfavourable (see Table 7.3).[17] The teacher pupil ratios revealed the uneven distribution of teachers among the different ethnic groups, especially those in the north. The Ovambos registered the highest pupil/teacher ratio in 1988 (see Table 7.4). Noticeable among the white ethnic group's totals was the drop in numbers of both teachers and pupils between 1980 and 1988, which was a direct outcome of the ongoing exodus of whites since the 1970s.

Table 7.3 Pupil/Teacher Ratios from Sub-Standard A to Standard X, 1980 and 1988

Ethnic Group	1980			1988		
	Pupils	Teachers	Ratio	Pupils	Teachers	Ratio
White	18,303*	1,362*	13:1*	14,555	1,212	12:1
Coloured	31,070	1,069	29:1	36,918	1,655	22:1
Black	186,009	5,066**	37:1	274,153	7,960	34:1
DNE***	—	—	—	42,000	1,698	25:1

* Figures for 1981.
** 179 of these were white.
*** Figures include all three major ethnic groups.
Source: Adapted from AGN 2, 1982:26, 65, 71, 92; Ellis, 1984:83; South West Africa Department of Economic Affairs, 1988:39 – 49

In black primary and secondary schools, teacher shortages persisted, especially in mathematics, science, and English. This was also a problem in white schools, especially in mathematics.[18] As a result, the level of teaching in these subjects was poor. This was significant, because these were the very subjects required for technical disciplines where limited numbers of pupils were able to succeed.

An alarming feature of this decade was the loss of teachers from the profession. This had many causes. White teachers were among those leaving the country, a trend which accelerated with the military exodus at the end of the decade. Black teachers had continued to flee the war zone in the north. Their departure was sparked mainly by the harassment from

Table 7.4   Pupils, Teachers, and Schools by Individual Ethnic Group, 1988

Ethnic Group	Pupils	Pupils as % of Total	Teachers	Pupil/ Teacher Ratios	Schools*
Caprivian	20,935	5.6	811	26:1	71
Coloured	15,946	4.3	658	24:1	37
Damara	9,921	2.6	426	23:1	23
Herero	16,595	4.4	613	27:1	40
Kavango	34,563	9.2	1,147	30:1	237
Nama	11,877	3.2	532	22:1	38
Ovambo	193,219	51.6	4,920	39:1	507
Rehoboth Baster	10,000	2.7	465	22:1	39
Tswana	1,068	0.3	43	25:1	2
White	17,224	4.6	1,212	14:1	66
DNE**	42,921	11.5	1,698	25:1	93
TOTAL	374,269	100	12,525	30:1***	1,153

* Includes technical schools and institutions, agricultural and special schools, specialised education and industrial schools.
** The DNE was responsible for the Bushmen's schooling. In 1988 there were thirteen schools (one offering matriculation) and a total of 1,620 pupils.
*** Ratio figures calculated from the totals of columns 2 and 4 and rounded to the nearest decimal.
Source: Adapted from South West Africa Department of Economic Affairs, 1988; DNE, 1988:57; Interview, Inspector of Education, (Bushmen), DNE, 14/10/1988

the South African army stationed in the north and the general dissatisfaction with the system.

Among those qualified teachers who remained in Namibia, those with higher qualifications could obtain better-paid or more attractive private sector or civil service jobs.[19] For this reason, resignations persisted despite a significant alteration in the government's policy since the late 1970s. From that time onwards, it raised the salary grades of black and coloured principals and teachers with Standard X qualifications and above to match those of their white counterparts with the same qualifications.

Total resignation figures were not available, nor was there any information regarding their ethnic composition. From 1980 – 1987, the number of teacher resignations from the DNE alone was 776. Virtually with every successive year of that period there was a marked rise in teacher resignations, reaching a high point in 1986/1987 of 187. This figure represented 13 per cent of the DNE's teaching force of 1,460 that year.[20] This trend of mass resignation was also prevalent in the individual ethnic administrations' schools, resulting in a serious lack of teachers in Namibia by the end of the 1980s. The official 1988 human resource survey reveals that out of a total of 468 listed vacancies in the educational sector at least 355 (76 per cent) were registered among teachers.[21]

TEACHER QUALIFICATIONS

It is reasonable to assume that there is a strong connection between the level of formal education and professional training of the teaching force, and the quality of teaching. One of the annual reports of the DNE ascribed the unsatisfactory quality of teaching to insufficient training, lack of knowledge of subjects, and poor language competence of the teaching force.[22] Almost every annual report of the DNE from 1981 to 1987 mentions the insufficient number of qualified teachers. By 1981, 29 per cent of all teachers in the country were professionally unqualified and only one quarter had attained a Standard X plus professional qualifications.[23] One official report noted that the problem was more evident in certain regions:

> Where there is the largest concentration of the population and the most urgent need for education, provision of education is poorest in terms of number ratios and level of training. Caprivi, Kavango and Owambo together have 65% of the total school population, while 54% of the total teaching corps works there. Of these teachers only 7% have qualifications higher than Std. 10 level, while 30% have qualifications lower than Std. 8.[24]

This meant a continuation of poor instruction and hence low-level pupil performance. Even when pupils succeeded in progressing to secondary school, insurmountable problems arose because they were unable to master the basic concepts of the junior standards. The least qualified teachers continued to be confined to the primary schools. In summing up the overall quality of the teaching force, the 1985 Education Committee stated that this profession seemed unable to recruit, motivate or maintain the best-qualified human resources in the country.[25]

By 1988, out of a total of 12,525 filled teaching posts in the country, the largest category of teachers (30 per cent) had Standard VII or a lower basic education plus two to three years' teacher training or Standard VIII or IX without training (see Table 7.5). It was reported that the subject knowledge of these poorly qualified teachers "is inadequate to serve as a basis for further in-service training for subject advisers to build on".[26]

Table 7.5 reveals that the majority of teachers in Namibia were underqualified. Teachers without a Standard X comprised 64 per cent of the teacher total in 1988 and 62 per cent in 1989. The percentages for Kavangos, Hereros and Ovambos were 90, 85 and 81 per cent respectively (see Table 7.6).

A 1989 United Nations Development Programme assessment estimated that 88 per cent of the country's teachers were un- or underqualified.[27] It must also be borne in mind that, for the period 1985 – 1989, the number of teaching posts

Table 7.5 Number and Qualifications of all Teachers,
1985 – 1988

	1985	1986	1987	1988
TOTALS				
No. of approved Posts	10,489	11,285	12,066	12,688
No. of Posts filled	10,372	11,121	11,945	12,525
Category of Teacher				
ZA	1,702	1,471	1,226	864
ZB	3,208	3,309	3,513	3,726
ZC	2,264	2,617	2,936	3,129
ZD	178	229	186	296
ZZ	355	564	932	1,096
A	211	191	279	335
B	509	582	559	593
C	840	890	896	943
D	886	1,036	1,164	1,247
E	170	184	195	229
F	26	26	32	39
G	23	22	27	28

Notes: ZA – Std. VII or lower with no teacher training.
ZB – Std.VII or lower with two or three years' training or only
Std. VIII or IX.
ZC – Std.VIII or IX with two years' teacher training or only Std. X.
ZD – Lower than Std. X (promotion posts: heads of departments,
deputy principals, principals).
ZZ – Std. X with two or more years' pre-tertiary training.
A – Std. X plus one year teacher training.
B – Std. X plus two years' teacher training.
C – Std. X plus three years' teacher training.
D – Std. X plus four years' teacher training (BA plus teachers'
diploma).
E – Std.X plus five years' teacher training (Honours degree plus
teachers' diploma).
F – Std. X plus six years' teacher training (MA plus teachers'
diploma).
G – Std. X plus seven years' teacher training (Ph D plus teachers'
diploma).
Categories A to G include both universities and technikons.
Source: South West Africa Department Economic Affairs, 1988:38

Table 7.6   Teachers' Qualifications According to
Individual Ethnic Groups, 1988

Ethnic Group	CATEGORY OF TEACHER				
	Std. X or Lower	%*	Std. X and Further Qualifications	%*	Total
Caprivian	565	70	246	30	811
Coloured	197	30	461	70	658
Damara	298	70	128	30	426
Herero	519	85	94	15	613
Kavango	1,034	90	113	10	1,147
Nama	338	64	194	36	532
Ovambo	3,986	81	934	19	4,920
Rehoboth Baster	184	40	281	60	465
Tswana	12	28	31	72	43
White	14	1	1,198	99	1,212
DNE	868	51	830	49	1,698
TOTAL	8,015	64	4,510	36	12,525

* Percentages in each individual group's teacher totals.
Source: Adapted from South West Africa Department of Economic Affairs, 1988:39 – 49

filled had been consistently below the number of approved posts, which further magnified the dire situation of the teaching force. Table 7.7 indicates gross disparities between ethnic groups in pupil/teacher ratios and in the ratio of pupils to qualified teachers, the latter ratio being particularly disadvantageous in the case of the Kavangos, Ovambos and Hereros.

Table 7.7   The Ratios of Pupils to Qualified Teachers, 1988

Ethnic Group	Pupil/Qualified Teacher*	Overall Pupil/Teacher
Caprivian	85:1	26:1
Coloured	35:1	24:1
Damara	78:1	23:1
Herero	176:1	27:1
Kavango	306:1	30:1
Nama	61:1	22:1
Ovambo	207:1	39:1
Rehoboth Baster	36:1	22:1
Tswana	34:1	25:1
White	14:1	14:1
DNE	52:1	25:1

* Standard X plus teacher training.
Source: Adapted from South West Africa Department of
Economic Affairs, 1988

These tendencies indicated the continuation of the already vicious cycle in black education, whereby output at secondary school level adversely affected the quality of the teaching force which in turn affected pupil performance. Nevertheless, department heads, deputy principals, and principals (category ZD in Table 7.5) were selected largely on the basis of post-matriculation qualifications. In 1988, 2.4 per cent had only a Standard X or lower qualification (see Tables 7.5 and 7.8).

Table 7.8   Teachers' Qualifications, 1988

	White	Coloured	Black	DNE
CATEGORY				
(1) Std. X or Lower	14	719	6,414	868
(2) Std. X + Further Qualifications	1,198	936	1,546	830
Total Number of Teachers	1,212	1,655	7,960	1,698
Total Excluding DNE	10,827			
GRAND TOTAL	12,525			
Heads of Departments, Deputy Principals and Principals with Qualifications Lower than Std. X	—	30	241	25
PERCENTAGE OF ETHNIC CATEGORY TOTALS				
(1) Std. X or Lower	1	43	81	51
(2) Std. X + Further Qualifications	99	57	19	49

Source: Adapted from South West Africa Department of Economic Affairs, 1988:39 – 49

TEACHER TRAINING PROVISION

Teacher training institutions and the Academy for Tertiary Education

By 1982 there were nine centres offering full-time teacher training: the same seven for blacks which were operating during the previous decade; the Khomasdal Teacher Training College for coloureds, Rehoboth Basters, and Namas; and the white Teacher Training College in Windhoek. All the institutions remained ethnic specific.[28] The new multi-racial Academy for Tertiary Education, established in Windhoek in 1980 in accordance with the Academy for Tertiary Education Act, No. 13 of 1980, was to play a major role in the provision of teacher training in Namibia. The Academy did not enjoy an autonomous status in the sense that it could not confer its own degrees and diplomas but prepared students for the awards of the University of South Africa (UNISA) and a technikon college in Pretoria respectively.

The establishment of such an institution was an important step in confronting the crisis in Namibia's human resource output. But this was not the only factor which prompted the government to establish the Academy. By the early 1980s, the government was faced with the embarrassing fact that a larger number of Namibians outside the country were receiving university, tertiary, and skills training than those inside Namibia. For example, by 1979 the United Nations Institute for Namibia (UNIN), then seen to be the nucleus of a future University of Namibia, had already enrolled 298 students, most of whom were drawn from pupils who had fled Namibia during the mid-1970s.[29] The Academy was therefore in part intended to counteract the impact of UNIN, placate the educational demands of blacks, and defuse international criticism of South Africa's policies in Namibia by making the country appear to be moving towards greater self-sufficiency in certain spheres. The Academy was a vital instrument of South Africa's Namibian political strategy of increasing the number of black and coloured recruits for higher jobs in government and commerce, thereby boosting the formation of a pliant nascent middle class.

A new Academy Act, No. 9 of 1985 not only altered the local institution's name to the Academy but also gave it a greater degree of autonomy than before, enabling it to award its own degrees, diplomas, and certificates, while also altering its structure to embrace a university, a technikon, and a college for out of school training. Generally speaking, the Academy remained firmly within the parameters of South African control. The high- and middle-level administrative and clerical staff who, in 1988, numbered approximately 350, were predominantly white Afrikaners. Many had come from South Africa, especially those at middle and top levels.[30]

The Academy's central administration controlled its finances, personnel, academic administration, and logistical services. The Central Government, however, was empowered to approve or disallow any new programme, department or faculty at the Academy. At least three Central Government cabinet members served on the Academy's Council. The Central Government also provided a major portion of the Academy's funding which, by 1988/1989, represented the third largest item in the country's entire education budget, after the DNE and the South West African Broadcasting Corporation (SWABC).[31] The Academy augmented its government subsidy by tuition and boarding fees, and donations from the private sector.

Black and coloured students quickly came to outnumber whites at the Academy. The ethnic breakdown for 1986 was as illustrated:

White	597	(17%)
Coloured	703	(20%)
Black	2,191	(63%)
TOTAL	3,491	(100%)

(The Academy Census 1986:8)

By contrast, in 1988 approximately 3,500 Namibians (mostly white) were attending universities and technikons in South

Africa.[32] The Academy seems to have been designed primarily to offer continuing education to Namibians whose formal schooling had been interrupted and upgrade qualifications for Namibian teachers. In this way, it provided a counter-incentive to those young Namibians who had plans to quit the country so as to further their education. The desire for further education was clearly evidenced in the numerous applications to the Academy from the start. In 1981 it was reported that hundreds of blacks and coloureds were turned away due to lack of room.[33] Concerning teacher training, the Academy certainly had an important role to play, especially for educationally disadvantaged groups.

By 1988 teacher training was offered at the Academy's University, the College for Out of School Training (COST), the Distance Teaching Section (which serviced the three components of the Academy), and the three satellite campuses at Ongwediva, Rundu and Katima Mulilo. The establishment of the Academy meant that for the first time students were able to train for secondary school teaching in Namibia. All teacher training courses requiring a Standard X entry qualification for blacks could be taken only in Windhoek, while the accredited campuses in the north and the training centres run by the 'homeland' administrations were only allowed to offer the Education Certificate Primary (ECP) post-Standard VIII courses. The Academy offered the following teacher qualifications in 1988:

The University: Faculty of Education
- Bachelor of Primary Education (B Prim Ed), four years' full time, post-secondary
- Bachelor of Education (B Ed), one year full time and two years' part time, postgraduate
- Higher Education Diploma (HED), one year full time and two years' part time, postgraduate
- Higher Education Diploma Secondary (HED Sec), four years' full time, post-secondary
- Education Diploma Primary (ED Prim), three years' full time, post-secondary

173

- Education Diploma Primary Academy (ED Prim Academy), one year full time and two years' part time, post-secondary
- Higher Education Diploma Primary (HED Prim), one year full time and two years' part time, post-secondary
- Higher Education Diploma Technical (HED Tech), one year full time and two years' part time, post-secondary
- Secondary Education Certificate (SEC), two years' full time, post-secondary
- Diploma in Special and Remedial Education (DSRE), one year full time, postgraduate plus two years' teaching experience — not on offer after 1988

Distance Education Section (courses on a part time basis)
- Higher Primary Education Certificate (HPEC), three years', post-secondary
- Education Certificate Primary (ECP Senior Primary only), three years', Standard VIII
- Education Diploma Primary (ED Prim), two years' post-secondary — as of 1989

College for Out of School Training
- Education Certificate Senior Primary (ECP), two years' full time, Standard VIII
- Education Certificate Junior Primary (ECP), two years' full time, Standard VIII

The number of students enrolled in teacher training or other education courses, both full and part time, was 63 per cent of the entire student total of 4,594 in 1988 (see Table 7.9). Entrance into degree courses in education required a matriculation exemption issued by the Joint Matriculation Board of South Africa or a senior school-leaving certificate issued by one of the education departments in South Africa, for entrance to certain undergraduate diploma and certificate courses. The ECP (Senior Primary) by distance education required a Standard VIII certificate; the HPEC, which was unique to the Distance Education Section of the Acade-

Table 7.9   Enrolment in Education Courses at the
            Academy and its Accredited Campuses,
            1988 and 1989

Courses	1988	1989
University		
B Prim Ed	14	10
B Ed	55	51
HED (Postgraduate)	40	52
HED (Secondary)	136	233
HED (Prim)	11	7
HED (Technical)	16	8
ED Prim	39	79
ED Prim (Academy)	4	2
SEC	15	14
Higher Education Post Diploma*	—	6
TOTAL	330	462
Distance Education		
HPEC	243	313
ECP (Senior Primary)	684	961
ED Prim*	—	15
TOTAL	927	1,289
College for Out of School Training		
ECP Junior Primary	48	—
ECP Senior Primary	218	—
TOTAL	266	
Accredited Campuses		
ECP	1,354	—
GRAND TOTAL	2,877	—

* Only as of 1989.
Source: Adapted from the Academy Statistics, November 1989;
International Conference on Teacher Education for Namibia, Lusaka,
21 – 27 September 1989:37

my, a school-leaving certificate; and the ED Prim, a matriculation exemption. The ECP courses at the College for Out of School Training also required only a Standard VIII certificate, the lowest educational requirement for a teaching qualification.

The Academy's satellite campuses at Ongwediva and Rundu also offered the ECP Junior and Senior Primary courses, while the Katima Mulilo campus offered only the ECP Senior Primary course, since the Caprivian Education Authority claimed to have sufficient junior primary teachers in 1988.[34]

Within the Academy's overall structure, the number of students in primary teacher training courses far exceeded those pursuing secondary school training, who numbered only 246 or 9 per cent of the total (see Table 7.9). By far the largest number of trainees were enrolled in the ECP courses at the accredited campuses in the north. These figures are a vast improvement over previous totals. Even in Distance Education, the 1989 ECP enrolments showed a considerable increase over those of 1988.

Students taking the ECP courses were able simultaneously to qualify for a matriculation (Senior Certificate) and a teacher's certificate. This ECP qualification, recognised only in Namibia, had some fundamental weaknesses. It concentrated on the matriculation subjects so that the education component of the course suffered. For instance, not nearly enough time was devoted to practice teaching and school organisation and administration. School administration, for example, was covered only during the last half of the final year, while practice teaching comprised two weeks during the final year. Another criticism of the programme was the dearth of experienced and qualified teacher trainers.[35] Kazapua claimed that it was mostly the academically weaker pupils, incapable of performing well within the school system, who opted for the ECP courses.[36] They saw it as another route to obtaining a matriculation qualification.

Nevertheless, bearing in mind the dearth of places for entry to senior secondary schools, the ECP was a way to widen access to matriculation qualifications by another route. It was also an important step in attempting to lower the number of teachers without Standard X qualifications. The majority of teachers in Namibia belonged to this category, as we see in Table 7.5. This programme must certainly have helped reduce the number of such teachers between 1985 – 1989. The ECP programme also lowered the number of primary-trained teachers in secondary schools without matriculation certificates. Despite its shortcomings, the ECP course was a realistic attempt to address the problem of raising educational standards. The intention was admirable. All the same, many Namibian educators regarded the ECP as a typical Bantu Education-style 'special' programme for black teachers and it was replaced within the first year of independence.

Most of the teacher training programmes offered by the Academy prepared students superficially, if at all, for administrative tasks in education. The Distance Education HPEC course, in its section Comparative Pedagogics, offered a very basic introduction. The ECP's Senior Primary course in the subject was even more elementary. The ED Prim qualification had no administrative component. All other centres which offered the ECP courses provided educational administration as an optional subject.

At university level, the only courses offering an administrative component were: the postgraduate B Ed degree (where the subject was optional), the HED Sec course, and the ED Prim diploma.[37] The enrolment in these three programmes was small, totalling 230 or 8 per cent of the entire teacher total in 1988 (see Table 7.9), and educational administration was compulsory in only two of them.

Generally, the Academy provided a more superior quality of teacher training than had been on offer before in Namibia. Its admission requirements were higher: Standard VIII was the minimum admission requirement for one of its certificate courses, while all the others required a Standard X or higher qualification. One of the most important features was that the structure of the courses differed from the training offered before to black teachers. At the Academy, there existed a more "traditional western type of teacher education, instead of the teacher training system for Africans, specially designed to fit into the framework of Bantu education".[38] Among the negative criticisms meted out against all the Academy's and other training institutions' teacher training was that the curriculum was too academic and practical training far too short. In many instances the latter was confined to two weeks with four weeks regarded as the minimum. Additionally, at the pre-independence review of teacher education the need for training in educational management was noted.[39]

Many of the staff of the University's education faculty were graduates of the more conservative Afrikaner universities in South Africa, which called into question the ideological and epistemological context of the Faculty's educational theory and practice. Several academics at this establishment saw it as "dominated by Afrikaner Nationalists who operate in support of the Verwoerdian dreams of segregation and white domination — to the detriment of the interests of Namibia".[40] The onset of independence clearly spelt the need for urgent changes to the Academy.

Recent changes at the Academy

Early in 1991, a Presidential Commission on Higher Education — comprising both local and international experts from the private sector, academia, and government — was established under Professor J.D. Turner. The Commission, among other things, aimed to:

☐ establish the needs, demands, and scope of higher education;

☐ determine the organisation and structure of the higher education system, including the nature and location of higher education institutions; and

☐ determine the extent of the higher education system in the medium and long term in relation to national human resource needs.[41]

The Commission's recommendations, submitted in September 1991, laid the groundwork for the creation of the

University of Namibia (UNAM).[42] The University came into existence after the passing of the University of Namibia Bill in August 1992. Prior to this date, the former structures of the Academy were maintained as they had been in the late 1980s. The Technikon and College for Out of School Training are to be merged into a Polytechnic of Namibia which, though independent of UNAM, will work in co-operation with it.

Since independence, new departments have come into existence within the Faculty of Education and new courses, many of which are more Namibia-specific, are available. However, the same emphasis is given to educational administration and management as was prior to independence. One of the diploma courses, the ED Prim, is to be phased out in 1993. This is because the Ministry of Education and Culture is offering a new three-year, pre-service Basic Education Teacher Diploma (BETD) at its teacher training colleges in Windhoek, Ongwediva, Rundu and Katima Mulilo. This is in line with the new Basic Education Reform Programme for schooling in Namibia. Administration and organisation of education are absent from the BETD's curriculum.

After independence, staff changes occurred at the upper levels of the former Academy's administration, namely, the appointment of black Namibians to the posts of Vice Chancellor, Dean of Students, Dean of Studies, and Registrar. The head of the Strategic Planning and Development Unit is a West Indian who was employed at UNIN. Former staff were not dismissed and those in high-level posts were merely moved laterally. However, some of them chose to leave. The Rector of the Academy, for example, resigned and subsequently resumed his career at a technikon in the Transvaal. By early 1991, the acting chairman of the Academy Council confirmed that resignations at the institution had left many vacancies.[43]

Within the Faculty of Education, at least six of the former 1988 staff were no longer employed in 1993. The number of black staff has also risen considerably from one in 1988 to at least ten at the time of writing. In fact, this faculty boasts the largest number of black staff at the University, some of whom are in Namibia only on limited contracts. A staff development programme exists which aims to recruit and train Namibians wishing to pursue university careers. Currently, there are few candidates on this programme.[44]

Another important change since independence is that student intake within the University has increased considerably. This was particularly evident in 1992 due to a deliberate 'open door' policy. Enrolments rose from 2,367 to 2,750 (16 per cent).[45] During the colonial period, a strict limit was kept on the number of students entering the University, due either to the lack of facilities and staff or simply as part of the deliberate strategy to keep Namibia's majority disadvantaged.

TEACHER SUPPLY

Just as the number of black pupils had risen over previous years', so there was a significant rise in the number of black teacher trainees within the country during the 1980s. In 1982 there were 905 trainees enrolled in Namibia (see Table 7.10). By 1988 the figures for the Academy and its various branches alone came to 2,877. This represented a 218 per cent rise over the 1982 enrolments and would have been higher if enrolments at the other teacher training centres were included. The rise in enrolments was extremely encouraging but, in order to ascertain whether this increase was adequate, we must also take note of the number of successful passes and the annual growth of school enrolment, put at 5.6 per cent in 1982.[46]

According to official sources, about 60 per cent of the candidates pursuing teacher training courses at the Academy's satellite campuses qualified.[47] Internationally, a 40 per cent failure rate in professional training would be regarded as completely unacceptable. The situation in the individual colleges was far worse than the average. At the Ongwediva campus run by the Ovamboland Administration, practically all the first-year ECP Junior Primary trainees failed in 1988, while less than half the second-year ECP students passed (147 out of 303). At the Rundu campus run by the Kavango Administration, the pass rate for second-year ECP teacher

Table 7.10 Teacher Trainee Enrolment in Namibia, 1982

Training	Year of Study				Total
	1	2	3	4	
PRE-TERTIARY Std. VIII + 2 Years	312	173			485
Std. VIII + 3 Years		22	36		58
TERTIARY Std. X + 3 Years	59	25	22		106
Std. X + 4 Years	95	55	44	62	256
PRE-TERTIARY Non-Final Year					334
TERTIARY Non-Final Year					278
Total Non-Final Year					612
PRE-TERTIARY Final Year					209
TERTIARY Final Year					84
Total Final Year					293
GRAND TOTAL Final and Non-Final Years					905

Source: AGN 3, 1983:82

trainees was 34 per cent (twelve out of 35).[48] No figures were available for the Katima Mulilo Training campus run by the Caprivian Administration but, there too, it was reported that pass rates were low. These low pass rates must also have been partly attributable to the boycotts and general unrest among black students during the late 1980s, especially in the north where most of the trainees were concentrated.

Within the Academy's Faculty of Education in 1988, a mere 88 (27 per cent), out of 330 students, passed. This was an improvement over the total of 23 and 53 in 1986 and 1987 respectively. No pass rate figures were available from the white Windhoek Teacher Training College where 120 students (about 30 from South Africa) were enrolled in 1988, but it was reported that the success rate was low. In 1988, 175 trainees were enrolled at the Khomasdal Teacher Training College which that year had an overall pass rate of 65 per cent, but 80 per cent of its students came from South Africa. They were obliged to return to teach there on completion.[49]

The issue of low pass rates was compounded by a further problem. The 1985 Education Committee reported that too few trainees were enrolled in teacher training to satisfy the needs of normal population growth, put at 3.6 per cent. It was estimated that 1,100 teachers would be needed in 1985 alone.[50] As it is not known how this estimate was arrived at, it cannot be properly assessed. However, the figure corresponds to the UNIN estimate that 1,000 new teachers are needed a year to meet annual growth alone. This figure increases to roughly 1,200 per year for a period of five years up to 1990 when taking into account the shortage of teachers.[51] The overall number of teachers required will rise even further if we consider how many teachers leave the teaching profession or the number of teachers necessary to replace unqualified teachers.

By 1989 there were approximately 1,500 first-year teacher trainees, excluding students at the Windhoek Teacher Training College. Given that some of those enrolled already worked as teachers, and taking into account low pass rates, even this rise in enrolments was insufficient to meet estimated needs for new teachers alone.[52] This reality pointed to the urgent need for more better-qualified teachers.

CENTRAL GOVERNMENT SUPPORT FOR TEACHER TRAINING

Among the efforts of the state to meet the need for more and better-qualified teachers was the Government Service Bursary

Scheme. This helped to boost the overall trainee total to some extent. After having qualified, candidates with awards from this scheme had to work for the Namibian Government Service for the same number of years as their sponsorship. For teacher trainees this meant taking up employment with the DNE or one of the ethnic administrations.

Most of the awards in this scheme went towards teacher training, with more than 80 per cent of the candidates at the Academy.[53] Out of the total of 107 bursaries for teaching in 1988, at least 75 were awarded to unqualified teachers.[54] This scheme was small in comparison to the ethnic authorities' bursaries (see Table 7.11), despite the Central Government's larger resources.[55]

THE ROLE OF THE PRIVATE SECTOR AND OTHER ORGANISATIONS IN ASSISTING TEACHER TRAINEES

Among private sponsors, the contribution of Consolidated Diamond Mines (CDM) to teacher training was negligible. From the inception of its bursary scheme in 1979 until 1988, CDM had awarded only five bursaries for educational studies in South Africa, Namibia, and Wales out of a total of 83. Of the five only one candidate, a black, passed and was employed by CDM and thereafter went to work for the DNE. A coloured candidate was still a student in 1988. The remaining students, two blacks and one white, did not pass their courses.[56] The aim of CDM's sponsorship was to assist students to study in those areas "appropriate for use in the company's Manpower Development Programmes" with a view to employment within the company. The period of contract to the company equalled the number of years of sponsorship.[57]

Postgraduate Namibians also had recourse to the Rössing Foundation's scholarship scheme which provided assistance for study at South African, American or British universities. Successful candidates were not contracted to work for their sponsor, but they had to return to Namibia on completion of their studies. By 1988, 23 scholarships had been awarded, five of which (all blacks) were in education. All these students passed their degrees, two having gone to Britain.[58] One of the

Table 7.11   Teacher Trainees on Bursaries from the
              Respective Authorities and the Government
              Service Bursary Scheme, 1988

Authority	TEACHER TRAINEES		
	Primary School	Secondary School	Total
Caprivi	93	10	103
Coloured	180	—	180
Damara	10	31	41
Herero	12	24	36
Kavango	133	12	145
Nama*	—	—	—
Owambo	1,072	—	1,072
Rehoboth Baster	37	41	78
Tswana	—	—	11
White	154	273	427**
Government Service	—	—	107
GRAND TOTAL			2,200

* A total of 68 awards were made in 1988, but it was not specified how
many of these were in education.
** Out of this total, 267 were studying in South Africa, seven of whom
were for primary school teaching.
Source: Personal communications and interviews with the respective ethnic authorities, 1988 and 1989; Government Service Commission *et al*,
1988:39

two candidates who went to Britain was later employed in a high-level administrative capacity within the education department of one of the ethnic administrations, and the other occupied a senior position in the DNE and subsequently directed a vocational training centre sponsored by a German donor agency. In 1988 no scholarship candidates were involved in educational studies on this particular scholarship programme. In 1987 the Rössing Foundation launched a bursary scheme uniquely for study in Namibia at the Academy. By 1988 a total of 53 awards had been made: four of the recipients pursued degrees in education and six trained as secondary school teachers.[59]

In 1988 a branch of the Otto-Benecke Foundation in Windhoek, financed by the West German Government, gave awards to Namibians for study at universities in South Africa. That year 25 awards were made, predominantly to blacks. Only two of these recipients were in education.[60] Of the applicants for Otto-Benecke awards from within Namibia, 60 to 70 per cent did not qualify because their Standard X examination aggregates were too low.

The Sam Cohen Scholarship Trust, a private scheme open to all ethnic groups within the country, voiced similar concerns about most applicants' poor academic records. This scheme, which stipulates that candidates must return to Namibia on completion of their studies, sponsors approximately sixteen candidates per year at universities in South Africa. To date, none of the scholarship holders have pursued studies in education; preference has been shown to those wishing to study in scientific and technical fields.[61]

The University Centre for Studies in Namibia (TUCSIN), based in Windhoek, has run a scholarship scheme since 1984. It was funded by the German Academic Exchange Service (DAAD), the Fulbright Scholarship Programme, and the American Council of International Programmes. TUCSIN provided ten scholarships a year mainly to black and coloured Namibians for studies at the undergraduate level at universities in South Africa and Germany. Scholarship quotas were not always filled because of the requirement for a good matriculation exemption, as well as the preference shown to candidates in the natural sciences. Out of the 37 awards made since 1984, only one undertook training for secondary-level teaching.[62]

There were more encouraging results in terms of teacher training assistance with the scholarship programme of the Council of Churches in Namibia (CCN), begun in 1983. Funding came mostly from overseas donors and from local church contributions for study in South Africa, both at university and pre-university levels.[63] Out of a total of 102 awards in 1988, 95 were new awards and 45 were in education studies at university level. The majority of these scholarships were for teacher training, and at least 20 of the candidates were studying at the black University of Fort Hare in the Eastern Cape. In addition to providing assistance for university-level studies, the fund awarded travel grants to nine additional students in 1988 to attend a two-year upgrading and general bridging course at Khanya College in South Africa and enable students to eventually continue tertiary-level studies. As with other scholarship programmes, one of the biggest problems facing this scheme was finding suitable candidates with good matriculation qualifications.

The continuing development and expansion of the non-government scholarship schemes in the 1980s was an encouraging step in the right direction. However, because the number of coloured and especially black matriculants remained very limited, qualified applicants for awards were not always available. The impact of such programmes, especially in educational studies, remained limited and progress was slow. Moreover, company schemes served a public relations function rather than addressing the country's real human resource requirements. Some, like the CDM programme, were geared towards fulfilling the sponsors' human resource needs. For Namibian scholarship programmes to have any real impact in helping to overcome the country's crucial human resource requirements, there is a need for more co-ordinated, carefully researched, needs-based approaches.

CONCLUSION

We conclude by summarising the answers to the four questions posed at the beginning of this chapter, namely:

☐ What impact did governmental expansion of formal education for black Namibians have on the number and quality of teacher trainees?

☐ What was the availability and quality of the teaching force by the late 1980s?

☐ Was the provision and quality of training suitable to satisfy the requirements for trained teachers?

☐ Did the private sector's role in educational provision have a meaningful impact on the number of teacher trainees?

Although the state, and to a lesser degree the private sector, increased formal provision, the number of coloured and particularly black students who benefited from senior-secondary and advanced training were too small to make a substantial impression on high-level human resource needs. As before, the system remained incapable of producing sufficient numbers of matriculants for tertiary-level training. In turn, this meant perpetuating the pattern of poorly qualified candidates entering teacher training. The number of qualified teachers, especially secondary school teachers, was still insufficient to supply the ever-growing school population. In addition, losses caused by resignations and departures also had to be considered as well as the need to upgrade the many unqualified teachers who comprised the majority of Namibian teachers. Moreover, the private sector and other organisations made very little impact in raising the number of teacher trainees, despite their financial contributions to training in the form of scholarships.

This did not augur well for the future. Independence under a majority SWAPO Government was likely to result in the expansion of formal education, as occurred in other African countries on independence. Consequently, the demand for more qualified teachers would greatly increase. By the late 1980s, there was also the possibility that the onset of a black majority government would lead to the rapid departure of white professionals, as had occurred in Zimbabwe. In the northern areas, where South African military personnel had been co-opted to the teaching force, this loss had already been felt by the end of 1989 with the withdrawal of South Africa's forces.

The insufficient number of trained teachers, especially for secondary-level schooling, meant that there would be fewer people able to move into educational administrative posts and other departments, should the need arise at independence. Drawing on qualified black primary school teachers would mean relying on resources which were scarce and mostly poorly trained. These findings were alarming, especially since teachers constituted the largest occupational group of educated blacks and coloureds. In this they were the most competent source of talent available to the new government. The opening of more job opportunities to educated blacks, most of whom for years were confined to the teaching profession, could have lured many away from teaching and also acted as a disincentive to those contemplating teaching as a career. What could occur was that the most experienced and qualified individuals would be encouraged to move into other spheres of public service, should these jobs become vacant.

In the light of these findings, it is now necessary to examine the educational administrative system in terms of its structure and staffing, as it existed by the end of the decade, in order to determine the extent of the present and future resource needs there.

NOTES

1. AGN 5 1983:71.
2. ACHSR 6:1985:23.
3. AGN 5 1983:72.
4. DNE 1988:1, 2; South West Africa Department of Economic Affairs 1988:19, 28.
5. Both 1988 and 1989 were characterised by school boycotts and closures across the country, while most Namibian schools closed on 27 October 1989 in preparation for the November independence elections. This all resulted in disruptions to students' studies and the October closures meant less time was available for students to complete the Standard X syllabus, placing further pressure on already generally poorly prepared black matriculants (DNE 1988:1; The Namibian 14/07/1988, 11/09/1989, 15/12/1989).
6. SAIRR 1982:440; Thomas 1983:73.
7. AGN 5 1983:38.
8. König 1983:32.
9. *ibid.*
10. DNE 1987:58, 59; South West Africa Department of Economic Affairs 1988:28.
11. Melber 1984:3.
12. Ellis 1984:27.
13. Concordia Brochure 1988.
14. DNE 1987:59.
15. Interview, Director, Rössing Foundation, 18/10/1988.
16. AGN 5 1983:81.
17. The school statistics conceal certain facts. The ratio of teachers to schools still remained lowest in black schools where, at the lower primary level, 'platoon' or double sessions were often held. This meant that the teachers had to run morning and afternoon classes for Sub-Standard A and Sub-Standard B. Moreover, most of the lower primary schools for blacks were small, but their existence bolstered the overall number of black schools. In sparsely-populated communities classes were small (UNIN 1981:15; 1986:512).
18. Interview, Director, White Directorate of Education and Culture, 20/10/1988; Administration for Whites 1987:75.
19. In the Caprivi, for example, the practice of retaining inadequately qualified teachers meant that no vacancies were available for newly qualified teachers who had to seek work elsewhere (Thirion Commission, Volume I, Part I, 1983:83).
20. Government Service Commission *et al* 1987:114; South West Africa Department of Economic Affairs 1988:48.
21. Department of Economic Affairs 1988:2.
22. DNE 1985:31.

23. AGN 5 1983:80.

24. Education Committee 1985:7.

25. *ibid.*, 11.

26. International Conference on Teacher Education for Namibia, Lusaka, 21 – 27 September 1989:34.

27. The Namibian, 18/05/1989.

28. The teacher training institutions in Namibia had their examinations set and marked in South Africa. Course structure, content and the rules governing practice teaching were also all determined in South Africa. This changed with the passing of the National Education Act, No. 30 of 1980, which resulted in courses, subjects, rules and regulations regarding tertiary education emanating from Windhoek via the Directorate of National Education and later on the DNE (Mukendwa 1986:82).

29. Rogerson 1980:678.

30. Interview, Rector's Secretary, 31/1/1988.

31. DNE 1988:2.

32. Interview, Director of the Bureau of Research, the Academy, 31/10/1988.

33. Legum ed. 1981/1982:B672.

34. Interview, Faculty Officer, Academy Accredited Campuses, 27/11/1988.

35. Mukendwa 1986:82.

36. Kazapua 1984:39.

37. The B Ed degree is a postgraduate degree in the South African system, usually for experienced graduate teachers. It often functions as an in-service qualification for aspiring administrators. Only 24 hours were devoted to the B Ed Academy degree's administrative component which meant that the topic could only be dealt with superficially. In contrast, 54 hours a year were devoted to the administrative component of the HED (Sec) and ED Prim qualifications (Interview, Lecturer in Comparative Pedagogics, Faculty of Education, Academy, 31/10/1988).

38. Mbuende 1987:53.

39. International Conference on Teacher Education for Namibia, Lusaka, 21 – 27
September 1989:33, 35.

40. The Namibian, 17/03/1989.

41. Presidential Commission on Higher Education, 1991:i.

42. Although the Commission's report was submitted to the Cabinet and the press, its recommendations were never published nor widely distributed. Furthermore, only some of its proposals have been or are being implemented. The Dean of Studies at UNAM claimed that the recommendations had to be prioritised in terms of feasibility and finance (Interview, Dean of Studies, UNAM, 4 and 5/08/1993).

43. The Namibian, 1/02/1993.

44. Interview, Dean of Studies, UNAM, 4 and 5/08/1993.

45. UNAM Registration Statistics, 1992, 1993.

46. AGN 5 1983:82.

47. Interview, Faculty Officer, Academy Accredited Campuses, 27/11/1988.

48. This campus also reported that, owing to the further increase in teachers' salaries in 1988, many of its trainees quit their training to take up posts as unqualified teachers in better-paid temporary posts (International Conference on Teacher Education for Namibia, Lusaka, 21 – 27 September 1989:36).

49. International Conference on Teacher Education for Namibia, Lusaka, 21 – 27 September 1989:35, 36, 37, 38, 75.

50. Education Committee 1985:7; AGN 5 1983:38.

51. UNIN 1984:28.

52. International Conference on Teacher Education for Namibia, Lusaka 21 – 27 September 1989:38.
    Unqualified teachers made up the greatest proportion of the Namibian teaching force in 1985.

53. Interview, Central Personnel Institution, 13/10/1988.

54. Government Service Commission *et al* 1988:39.

55. The total number of Central Government bursaries awarded in 1988 was a large decline over most previous years' awards. Prior to 1985, such government awards were made by the DNE: 118 in 1981, 128 in 1983 and 116 in 1984. In 1985 the Central Personnel Institute of the Government Service Commission took over responsibility for bursary awards. No figures were available for 1985 and 1986. In 1987, 57 education bursaries were awarded. That year the DNE also made fourteen awards available to "needy, indigent students" (DNE 1981:4, 1983:4, 1984:6, 1985:7, 1986:8, 1987:8; Government Service Commission *et al* 1988, Annexure A).

56. Personal Communication, Education Co-ordinator CDM, 2/11/1988.

57. CDM undated:2, 4.

58. Interview, Director, Rössing Foundation, 18/10/1989.

59. *ibid.*

60. Interview, Scholarships Programme, Otto-Benecke Foundation, 22/11/1988.

61. Personal Communication, Sam Cohen Trust, 1988 – 1991.

62. Interview, TUCSIN, 17/10/1988.

63. It appears that the CCN scholarship programme did not provide bursaries at the Academy in Windhoek because teaching was mostly through the medium of Afrikaans (Interview, Director, CCN Department of Formal Education, 20/10/1988).

Educational administration: the final decade of South African rule

8

An ever-expanding education bureaucracy

… the apartheid policy in … occupied Namibia require(s) an ever-expanding bureaucracy to duplicate the same discriminatory administrative structures and procedures for each of the … ethnic groups…. This requires … structures and personnel without regard for efficiency.

UNITED NATIONS INSTITUTE FOR NAMIBIA, 1986

INTRODUCTION

Thus far we have traced the gradual evolution of Namibia's educational administrative structure. Decentralised missionary involvement in black and coloured education and state-controlled white education during the German occupation of 1884 – 1915 were followed by a short period of South African military rule that saw no alteration to the inherited German structure. It was only following South Africa officially becoming mandatory of the country in 1920 that attempts were made to centralise educational control in the South West Africa Department of Education. After 1968, the management of black and coloured education was transferred to the corresponding ethnic departments in South Africa via regional offices in Windhoek.

During the 1970s, the process of devolving educational control to certain local ethnic authorities was set in motion. The establishment of the Directorate of National Education in 1979 attempted both to bring the education systems of the three major ethnic groups within one structure and to shift control from South Africa to Namibia. In 1980 the Directorate was converted into the Department of National Education (DNE), while new legislation led to further ethnic decentralisation. By the end of the decade, this had resulted in ten ethnic Directorates of Education and Culture in addition to the centralised DNE.

To understand the evolution of the educational administrative structures as they existed by the end of the 1980s, we must firstly be familiar with:

☐ the system of government in Namibia; and
☐ the legislative processes which led to the establishment of the individual educational administrative structures.

Thereafter, we attempt to answer the following questions:

☐ What was the cost of the fragmented educational administrative system in terms of state expenditure and staff requirements?
☐ What were the qualifications and training of educational administrators within the DNE and each of the ten directorates?
☐ Were there any evident patterns of ethnic and gender bias in the distribution of staff at certain levels within the administration?

The answers to these questions will provide a clearer picture of the effects of the apartheid system of educational administration and staffing on the country's educational administrative resource potential at the time of independence.

GOVERNMENTAL STRUCTURE

After 1985, a three-tier system of government was organised as follows:

(a) The **first tier** was the Central Government, called the Transitional Government of National Unity from 17 June 1985. It exercised legislative, executive and judicial powers. The legislative powers were vested in the National Assembly. This comprised of 62 members with nine standing committees which, in turn, consisted of at least one member from every political party represented in the Assembly. The largest party was the Democratic Turnhalle Alliance with 22 seats. Five other parties had eight seats each. All legislation had to be approved by South Africa's representative in Namibia, the Administrator-General, since ultimate power still rested with South Africa.

Executive powers were vested in the Cabinet. This consisted of eight ministries, one of which was the Ministry of National Education (including the DNE) and the Central Personnel Institution.

(b) The **second tier** was made up of nine ethnic representative authorities: the Caprivians, coloureds, Damaras, Hereros, Kavangos, Namas, Ovambos, Tswanas and whites, as well as the Government of Rehoboth.[1] The affairs of the Bushmen were controlled by the Central Government. The other ethnic authorities enjoyed legislative and executive powers, but their ordinances had to be ratified by the Administrator-General, once again demonstrating that ultimate power rested with South Africa. The ethnic authorities were financed by personal taxation of each ethnic group's population and from the Central Government. The accounts of the representative authorities were subject to audit by the Central Government's auditor general.

(c) The **third tier** consisted of municipal authorities, the peri-urban development boards and village management boards. Blacks and whites had separate councils. The black boards enjoyed only advisory powers and were represented on white councils by white officials. The coloureds also had consultative committees which were also represented by whites on municipal councils.

LEGISLATIVE DEVELOPMENTS AFFECTING THE EDUCATIONAL ADMINISTRATIVE STRUCTURE

Three pieces of legislation enacted in 1980 determined the way that educational administration was structured. These were:

□ the Representative Authorities' Proclamation (Proclamation AG 8 of 1980);
□ the Government Service Act, No. 2 of 1980;
□ the National Education Act, No. 30 of 1980.

The Representative Authorities' Proclamation (Proclamation AG 8 of 1980) established representative authorities for the Rehoboth Basters, Bushmen, Caprivians, coloureds, Damaras, Hereros, Kavangos, Namas, Ovambos, Tswanas, and whites. The Bushmen were controlled by the Central Government.[2] The Rehoboth Basters retained the administrative structure established in 1976 and continued to be referred to as the Government of Rehoboth rather than a representative authority.

Each of the representative authorities was responsible for the provision of pre-primary, primary and secondary school education, and primary school teacher training up to Standard IV, as well as "the establishment, erection, maintenance and management of, and the control over, schools, training colleges, hostels and other institutions for or in connection with the provision of education or training...."[3] To carry out these functions, each ethnic administration established its own Directorate of Education and Culture. Additionally, because the Academy's three satellite teacher training campuses were situated at Ongwediva, Rundu, and Katima Mulilo, the representative authorities of Owambo, Kavango, and the Caprivi respectively had to provide the facilities and lecturers and pay the latter's salaries.

Proclamation AG 8 of 1980 constituted the fruition of the 1964 Odendaal Commission's recommendation that self-governing ethnic entities manage educational matters "with their own controlling machinery", the process having been set in motion in the 1970s.[4] The apartheid ideal was still being perpetuated; the only difference was that multiple ethnic divisions now replaced the traditional segregation between coloureds, blacks, and whites. Simultaneous with the realisation of ethnically decentralised control was the apparent contradictory move towards greater centralised control over those aspects of education that fell outside the auspices of the ethnic administrations' directorates.

The creation of ten ethnic authorities with administrative divisions to carry out their new responsibilities seemingly enhanced the employment opportunities for blacks and coloureds in top- and middle-level posts, previously reserved for whites, thereby boosting the formation of an elite class among these ethnic groups. However, a closer examination reveals the predominance of whites in almost all important positions.

The Government Service Act, No. 2 of 1980 aimed at creating an "independent" government service in Namibia. This resulted in the abolition of the former ten directorates, of which the Directorate of National Education was one, and the creation of sixteen departments. As a result, the Directorate of National Education was replaced by the DNE.

The National Education Act, No. 30 of 1980 replaced the South African Bantu Education Act, No. 47 of 1953, as well as all amendments thereto, in defining the DNE's functions. The DNE was to control all primary and secondary education which did not fall to a representative authority or the Government of Rehoboth. This included most private schools and those with a heterogeneous school population.

In instances where representative authorities chose not to exercise their educational responsibilities, these could be performed by the DNE. This was the case with the Bushmen and the Tswanas, though by the late 1980s the Tswanas had their own Directorate of Education and Culture, albeit a very basic one. The DNE was also to provide professional services at primary and secondary school level to the representative authorities on request.

The National Education Act also provided for the establishment of three bodies, the first two being a National Education Board and an Examination Board. Then at the end of 1987, the Curriculum Management Committee was established to advise the Examination Board on matters relating to the curriculum. The DNE's Directorate of Educational Auxiliary Services acted as the secretariat to these three bodies.

The Education Board consisted of representatives both from the DNE and the various ethnic authorities' Directorates of Education and Culture. These comprised the Secretary of National Education and two other officials from the DNE's head office, and all the heads and one official of each ethnic Directorate of Education and Culture. This ensured that representation was restricted to the providers of education, while practising educationists were excluded.[5] The Board's tasks were:

☐ to advise and make recommendations to the Administrator-General on general education policy;
☐ to advise and make recommendations to the Administrator-General on any other matter pertaining to education which the Administrator-General refers to the Board for its advice and recommendations; and
☐ to report to the Administrator-General on any matter concerning education which the Administrator-General refers to the Board for investigation and report.[6]

In reality the Board was relatively powerless for, despite its membership, its responsibilities did not extend to the ethnic administrations and the Government of Rehoboth. Although it was the sole national advisory body for education in the country, it could not direct, monitor or sanction educational practices, nor did it possess the necessary liaison mechanisms to gather information and present its findings or to enforce educational policy.

The Examination Board consisted of representatives from the DNE, the ethnic administrations, and a representative from the Board of the Academy for Tertiary Education. Its function was to prescribe the minimum standards and requirements for courses and syllabuses, to conduct examinations, and to issue certificates to schools and other institutions. However, it did not succeed in fully exercising the powers bestowed upon it by law, nor did it possess the necessary infrastructure or regulations with which to monitor examinations.

The Standard VIII examination (which was also a selection process for pupils wishing to continue to Standard X) was an external one run by the Examination Board for South West Africa/Namibia. Standard X pupils sat for the Cape Senior Certificate. A few private schools used the South African Joint Matriculation Board (JMB). Mention has also been made of the private schools in Namibia, namely, Martin Luther High School, at Okombahe, and the Gibeon and Berseba secondary schools, which taught the syllabus used in Botswana, Lesotho, and Swaziland (see page 153, Chapter 6, note 14). The Standard VIII and X examinations of the DNE's Non-Formal Education Division were conducted from Pretoria.

Namibia clearly had little capacity for a public examination system of its own, and by 1989 it did not yet have its own curriculum at secondary school level. Work on curriculum development had commenced only in 1985 with a view "to essential adaptations and changes".[7] The co-operation of universities in South Africa was enlisted in this project.

OVERVIEW OF THE EDUCATION SYSTEM

The education system as a whole, in terms of standards, structure, content, and requirements, was virtually all South African-based. As such, it was lacking in national character, confirming the ineffectiveness and powerlessness of the boards as independent policy-making bodies. An official report on the education system in Namibia considered that the prevalence of ethnically separate state control over educational provision was the most serious stumbling block to attaining a national educational policy.[8] But the problem extended beyond the actual administrative structure. It was not until 1988 that posts for curriculum planners and designers were advertised, and only then was a planning network built up. However, not all posts were filled.[9]

As for the DNE, its functions appeared to be confined more to day-to-day administration than to decision making and policy formulation. This was evidenced in the powers given to its secretary, the chief executive officer. He could issue regulations concerning the medium of instruction, religious education, school committees, courses and admission requirements, the registration of private schools, the composition and duties of school committees, control of school funds, conditions of service for teachers, and the admission and expulsion of pupils and teachers. Ultimate control rested with South Africa's representative in Namibia, the Administrator-General, who was, in turn, accountable to the South African State President. He had the power to issue educational acts or to repeal and amend educational acts of the Republic of South Africa applicable to Namibia, subject to the South African State President's approval. These arrangements, plus the continued reliance on educational bodies in South Africa, underlines that the DNE was no more than an amalgamated branch office of South Africa's corresponding black, coloured and white education bodies. Thus, any changes which occurred could be changes in name alone.

EDUCATIONAL EXPENDITURE

The DNE had its own vote in the South West Africa/Namibia budget, while all the ethnic Directorates of Education and Culture were budgeted from within their respective ethnic authorities who received money from the Central Government specifically for education. But these funds were often directed by the ethnic authorities to fields other than education, and not all the authorities made available sufficient resources for educational spending.[10] The black ethnic authorities' educational funds were augmented by school fees paid by impoverished tax payers.

Table 8.1   Central Government Expenditure on Education
in Rands (Million), 1987/1988

Ethnic Group	Rands (m)	% of Total	Enrolment[+]	% of Total	Expenditure per Pupil
Caprivian	10.9	4	19,453	5	560
Coloured	14.1	5	15,696	4	898
Damara	8.0	3	9,512	3	841
Herero	11.4	4	16,043	4	711
Kavango	17.1	6	32,270	9	530
Nama	10.6	4	15,351	4	691
Ovambo	74.7	25	189,533	52	394
Rehoboth Baster	9.4	3	10,000	3	940
Tswana	0.96*	0.32	1,016	0.3	945
White	21.5	7	16,823	5	1,278
DNE**	99.3	34	38,707	11	992
The Academy	17.6≠	6	—	—	—
TOTAL	295.56	—	364,404	—	—

* The actual amount was R963 000.
** Only R38 394 300 went towards school education.
+ Figures of pupils in 1987.
≠ Figures for 1986/1987.
Source: Adapted from Pütz *et al*, 1987:233, 238, 239; DNE,
1987:6; South West Africa Department of Economic Affairs,
1988:21 – 28; Academy Statistics, November 1988

A breakdown of the Central Government expenditure on education is shown in Table 8.1 for the period 1987/1988. Out of the total, 34 per cent went to the DNE, followed by the Owambo Authority's 25 per cent. Whites came third with 7 per cent of the total. The DNE's education budget also included tertiary-level education for all ethnic groups (except for the Academy which had its own subsidy). The Ovambos made up 52 per cent and the whites only 5 per cent of the total school-going population (see Table 8.3). The Ovambos had the highest pupil totals in the country, yet by far the lowest expenditure per pupil.

The coloured and black ethnic authorities suffered a dual disadvantage in that not only were their budget allocations much less per pupil than those of the whites but there was also no provision prohibiting these funds from being earmarked elsewhere.[11] Their situation was compounded by corruption and mismanagement. For example, in the Caprivi Directorate of Education and Culture, irregularities were evident in the payment of salaries, as the Thirion Commission of 1983, a judicial commission of inquiry into the mismanagement of state funds, uncovered.[12]

Administrative costs consumed no less than 60 per cent of the education budget in 1986/87, 55 per cent in 1987/88, and 53 per cent in 1988/89. In the same years, formal education expenditure accounted for 35, 39, and 40 per cent of the education budget respectively. The rise in formal education expenditure reflected substantial enrolment increases in the last years of South African rule.[13] The amount spent on running eleven education structures in 1987/1988 came to roughly 18.3 per cent of the total territorial budget allocation for that year, which marked a rise over the estimated 11.2 per cent of public spending in 1980.[14] Despite the increased expenditure on education in Namibia, which resulted in some improvements in educational provision and output in the late 1980s, the system still had a long way to go towards making up for past neglect and satisfying the human resource shortages. A senior official of the DNE summed up the situation by saying that the educational system in Namibia was overly expensive and the structure absurd.[15]

THE DEPARTMENT OF NATIONAL EDUCATION: ORGANISATIONAL STRUCTURE, STAFFING, AND TRAINING, 1988

STRUCTURE OF THE DNE

This Central Governmental department, headed by a secretary, was divided into four directorates each with its own director:

☐ The Directorate of Educational Control[16]
☐ The Directorate of Educational Auxiliary Services
☐ The Directorate of Culture
☐ The Directorate of General Services

These four directorates were further divided into divisions, subdivisions, sections and subsections. The aims and functions of each directorate were as follows:

The Directorate of Educational Control was to promote and manage formal and non-formal education through inspection and subject advisory services. The task of the Directorate of Educational Auxiliary Services was the planning of and research into curricula and extracurricular affairs, and physical facilities. Sports, conservation, development, and the promotion of the cultural heritage of the people of Namibia through research, administration of the museums, archives and language services fell to the Directorate of Culture. The duties of this Directorate's Monuments Section remained under the South African Monuments Council, on which only two Namibians served. All auxiliary administrative functions, namely, financial, stock, personnel, and general office administration, were undertaken by the Directorate of General Services.

After 1980 the DNE underwent several structural changes. There were considerable additions to the number of posts, many of which by 1988 remained unfilled. Early in 1987 two significant new subdivisions were created within the Non-Formal Education Division of the Directorate of Educational Control: the Teachers' Centres Subdivision and the Distance Teaching Subdivision. The Teachers' Centres aimed to provide a resource for practising teachers, thereby contributing to an improvement in the quality of teaching. Assistance was in the form of monthly voluntary in-service training for teachers employed at schools registered with the DNE. By 1989 there was a total of three Teachers' Centres: Katutura, Tsumeb, and Otjiwarongo. The Distance Teaching Subdivision aimed to assist un- and underqualified teachers in the DNE's service to obtain suitable qualifications and in this way to improve overall educational standards in Namibia.

What appeared to be lacking in the DNE's complex infrastructure was a central planning body to co-ordinate all education and training. The absence of such a body and the powerlessness of the National Education Board and the Examination Board, as revealed previously, all pointed towards a continued reliance on the relevant organisations in South Africa.

STAFFING

There were six categories of staff within the DNE in accordance with all the public administrative structures in Namibia: administrative, professional, executive, technical, secretarial, and ancillary. Prior to discussing staffing trends, it is useful to understand the line of promotion in the education structures. Within the schools, this ran from teachers to heads of department to deputy principal to principal. A principal could become a subject adviser and thereafter an inspector or educational planner. Thereafter, it was possible to be promoted to management posts.

The prerequisite for any professional post at head office was a Higher Education Diploma or at least a Primary School Teachers' Diploma, while for more generalised administrative duties, like clerical work, a Standard X certificate sufficed.[17] People who were trained or experienced in technical fields like computers, statistics, and accountancy (not necessarily at degree level) were also employed.

The middle- and top-level administrative staff within the Directorates of Educational Control and Educational Auxiliary Services predominantly came from teaching backgrounds, most having been trained at South African universities or colleges. Almost all the educational planners within the DNE had an educational background and practical experience in teaching. Some had advanced qualifications like Masters degrees in educational and curriculum planning and design.[18] However, minimum employment requirements were sometimes dropped so as to enable more blacks and coloureds to apply for posts, according to an interview with the Head of the DNE's Formal Education Division.[19]

Racism in job allocation

By the late 1980s, the DNE employed 1,100 people (excluding teachers), 351 in Windhoek. Within the head office, a clear ethnic pattern was evident (see Appendix A). The DNE's head office management and professional structure was dominated by whites, many of whom were South Africans. Only a small number of coloureds and even fewer blacks filled professional posts, and they were mostly confined to the Directorates of Educational Control and Auxiliary Services. Coloureds therefore continued to fulfil an historical intermediate position. Those blacks and coloureds who did not hold professional posts were rarely promoted to management level. In 1987 there were nineteen black educationists within the head office structure, and blacks in general made up only 24 per cent of the DNE's staff. Most blacks were employed in semi-skilled and unskilled occupations, although some were employed in secretarial, clerical, and accounting posts.

This tendency towards racism in job allocation led the 1990 information secretary of the Namibian National Students' Organisation (NANSO) to say that staff were appointed on the basis of their commitment to the apartheid ideology, nepotism, and favouritism rather than on the strength of suitable training and experience.[20] Yet, aside from the fact that there were few coloured and even fewer black teachers and other professionals available to fill professional posts within government, it was not surprising that white South Africans dominated at those levels. There was a dearth even of trained white Namibians.

Personnel recruitment for Government Service jobs was primarily conducted in South Africa at white tertiary education institutions like the University of Stellenbosch, the Cape Technikon, the University of Pretoria, and Pretoria Technikon between July 1987 and June 1988. As one report stated, visits concentrated "on Universities where a large number of South Westers study".[21] The only local recruiting efforts were made during a one-day careers exhibition at the Otjiwarongo High School, which was attended by pupils from various schools in the north, and the Windhoek Agricultural Show. Talks on the Government Service's Bursary scheme were also delivered at two Windhoek high schools. Posts were advertised in internal circulars and the local, South African and overseas press.[22]

Sexism in job allocation

As far as the gender make-up of the education-specific professional staff within the Directorate of Educational Control was concerned, women were confined to the posts of subject advisers. No women attained the rank of chief subject adviser. However, the deputy head of the Teachers' Centre within the Non-Formal Education Division was a woman. There were more female teachers in the Distance Teaching Subdivision of Non-Formal Education, but men outnumbered women in this division's subject advisory services, and there were no women inspectors in this or in the Formal Education Division. All other professional occupations within these two divisions were occupied by men.

The only professional woman within the Directorate of Auxiliary Services was a black language assistant. Professional women were better represented in the Directorate of Culture, where they were employed as deputy director of the Archives, Library, and Language Service Division; head of the Language Service Division; archivists; librarians; and as specialists within the Departmental Service's European Languages',

Natural Sciences', Humanities', Exhibition and Information Sections. Other occupations commonly assigned to women were those of typists, private secretaries, record clerks, clerks, and cleaners. Coloured and black women predominated in the lowest occupations.

Within the General Services Directorate, there were six female accountants most of whom were white, while a woman headed the subdivision Examinations. Apart from these professional posts, women tended to be confined to the lower-level posts of secretaries, clerks, and so forth, black women occupying the lowest occupational levels. Generally speaking, white women had far greater access to professional posts than women from other ethnic groups. Men were clearly the most prominent in the majority of professional and virtually all management-level posts, while women in general and black women in particular were discriminated against.

TRAINING

The shortage of qualified and experienced staff was highlighted by the DNE in virtually all its annual reports from 1980 to 1987. These personnel shortages were especially prevalent in supervisory and administrative control posts. This meant that there were fewer professionals available to deal with the requirements demanding their expertise which, in turn, reduced the quality of services rendered. Supervisors were required to train staff on the job, ostensibly because "only a small percentage was willing to do work of an acceptable standard".[23] The few available experienced and expert personnel in supervisory and controlling levels were likely to apply for the many vacant higher-graded posts in other government service departments or within the representative authorities. Attempts to procure the services of officers from South African departments were not always successful, and the DNE therefore had to resort to requesting pensioned Namibian officers to take up temporary posts.

Training at head office and the Academy

In the earlier part of the decade, the prevailing personnel shortages were said to be the reason for not providing formal or in-service training.[24] More regular in-service training began in 1981 at head office. This training at the DNE was organised by the Central Personnel Institution (CPI). The CPI, originally a regional office of the South African Public Service Commission, was established in Windhoek in 1979. It was responsible for all personnel administration at Central Government level as well as for three representative administrations, namely, the Tswanas, Kavangos, and Caprivians. Among the many functions performed by its Training and Publicity Division were:

> the assessment of departmental training needs; co-ordination of all external training between departments/administrations; activation of departmental training and the identification and elimination of overlapping training.[25]

The CPI's subdivision, Administrative Training, drew up courses and seminars to satisfy identified training needs, and it co-ordinated all administrative practice courses. CPI also provided advisory services to all departments to assist them to increase their efficiency. In 1986 this resulted in the structural changes to the DNE mentioned above. Although staff who participated in the CPI-run courses came from the DNE's four directorates, it was staff from the Directorate of General Services who participated most frequently in such programmes.

CPI courses were usually two to seven days long, but some lasted nine weeks. The most common training provided by CPI included orientation, supervision, public appearance, legislation and delegation, instruction, secretarial, personnel evaluation, and registration management. The CPI also ran a course for subject advisers for one week in 1985, but it was not repeated. Additionally, the CPI organised day-long seminars for leadership officers. From 1986 onwards, a middle-level administrative practice course was introduced. Top-level short courses for all Central Government departmental heads were also held on topics such as public administrative practice and accountability.

Apart from short-term, general administration training by the CPI, the Academy offered a longer-term course in public administration. The CPI training unit collaborated in the compilation of the Technikon's part-time, three-year Public Administration diploma course. Most students taking this course were already employed in lower-middle and management level. The course itself was broad-based and geared to daily administrative jobs in the government service. Its components were:

□ The Nature and Context of Public Administration;
□ Foundations and Guidelines of Public Administration;
□ Identification of the Generic Administrative Process, that is, Policy and Policy-making, Organising, Financing, Public Personnel Administration, Procedures and Methods, Control and Rendering Account, Macro- and Micro-Administration, Environmental Factors Influencing Public Administration, and Institutional Hierarchy.[26]

Although the syllabus was much the same in content and standard as other such courses in South Africa, the diploma was not recognised in South Africa. Even though some attempts had been made to make the contents relevant to Namibia and to localise them, the course itself was heavily based on the South African author J.J.N. Cloete's model for the 'homeland' concept of administration. This meant that administrative training was biased in favour of the concept of separate ethnic development. It is doubtful that white lecturers in this course questioned these ethnically determined pre-suppositions.

Because the CPI's training unit suffered from shortages of training personnel, it had to rely heavily on the Technikon for trainers. As a result, when the first batch of eight graduates completed the course in 1987 many of them moved into the CPI's training unit as trainers.[27]

A three-year degree course in public administration was introduced at the Academy in 1986 in response to the government's need for planners and researchers. On completion of their degrees, candidates went into research and planning jobs either in government or in the private sector. Although the university-level course was more theoretical in its approach, the same six generic administrative processes as those offered in the diploma were covered. However, it also delved into the history and philosophy of each of these processes. The course was Namibia-oriented, although it was based on one offered at the University of Cape Town.[28]

The DNE also ran short courses to meet particular needs which had been identified. The trainers on such departmental courses were preferably local or from South Africa. If the CPI had experts in a particular field, then training was referred directly to them. The Directorate of Educational Control organised an annual one-week principals' course, while other courses took place on an *ad hoc* basis, such as a course for chief inspectors, inspectors, and principal subject advisers in 1986. In 1987 the Directorate of Educational Auxiliary Services ran a course in assessing school readiness for six subject advisers, one educational planner, and two teachers. No other mention was made of training subject advisers or inspectors; therefore, we can assume that they remained untrained, having to rely chiefly on personal experience. Another *ad hoc* course was the Directorate of Educational Auxiliary Services' symposium on educational planning for non-formal education in developing countries.

Additional short-term training for the DNE in general took the form of seminars, conferences, courses, and so forth. These were either organised locally by the private sector, for example, the Rössing Foundation or the Academy or they took place outside Namibia at various institutions in South Africa and elsewhere. This training was also geared towards middle-level professionals and covered areas such as curriculum development, guidance, language teaching, and counselling.

The 1986 annual report of the DNE mentions the rapid changes occurring in the business, economic, and political spheres within Namibia. These changes had implications for education. The officers within the Directorate of Auxiliary Services were under pressure to make meaningful plans for the future. It was stated that planners would require special skills in order to devise useful strategies for educational provisions and innovation. That year five people from the DNE were sent to South African universities for postgraduate training in curriculum design and planning, for periods of two to three years. They received bursaries from the private sector — the majority of the five were originally from South Africa.[29] This was the first time long-term training of professionals was mentioned.

Administrative training within schools

Regular in-service training in school administration and organisation was given to principals, deputy principals, and heads of departments. The training was done by the DNE's inspectorate. The annual one-week course for principals was compulsory for all black, coloured and white principals. This meant that principals with differing levels of experience and training were combined in one course on administrative and management training. These courses resulted in improved motivation of the principals which, in turn, had a positive effect on the teachers, resulting in the growing improvement in pupil achievement.

During visits to schools, the inspectorate and subject advisers also assisted teachers with aspects such as general school organisation, class administration, lesson planning, subject method, control, and evaluation. Refresher and orientation courses for teachers were also run by the DNE at its various schools. In 1983 there were 71 such courses in a variety of subjects, which dealt with effective teaching techniques and the syllabus rather than with administrative issues. These were attended by 1,356 teachers.[30] Teachers participating in the distance teaching project to raise their qualifications also received visits from the DNE's subject advisers.

213

An important change in the approach to advisory services was adopted in 1986. Instead of individual subject advisers visiting schools, a panel of subject advisers headed by an inspector of education visited an identified school. The purpose was to upgrade the whole school by assisting individual subject teachers, subject heads, and personnel holding promotional posts. In this way emphasis shifted from inspection to consultation and counselling.

In 1987 courses were organised for subject advisers, principals, deputy principals, and school departmental heads to inform them of the changed role of school inspection and enable them to make informed decisions regarding the needs and shortcomings of individual schools. No mention was made at any point of training the inspectors for their new tasks.

Critique of training

Between 1981 and 1987 the majority of CPI-run courses appeared to have been geared towards lower- and some middle-level staff at the DNE rather than the professionals.

Much of the basic administrative subject matter covered in both the Technikon and University courses could well have been pertinent to educational administration but, to have any real impact on the staff of the DNE, the training should have been more education-specific. As for the DNE's management staff, they appeared to have had little exposure to training other than the general CPI courses for the heads of all Central Government departments and the legislation and delegation course offered in 1982. There was no training for top-level officials within the DNE which was specific to educational administration.

Other than a few courses lasting a few days, there appears to have been no in-service training for educational professionals (inspectors, planners, curriculum advisers, and subject advisers). Curriculum advisers' exposure to training was on-the-job and took the form of forums for discussion on certain issues. The long-term postgraduate training in curriculum planning and design, which commenced in 1986, was not, it appears, a regular feature of professional training within the DNE.

Such a lack of training is astounding, especially where subject advisers were concerned, in view of their important role in upgrading the quality of the teaching force. Other than the four subject advisers who attended the CPI instructors' course in 1985, this group of professionals had received no training on how to train. Most subject advisers were teachers who were bound to rely almost wholly on their own experience. However, moves were afoot to introduce more in-service courses or workshops and seminars for subject advisers and inspectors in early 1989.

At school level, the effectiveness of the subject advisers' courses for teachers was said to be minimal. In areas like Ovamboland, training needs were enormous, yet subject advisers were able to visit only two or three times a year. Often they had to visit several schools during one trip and their impact was only superficial. They had to cover great distances and much time was necessary for the travel alone. These problems highlighted the need for additional training facilities and professional staff. Follow-up visits to monitor progress and reinforce training were seldom possible due to time constraints. As for the annual principals' course, according to one official, this did not "tackle the issue of how to manage", while courses in general, in his opinion, tended to neglect all forms of personnel management.[31] The Director of Education Control said that there should be a system of set regular courses of longer duration, which principals should be required to attend throughout their service.[32]

It was clear that there was no uniform method of training or back-up within the DNE. Neither was there a specialised division to identify training needs or to design training according to the defined needs. Where skills were lacking, these were imported from outside or else people with experience were relied upon. Often this meant relying on people whose ideas were drawn from the past and who lacked knowledge of new and innovative techniques. How suitable would these serving administrators be in terms of their ideological commitment and competence for the challenges that independence would bring?

The interviews conducted within the DNE revealed that middle-level professional staff, especially the subject advisers whose work took them to most areas within the country, were more in touch with the need for administrative and management training than were the top-level staff.[33]

If these glaring inadequacies were so prevalent in the generously-financed state-run educational administrative structure, what were the trends within each ethnic authority's Directorate of Education and Culture?

THE TEN ETHNIC DIRECTORATES OF EDUCATION AND CULTURE

By 1989 the Caprivian, Damara, Herero, Kavango, Nama, Owambo, Rehoboth Baster, Tswana, coloured, and white ethnic authorities each had their own Directorate of Education and Culture. This amounted to a form of ethnic decentralisation promoting the goal of ethnic fragmentation. In discussing each directorate, an attempt is made to gauge its staff total as accurately as possible, as well as the ethnic distribution of posts. However, not all the posts indicated in the 1988 figures were occupied, while some new posts were added at a later date.

STRUCTURE AND STAFFING

A familiar pattern of ethnic discrimination emerged within the administrative structures in terms of infrastructure and professional staffing. Table 8.2 reveals that in 1988 there were 8,830 staff administering the needs of 374,269 school-going pupils. After independence, a senior consultant to the Minister of Education stated that this "far exceed(s) the number of staff who one would anticipate as being necessary for a nation of the size and population of Namibia".[34] Although this figure may appear large initially, further examination indicates that the actual number of educational professionals within all the structures made up only 4 per cent of the overall administrative staff total, the largest number of whom were concentrated in the DNE followed by the White Directorate.

Table 8.2   Administrative Staff Totals and Number of Educational Professionals of the Department of National Education and the Ten Ethnic Directorates, 1988

Ethnic Authority	Administrative Staff*	% of Total	Educational Professionals**	% of Total
Caprivian	375	4.2	12	4.0
Coloured	555	6.3	25	8.0
Damara	642	7.3	18	5.4
Herero	918	10.4	26	8.0
Kavango	743	8.4	15	5.0
Nama	437	5.0	30	9.0
Owambo	2,158	24.4	22	7.0
Rehoboth Baster	353	4.0	18	5.4
Tswana	98	1.1	1	0.3
White	1,451	16.4	42	13.0
DNE	1,100	12.5	123	37.1
TOTAL	8,830	—	332	—

* Figures include school administrative staff such as deputy heads and principals.
** Cultural officials and language practitioners have been included in this category.
Source: Interview, CPI, 14/10/1988; Interviews DNE, 1988; Personal Communications with Individual Ethnic Authorities, 1988 and 1989

Table 8.3 indicates that the DNE and the White Directorate oversaw the educational needs of only 11 and 5 per cent respectively of the overall school-going population, compared with the 52 per cent which fell under the auspices of the Owambo Directorate. Although whites were one of the smallest ethnic groups, they had the best-staffed and most developed administrative structure.[35] The pattern of professional organisation in the directorates also varied considerably. The White Directorate boasted four specialised divisions staffed by professionals such as planners, school psychologists and language therapists, in addition to subject advisers and inspectors. So effectively organised, staffed and equipped was this directorate that its director claimed it was self-sufficient enough to operate autonomously.[36] The Owambo Directorate in contrast, despite having to administer the largest percentage of the country's total school-going population, had a structure far less complex than that of the whites and the DNE. However, its structure was still the most complex of the remaining ethnic directorates. Yet the number of its educational professionals made up a mere 7 per cent of its educational staff totals (see Table 8.2). The most basic structure was that of the Tswanas with its single professional post of inspector. The DNE executed most of its functions.

The Caprivian and Owambo Directorates were the only black structures which had educational planners, while the Damaras alone of all the black directorates had a school psychologist. The professional staff within the black head offices were limited to inspectors and, in the case of the Damara and Herero, to a combination of inspectors and subject advisers. The other black directorates did not have subject advisers. The Namas, coloureds and Rehoboth Basters all had at least one educational planner and, in the case of both the Rehoboth Basters and Namas, school psychologists. All three had inspectors and subject advisers. Of interest is the fact that all the ethnic directorates, bar that of the whites, had a division for Cultural Affairs or Cultural Promotion (as it was referred to for the coloured and Rehoboth Baster Directorates) to foster and stimulate ethnic identity. Cultural matters concerning whites were determined predominantly in South Africa. Finally, not all of the educational professionals working in the ethnic directorates were sufficiently qualified to carry out their designated tasks. This was particularly true of those working for black education directorates as discussed below.

Table 8.3   Pupils and Teachers of Individual Ethnic Groups as a Percentage of Each Category's Overall Total, 1988

Ethnic Group	Pupils	% of Total	Teachers	% of Total
Caprivian	20,935	5.6	811	6.5
Coloured	15,946	4.3	658	5.2
Damara	9,921	2.6	426	3.4
Herero	16,595	4.4	613	4.9
Kavango	34,563	9.2	1,147	9.2
Nama	11,877	3.2	532	4.2
Ovambo	193,219	51.6	4,920	39.3
Rehoboth Baster	10,000	2.7	465	3.7
Tswana	1,068	0.3	43	0.3
White	17,224	4.6	1,212	9.7
DNE	42,921	11.5	1,698	13.6
TOTAL	374,269	—	12,525	—

Source: Adapted from South West Africa Department of Economic Affairs, 1988

Ethnic tendencies in staffing patterns

The ethnic occupational patterns evident within the DNE tended to be mirrored in most of the black education directorates, especially when it came to top-level decision making posts (see Appendix B). It is essential to examine the extent of this tendency, since this in turn will enable us to ascertain the supply and potential of educational administrators from Namibia's majority communities. Such an examination is necessary, firstly, in view of the possibility in the late 1980s of a large-scale white exodus like that which occurred in Zimbabwe at independence. This could have spelled the possible collapse of the administrative structures. Secondly, if a majority government came to power, it would almost certainly adopt a policy of affirmative action in job allocation, especially in the civil service. Would it, however, be able to realistically introduce such a policy if, for example, there was a shortage of trained educational adminstrators among coloureds and blacks?

The Owambo Directorate was the sole exception to the tendency of white professional monopoly. However, in all the other black ethnic directorates the directors or deputy directors were white, most of whom were originally from South Africa.[37] Some of these whites had served within the DNE. When they took up jobs within the ethnic authorities this often meant a promotion.

Within the middle-range professional occupations, namely, inspectors and subject advisers, there appeared to be a better mix of blacks and whites as a result of advancement of black professionals during the 1980s. The Owambo, Caprivian and Kavango Directorates had blacks in the post of head inspector. None of these three directorates had subject advisers, which was alarming, especially in view of those professionals' role in upgrading the quality of teachers. The Hereros had the largest number of subject advisers. Those structures which had the least number of black professionals at head office were the Herero, Damara and Nama Directorates.

For the coloureds and Rehoboth Basters, there was a more equitable ethnic distribution. But, as mentioned before, these two groups enjoyed better educational provision, pupil output at tertiary level, and training than most blacks. Therefore, their professional pool of supply was larger.

Women, on the whole, did not feature at all in any of the top-level posts. Within middle-range occupations, there was a small minority in education-specific occupations. In 1988, out of all the black directorates, there were only two female black subject advisers and they were in the Damara and Herero Directorates. Women were mostly consigned to clerical posts, the more senior of which were at times occupied by whites (for example, the posts of head and senior clerks within the Nama Directorate, one of whom was a South African, and the typist in the Caprivi Directorate).

Staff potential

Despite evidence of a more equitable ethnic mix within middle-range posts, especially in the Caprivian and Kavango Directorates, some alarming conditions have been reported in a study by a Namibian educationist who was the Caprivi head inspector at the time the fieldwork was done. He was a Rössing Education Foundation scholarship candidate who successfully obtained both a Diploma and Masters degree in Educational Planning in London. Regarding the East Caprivi, he claimed that inspectors and subject advisers were normally poorly qualified or often never trained at all. Appointment was not according to merit, but placement was done by the Traditional Tribal Authorities who themselves were not always well educated or trained. Some of the inspectors and subject advisers had only Standard VIII and a Lower Primary Teachers' Certificate (LPTC) and very few staff with a matriculation and LPTC had been appointed to these posts. Inspectors and subject advisers were not necessarily specialised in any subject area. Hence they were unable to inspect schools efficiently or to offer proper guidance to teachers, some of whom knew more about a subject than them. This contributed to the poor teaching problem which in turn affected pupil performance and often resulted in wastage.

In addition to not having satisfactory professional qualifications or training, some subject advisers also lacked the necessary experience. Owing to their inability to perform their proper functions, this group of 'professionals' resorted to carrying out administrative office work and went to schools only when they had to deliver school books or transfer a teacher.[38]

The lack of properly qualified indigenous staff in middle-level occupations was probably echoed in other educational directorates but possibly to a lesser degree in those of the coloureds and Rehoboth Basters and especially that of the whites. An official report in the early 1980s, discussing the representative authorities, made reference to the "fundamental problems in terms of provision of professionally trained people for education and educational control".[39] The 1985 Education Committee Report also made reference to the lack of qualifications and experience among staff in educational administrative structures and it stressed the dearth of capable head office personnel "for optimal service and management of education".[40] Generally, it was said that blacks lacked the expertise, qualifications, and experience to take up higher posts, a direct result of the apartheid system.[41]

In 1983 it was reported that the Owambo administration suffered shortages of senior personnel. These were directly attributed to the lack of officials with qualifications and experience in administration. There were also difficulties in finding suitable candidates elsewhere to fill the posts.[42] The Owambo Directorate of education was likewise said to be understaffed. Some of the inspectors, for example, had 45 schools per circuit, while DNE officials had a maximum of fourteen or fifteen.[43] By 1988 one of the higher-level members of staff within the DNE went so far as to describe the situation in the Owambo Directorate as catastrophic.[44]

The deficit of qualified, experienced staff had a direct impact on the efficiency of each authority's educational administrative practices. An official report in 1983 mentioned that some of the ethnic authorities succeeded in satisfactorily carrying out their educational functions, while others found this extremely difficult for various unstated reasons. On the whole, though, most ethnic authorities were reported to have had difficulties in managing their educational systems.[45] A later report in the mid-eighties made a direct correlation between optimal service and management of education, and the lack of capable head office personnel in some of the ethnic directorates of education.[46] The functioning of the White Directorate, in contrast, was described in 1987 as being "extremely healthy and effective".[47]

In black ethnic authorities the situation was compounded by corruption, directly attributable to the fact that "there are no trained personnel around to keep an eye on things and ensure that correct office procedure is observed".[48] Here a direct link is made between mismanagement and the lack of training. It was also reported that with the system of multiple governments and so few trained people, "there are plenty of people on the make ... many of them seconded white civil servants".[49] This was especially alarming since whites held most of the high-ranking posts within the black educational directorates and a sizeable portion of the middle/professional-level posts.

Overview

While being afflicted with a dearth of qualified and trained staff, the structures of various directorates were also inadequately developed. A report on education in the early 1980s, in addition to highlighting the lack of experience in advisory and planning services among ethnic authorities, drew attention to their infrastructural requirements.[50] In reality, the ethnic directorates had no meaningful say in the planning, control, and organisation of their education and there was no co-ordination among the various ethnic directorates. Much responsibility and advice was still forthcoming from the DNE which both monitored their education and administered examinations. The 1985 Education Committee report called for an education system managed and supported by a strong central department of education. This central department would have regional bodies to assist with its administrative tasks and it was also suggested that there be local (school) level control so as to cater to the specific needs of the individual and the community.[51] By the end of the 1980s, this proposal had still not been realised.

Although the system appeared to be decentralised, in reality this was only so in a very basic administrative sense. Real control over educational policy remained indirectly vested in South Africa via its Administrator-General in Namibia, who could accept certain changes to educational policy only once he had the approval of the South African State President. The DNE appears to have been the conduit for carrying out South African-defined educational policy in the country.

A combination of inherited educational disadvantages, lack of funds, insufficient professional and experienced staff, as well as structural shortcomings resulted in a semi-decentralised, ethnically fragmented, generally poorly run educational administration. The outcome of such administration was evident in the difficulties of educational provision for Namibia's comparatively small population. The overall inability of most ethnic authorities' directorates to control their own education satisfactorily is evident in the amount of assistance they received from the DNE and, in some instances, from the White Directorate of Education and Culture with staff training.

TRAINING

As with the DNE, none of the ethnic directorates had training divisions within their structures. However, the subject advisory divisions within the Damara, Herero, Nama, Rehoboth Baster, Coloured and White Directorates provided some form of training for teachers, even though these divisions were not managed for training purposes. Thus training within the head offices had to be sought elsewhere. This was provided by the CPI, the DNE, and the White Directorate of Education and Culture. Occasionally, some ethnic directorates released their professional staff for further medium- or long-term training. For example, in 1985 an Ovambo inspector of schools pursued a three-month inspection and supervision course in London, while one of the Caprivian Directorate's staff went to London to do both a diploma and Masters degree course.[52] Long-term training such as this, however, was not a common feature among the directorates. This was either because they lacked enthusiasm for any form of training or because they could not cope with having staff, already in short supply, absent for long periods from the directorates.

CPI training, which was provided on an agency basis, tended to be very generalised and short-term and was in no way education-specific. For example, in 1982 two short induction courses were held for officials from the Kavango and Caprivian authorities' administrations. Rehoboth officials attended a similar course in 1986. Other short-term training included supervisors' courses in 1983 and 1984 for the Damara and Caprivian authorities respectively. Discussions and seminars were also held on general themes for all the Central Government departments and the representative authorities. In 1984 such discussions revolved around 'Economising Action'.

The CPI, as with the Central Governmental departments, also provided advisory and inspection services to all the ethnic authorities to help them increase their efficiency. In 1988 eight formal visits were made by its staff to various representative authorities. These, however, were minor investigations due to shortages of suitably trained officers within CPI. The acute shortage of trained training officers was evidenced by the fact that there was only one CPI Training and Publicity Officer responsible for all facets of training officials in the Owambo, Caprivi and Kavango administrations. These administrations were among the largest in 1987, with 55 per cent of the staff of all ethnic administrations in that year. The effectiveness of training emanating from the CPI's training office was therefore very limited.[53]

The DNE provided training to other directorates on request. Regular training assistance mostly took the form of one-week courses for principals in efficient school administration, subject advisory services, and in-service teacher training, given by subject advisers and inspectors. Short courses run by two inspectors from the Formal Education Division of the DNE were also provided for inspectors. Other training included providing psychological services to pupils, especially study guidance and subject choice for pupils, guidance in administration techniques for the staff managing the school hostels, and advisory services to the inspectorate.

All the ethnic authorities excepting whites relied on the DNE's training assistance. Training was fairly extensive, as was revealed by the 1987 report on subject advisory services to the Owambo, Kavango, Caprivian, Coloured and Tswana Directorates. During that year, 2,227 teachers attended the 99 courses offered, while 605 schools were visited and 1,238 teachers assisted there.[54] It appears that training was mainly directed at staff within schools rather than officials in the head office structures. Any training which occurred within the administrative structures appears to have been on-the-job where experienced staff trained less experienced employees. The Caprivian Directorate, however, claimed that from time-to-time the DNE offered short in-service training to its subject advisers.[55] The Coloured Directorate stated that its inspectors underwent in-service training and in turn trained their subject advisers.[56]

According to the DNE'S Director of Educational Control, the Nama, Damara, Coloured, Baster and White Directorates received more limited assistance than the five remaining black ethnic directorates. This could presumably have been because the training provided was not strictly needed. The Damara were said not to turn to the DNE, simply to show their rejection of the Central Government. Instead, they approached the White Directorate for training assistance.[57]

The White Directorate's sophistication, compared with the other ethnic directorates, was not limited to a superior structure and more numerous and better qualified staff, but also encompassed the in-service training it extended to its employees. In 1986 alone, training was provided for subject heads and subject teachers and there were courses in school management guidance for principals, deputy principals, heads of department, and hostel superintendents. The training consisted of basic as well as specific training in school management and guidance in administrative, organisational and professional areas. At least 29 subject advisers attended a course on subject management. Education management training for principals, deputy principals, department heads, and superintendents was provided in 1987 on an intensive basis.[58]

This directorate strongly emphasised good management techniques. For example, at head office level, inspectors were sent on a year-long business management course to South Africa. On completion, they worked together with other members of staff in the directorate to develop an education-oriented management course, adapting the techniques of business management to the needs of educational administration. The trained inspectors were then responsible for guiding all principals, deputy principals, and hostel superintendents in management. In addition, all staff who received promotion had to participate in one to two weeks of management training. The Professional and Auxiliary Services' Division also provided guidance, advice, and support to educationalists at all levels within the directorate regarding organising, planning, control, and communication in order to bring about effective staff management.

In a further bid to improve professional qualifications, the directorate annually made available to teachers five bursaries for one year of postgraduate study in South Africa and one additional such bursary for study abroad. In return, successful candidates had to work for the directorate for three years. In 1988 three such postgraduate bursary awards were made.59

The White Directorate was also able to extend its training provisions to other ethnic authorities on request. In 1986 a course was run for 79 principals, deputy principals, and departmental heads of the Herero Directorate and in 1987 there was a course in school management for school principals from this directorate. Advice was also given to that directorate's top management in 1986 regarding general problems. In the same year, 75 of the Damara Directorate's principals, deputy principals, and heads of department attended a course in basic school management. In 1987 a similar course was held for 39 Baster principals, while the staff of that ethnic directorate were involved in short information sessions in management and planning.[60]

In 1986 subject advisers from the White Directorate visited some Damara and Baster schools to help identify and provide guidance on areas of need and a psychologist from the Coloured Directorate was trained by the White Directorate. That year the Rehoboth Directorate's subject advisers attended a course covering communication, interviewing, dealing with conflict, and programme design.

Critique of training

On the whole, there was no concerted effort to train members of staff in ethnic directorates in areas which would enable them to take on more responsibility to manage and plan their own education. Proof of this was seen in the lack of training provided to professional staff involved in planning, psychology, and curriculum services, let alone those involved in actual management functions. Instead, in-service training was levelled more at middle-level staff such as heads and teachers, and it appears to have been geared towards efficiency in the day-to-day running of schools. As such, the existing training tended to perpetuate the ethnic authorities' dependence on the DNE and to a lesser degree on the White Directorate of Education and Culture.

CONCLUSION

The division of the educational administrative system into eleven 'independent' structures was both fragmented and wasteful. This resulted in unnecessary duplication of human resources, facilities, and administrative structures. The government spent huge sums of money on all these services. As one official report recognised, this was a luxury that a developing country such as Namibia could ill afford.[61] But not only was it a luxury, it was also an expression of South Africa's policy of 'homeland' administrations which were marred by corruption and incompetence, not least due to the lack of properly trained staff. In this, the policy totally disregarded the true needs of Namibia as a whole.

Furthermore, the entire education system, reflecting both the political reality of dependency and the excessive shortages of professional staff, was still heavily reliant on South African educational bodies. Though the DNE lacked effectively trained administrative staff, it was clearly the ethnic director- ates with the largest concentrations of pupils that suffered the greatest staff shortages.

Within the DNE, there was an overall deficit of well-man- aged, regular, in-depth training programmes geared specifi- cally to the needs of the educational staff at all levels. The lack of management and administrative training was further mag- nified within all the ethnic directorates, bar that of the whites. The White Directorate seemed to be the only structure with few administrative problems and did not have to rely on the DNE to assist with training. Indeed, the White Directorate had sufficient numbers of trained professionals to assist in train- ing the staff of other directorates on request.

By the late 1980s, Namibia not only lacked sufficient pro- fessional educators and educational managers, it also was unable to train enough specialised staff within its borders. But what of those Namibians in exile? In examining the training of Namibians living outside the country, we will be able to gauge their ability to fulfil the educational administrative staff needs of an independent Namibia.

NOTES

1. Representative authorities were the ethnic organisational structures established to administer and manage the affairs of the country's different population groups. Because the Rehoboth Basters had had their own government since 1976, their administrative structure was always referred to as the Government of Rehoboth rather than an administration (Administrator-General 1980:2; AGN 5 1983:51).

2. The Bushmen in particular lacked educationists. In 1985 one Bushman teacher was listed, while for the period 1986 to 1988 there were none. Teachers in Bushman schools were predominantly white, many of whom were national servicemen and these schools had only white principals (DNE 1985 Schedule A:11; 1986:92; 1987:87; 1988; Interview, Inspector of Education (Bushmen), 14/10/1988).

3. Administrator-General 1980:18, 38; AGN 5 1983:53.

4. Republic of South Africa 1964:245.

5. AGN 5 1983:50.

6. National Administration of South West Africa 1980:12, 14; Education Committee 1985:5.

7. DNE Annual Report 1985:41.

8. AGN 5 1983:101.

9. Interview, Director of Educational Control, DNE, 12/10/1988.

10. AGN 5 1983:99; Education Committee 1985:20.

11. AGN 5 1983:99.

12. Thirion Commission, Volume I, Part 1, Seventh Interim Report, 1983:83.

13. Included in the overall budget totals for each year were the subsidy to the Academy and all costs for the SWABC. The latter two came to R28,565,400 (23 per cent) and R33,290,000 (26.9 per cent) respectively in 1988/1989 and as such ranked second and third after the allocation to formal education (DNE 1988:2).

14. Pütz *et al* 1987; ACHSR 1985:72.

15. Interview, Head, Formal Education Division, DNE, 11/10/1988.

16. It is interesting to note that although the Afrikaans translation of the Directorate of Educational Control is "Direktoraat van Onderwysbeheer", which translates into educational management/administration, the word control has been used instead in all the DNE's publications.

17. Interview, Subject Adviser, Non-Formal Education Division, DNE, 2/11/1988.

18. Interview, Director of Educational Control, DNE, 12/10/1988.

19. Interview, Head of Formal Education Division, DNE, 11/10/1988.

20. The Namibian, 9/02/1990.

21. Government Service Commission *et al* 1987:41.

22. *ibid.*, 42; 1988:33, 42, 43.

23. DNE 1982:8.
24. *ibid.*, 1980:7.
25. Government Service Commission *et al* 1987:7, 22; 1988:16.
26. Interview, Technikon Lecturer, 31/10/1988.
27. Interview, Director, Technikon, 31/10/1988; Government Service Commission 1988:35.
28. Interview, Director, Technikon, 31/10/1988; Dean, Faculty of Economic and Management Studies, the Academy, 1/11/1988.
29. Interview, Director, Educational Control, DNE, 12/10/1988.
30. DNE 1983:14, 25, 26.
31. Interview, Subject Adviser, Formal Education Division, DNE, 4/11/1988.
32. Director of Educational Control, DNE, 11/10/1988.
33. A mimeograph written by three senior subject advisers within the Formal Education Division called for improvement in school administration, by upgrading the abilities of administrators through the establishment of centres for on-going training for school personnel during their periods of service (West *et al* 1988).
34. Turner 1990:3.
35. In 1987 the white representative authority received the second largest financial contribution to education in Namibia (R21,532,000), despite having fewer pupils and schools than some of the other directorates (see Table 8.3). The Owambos received the highest subsidy of R74,711,000. It must be noted, however, that personal income taxes accrued to the second tier ethnic governments. Since whites had always paid higher taxes than all the other ethnic groups by virtue of their privileged financial status, the white administration was the wealthiest in the country (Pütz *et al* 1987:233; SAIRR 1982:616).
36. Interview, Director, White Directorate of Education and Culture, 20/10/1988.
37. Interview, Director, Educational Control, DNE, 12/10/1988.
38. Interview, Subject Adviser, Formal Education Division, DNE, 4/11/1988; Mukendwa 1985:38.
39. AGN 5 1983:137.
40. Education Committee 1985:13, 77.
41. Interview, Director, Educational Control, DNE, 12/10/1988.
42. Thirion Commission, Volume I, Eerste Tussentydse Verslag, 1983:175.
43. Interview, Subject Adviser, Formal Education Division, DNE, 4/11/1988.
44. Interview, Head, Formal Education Division, DNE, 16/10/1988.
45. AGN 5 1983:85, 102.
46. Education Committee 1985:77.
    Concerning the Caprivi administration, the Thirion Commission

reported that " staff administration leaves much to be desired. It is doubtful whether the personnel in charge of staff administration have the knowledge or experience to restore proper administration or even to rectify the errors and irregularities revealed ...." The Herero and Kavango Directorates were also singled out for their inefficiency (Thirion Commission, Volume I, Part I, Seventh Interim Report, 1983:77, 78; Interview, Subject Adviser, DNE, 4/11/1988).

47. Administration for Whites 1987:66.
48. SAIRR 1984:606.
49. *ibid.*
50. AGN 5 1983:96.
51. Education Committee 1985:46, 47.
52. Mukendwa 1985:89; Interview, Director, Rössing Education Foundation, 8/10/1988.
53. Government Service Commission *et al.* 1987:94; 1988:35, 36, 46.
54. DNE 1987:34.
55. Personal Communication, Educational Planner, Caprivian Directorate of Education and Culture, 7/11/1988.
56. Personal Communication, Inspector, Coloured Directorate of Education and Culture, 16/11/1988.
57. Interview, Head Subject Adviser, DNE, 4/11/1988.
58. Administration for Whites 1986:123; 1987:68.
59. Interview, Director, White Directorate of Education and Culture, 20/10/1988.
60. Administration for Whites 1986:123; 1987:68; Personal Communication, Director, Government of Rehoboth 28/11/1988.
61. AGN 1983:88.

Preparing for independence: training programmes in Africa and abroad

9

International assistance to post-secondary education training (1): governmental and non-governmental organisations and institutions

The efforts outside ... Namibia ... to train
people in technical and managerial occupations
are an important contribution to closing
the skills gap between the races in the future.
G. GERHART, 1983

INTRODUCTION

Many African countries are still suffering from the long-term effects of attaining independence without the necessary stock of skilled and experienced human resources to change and run their governmental, economic, and educational systems. Mozambique is a case in point. After the mass exodus of Portuguese managers, professionals, and technicians in the early 1970s, the country was left without a working civil service. This was one of the harshest legacies of colonial rule.

Southern African liberation movements like SWAPO of Namibia, the African National Congress (ANC) of South Africa, the Zimbabwe African National Union (ZANU), and the Zimbabwe African People's Union (ZAPU) have always recognised the importance of education. They are aware of the vital contribution education can make to national development because of its role in producing skilled resources. These liberation movements all adopted manifestos and policy statements which included educational goals and commitments because education was seen to be central to the liberation struggle and post-independence development. These movements' early formulations of education policy were dominated by the total rejection of and resistance to the oppressive, colonialist education policies, and the demand for equality in education.

As a result, by the early 1980s some of the movements had established their own schools and were running their own educational programmes in the frontline states and other friendly countries. Before independence, ZAPU and ZANU were even able to open schools in liberated areas within Zimbabwe. SWAPO's political programme also stressed the need for "the urgent training of technical and professional cadres at institutions of technical and higher learnings in different parts of the world as well as the newly established United Nations Institute for Namibia".[1]

In this chapter, there is a brief overview of SWAPO's activities in the provision of school and basic adult education to exiles, as well as a review of SWAPO's extensive teacher training programmes. More important, however, is the analysis of the output from SWAPO's direct training programmes as well as certain scholarship schemes in Africa and elsewhere. Through these schemes, Namibians were trained as teachers and in other education-related fields. Mention is also made of those who undertook public administration training, to indicate the availability of trained potential public administrators and possibly public enterprise managers who could take on more generalised administrative posts in the educational sector. The aim of the current analysis is to provide an indication of the number and potential of the educational specialists and teachers who trained in exile and who have in principle become available to the post-independent Namibian education system. Unfortunately, this analysis has had to rely on incomplete data.

LIMITATIONS TO THE DATA

Neither this chapter nor the next make any pretence at providing a complete picture of the number of Namibians trained or experienced in educational fields abroad. The search for statistical data commenced in the latter half of the 1980s when the reality of Namibia's independence was still very uncertain and fraught with much indecision on South Africa's part. This had a direct influence on the ability to gain access to certain data. Information on the number of Namibians in tertiary-level education and related areas of study was requested from various non-governmental, bilateral, and international aid agencies, as well as ministries of education and statistical offices in various countries. The annual reports of the United Nations training and scholarship schemes for Namibians were also consulted and additional information was obtained through personal communication with the United Nations Institute for Namibia (UNIN).

It has been difficult to obtain accurate information through mailed requests. Such applications are often treated with suspicion. Details concerning Namibian students were frequently considered confidential, especially when the struggle for independence was still in progress. SWAPO was reluctant to divulge detailed information on various education projects because these were not always successful owing to the participants' severe educational handicaps. Some countries like West Germany, the then German Democratic Republic, France, the Soviet Union, Australia and New Zealand and, until the mid-1980s, the United States did not compile statistics on foreign students by country and field of study. Most foreign students were merely classified according to region. Norway, Sweden, and Denmark simply claimed that such information was not available. Even where the information had been compiled, the amount of time officials needed to gather it acted as a deterrent. On other occasions when the information was provided, further requests for up-dated details were not supplied because of staff changes. No East-bloc countries, including Cuba (listed as having Namibian students according to a 1985/1986 UNESCO questionnaire survey), responded to written requests, although Poland made an attempt to circulate the author's requests among various governmental departments.

A further difficulty was that the available data did not necessarily indicate the number of students who had completed their studies. This statistic was provided only in the United Kingdom university survey for the period 1972 – 1989 and, as of 1982, in United Nations Council for Namibia reports on scholarships under the United Nations Fund for Namibia (see Chapter 10). The latter, however, did not provide a detailed breakdown of students according to their fields of study. Since the United Nations-sponsored programmes appear to have been the most comprehensive and best documented, more attention was devoted to analysing them in terms of training teachers and educational administrators. A more fragmented picture emerges from reviewing other aid programmes.

To compensate for the absence of statistics from individual scholarship programmes, data, where available, are given on the number of Namibians studying in a specific country. However, as stated above, not all countries compiled such information. Moreover, some programmes did not differentiate between United Nations-sponsored and other Namibians, nor between exiles and those able to return home. This was the case with data on the overall number of Namibians studying in Canada, the United Kingdom, and the United States. By contrast, statistics on Namibians in Africa and India are limited to specific scholarship programmes.

As with the United Nations projects discussed in the next chapter, the overall picture is too vague to permit an accurate assessment of the number of exiled trained Namibians on such scholarship schemes. This, as well as the dearth of accurate data on the number of trained professionals within Namibia (see Chapters 7 and 8), inhibits the assessment of educational staff needs in the country and the potential to overcome these. Most estimates on the skilled human resource requirements within the country in the immediate post-independence period have been calculated on the premise of a large-scale white exodus which has simply not occurred (see Chapter 13). In view of these uncertainties, we have kept to making only general observations on such issues.

SWAPO'S ROLE IN EDUCATIONAL PROVISION AT SCHOOL LEVEL

The first exodus of Namibians this century dates back to 1904, when about 1,000 Herero succeeded in reaching Bechuanaland (Botswana) after fleeing the German extermination campaign against them. The next exodus commenced in the early 1960s, when many leading nationalists quit the country for fear of their safety, especially after the Windhoek shootings in December 1959. They headed for Dar es Salaam where offices for both SWAPO and the South West Africa National Union (SWANU) were established. The persistent inequalities and lack of opportunities for black Namibians resulted in the continuation of the exodus of Namibians. They sought refuge in neighbouring countries with the intention of joining the externally-based nationalist movements of SWAPO and SWANU and also to further their education.

Already during the 1960s, SWAPO had begun sending a number of young Namibians to various educational institutions abroad with the help of the United Nations Educational and Training Program for Southern Africa (UNETPSA). These young men and women paved the way for a comprehensive scholarship programme which by the early 1980s had benefited about 5,000 students.[2] The intensification of the liberation struggle, with the commencement of SWAPO's armed struggle in August 1966, and the collapse of the Portuguese empire and subsequent independence of Angola and Mozambique in the mid-1970s resulted in a considerable increase in the number of young refugees intent on either joining the armed struggle or attaining a better education. By 1983 the United Nations High Commissioner for Refugees (UNHCR) estimated that there were 70,000 Namibian refugees in Angola and 33,000 in Zambia of whom approximately

40,000 and more than 2,000 respectively were living in SWAPO settlements in Angola and Zambia. Over half the refugee population in these settlements consisted of teenage or younger children.[3]

SWAPO's Department of Education and Culture was formed in 1968. It played a major role in providing education to Namibian exiles through various education projects, pre-school facilities, primary and junior secondary schools at Kwanza Sul in Angola and Nyango in Zambia (opened in the early and mid-1970s respectively), as well as the provision of distance and adult education at its settlements in Angola and Zambia. The two SWAPO schools at Nyango and Kwanza Sul went up to junior secondary level and schooling was compulsory for all school-age pupils in the refugee settlements. SWAPO-run schools were also established on the Isle of Youth in Cuba. Between 8,000 to 10,000 children were said to have attended SWAPO's school in Angola and 2,000 in Zambia, while in Cuba by the late 1980s there were approximately 1,200 primary and secondary school pupils.[4] Vocational training was provided for 500 pupils at the SWAPO secondary technical school established in 1986 at Loudima in Congo. A Vocational Training Centre for Namibians was inaugurated at Sumbe in Angola in 1984 for 200 students.[5] Those completing the SWAPO primary or lower secondary education courses, prior to the establishment of the Loudima secondary school, were able to complete senior high school in appropriate schools throughout Africa.

On the whole, SWAPO was said to provide "education of relatively high quality" and one official from the British Overseas Development Administration (ODA) commented that Namibian exiled pupils appeared to be better qualified than their compatriots within the country.[6] By 1983 the total number of Namibians enrolled in or having completed secondary or tertiary education under the auspices of SWAPO was estimated to have exceeded 3,000.[7] In fact, more Namibians were pursuing tertiary and technical education outside Namibia than were enrolled within the country by that date.[8] All these achievements came about with the extensive assistance of the

United Nations, the Commonwealth and bilateral and non-governmental agencies, organisations, and institutions. The extent of such assistance was made evident in a survey on support to refugees from South Africa and Namibia conducted for the Ford Foundation (see Gerhart 1983). Here we limit our focus to teacher training programmes.

SWAPO'S TEACHER TRAINING PROGRAMMES AND THEIR OUTPUT

SWAPO, in addition to providing school-level training, also embarked upon extensive primary school teacher training programmes. A common difficulty experienced in the settlement schools was the shortage of qualified teachers. A report on education in exile summed up the situation, saying that most teachers were untrained and at secondary level "the lack of teachers ... is more acute".[9] The problems therefore mirrored those within Namibia. SWAPO also recognised the important influence trained teachers have on the quality of primary and secondary education. Its teacher training programmes placed specific emphasis on English language training since English was to become the official language in a country previously dominated by Afrikaans. Such training was based on bilateral agreements between SWAPO's Department of Education and Culture, donor agencies, and training institutions in various countries.

SWAPO's programmes consisted of both in-service training (henceforth INSET) and institutional pre-service teacher training. Here we examine the following:

☐ the SWAPO Department of Education and Culture's INSET Programme;

☐ the Integrated Teacher Training Programme (pre-service);

☐ the United Kingdom Teacher Training Programme for Namibian Teachers of English (pre-service).

THE INSET PROGRAMME

SWAPO's INSET programme was carried out in the early 1980s in conjunction with the in-service training provided by the United Nations Institute for Namibia (see Chapter 10) for untrained teachers in the SWAPO refugee settlements, some of whom had a very low level of education.[10] The programme was run at Kwanza Sul in Angola, the larger of the organisation's two settlements in Angola and Zambia. The project, which was conducted in close co-operation with institutions of higher learning in Africa and Europe (no details or names thereof were provided) and with Swedish expatriates, was intended to train primary school teachers through short courses. These courses took the form of workshops and seminars which were geared to encourage participants to continue with further full time teacher training. The aim was not only to improve the general quality of serving teachers who were drawn from primary and secondary levels but also to act as a preparatory course for full time teacher training.

No figures, not even approximations, are available of the number of candidates in the project. Since the participants were all acting teachers, the training did not increase the number of available teachers but, rather helped improve the professional competence of existing teachers. A serious drawback experienced by the INSET programme was the low level of education of certain participants and the lack of skilled personnel to direct the scheme.[11]

THE INTEGRATED TEACHER TRAINING PROGRAMME (ITTP)

This three-year, full-time training programme for primary school teachers dated from 1986. Half of the programme was conducted at Kwanza Sul and the rest at the University of Umea in Sweden.[12] The training was unconventional because of the relative stress on linking theory and practice. About 60 per cent of the programme was conducted outside an established teacher training college and trainees were encouraged to produce their own teaching materials. The idea was to train the trainees in the environment in which they would eventually work. The course therefore included specific knowledge relevant to the needs of the Kwanza Sul school.

The trainees' educational backgrounds, teaching, and learning experiences were very varied. Among the first group of fifteen trainees who graduated in 1989, six had an 'O' level pass from West Africa but no teaching experience. The remaining nine students had received primary and some secondary education from Namibia and had taught at the SWAPO schools. Some of the nine had received vocational training while in exile and one trainee had undertaken the three-year Management and Development Studies course at UNIN.[13] Since the programme focused on improving the professional quality of a small number of teachers from Kwanza Sul, its contribution to the overall teacher output was not great. Nevertheless, it provided a model for an alternative form of teacher training in independent Namibia.

SWAPO's teacher training projects were limited to teachers at the primary school level. At no point did the movement develop a teacher training system to cater for the secondary schools' system. The majority of its schools were primary, while SWAPO candidates who wished to train for secondary-level teaching could do so via the various scholarship assistance schemes on offer.

THE UNITED KINGDOM TEACHER TRAINING PROGRAMME FOR NAMIBIAN TEACHERS OF ENGLISH

This project, in operation since 1982, was funded by the ODA and administered by the British Council (BC).[14] Training took two-and-a-half years and was divided into:

- intensive pre-course training in Lusaka at the British Council;
- specific English language training at Bell School of English, Saffron Walden, for 12 weeks;
- one year at Selly Oak Colleges, Birmingham, acquiring a broad educational background;

❑ one year at Moray House College, Edinburgh, Scotland, to prepare for the diploma in Teaching English as a Foreign and Second Language (TEFL/TESL).

The average number of participants each year was fifteen. Many had two to three years' teaching experience, some had more, while others had virtually none. The trainees were drawn largely from the teaching force in the SWAPO Health and Education Centres in Angola and Zambia, with a small number, directly from Namibia, who had joined the course for the Moray House training.

During the year at Moray House College, students for the first time formed part of a larger group of teachers from various countries rather than being confined to a course tailored to their specific needs. In addition to the TEFL/TESL diploma training, students were able to explore or extend their competence in areas such as mathematics, educational administration or literacy training. A 1989 report claimed that since its inception, over 100 students successfully completed this training.[15]

After this two-and-a-half year training, some trainees, on average five or six per year and eleven in 1989, went on to follow B Ed, diploma, or M Ed programmes in Britain with financial assistance from the ODA or Scandinavian and other agencies via the Africa Educational Trust. In 1986, for example, three Namibians from Moray House College went on to do B Ed studies at Bristol University.[16]

The number of students pursuing further studies on completion of the course — assuming an average of five students per year per group since 1983 and eleven in 1989 — would be around 41. This is encouraging, especially since some of this number were pursuing postgraduate level studies. An example of such studies was the diploma course in educational management and administration at Moray House in which three Namibians were enrolled in 1986.[17]

The Teacher Training Programme for Namibian English Teachers, although geared to primary school teachers like INSET and ITTP, was not limited to trainees from Kwanza

Sul. Since the participants were all acting teachers, this programme did not augment the number of available teachers. Instead, it served to improve existing teachers' professional competence. It also added to the number of Namibians embarking on university-level educational studies. The overall estimates are encouraging although it was not possible to discern the students' areas of postgraduate specialisation. The following section provides statistics on the number of Namibians in educational studies as a whole in the United Kingdom.

NAMIBIANS STUDYING IN THE UNITED KINGDOM

The highest number of Namibian students in Europe were believed to be in Britain.[18] In addition to assistance provided by the British Government through the ODA and the British Council (BC) to both exiled and other Namibians, other non-governmental organisations provided scholarships mostly to exiles. These included World University Service (WUS, United Kingdom), Christian Aid and the Africa Educational Trust (AET).

WUS had a small scholarship scheme in Britain dating back to 1980. WUS did not provide statistics but indicated that this programme was small and mostly in technical/scientific fields, including 'access' courses to enable Namibians to qualify for entry to higher education.[19] Christian Aid, which also began sponsoring Namibians in 1980 and did so from 1980/1981 to 1988/1989, assisted a total of 43 Namibians, seven of whom were enrolled in educational studies, five at undergraduate level and the remainder at postgraduate level. Students receiving Christian Aid sponsorship were a combination of refugees and non-refugees.[20] The AET did not volunteer information on the number of Namibians it assisted nor their fields of study, for reasons of confidentiality.

Table 9.1 provides overall totals of Namibian students in all fields of study in the United Kingdom for the period 1974/75 to 1987/88. These figures were calculated from

Table 9.1   Namibian Students at Universities and Public
Sector Institutions of Higher and Further Education in the United Kingdom, 1974/75–1986/87*

Year	Under-grad	Post-grad	Total	Further Ed	Poly	UK Other	Grand Total**
1974/75	2	5	7	7	—	—	14
1975/76	4	1	5	—	—	8	13
1976/77	1	1	2	—	—	2	4
1977/78	4	4	8	12	2	3	25
1978/79	2	4	6	14	2	3	25
1979/80	2	2	4	13	3	20	40
1980/81	4	5	9	22	14	16	61
1981/82	13	5	18	19	14	1	52
1982/83	24	7	31	25	17	2	75
1983/84	19	13	32	35	12	4	83
1984/85	15	22	37	21	10	—	68
1985/86	15	22	37	34	6	—	77
1986/87	18	28	46	21	11	—	78
1987/88	20	47	67	19	18	—	104
TOTALS	143	166	309	242	109	59	719

* Central Institutions in Scotland only from 1984/85.
** This total covers all the Namibians training in the United Kingdom.
Notes: (1) The data have been compiled from British Council surveys
and other official sources. The various bodies collecting the
data used different survey dates and methods so caution
should be exercised. Much of the information is derived
from student admissions or registration documents.
(2) The statistics on institutions other than the universities, further and higher education establishments, and the public
sector in general are partial, therefore the grand total is an
approximation. Students on short courses in certain private
institutions have not been included.
(3) As of 1984/85, statistics on women were given separately:
1984/85 nineteen (six at university)
1985/86 eighteen (three at university)
1986/87 fifteen (six at university)
1987/88 twenty-seven (fifteen at university)
Source: Adapted from British Council Statistics of Overseas Students in
the United Kingdom, 1976 — 1986; 1988; 1989

British Council statistics which were presented in detailed format only from 1974/75. For the period 1974/75 to 1987/88, a total of 719 Namibians had been enrolled at institutions in the United Kingdom, 309 (43 per cent) of whom were at university level.

Namibians at universities, polytechnics and institutions of higher education made up 92 per cent of the overall total of 719 by 1987/88. No figures were available for the students who had completed their studies by 1987/88.

Between 1972 and 1979, no students were listed as having done educational studies at any United Kingdom universities.[21] Table 9.2 provides a statistical breakdown of all Namibian university students undertaking educational studies in the United Kingdom as at 31 December of each year. Short courses, for example, of four months' duration, were not included in these figures.[22] Undergraduates in educational studies made up 16 per cent of the total number of Namibian undergraduates in all subjects for the period 1979 – 1989. Out of the 44 Namibian undergraduates who completed their studies during the ten years (see Table 9.3), those in educational studies made up 14 per cent. Postgraduates in educational studies constituted 52 per cent of the number of postgraduates in all fields from 1979 – 1989. Those enrolled in education courses who completed their studies comprised 61 per cent of the successful postgraduate totals for the ten-year period under discussion.

Only three Namibians completed postgraduate studies in public administration and one student completed undergraduate studies for the period 1979 – 1989. As with education studies, there were more postgraduates than undergraduates in this field (see Table 9.3).

The data from the individual sponsorship schemes also help to expand the picture. For example, ODA, through its Technical Co-operation and Training Programme (TCTP), administered by the British Council, sponsored Namibians at a variety of educational establishments in the United Kingdom.[23] In 1986, for example, six Namibians studied for diplomas and one for a certificate in public administration and another student was enrolled in a postgraduate educational administration/public administration course at a polytechnic. Ten more Namibians were training for the diploma in English language training at an institute of higher education. The total number of Namibians sponsored by this programme, pursuing degrees and diplomas in education at

Table 9.2   Full-Time Namibian Students in Educational Studies at United Kingdom Universities, 1979 – 1989*

Year	Ed Under-grad	No. Com-pleting	Total Under-grad +	Ed Post-grad**	No. Com-pleting	Total Post-grad+
1979	—	—	4	2	—	2
1980	—	—	4	4	1	5
1981	1	—	13	2	1	5
1982	1	—	24	1	2	7
1983	1	—	19	6	—	14
1984	1	—	16	10	3	23
1985	4	1	16	7	2	22
1986	3	2	18	15	3	28
1987	3	—	20	28	10	47
1988	7	—	20	21	15	39
1989	7	3	20	22	16	37
TOTALS	28	6	170	118	53	229

* Courses of nine months or longer. Figures do not include short courses.
** Includes the one-year teacher training course at postgraduate level.
+ Total for Namibian students in all subjects.
Source: Personal Communication, Universities Statistical Record, 31/10/1989

universities for the period 1982/83 – 1986/87, came to seventeen of whom two were enrolled for Masters courses in educational administration and another for an M Phil in educational planning.[24] These students are included in Tables 9.2 and 9.3.

Table 9.3   Full-Time Namibian Students in Public
Administration Studies at United Kingdom
Universities, 1979 – 1989*

Year	Admin Under-grad	No. Com-pleting	Total** Under-grad Com-pleting	Admin Post-grad	No. Com-pleting	Total** Post-grad Com-pleting
1979	—	—	1	—	—	2
1980	1	—	1	—	—	1
1981	1	—	1	—	—	1
1982	1	—	1	1	—	2
1983	1	1	3	1	—	4
1984	1	—	6	1	1	5
1985	—	—	9	—	—	5
1986	—	—	4	1	—	6
1987	—	—	2	1	1	15
1988	—	—	7	2	—	23
1989	—	—	9	1	1	23
TOTALS	5	1	44	8	3	87

* Courses of nine months or longer.
** Totals for Namibian students in all subject areas.
Source: Personal Communication, Universities Statistical Record,
31/10/1989

To gain a more complete picture of the total number of Namibians in both education and public administration studies, we also have to take into consideration students graduating from polytechnics and other institutions of higher learning for which separate data are not available.

THE COMMONWEALTH SECRETARIAT'S FELLOWSHIP AND TRAINING PROGRAMME

This Commonwealth Secretariat Programme aimed to assist developing countries to increase their pool of skilled human resources in areas important to national development. It was set up in 1972 as a division of the Commonwealth Fund for Technical Co-operation (CFTC). Within it a special Commonwealth Programme for Namibians was established in 1975 to assist exiled nationals. The Commonwealth Secretariat worked closely with the United Nations on this programme.[25]

By 1987 almost 600 Namibians had been supported on full time courses at institutions in fifteen, mostly developing, Commonwealth countries.[26] Most of the awards were in technical and vocational fields. The courses had a built-in instructor component which enabled successful trainees to further develop the skills of other Namibians in the refugee camps, since most trainees returned to Angola and Zambia. By 1990, 1,500 candidates had received full-time professional, technical and vocational training in 21 countries under the CFTC. This was a prodigious output for fifteen years and a sizeable contribution to human resource development.[27]

In 1985/86 a particularly large cohort of Namibians embarked upon teacher training in various countries. Twenty Namibians commenced a three-year primary English teachers' course at Peradeniya College, Sri Lanka. Most of these trainees had completed only seven years of education and possessed a poor knowledge of English. The course was therefore altered to overcome these deficiencies and to make the subject matter more relevant to the trainees' African background. That same year, a further four Namibians were sent to Port Loko Teacher Training College, Sierra Leone, to attend an English language training course, and another fourteen attended adult literacy instructors' courses in Kenya at Kitui.[28] This teacher training fell under the Secretariat's English Language Programme for Namibians (ELPN), launched in 1983 in Lusaka. It was part of the Fellowship and Training Programme. By 1989 at least 40 Namibians (all women) had trained as English language teachers under this programme and a further 30 had completed adult literacy instructors' courses.[29]

Training in education under the Commonwealth programme was not only limited to increasing or enhancing the quality of Namibia's teaching stock. By 1987 about ten Namibians had trained in educational planning at the National Institute of Educational Planning and Administration (NIEPA), India and the Eastern and Southern African Management Institute (ESAMI) in Tanzania. The courses were three months long and led to a diploma. Although graduates were preferred for this training, Namibian candidates were selected from SWAPO's Department of Education and Culture on the basis of their experience and competence rather than their formal academic qualifications. On completion of the training, the candidates returned to work with SWAPO.

Such training, however, was not specifically adapted to Namibians' needs. Most Namibians attending the courses were not graduates, which must have placed them at a considerable disadvantage despite their experience. Moreover, the courses were too short to enable the Namibians to overcome their academic handicaps. Notwithstanding the fact that a fair number of Namibians had undergone training in educational planning, training in this field was not identified as being a major area of need by SWAPO.[30]

Administrative training in general appears to have received little attention in the Commonwealth Programme for Namibians. By 1986 only three to four Namibians had trained in management administration.[31] Educational administration training was totally lacking despite the administrative shortcomings within certain SWAPO schools and the Namibian

Extension Unit (see Chapter 10). Since the Commonwealth Programme was responsive to SWAPO-defined needs, it may be inferred that educational administration was not seen as a key area by the organisation.

Following the Commonwealth Heads of Government meeting at Kuala Lumpur in 1989, a small team of experts was sent to Namibia after the elections of 1989 to identify those areas of need with which the Commonwealth would be able to help collectively. Among the issues raised by the team with the government-elect in late November 1989 was the re-structuring of the civil service and local government in order to help overcome the legacies of apartheid in these sectors. The Commonwealth agreed to send an advisor on this matter. It was suggested that two or three of the most senior officials in each ministry undergo attachment to comparable ministries of Commonwealth countries and attend specially designed courses in public administration.[32] This was the first time that the Commonwealth's attention had been directed toward top-level administrative training.

TRAINING ASSISTANCE FROM THE UNITED STATES

The American non-governmental organisations providing most scholarship assistance to exiled Namibians were the African-American Institute (AAI) through its Southern Africa Training Program and the Phelps-Stokes Fund (PSF) for undergraduates only.[33] Although the majority of AAI's southern African candidates went to the United States, it also provided assistance for training in Africa. Throughout the 1960s, the AAI sponsored a total of 20 Namibians (field of study not stipulated). In 1983 it assisted fourteen Namibians teaching in the SWAPO refugee camps to enrol in teacher training courses in Sierra Leone.[34]

By 1984 the AAI was sponsoring a total of 50 Namibians (37 in Africa and thirteen in the United States). Of this total at least sixteen were in education or teacher training. Priority was clearly given to Africa-based training since this was less

expensive. In 1985 the number of Namibians on the programme rose to 110, ten in America, of whom two were
pursuing education studies, and 100 in Africa, of whom
eleven were enrolled in education studies.[35] Between 1978
and 1984 the PSF supported one student in educational
studies and one public administration candidate for the years

Table 9.4   Namibian University Students in all Fields of
Study in the United States, 1975/76 – 1987/88*

Year	Total Students Each Year
1975/76	1
1976/77	5
1977/78	5
1978/79	—
1979/80	41
1980/81	28
1981/82	44
1982/83	68
1983/84	54
1984/85	86
1985/86	74
1986/87	—
1987/88	22
TOTAL	428

* The data presumably includes both exiled and other
Namibians on a variety of sponsorship programmes.
Source: Personal Communication, Institute of International
Education, United States of America, May 1987; UNESCO Office of
Statistics, Questionnaire on Statistics of Education at the Third Level,
1985/86

1984 – 1988. Further information from these two American-based organisations was not forthcoming.

Since students on these two programmes were mostly refugees, we can assume that those doing educational studies would have returned either to teach in the SWAPO schools or taken up employment in the SWAPO Department of Education and Culture on completion of these courses. Table 9.4 shows the number of university-level students studying in the United States as a whole (exiles and others) since 1975/1976.

NAMIBIANS STUDYING IN CANADA

Undergraduate and postgraduate Namibian students in Canada numbered 24 over the period 1975/76 – 1989/90 (see Table 9.5).

At least ten Namibians were in elementary/secondary teacher training; three of these were postgraduates. Six were in physical education and the remainder in unspecified non-teaching fields of education.[36] The number of Namibians in education as a whole constituted 16 per cent of overall Namibian student totals, but it is not stated how many completed their studies.

WEST GERMAN SUPPORT TO NAMIBIANS

Statistics on the number of Namibians in Germany and their fields of study were not available simply because they have not been compiled. The Otto Benecke Foundation appears to have been the most active organisation in that country in terms of assistance to a sizeable number of Namibians who were sponsored by SWAPO, SWANU or who had no political affiliations. Between 1978 and 1985, it had assisted more than 500 Namibian refugees in vocational training in both Germany and Africa. Concerning education studies, however, most training was confined to Africa. In 1986, for example, at least eleven Namibians were doing teacher training in Sierra Leone with the help of the Otto Benecke Foundation.[37]

Table 9.5   Namibian University-Level Educational Studies
Students in Canada, 1975/76 – 1989/90

Year	Education			Total all Fields
	Undergrad	Postgrad	Total	
1975/76	—	1	1	4
1976/77	1	—	1	4
1977/78	2	—	2	4
1978/79	1	—	1	7
1979/80	2	—	2	11
1980/81	2	—	2	14
1981/82	1	1	2	10
1982/83	2	1	3	11
1983/84	1	2	3	16
1984/85	1	1	2	8
1985/86	1	1	2	15
1986/87	1	1	2	17
1987/88	—	—	—	7
1988/89	1	—	1	12
1989/90	—	—	—	9
TOTAL	16	8	24	149

Source: Personal Communication, Statistics Canada, Post-
Secondary Education Section, 13/07/1987, 23/11/1987, 19/11/1990

NAMIBIANS AND THE NORDIC COUNTRIES

FINLAND

Finland, with its historical link to Namibia via nineteenth century Finnish missionary work in Ovamboland, has always taken a keen interest in Namibia. It gave predominantly to United Nations projects but also directly assisted SWAPO with humanitarian aid, chiefly in the form of scholarships for students sent by the movement. This was tied up to a large degree for use in Finland. Information on the overall number of Namibians studying in Finland was considered confidential; the data here are therefore incomplete. Between 1975 and 1985, there were at least 80 Namibians pursuing university-level studies. Most of them were exiles although a small number had come from within the country. Their fields of study were not stipulated. Some of the Namibian SWAPO students, as well as those from within Namibia who were studying in Finland, were also sponsored by various non-governmental organisations.

The government of Finland, via the Finnish International Development Agency (FINNIDA), played a role in assisting Namibian exiles as well as a few Namibians from within the country. During the period 1976 – 1986, for example, it granted 138 scholarships at universities and other educational institutions in Finland to SWAPO, three of which were in education at university level. By 1987 two Namibians were pursuing educational studies at postgraduate level.[38]

In addition to scholarships, FINNIDA also organised training programmes. In 1983 FINNIDA ran a three-month management course for fifteen participants from SWAPO's administration. This was probably a very broad-based course since it covered the organisation's entire administration and the length of the course would have prevented any specialisation. Two years later, FINNIDA organised a nine-week training course for nine instructors from Nyango, Zambia, in wood- and metalwork. FINNIDA also organised two-year pre-university training courses for seventeen Namibians in 1986. This training was specially modified to Namibians' needs with

English as the medium of instruction throughout. It was described as being one of the largest of FINNIDA's educational programmes. Although the Namibians on this course entered technical fields rather than educational studies, such pre-university training was important and represented a realistic attempt to overcome educational handicaps before placing students in an academic environment.

SWEDEN

Sweden was also very active in assisting Namibian refugees, mostly through grants to the AET, WUS, the Commonwealth Secretariat's Fund for Technical Co-operation, United Nations scholarship programmes, and the University of Zimbabwe. The Swedish International Development Authority (SIDA) also provided direct aid to SWAPO. In 1984/85 SIDA financed a nine-month course in financial management for eleven exiled Namibians from Angola in Sweden and arranged courses for administrators, teachers, and nurses.[39] It is not clear where such training occurred nor how many Namibians participated, since any information regarding SIDA's humanitarian assistance was considered confidential. Moreover, Sweden claimed not to compile data on the foreign students studying there.[40] The picture here regarding Namibians and their areas of study was too scattered to provide even a rough estimate of numbers.

DENMARK

Denmark channelled most of its assistance to Namibians through the United Nations and private non-governmental organisations like those mentioned under Sweden, including the Lutheran World Federation. Unlike FINNIDA and SIDA, Denmark did not directly assist SWAPO. No statistics were compiled on the number of foreign students studying in Denmark. This rules out any estimation of the number of Namibians studying there.[41]

NORWAY

Norway gave active support to SWAPO both directly and via the various United Nations programmes and non-governmental agencies mentioned above, as well as through programmes based in Norway: the Norwegian Students' and Teachers' International Assistance Fund; the Church of Norway (Council on Foreign Relations), and the Namibia Association at Elverum. As with the other Nordic countries, allegedly no data were compiled in Norway regarding Namibian students and their fields of study.[42]

SUMMARY

SWAPO's teacher training programmes were restricted to primary school teachers. The movement did not develop a teacher training system to cater for the secondary school system. On the whole, most teacher and other training in education was undertaken in the United Kingdom, Canada, the United States, the Nordic countries, a number of Commonwealth or Anglophone African countries, India, and Sri Lanka. By far the largest number of education students was in teacher training, especially English language teacher training. Indeed, by 1989, 100 or more students had completed English language teacher training in the United Kingdom and 40 or so primary school English language teachers had trained in Sri Lanka and Sierra Leone under the Commonwealth Secretariat's programme for Namibians. Sixteen adult literacy instructors were also trained in Kenya. The majority of Namibian students were selected from among the existing teaching force in SWAPO schools in Africa. On completion, most students are believed to have returned to those SWAPO schools.

It is impossible to ascertain much about other areas of specialisation from the statistics provided. What is certain is that the SWAPO teacher training programmes and projects of the Commonwealth Secretariat devoted little or no attention to educational administration either as a course of instruction or as a component of teacher training. Namibians who enrolled in educational administration studies might also have struggled to gain experience after their courses. It was generally difficult for exiles to get work experience once qualified, and job opportunities in the settlements were limited. SWAPO's Department of Education and Culture was a likely employer of trainees in educational administration, in addition to SWAPO schools; but it was small, with only about six to seven trained people.

What was the potential of Namibia's trained exiles to help overcome some of its human resource shortages in education? Only after examining the major United Nations' education projects will we have a clearer idea. The following chapter on United Nations projects for Namibia completes the picture of external training of Namibians in education.

NOTES

1. SWAPO 1981:13.
2. SWAPO Department of Education and Culture 1982:27.
3. Dodds and Inquai 1983:32; Gerhart 1983:11.
4. United Nations Commissioner for Namibia, 13 December 1989:30; Ellis 1984:57.
5. Inter-Agency Mission Report to the People's Republic of Congo, 20 April – 10 May 1982:8; United Nations Commissioner for Namibia, 15 March 1985:13, 26.
6. Mbuende 1987:62; Interview, Central and Southern Africa Department, ODA, 1/12/1986.
7. Legum ed. 1984:B701.
8. Gerhart 1983:12.
9. Dodds and Inquai 1983:33.
10. Teachers in SWAPO schools were drawn from two major groups, namely, Namibians educated in Namibia and those educated outside the country. Teachers' qualifications ranged from poor to moderate to highly qualified. Those teachers who were poorly or moderately qualified were those who, at most, had completed only primary or secondary schooling. These were the young Namibians who had left the country before completing their schooling. The category also included teachers trained in Namibia. The highly qualified teachers in SWAPO schools were drawn from Namibians trained abroad at universities or technical institutions (Mbuende 1987:72; Mbamba 1982:132).
11. Mbuende 1987:65.
12. Among the problems encountered in training at Kwanza Sul were shortages of necessary equipment, laboratories, library materials, disease, and at times, the unstable security situation. These factors not only hindered the programme's progress but possibly lowered the standard of teacher training in comparison to international levels.
13. International Conference on Teacher Education, Lusaka, 21 – 27 September 1989:160.
14. SWAPO students had been going to Selly Oak Colleges since 1977 to do basic one-year courses in social work and child care. The courses were soon replaced with a more broadly based flexible training, leading to a Certificate of Further Education. This enabled some of the Namibians to either return to the SWAPO camps and centres or continue with further studies. These Selly Oak courses, eventually phased out in 1981, paved the way for the English language teacher training courses started in 1982 (Pat Bryden, Background Papers Seminar on Education for Namibians in the UK, 7 June 1982:1, 2, 3, 4).

15. International Conference on Teacher Education, Lusaka, 21 – 27 September 1989:162.

16. Personal Communication, British Council, Technical Co-operation Training Department, Country Officer Namibia, 14/07/1987.

17. Personal Communication, Moray House College, 31/10/1986.

18. CCN/RRR Newsletter, 18/08/1989.
    Very small numbers of exiled Namibians appear to have undertaken educational studies in other countries in Europe. This could simply have been because of the wish to encourage proficiency in English. In 1982/83 four UNIN graduates commenced language teacher training in France (Personal Communication, UNIN, Senior Documentalist, 7/03/1989).

19. Personal Communication, World University Service (UK), 21/10/1985.

20. Personal Communication, Christian Aid, 8/10/1990.

21. Personal Communication, Universities Statistical Record, 23/10/1989.

22. Between 1979/80 – 1985/86, fifteen Namibians, three of whom came directly from Namibia, participated in the short Distance Teaching course at the Institute of Education, University of London and one Namibian employed within the country participated in the three-month Inspection and Supervision course in 1985. During the same period, four Namibians from within the country undertook postgraduate studies in education at the Institute. In 1990 a further two Namibians (one from the Council of Churches in Namibia Education Unit and one from the Namibian Extension Unit, Zambia) attended the Distance Teaching course in London (Personal Communication, University of London, Institute of Education, Department of International and Comparative Education, November 1989; CCN/RRR Newsletter, 12/04/1990).

23. The trainees were predominantly from SWAPO, though one-third at least were from within Namibia, having been nominated by the Namibian Council of Churches. ODA determined the key training areas for candidates, for example, it stressed health and nursing, yet it was flexible and allowed students to do studies outside these areas as well (Interview, Central and Southern Africa Department, ODA, 1/12/1986).

24. *ibid.*
    The number of university students by field of study as supplied by ODA does not always tally with the statistics in our tables. For example, in 1984 ODA was sponsoring three Namibians at university doing a Masters in public administration. Table 9.3, however, lists only one postgraduate in this field. These variations could be the result of different methods being used to calculate the data, namely,

the number of students originally registered as opposed to actual numbers eventually doing the courses.

25. The Commonwealth Secretariat had entered into a co-financing agreement with organisations such as the Swedish International Development Authority, World University Service, the United Nations Educational and Training Program for Southern Africa, the United Nations Commissioner for Namibia, the Africa Educational Trust, and the Association of Canadian Community Colleges. Statistics on Namibians in postgraduate education courses with joint funding from the UNETPSA and the Commonwealth Programme are therefore also included in the statistics provided in Table 9.5 (Commonwealth Secretariat, 8/10/1986:1).

26. Commonwealth Secretariat 1987:6; Commonwealth Secretary-General Report 1981:34.

27. Commonwealth Secretariat 1990:3.

28. International Conference on Teacher Education, Lusaka, 21 – 27 September 1989:8; Interview, Commonwealth Secretariat, Chief Project Officer Fellowship and Training Programme, 7/06/1990; United Nations General Assembly A/42/628, 9 October 1987:9 – 11.

29. Commonwealth Secretariat, 8/10/1986:2, 3; Interview, Commonwealth Secretariat, Chief Project Officer, Fellowship and Training Programme, 7/06/1990.

30. Unlike the ODA's TCTP, which stipulated key areas of training, the Secretariat was responsive to SWAPO's demands concerning training needs (Interview, Commonwealth Secretariat, Chief Project Officer, Fellowship and Training Programme, 24/02/1987).

31. *ibid.*

32. Commonwealth Secretariat 1990.

33. From 1984 the Ford Foundation, based in New York, also provided scholarship assistance, but this was for Namibians from within Namibia to study in Zimbabwe. An initial nineteen black Namibians were selected after completion of their 'A' levels. Of these only five were to enter education studies. Five more Namibians from within the country were to receive scholarships from this organisation to pursue studies at colleges and universities in America in 1986. No further information was forthcoming from the Ford Foundation regarding this assistance (Personal Communication, Ford Foundation, Assistant Program Officer, 13/09/1985).

34. Gerhart 1983:54.

35. Personal Communication, AAI, 8/07/1985, 13/08/1985.

36. Personal Communication, Statistics Canada, Postsecondary Education Section, 13/07/1987, 23/11/1987.

37. Personal Communication, UNIN, Senior Documentalist, 7/03/1989; Interview, Head of Scholarship Programmes for Developing Countries, Otto Benecke Foundation, 22/12/1986.

38. Personal Communication, Central Statistical Office of Finland, 10/07/1987; Personal Communication, FINNIDA Programme Officer, 8/04/1987.

39. SIDA 1986a:15; SIDA 1986b:17; Personal Communication, SIDA, Desk Officer for SWAPO, 26/07/1985.

40. Personal Communication, SIDA, 5/05/198; Personal Communication, Swedish National Board of Universities and Colleges, Admissions Office, 9/11/1987.

41. Personal Communication, Danish Ministry of Education, International Relations Division, 1/08/1987.

42. Personal Communication, Norwegian Central Bureau of Statistics, 21/07/1987.

10

International assistance to post-secondary education training (2): United Nations programmes

This is the first time in the history of a non-self governing country that the international community has taken the initiative before liberation of preparing the infrastructure and administration that will be required as soon as freedom is achieved.

K. KAUNDA, 1976

INTRODUCTION

United Nations assistance to Namibians took the form of a variety of training programmes outside the country which aimed at developing the country's skilled human resource potential. The scope of this chapter is confined to those programmes dealing with teacher and educational administration training, the aim being to ascertain:

□ the availability of externally trained teachers who were also likely to constitute a pool from which future administrators could be drawn; and

□ whether emphasis was placed on the specialised field of educational administration training and if sufficient Namibians were being trained in this area.

UNITED NATIONS-ASSISTED TRAINING PROGRAMMES

Through the United Nations Council for Namibia, the United Nations assumed direct responsibility for Namibia in 1967 after having revoked South Africa's mandate there in 1966. Thereafter, the United Nations (UN) was obliged to assist and prepare Namibians for independence. This accounts for the leading role the UN has played in backing SWAPO's plans and programmes since 1973, when the movement was named as the authentic representative of the Namibian people by the United Nations General Assembly. SWAPO participated actively in the Council's work, and the Council always consulted the movement regarding the formulation and implementation of its programmes and work or matters of interest to the Namibian people. Assistance to Namibians has taken the form of a number of projects which are discussed below.

THE UNITED NATIONS FUND FOR NAMIBIA

Constructive action to anticipate Namibia's independence was taken when the United Nations Fund for Namibia was established in 1970. This became operative in 1972. Its task was to amass finances for various projects for Namibia. The Council for Namibia was responsible for the management and administration of this Fund through its Committee on the United Nations Fund for Namibia. The major source of financing was voluntary contributions which came from governments, different national organisations and institutions, specialised agencies, and other organisations and bodies within the United Nations system, as well as governmental and non-governmental organisations, and private individuals.[1]

The Fund's resources were concentrated in three main programmes:

☐ The Nationhood Programme;
☐ The United Nations Institute for Namibia(UNIN); and
☐ Educational, social and relief assistance.

The implementation of these programmes was the responsibility of the United Nations Commissioner for Namibia who was the executive and administrative arm of the Council for Namibia.

THE NATIONHOOD PROGRAMME

This programme was established by the General Assembly in 1976 and launched by the United Nations Council for Namibia in 1978. It comprised a comprehensive and consolidated assistance programme aimed at Namibia's nationhood and involving specialised agencies and other bodies in the United Nations system. It was the first programme of its kind in the history of the United Nations. This Programme was alleged to have been limited to Namibians who were members of SWAPO.[2] The Programme was to cover three areas:

☐ pre-independence projects;
☐ transitional projects;
☐ post-independence projects.

The two major components of these projects were:

☐ human resource training carried out in a wide range of countries in Africa, the West, and certain East-bloc countries; and
☐ the preparation of sectoral surveys and analyses of the Namibian social and economic structures to help identify development priorities.

The importance of human resource training was evidenced by the fact that by 1984 at least 85 per cent of the total funding of approved projects went towards formal and non-formal education and training. According to one source, although *on paper* the Programme would give Namibia "the best data base for national planning any African state has had at independence; ... in reality it is likely to be rather less".[3] As we shall see, this was also true of its training programmes.

Projects under the Nationhood Programme

Initially, 77 pre-independence projects were proposed by the various United Nations executing agencies. Of these, 46 were approved and begun in the first half of 1980. These covered various economic and social fields and addressed key problems in Namibian development. UNIN was a major source of candidates for training projects within the Nationhood Programme.

One of the areas the projects focused on was social infrastructure and administration which included education and public administration. The projects are discussed according to two categories: firstly, those dealing solely with teacher and educational staff training and, secondly, those projects involving public administration and public enterprise training.

Training in education

The first training projects in the Programme, with UNESCO as the executing agency, were:

☐ Preparing of Plans for a New Educational System (NAM/79/018); and
☐ Fellowships for Teacher Trainers and other Educational Personnel (NAM/79/019).

Both projects were short-lived. By August 1982 UNIN, SWAPO, and the Commissioner for Namibia agreed to cancel these and transfer the funds to the teacher training Programme at UNIN (see below). No reasons for this decision were announced. Despite the cancellation, it is important to examine the projects because of the importance of some of the points they raised regarding the skilled human resource requirements of a future education system in Namibia.

The project **Preparing of Plans for a New Educational System** had the following objectives:

1. To assist in outlining possible educational policies and principles for Namibia.
2. To outline possible alternative educational strategies at all levels of education and to study their implications.

3. To study the possible patterns and structures for an educational system including the possibility of delimiting the boundaries between school and out-of-school education.

4. To make estimates of student population (school, adult programmes) and teacher and instructor needs.

5. To undertake a comprehensive educational mapping exercise.

6. To identify possible resources — human, physical and financial — to meet the needs of the system, including local and external resources.

7. To examine the various alternative arrangements for organizing higher education and research, e.g. establishing a new university based on a known model, developing the Institute of Namibia into an institution meeting the unique needs of Namibia and some other formula.[4]

This project aimed to assist UNIN in researching possible educational strategies for an independent Namibia. These would then be used "to determine the requirements for a transition to universal effective literacy, mass continuing adult education, universal primary education, secondary, technical and university education".[5] Educational planning expertise was to be provided and there were to be two planning workshops to discuss and examine the results of the studies and survey.

An important motivating force was the realisation that an independent Namibia would have to change its colonial educational system drastically to overcome its inadequacies. Points (4) and (6) of the project's objectives were of particular interest. The provision of estimates of the student population and teacher needs was expected to help determine how many teachers needed to be trained in the pre-independence period. This exercise involved examining the situation both within Namibia and in the SWAPO refugee schools in Angola and Zambia, since they too suffered a shortage of sufficiently trained and qualified teachers especially at secondary level. It was hoped that the identification of human resources available within and outside the country would throw light on internal and external teacher and administrative personnel needs, thereby enabling better estimates of training requirements so that appropriate training programmes could be established to meet them. This would also help clarify how many expatriate personnel would have to be relied upon if there weren't enough trained Namibians.

Although the implementation of the projects was made difficult by the dearth of reliable socio-economic data on Namibia and the lack of access to the country, at least researchers could focus on the immediate needs within the refugee centres. A 1979 study carried out among teachers in the SWAPO schools in Angola and Zambia had already highlighted the lack of sufficient and qualified teachers and expertise in school administration.[6] Both schools were reported to be experiencing day-to-day problems and needed better functioning administrations. Two reports in 1983 and 1984 confirmed the need for more trained teachers in the SWAPO schools.[7]

These problems anticipated on a small scale the difficulties a new government would face at independence when confronted with the task of administering many more schools, especially given the anticipated surge of enrolments after independence. Trends in Angola, Mozambique, and Zimbabwe revealed that within two years of independence the school population had doubled. This would magnify the problem of teacher shortages as well as the need for well-administered educational services. The two projects of the Nationhood Programme were expected to supply a cadre of well-trained teachers and educational administrators to the refugee schools and set up in-service training programmes for already employed, yet underqualified, teachers. The programme would then be evaluated to test its possible application within Namibia after independence.

The immediate objective of the **Fellowships for Teacher Trainers and other Educational Personnel** project was to provide training and work experience for Namibians. Ostensibly, this would enable them to take on important roles in the planning, development, and administration of an educational system in independent Namibia, thereby reducing reliance on expatriate resources. The project was to take the form of twelve-month fellowships mostly in Africa. Namibians would have a chance to participate in special courses, study tours, and secondments in fields needed for the development, organisation, and administration of an education system. Despite these objectives, emphasis was placed virtually entirely on training teacher trainers. This was surprising, especially since there were at least three obvious factors which enhanced the importance of the project's proposals for building up the country's educational administrator potential:

☐ There was a general shortage of professional educational administrators in Namibia because of the policy of total reliance on South African staff and structures;

☐ Very few black and coloured Namibians were involved in decision-making within the education system. This meant that they lacked the concomitant experience in educational administration beyond the level of carrying out instructions;

☐ The belief prevailed that independence would herald the exodus of at least 75 per cent of the white personnel. This could have resulted in a serious skills' vacuum since virtually all high- and middle-qualification posts crucial to the country's economic and social structure were in white hands. In a study conducted in the mid-1980s, UNIN predicted that, in terms of middle- and high-level white Namibian and expatriate personnel, about 12,000 to 19,000 would probably quit the country at independence.[8] Already in the early 1980s, Simon noted that serious problems were being experienced in filling existing posts throughout the public sector, especially in the higher ranks. By 1983 there reportedly were 3,700 vacancies in the public sector, roughly 30 per cent of central government departments.[9] These problems were in part due to the continuing exodus of whites from Namibia because of the political and economic uncertainties and the lure of higher salaries in the private sector and the municipality.

In education, even if fears of a mass white exodus proved unfounded, the possibility that a new government would expand educational provision meant that many more educational administrators would be needed, especially inspectors, subject advisors, and other middle-level administrative staff. Additionally, the likelihood of a process of affirmative action would add pressure to the already limited skilled black and coloured personnel at administrative levels. In the light of these potential developments, it would seem obvious for any training programme involved with training staff for an education system to focus on educational administration training as well. Yet in the section describing the project's activities, it was stated that training in fields such as educational administration and educational planning would only be optional.[10]

When the two projects were cancelled, they were replaced by the **Teacher Education Programme** (NAM/82/009). This aimed to assist UNIN in establishing a two-year residential teacher education programme which was to include vocational courses and workshops for Namibian teachers and teacher trainers. Strategies were also to be formulated for linking teacher education and curriculum development in an independent Namibia. This project, which was completed in 1986, is discussed later (see page 284).

The projects were cancelled at a time when the SWAPO Department of Education and Culture called for the training of educational cadres. In addition to teacher training, teacher upgrading, and training teacher trainers, one of the projects had also included training educational administrators. SWAPO stated:

> it is of paramount importance that a core cadre of educational administrators and planners is trained. These will be the people who could take leadership roles in the field of education.[11]

The project **Training in English Language and Administrative Skills** (NAM/84/004) was introduced in 1984. This project was tailor-made to strengthen SWAPO's administrative machinery by providing training in specialised English language and administrative skills for middle- and high-level officials.[12] The administrative skills training component of the project was limited to budgeting, basic accounting, and bookkeeping. These administrative skills were so basic that it could be assumed the target group would be better suited to jobs within the lower- and middle-level ranges, rather than the middle- and high-level groups stated by the project. Ten SWAPO officials completed the nine-month training in the United Kingdom by December 1984 when the project ended.[13]

In 1988 the project **Training in Administrative Skills and English Language** (NAM/88/003) was introduced. This was a replica of the project introduced in 1984 (NAM/84/004) except now its target group was more general, 'SWAPO officials', as opposed to 'middle- and high-level' SWAPO officials. The project was classified under the rubric of public administration, economic planning, and judicial systems. By June 1989, eleven students had completed their training in the United Kingdom, bringing the total number of trainees up to 21.[14]

The Field Attachment Programme for Namibians (NAM/84/013) provided one year of in-service training to those in possession of basic technical or theoretical academic training. This took place mostly in Africa and spanned many fields. By mid-1989, none of the identified candidates for placement had been seconded to education-related areas, except in 1987 when one French teacher trainee commenced training in France.

The project **Assistance to Establish a Pilot Vocational Training Centre** at Sumbe in Kwanza Sul, Angola (NAM/78/008/) was replaced by the scheme **Assistance to the United Nations Vocational Training Centre**, Cuacra, Angola (NAM/86/005). The latter establishment by mid-1987 had enrolled 202 trainees. This project provided training programmes both locally and abroad for the Namibian instructional and administrative staff of the centre. This was the only education-related programme which appears to have included such an administrative training component. No details were provided as to its length and level.

At least eleven of the initial 46 pre-independence projects within the Nationhood Programme appear to have had an administrative or managerial training component. Such training was lacking in virtually all the education projects bar those of the late 1970s, which were subsequently cancelled. Clearly there was a lacuna in educational administration and management training within the Nationhood Programme.

Public administration and public enterprise management
Both types of training featured fairly prominently in the Nationhood Programme with three important projects in the late 1970s and a fourth project in the late 1980s.

Preparation of Plans for a Public Administration System (NAM/79/027), in addition to proposing alternative administration systems for Namibia, entailed analysing the training needs of civil servants in Namibia as well as looking into corresponding training plans. Six senior fellows were to receive financial assistance from the project for their training. The idea was to upgrade the administrative skills within SWAPO. It is not clear whether the fellowships were ever taken up, but the project findings were reported to have been incorporated into the 1986 UNIN comprehensive study on Namibia, whereafter the project was closed.

The Fellowships in Public Administration (NAM/79/028) project's objectives were to train Namibians in administrative skills for the functioning of public administration after independence. Initially, twelve Namibians were to undergo three month's training.[15] By late 1982, only two students had been selected for study, one in the Institute of Financial Management in Dar es Salaam and another in immigration procedures in Zambia. The number of fellowships in this project was subsequently reduced to five in 1983. By that year, both the initial two students had discontinued their studies in Zambia and Dar es Salaam. This project ended up sponsoring a total of only two female students in co-operative management at Moshi Co-operative College in Tanzania in 1984.

They completed the diploma course in 1988 and 1989 respectively, one of the students having failed a year. Thereafter, the remaining student in the project returned to Namibia and the project was closed by mid-1989.

Training in Administration (NAM/86/002) aimed at preparing twelve Namibians in various aspects of administration to enable them to take up posts in an independent Namibian civil service. In 1986 four students enrolled in the two-year diploma course in public administration at the University of Ghana. Two commenced co-operative management training at Moshi Co-operative College, Tanzania. Two foreign service officers commenced a one-year diplomacy course at Dar es Salaam's Centre for Foreign Relations. Additionally, four Namibians completed short courses in administration at the Eastern and Southern African Management Institute (ESAMI) at Arusha in Tanzania.

By mid-1989, there were only three students continuing the course in public administration at the University of Ghana, the fourth having transferred to a vocational course, also in Ghana. That year only one of the two students in co-operative management in Tanzania completed her diploma course. In 1987 alternative sponsorship was found for the two foreign service officers who had initially been sponsored under this project, but no mention was made of them thereafter. Out of the initial twelve trainees, only five completed their training under the project by 1989. That same year five new students, who had been enrolled in the project to pursue a six-month course in electronic data processing in the United Kingdom, completed their tailor-made course. A further eleven students commenced a two-year programme in banking in India in 1989.[16]

Training in Public Enterprise Management phases I-V (NAM/79/034; NAM/81/002; NAM/82/002; NAM/82/008 and NAM/83/006). The objective of this project was to train future public enterprise officials for managerial positions. After two months of preparatory/remedial training at UNIN, candidates entered eight months' training at the International Centre for Public Enterprises for Developing Countries

(ICPE), Ljubljana, Yugoslavia. The final batch of trainees completed their training in September 1984, by which time a total of 69 Namibians had been trained during all five phases.[17]

The total number of Namibians trained in both public administration and public enterprise management came to roughly 76 by 1989. Because this figure was small in terms of the anticipated needs of the public administration system in an independent Namibia, it was unlikely that skilled Namibian administrators from this source would move into general administrative posts within the educational bureaucracy (see UNIN 1986:651, 652). The reality that the full quotas of fellowships for training in public administration were never filled and the fact that output was low was an indication of the difficulties experienced in finding suitable candidates; a situation which was mirrored within Namibia as well (see Chapter 7). The Office of the Commissioner for Namibia in one of its reports on the Nationhood Programme mentioned the fact that several fellowships remained unfilled due to the lack of suitable candidates. Furthermore, it stated that training in some sectors had been rendered difficult because of students' deficiencies in English, mathematics, and science as a consequence of the discriminatory educational system in Namibia.[18]

In summary, the Nationhood Programme's projects made little headway in attempting to overcome the problem of providing an independent Namibia with a more racially equitable distribution of trained educational administrators. Neither did it answer the administrative needs of the SWAPO schools. However, a more encouraging picture emerges from the training undertaken at UNIN.

UNITED NATIONS INSTITUTE FOR NAMIBIA

UNIN was launched in 1976 in Lusaka, Zambia and was supported financially by the United Nations Fund for Namibia and bilateral contributions. This Institute was to provide Namibians with the skills needed "for the future planning of, and participation in, the organization and administration of the various government departments and public services in an independent Namibia...."[19] Its other functions entailed serving as an information and documentation centre on Namibia, as well as undertaking research into various political and socio-economic aspects of the country. The research programme was to make available basic documents for policy formation by a future independent government. UNIN also played an important role in implementing some of the Nationhood Programmes such as the **Teacher Education Programme** (NAM/82/009).

Since independence for Namibia was the ultimate goal, UNIN was to exist for only five years, the time it was expected to take Namibia to gain its sovereignty. Even though the Institute remained the property of the United Nations, SWAPO was very much involved in its programmes. According to the movement's president, Sam Nujoma, some of SWAPO's "most able cadres" were assigned to its staff and students.[20] SWAPO officials played a leading role in its administration and policy-making and non-SWAPO students, it was claimed, found it difficult to pursue studies at the Institute.[21] Essentially, it was a training body for SWAPO with its students being drawn primarily from the refugee populations in Zambia, Botswana, and Angola. After independence, the Institute was expected to transfer to Windhoek; instead, it was closed down. Many of its books were sold off and its archival material has now been loaned to the University of Namibia.

UNIN offered training in the following areas:

☐ a three-year diploma course in management and development studies;

☐ a two-year certificate in magisterial studies;

☐ a two-year teacher training diploma as well as two to three weeks' in-service teacher training;

☐ two-years' secretarial training; and

☐ voluntary French and German language courses outside of regular working hours.

Diploma in Management and Development studies

This course was the core of the Institute's programmes and had the highest enrolment and number of graduates each year. It aimed at training middle-level public administrators and managers within the context of the country's public service needs. The first year of study was interdisciplinary with instruction in the Institute's five academic divisions. Students took courses from all these divisions.[22] The subject matter ranged across law, society, politics, administration, history, agriculture, economics, and education. English language training as well as mathematics were offered over two years. During the first year, a correlation was drawn between socio-economic problems and solutions for development in the world in general and, in particular, in newly independent African countries. Subject matter was very much Namibia-oriented, especially in fields like economics, agriculture, and history. In the second year, students specialised within one of the five academic divisions. They were also able to select courses which were inter-divisional, such as 'Research Techniques', 'Development Planning', and 'The Administration of Human Resources'. Usually, equal numbers of students were allocated to each division.

Within the Social and Education Division, a course entitled 'Comparative Approach to Contemporary Educational Systems' was offered. Among its objectives, the course aimed at enabling students to describe the various ways of administering education by examining the process of educational administration in various countries. Also included was the administration of education under centralised, regionalised, and localised systems. The course 'Education for Development in Namibia' described the process of planning, management, and administration of educational programmes and projects with emphasis on Namibia. These two courses were clearly educational administration specific.

Another course useful for administration was the inter-divisional section's 'Administration of Human Resources'. It aimed at providing students with an understanding of the organisation, structure, and functions of personnel management in the public service, as well as highlighting the major problems, issues, and solutions encountered in the field of personnel management, especially in governmental and semi-governmental institutions in newly independent African states, specifically in Namibia. The course 'Development Planning' provided students with the basic techniques and skills required of middle-level administrators involved in development planning. It also explored ways of interacting with administrators, politicians, and ordinary citizens. In doing so, trainees were familiarised with popular participation in plan formulation and implementation.

Students would have a broad theoretical foundation in general administration on completion of the second-year courses, as well as 'Organisation and Management of Social and Political Institutions', 'Planning and Administration of Social Services', 'Development Management,' and 'Office Administration', from the first year.

In their third and final year, students were seconded to various governments and organisations in Africa for nine months of practical training. Depending on their areas of specialisation, they were attached to government ministries, local authorities, courts, parastatal organisations or any relevant institutions in Africa.

Trainees were initially to be placed at the lowest point of entry in the middle-management level and were then to be encouraged to proceed to higher points within the level. Those trained in education within the Social and Education Division were seconded to the education ministries of Botswana, Tanzania, Zambia, and Zimbabwe. The secondment programme was divided into three phases:

☐ a two-month preparatory phase prior to actual placement (January-March);

☐ six months' attachment (April-September);

☐ the eight weeks' post-secondment phase in which students were to review their experiences and relate them to the Namibian context.

During the secondment phase, students were to be given practical work and duties, and written assignments by supervisors in the host institutions. They also had to participate in discussions with other students, research, and seminars. At the end of their practical experience, students were expected to have understood and acquired basic administrative and inter-personal office skills.

Table 10.1 provides a break-down of the number of second-year students in the Management and Development Studies programme for the period 1978 – 1984 according to their areas of specialisation. Table 10.2 gives the total number of graduates from the five academic divisions from 1979 up to and including 1989.

Table 10.1   Second-Year Student Enrolment in UNIN's Management and Development Studies Course, 1978 – 1984

Division	1978	1979	1980	1981	1982	1983	1984	Total
A&L	10	20	15	11	19	—	31	106
CLJ	16	19	20	15	20	19	24	133
Econ	15	17	18	13	21	—	33	117
HPC	15	18	20	14	20	—	27	114
Soc & Ed	18	19	21	13	20	20	35	146

Notes: (1) 1977 marked the first year of student intake into this course.
   (2) A&L   = Agricultural and Land Resources' Division
        CLJ   = Constitutional, Legal and Judicial Affairs' Division
        Econ   = Economic's Division
        HPC   = Historical, Political and Cultural Division
        Soc & Ed   = Social and Education Division
Source: Adapted from the UNIN Senate Report, July 1983 – June 1984:9

Table 10.2   Number of UNIN Graduates by Academic
Programme, 1979 – 1989

Year	Division								Total for M&DS
	A&L	CLJ	Econ	HPC	Soc & Ed	TT/U	Mag	Sec	
1979	9	15	15	14	13	—	—	—	66
1980	16	15	14	17	18	—	—	—	80
1981	15	14	11	17	17	—	—	33	74
1982	9	14	12	14	13	—	—	—	62
1983	16	16	20	20	20	—	—	44	92
1984	—	16	—	—	17	21	16	—	33
1985	29	20	33	26	33	29	—	45	141
1986	22	14	22	17	21	18	17	50	96
1987	24	17	32	24	24	36	—	—	121
1988	23	16	34	18	32	29	—	36	123
1989	—	—	—	—	—	29*	18*	—	118*
Divisional Totals	163	157	193	167	208	162	51	208	1,006
CUMULATIVE TOTAL FOR UNIN 1,427									

Notes: (1) 1979 was the first graduation year.
   (2) TT/U, Mag and Sec are not included in M&DS totals, since
        these are separate courses.
   (3) A&L   = Agricultural and Land Resources' Division
        CLJ   = Constitutional, Legal and Judicial Affairs'
                    Division
        Econ   = Economics' Division
        HPC   = Historical, Political and Cultural Division
        Soc & Ed = Social and Education Division
        TT/U   = Teacher Training/Upgrading Division
        Mag   = Magistrates' Training Programme
        Sec   = Secretarial Training Programme
        M&DS   = Management and Development Studies
   (4) * Estimates only.
Source: Personal Communication, UNIN Information and
Documentation Division, 7/03/1989

Out of the overall total of 888 graduates in Management and Development Studies for the period 1979 – 1988 (1979 was the first year of graduation), at least 494 (56 per cent) were women. This was important, especially in view of the systematic discrimination against women within Namibia as far as administrative jobs were concerned, as was seen in Chapter 8.[23] The greatest cumulative number of graduates in a specific course by 1988 was 208 in the Social and Education Division (see Table 10.2). For the years 1983 – 1986 alone, at least 58 students were seconded to ministries of education in Botswana, Tanzania, Zambia, and Zimbabwe.[24] However, placement in effective positions may have been a serious problem for UNIN. In 1984 UNIN failed to place 40 graduates who returned to SWAPO.[25]

Generally speaking, the overall output was encouraging, not so much in a numerical sense but in terms of the knowledge and skills with which graduates were equipped. This was all the more important if they were eventually to fill middle-level posts within the Ministry of Education or in regional administrative structures. On paper, this diploma appeared to be comprehensive and well-structured in terms of its theoretical and practical emphasis and orientation. It exposed students to valuable training and experience in the administrative sphere. Even in situations where secondment was not in a ministry of education, the theoretical knowledge and skills acquired from the first two years of the course could well have been sufficient to enable students to cope with basic day-to-day administrative tasks. There were, however, some drawbacks.

A UNIN Evaluation Team assessed the programme in 1987. One of its criticisms of the first-year course's structure was that it was too varied, resulting in only a superficial knowledge of the subject matter. Additionally, it maintained that courses at this level were pitched at either too high a level for the students to adequately understand and appreciate the contents, or that what was actually taught bore little relation to the prospectus. The amount of time devoted to the second-year courses was considered insufficient to produce Namibians who "will form the core of public service managers and administrators in independent Namibia".[26] The evaluators suggested that the scope of the courses be reduced and more attention be placed on training *managers* for Namibia in courses designed for such a purpose.

Furthermore, they were critical of the lack of correlation between the high academic level of courses offered at UNIN on the one hand and the poor academic background of the trainees, some of whom were below secondary standard. Admission requirements in terms of academic qualifications had not been rigidly applied. Another observer had commented earlier that since students ranged from seventeen to 40 years in age, the task of the instructors was that much more difficult.[27] These realities pointed to the fact that graduates from this course were not always of middle-level administrative calibre. One official interviewed, stated that students emerging from this course would be better suited to lower-level civil service posts.[28]

This view was borne out by top-level Zimbabwean educational staff, including the Minister for Primary and Secondary Education, concerning the groups of Namibians sent to their Ministry for training. Small groups of Namibian trainees from UNIN had been coming to the Zimbabwean Ministry of Education between 1985 and 1988, the last group comprising entirely of women. The overall feeling was that the level of the Namibian trainees' education was too low for them to have benefited fully from the secondment and that they experienced handicaps in English usage. One interviewee summed up by saying that the Namibian trainees were at the same level as Zimbabwean clerks, not education officers.[29] As a result, the students were passed on to the Ministry's clerks within the various sections. There their training was more observational than participatory. The trainees were attached to each section within the Ministry for two to four weeks. They were also exposed to courses on school supervision and management.[30]

Another drawback to this secondment scheme was that:

> the programme mission was never stipulated nor were guidelines of areas of interest focused upon. The

> Namibians were merely passed from section to section
> .... In addition to this, the attitudes of the Namibians
> was very disappointing.... As a group (in 1988) they
> were passive and not very interested.[31]

A further complaint listed that the actual six-month period of secondment was not long enough to enable students to study an entire education system in detail. Realistically this requires a full year. For a more in-depth study and broader understanding of the Ministry's divisions, attachments of six months should have limited the trainees to two divisions.

Already in 1986, a UNIN evaluation team had indicated that recipient countries and institutions were not always aware of the purpose of the secondments and therefore of the services that should have been provided. As a result, many attachments were not as rewarding as they might have been.[32] As for the Namibians' reticence, this could well have been due to their linguistic handicap and possibly to the disorienting effect of living in exile. Realistically speaking, the diploma course was an attempt to overcome some of the educational disadvantages of a wide-ranging age-group of Namibians with a medley of educational and work experiences. It provided a general base of knowledge in a number of areas, as well as practical exposure. This would better equip graduates for further academic or practical training since the course itself was not pitched at university level. But the graduates were clearly not yet sufficiently trained to take on middle-level civil service posts.

On completion of their courses, many graduates were absorbed into SWAPO's administrative and policy-making machinery or found work in the refugee settlements. Not all the graduates were able to find work. This was a common problem for most training programmes involving Namibians and meant that after having attained a certain level of theoretical knowledge in a particular field, students were not able to develop their newly acquired skills.

The diploma course was also a feeder programme from which both the Magistrates and Teacher Training/Upgrading programmes "recruit the majority, if not all, of their students".[33] Not all graduates from the Management and Development Studies course, who had specialised within the Social and Education Division and who continued with tertiary training, necessarily went into education. Between 1979 and 1985, for example, at least thirteen graduates from that division went to train in public enterprise management in Yugoslavia.[34]

Between 1980 and 1988, out of UNIN's cumulative student total of 1,262 for that period (see Table 10.2), 155 graduates (12 per cent) went on to tertiary-level training, mostly at university level. At least nine of these took educational studies, mainly in teacher training, and seven were in public administration which, being at university level, would have raised their employment level to the middle-range and higher.[35]

Even though it did not achieve its ideal of training middle-level civil servants, especially in the realm of educational administration, UNIN was unique in the sense that, for the first time in the history of the independence struggles in Africa, preparation and training for an infrastructure and administration were undertaken by the international community prior to independence. By 1989 UNIN had provided roughly 1,427 Namibians "with a level of education and training that could not have been attained were it not for the existence of the Institute".[36] Thus UNIN played a crucial role in the development of Namibian's human resources, providing the largest pool of educated Namibians from any single institution.[37] UNIN also made a significant contribution in the sphere of teacher training, which we examine next.

Teacher Training/Upgrading Programme

Established at UNIN in 1982, this programme was an attempt to overcome the shortage of qualified teachers both in the camps and within Namibia after independence once educational provision was expanded there. Two types of training were offered within this division:

□ a two-year residential teacher training programme at primary and lower secondary level leading to a diploma; and

❑ programmes of two to three weeks' in-service training for
SWAPO teachers during their vacation periods.

Both qualified and trainee primary teachers wishing to
upgrade their skills were admitted into the in-service programme. The programme included training in classroom
management, evaluation, testing, teaching skills, and methodology. Mention was made of extending the in-service training to include teacher supervisors to monitor trainees'
progress in Angola and Zambia. Successful diploma candidates were automatically employed at the SWAPO Education
and Health Centres in Angola and Zambia and some went on
to do degree programmes in education.

Output from the in-service training programme was impressive. Within a space of four years it had produced 384
trainees. Such training appears to have ceased after 1986 (see
Table 10.3). The output of 162 diploma graduates was disappointing since this meant that only 42 per cent had passed
out of the 384 students enrolled in the course for the period
1983 – 1989. The number of graduates was low, especially
when measured in terms of the needs within Namibia at
primary level, let alone the refugee schools. In the diploma
training, educational administration was one of the core
courses which, along with curriculum studies and methodology, was accorded three hours per week. Much of the educational administration training offered as part of teacher
training was descriptive and did not necessarily enhance
management skills.

In 1989, in addition to the two above-mentioned programmes, the Teacher Training Division offered the first part
of a four-year split B Ed degree with Warwick University for
training English language teachers. By September 1990, ten
students had commenced the second part of their course at
Warwick University, having completed the first part of the
course's training at UNIN. The ten were due to complete
their studies in 1993.[38] This co-operative venture aims "to
develop an appropriate professional education degree which
can successfully provide some of the educational practitioners

needed for Namibia's new education system after Independence".[39] Trainees will not only be geared to teach but also to train teachers or administer education in Namibia.

Table 10.3   Student Output from UNIN's Teacher
            Training/Upgrading Division, 1983 – 1989

Training Programme	Year							Total
	1983	1984	1985	1986	1987	1988	1989	
Diploma in Basic Education	—	21	29	18	36	29	29	162
In-Service Programme	156	78	72	78	—	—	—	384

Source: International Conference on Teacher Education for Namibia, Lusaka, 21 – 27 September 1989:180

It is likely that any specific administrative component in a course at this level would help prepare Namibians for middle-level posts. As it is, the administrative components of the English Language Training section of the course, which comprised 50 per cent of the first year of training at Warwick, include syllabus design, materials' development, distance learning techniques, examination setting and administration of language tests, organisation of an English department, and the management of English language teaching in schools. The only drawback to date is the small enrolment figure for such a vitally important course; this had already dropped from an initial intake of fourteen to ten.[40]

EDUCATIONAL, SOCIAL AND RELIEF ASSISTANCE

This section of the United Nations Fund for Namibia included scholarship assistance and training projects. Scholarships ranged from primary education to graduate degree programmes. Even though both primary and secondary education were provided within the Fund's scholarship programme, most Namibian refugees requiring schooling were assisted by the United Nations High Commissioner for Refugees (UNHCR), the Commonwealth Secretariat, and other organisations.

Fields of study included vocational, technical, scientific, remedial, and professional education and training. Unlike the UNIN and Nationhood Programmes' training, Namibians who benefited from the Fund's scholarships were not required to be members of SWAPO, although preference was shown to SWAPO affiliates. Table 10.4 indicates the total number of scholarships awarded in a ten-year period starting in 1976/77. No details were available on individual candidates and their specific fields of study. Those pursuing education or public administration studies were therefore included in the totals for each year.

Other projects connected to training included **UNIN Graduate Training** (NAF/80/005) which enabled selected UNIN graduates to train further with the help of fellowships for either one-year diploma courses or four-year BA degree courses. The purpose of this programme was to equip middle- and high-level professional and technical personnel for a future Namibian public service. It differed from the Nationhood project's **Field Attachment Programme** (NAM/84/013) in that the latter placed emphasis on in-service training after completion of the theoretical training, while this project stressed further training in the theoretical domain.

Areas of training were related to those offered at UNIN. In 1980 three students were studying public administration at the National Institute of Public Administration in Zambia. This project ended in 1982. It is not clear how many of the initial batch of fourteen students from this scheme completed their studies. By December 1982, only eleven were still in training. The project **Fellowships for UNIN Graduates** (NAF/83/003), which had the same aims as the previous UNIN Graduate Training scheme, was introduced in 1983. It supported a total of 28 students in various fields of study. By June 1989, sixteen students had completed their first degrees in law, economics, political science, and development studies at universities in the United Kingdom. None had graduated in education. But by that time, of the 26 students still continuing in degree programmes, there was at least one in education.[41]

Table 10.4   United Nations Fund for Namibia Scholarship
Holders, 1976/77 – 1986/87

Year	Students *	New Awards	Students Completing Courses
1976/77	94	—	—
1977/78	116	—	—
1978/79	116	—	—
1979/80	129	—	—
1980/81	109	—	—
1981/82	114	—	12
1982/83	126	49	26
1983/84	124	51	52
1984/85	140	54	26
1985/86	224	115	18
1986/87	215	79	31

* Figures include new awards and those still active in 1987.

Notes: (1)   Most tertiary-level studies in education and public administration appear to have been conducted in the United States and Canada.

(2)   The largest number of scholarship holders were concentrated in the United States. From the mid-1980s onwards, students in Zambia were the second biggest group after those in America.

Source: Adapted from United Nations Council for Namibia, A/32/24, 1977; A/33/24, 1978; A/34/24/Add I, 1980; A/35/24, 1980; A/36/24, 1982; A/37/24 1982; A/38/24 1984; A/39/24 1985; A/40/24, 1986; A/41/24, 1986; A/42/24, 1987

Further projects under this section of the Fund assisted twelve Namibians with remedial training (NAF/83/006) prior to their enrolling in the course in public enterprise management at the International Centre for Public Enterprises (ICPE) in Yugoslavia. The project was completed in early 1984. The project **Education in Guyana** (NAF/83/005) provided funding for ten Namibians to train at degree and diploma levels in Guyana in various fields, one of which was public administration. By late 1987, only eight fellows were pursuing studies. Two students out of this total, who appear to have been pursuing public administration, did not meet the requirements to receive their diplomas and returned to Angola.[42]

The project **Distance Teaching Training** (NAF/80/003) was introduced in 1980 to provide training in evaluation, writing, editing, and the production of learning materials for distance teaching. That same year two Namibians completed a three-month course at the University of London's Institute of Education and the project ended. It appears that such training was not repeated under any of the Fund's three main programmes.[43] Further projects involving distance teaching training fell under funding for the Namibian Extension Unit.

Project NAF/81/001, **Vocational Training in Denmark**, aimed to provide vocational training for one year but also included fifteen months' primary teacher training for teachers in the refugee schools. By 1983, 82 students had completed their training. Eighteen other Namibians commenced training in automechanics in May 1983 and completed the course by early 1984, the same year in which the project ended.[44] It is not possible to ascertain how many of the original group of 82 were in teacher training.

Another education project, **Training for Teachers of the Hearing Impaired** (NAF/88/007), provided training for eight Namibians with impaired hearing. They participated in a custom-tailored programme in the United States in sign language, sign language linguistics, leadership, English, and teacher education.[45] Since training of this kind had almost certainly not been available to Namibians, other than a few whites who trained in South Africa, these students would be much in demand within the country.

As the information now stands, it is clear that none of the projects under this part of the Fund's programmes focused on educational administration. Training in public administration appears to have been non-existent.

THE UNITED NATIONS EDUCATIONAL AND TRAINING PROGRAMME FOR SOUTHERN AFRICA (UNETPSA)

This programme, established in 1967 under United Nations auspices, was financed by voluntary contributions from United Nations member countries. It concentrated only on scholarship awards which were tenable anywhere in the world for A-level studies and above.[46] These scholarships were also administered by organisations such as the now defunct International University Exchange Fund, the British Council, and the UNHCR. Candidates did not necessarily have to be refugees. Nevertheless, endorsement of applicants by SWAPO was considered important.[47] UNETPSA evolved into the single most important scholarship training programme for Namibians by virtue of the large number of candidates it assisted.

Table 10.5 shows UNETPSA scholarship holders pursuing education, public administration, management and administration studies in relation to the total number of awards for each year for the period 1969/70 – 1988/89. Those enrolled in education studies were in many fields comprising teacher training, special education, adult literacy instructors' training, educational administration, curriculum development, English language teacher training, and doctoral research. The areas of specialisation were not always stipulated. Postgraduates in education made up 23 per cent of the 279 students in education studies, three of whom have been confirmed as educational administration students. The total number of students in education studies comprised only 7.4 per cent of the overall number of awards by 1988/1989. Students in public administration, administration and man-

Table 10.5 Namibian UNETPSA Scholarship Holders in
Education, Public Administration,
Administration and Management, and
Scholarship Totals, 1969/70 – 1988/89

Year	Ed Postgrad	Ed Total	Pub Admin etc. Postgrad	Pub Admin etc. Total	Total Awards
1969/70	—	3	—	—	56
1970/71	6	6	—	1	67
1971/72	4	4	—	1	78
1972/73	4	6	—	1	81
1973/74	5	9	—	3	73
1974/75	7	12	—	4	157
1975/76	5	8	—	3	163
1976/77	5	9	—	4	191
1977/78	2	6	—	5	236
1978/79	2	7	—	4	232
1979/80	3	7	—	4	215
1980/81	2	9	—	2	135
1981/82	3	7	—	3	125
1982/83	—	3	—	—	23
1983/84	1	4	—	—	49
1984/85	2	29	—	3	145
1985/86	2	54	1	4	342
1986/87	4	56	1	3	460
1987/88	5	22	—	2	479
1988/89	2	18	—	1	442
TOTALS	64	279	2	48	3,749

Notes: Among the countries where these awards were tenable were
Canada, the United States of America, Kenya, Zambia, the United
Kingdom, Sri Lanka, Lesotho, Sierra Leone, Liberia, Zimbabwe, and the
then Federal Republic of Germany.
Source: Adapted from the United Nations Secretary-General,
6/11/1970; 29/10/1971; 25/10/1972; 21/11/1973; 25/11/1974;
7/11/1975; 26/10/1976; 1/11/1977; 2/11/1978; 22/10/1979;
10/10/1980; 6/10/1981; 22/09/1982; 19/10/1983; 23/10/1984;
22/10/1985; 8/10/1986; 9/10/1987; 5/10/1988; 28/09/1989

agement studies made up 1.3 per cent of the overall scholarship total. This was very low in relation to the anticipated needs of the public service at independence.

By 1988/89 at least 541 Namibians had completed their studies out of the total of 3,749 UNETPSA Namibian scholarship holders.[48] No further breakdown by field of study was available. Assuming that the 1986/87 to 1988/89 awardees were still studying, the approximate success rate for the period 1969/70 to 1985/86 out of a total of 2,368 scholarship holders was a mere 23 per cent. The UNETPSA awards had no built-in remedial component, unlike certain training projects under the United Nations Fund for Namibia like the Public Enterprise Management Training programme and the UNIN courses. As the Office of the United Nations Commissioner for Namibia had reported (see page 275), the Namibians' poor educational background made it impossible for them to benefit fully from what was on offer, and this meant that additional years had to be spent on preparatory studies in language, mathematics, and even basic study skills. These serious educational handicaps explain their overall poor performance. Ellis pointed out that many agencies assisting Namibians were not always aware of the extent of this handicap and, as a result, they found that their programmes were not successful.[49]

TRAINING IN EDUCATIONAL ADMINISTRATION: THE INTERNATIONAL INSTITUTE FOR EDUCATIONAL PLANNING

Even though the initial two educational programmes, NAM/79/018 and 019, ostensibly to address needs in educational administration, were cancelled, UNESCO, through its regular scholarship assistance programme to liberation movements, was able to assist four Namibians nominated by SWAPO for educational administration training between 1980/81 and 1986/87. These trainees attended a seven-month programme in educational planning and administration at UNESCO's International Institute for Educational

Planning (IIEP) in Paris. The four trainees were a woman teacher from SWAPO's Kwanza Sul refugee school in Angola, a vice principal for Academic Affairs also at Kwanza Sul, a principal at Nyango, Zambia and a doctoral educational research student in Sweden.

The course was directed at practising educational planners and administrators, as well as those with responsibilities for training in these fields. It covered the design, preparation, implementation, and evaluation of strategies and plans for the development of education. This leads us to understand that trainees would come from within a ministry of education or planning body rather than from a school administration environment. The Namibian candidates did not entirely fulfil these prerequisites.

All four trainees received their diplomas from the IIEP despite the fact that, with one exception, they did not meet the entry requirements. One of the trainees went on to a distinguished career in educational research and administration with UNESCO's Regional Office for Science and Technology in Africa (ROSTA). The former vice principal for Academic Affairs became Education Co-ordinator with the Repatriation Resettlement and Reconstruction (RRR) Committee for returnees to Namibia in 1989.

The educational disadvantages and lack of professional experience of the Namibian trainees reflected the inadequacy of suitable candidates to avail themselves of the fellowships on offer. The fact that no Namibian trainees attended the IIEP in the years subsequent to 1986/87 and prior to independence in 1990 could well have been directly attributable to this. The problem was familiar to the various United Nations bodies involved with training Namibians. Yet no institution or sponsoring agency developed a professional course in educational administration tailored to Namibian needs. This might have proved more beneficial than sending candidates on a sophisticated training programme not entirely geared towards their requirements, as occurred with the IIEP programme. Alternatively, trainees who required it should have undergone access or bridging courses or remedial training to better prepare them.[50]

THE NAMIBIAN EXTENSION UNIT (NEU)

The Unit was launched in November 1981 in Lusaka, Zambia, with assistance from the Commonwealth Secretariat, the United Nations Commissioner for Namibia, UNIN, and SWAPO. The project was the first of its kind and aimed chiefly at providing basic education through distance teaching. It was directed at Namibian refugees between sixteen and 60 years of age with at least four years of primary education.[51] This programme was offered in conjunction with the adult education system operated by SWAPO in its refugee schools in Angola and Zambia. However, it was geared to those adults who for various reasons were unable to attend formal education. NEU's first priority was to compile remedial upper primary/junior secondary courses in English and mathematics in order to prepare students for secondary and vocational education and middle-level administrative and community leadership.[52]

NEU's target enrolment was 40,000. By 1986, 3,700 learners were enrolled and 2,000 had completed the introductory course. The staff numbered 54.[53] Not only did the Unit provide school-level courses to Namibians, it also trained tutors, field supervisors, and group leaders within the refugee centres in the skills of group leadership, group dynamics, and distance teaching methodology. Tutors were selected from among refugees in the settlements in Angola and Zambia and needed no formal qualification.

By 1986 the Unit had trained 336 group leaders, 130 tutors and twelve other members of staff who completed their training abroad. The latter, mostly tutors, attended the four-month distance teaching courses organised by the International Extension College, Cambridge, in association with the then Department of Education in Developing Countries at the Institute of Education, University of London. The Council of Churches in Namibia also sent trainees from within Namibia on this course, but their number was small, for example, only three in 1985. Teachers in the SWAPO schools in Zambia and Angola who had an interest in adult education were also selected for distance teaching training.[54] A Namibian from the NEU also studied for a diploma in adult education at the University of Zambia and one student was at the University of Warwick pursuing a diploma in teaching English as a foreign language.[55]

These training efforts meant that a cadre of staff specialised in teaching methods was gradually being built up. They would be able to relieve the load on the formal teaching system and provide adults with a chance to further their own education and skills. Furthermore, distance education was likely to be a considerably cheaper approach to educational provision (see note 53), an important factor for any developing country intent on building up its human resource potential.

After independence, the NEU's resources and materials were transferred to Windhoek and its activities were integrated into the programmes of the current Ministry of Education and Culture's Directorate of Adult and Continuing Education. This directorate is now headed by the former NEU director. Its potential clientele is anticipated to be far larger than that of the school system.[56] As an alternative system of educational delivery within Namibia, especially for a target population well in excess of the original 40,000, such a directorate must be efficiently run. Efficiency in turn requires well-trained administrators and management staff, as well as course writers and instructors. Already in 1986, it was reported that the NEU's administration and the co-ordination of its activities from the headquarters to the centres "leaves much to be desired".[57]

Shortcomings centred chiefly on problems encountered with the instruction methods as well as with administration and management techniques. For example, in Kwanza Sul, Angola, it was reported that learning activities were not very distinct from those of formal education. Group leaders were said to need upgrading training programmes. The field supervisor, who was the chief administrator of the programme in the field, was not sufficiently assertive in terms of explaining the objectives, structure, and purpose of the Extension Unit to the tutors who, in turn, lacked a clear understanding of the acceptable approach and correct strategies to promote such learning among adults. Additionally, there weren't enough tutors. There was a lack of cohesion among head office staff, while the delivery of course material was often delayed, especially in Angola which had the majority of students.[58] This shortage of skilled personnel to manage the programme was not a new feature of training/education projects for Namibians, as was shown previously with SWAPO's INSET project.

OVERVIEW OF THE UNITED NATIONS TRAINING PROGRAMMES

Since it is not possible to identify the number of United Nations Fund scholarship holders by field of study, as well as the number of Namibians undergoing teacher or educational administration training, it is difficult to estimate the output of teachers and administrators from such projects. Clearly, very little emphasis was placed on direct training in educational administration within any of the Nationhood Programmes' training projects.

The UNETPSA output in educational administration was also negligible, totalling an estimated three, while teacher training totals were generally not discernible because areas of specialisation were not always stipulated. The IIEP course was an exception in the sense that it provided four Namibians with training directly related to educational administration. This figure, however, is obviously inadequate and the difficulties several of the trainees had in coping with such a professional course without the prerequisite experience and education would have limited the impact of such training.

In terms of UNIN's contribution to the output of potential administrators, by 1988 graduates from its Education and Social Division totalled 208, some of whom would have specialised in public health (see Table 10.2). Although the number is substantial, especially by comparison with the other programmes, the calibre of most graduates was far from the requirement of middle-level administrators. Virtually all nine UNIN graduates who went on to do degree studies in education undertook teacher training.

By 1989 diploma trainees in UNIN's Teacher Training/Upgrading programme numbered 162 after five years. The in-service programme offered by the Teaching Division did not necessarily result in increased output of teachers but improved the qualifications of employed SWAPO teachers (Table 10.3). It is likely that, as with the diploma teachers, they would have been absorbed into teaching repatriated returnees especially in view of the need to continue with the type of education they were exposed to in exile, at least for the immediate post-independence period. In an interview with the SWAPO Education Co-ordinator for returnees in late 1989, it was confirmed that returnee children were being taught by returnee teachers.[59]

Finally, the NEU, despite some encouraging progress, also suffered from administrative difficulties. This pointed to the need for specially-trained, competent staff to run such an alternative system of education successfully. The output from training programmes and scholarships for public administrators was fewer than in education as a whole, which cancelled out the possibility of using such professionals to meet educational administrator shortages or as a potential back-up for possible educational administrator shortages.

CONCLUSION

By the late 1980s, Namibia did not have sufficient teachers to answer the needs of its school-going population. Many of the employed teachers were also underqualified. Encouraging and helpful though all the United Nations efforts have been in producing teachers, their output was small in relation to the country's needs.

Notwithstanding the fact that there are no precise figures for the number of Namibians trained as educational administrators, the number of United Nations projects in the field of educational administration is particularly disappointing. A tailored course for Namibians in this area was not forthcoming in any of the pre-independence projects. This shows lack of foresight in drawing up suitable training programmes prior to independence. It suggests the need to evaluate carefully the approach to training in the period after independence.

Bearing in mind the lack of sufficiently trained educational administrators both within the country and among its former exiles, what was the post-independence scenario likely to be? Before answering this question, we will examine another country's paradigm regarding staffing and training programmes. Zimbabwe, Africa's second youngest nation, had a colonial past tainted by racial inequalities similar to those in pre-independence Namibia. A review of the education system there, as well as the structural and staffing trends within the educational sector and the patterns which emerged after independence, should enhance our understanding of how best to overcome the shortage of trained educational administrators in Namibia.

NOTES

1. Prior to 1972 UN assistance to Namibians was channelled through other funds and organisations within the United Nations, namely the office of the United Nations High Commissioner for Refugees, the United Nations Educational and Training Programme for Southern Africa (UNETPSA), and the United Nations Trust Fund for South Africa (United Nations Council for Namibia, A/33/24 1978:15).

2. Namibia Digest No. 3 October 1986:5.

3. Legum ed. 1981:B755.

4. Committee of the United Nations Fund for Namibia, Conference Room Paper 112, 6 February 1979, UNESCO-7 Project Document Proposal, 22 November 1978:3.

5. *ibid.*, 4.

6. In 1979 at Kwanza Sul with its school population of roughly 2,000, there were 21 teachers, only five of whom were university graduates but not necessarily all in education. Nyango in 1978 had only twelve to fifteen teachers for its school population of about 600 (Mbamba 1979:20, 22, 24, 25).

7. United Nations Council for Namibia, Report at 39 Session of UNESCO International Conference on Education, Geneva, 16 – 25 October 1984:5; Dodds and Inquai 1983:33.
   Teacher shortages persisted. By 1989 in the SWAPO-run schools on the Isle of Youth in Cuba, 21 Namibian staff were responsible for educating approximately 1,200 primary and secondary pupils (United Nations Commissioner for Namibia, 13 December 1989:30).

8. UNIN 1978:4, 12; UNIN 1986:649.

9. Simon 1983:404; Kazapua 1984:60.

10. Report of the Committee on the United Nations Fund for Namibia, Conference Room Paper 112, 6 February 1979; UNESCO-8 Project Document Proposal, 22 November 1978:3.

11. SWAPO Department of Education and Culture 1982:53, 54.

12. United Nations Commissioner for Namibia Progress Report, 15 March 1985:27, 38.

13. *ibid.*

14. *ibid.*, 13 December 1989:38.

15. *ibid.*, 31 December 1980:24.

16. *ibid.*, 13 December 1989:36.

17. *ibid.*, 31 December 1980:24; 26 January 1982:44; 14 April 1983:31; 19 November 1982:38; 15 September 1983:32;15 March 1985:34.

18. *ibid.*, 31 December 1980:6.

19. UNIN Prospectus 1985/86:3, 4.

20. UNIN in Brief undated:3.

21. Thomas 1978:223.

22. The Institute had seven divisions: Agriculture and Land Resources; Constitutional, Legal and Judicial Affairs; Economics; Historical, Political and Cultural; Social and Education; Information and Documentation, and Teacher Training/Upgrading. The latter two did not provide courses leading to the diploma in Management and Development Studies (UNIN Prospectus 1985/86:8).

23. Personnel Communication, UNIN Information and Documentation Division, 7/03/1989.

24. The number of graduates from the individual divisions in each year does not necessarily correspond to the number on secondment within related ministries or institutions. For example, in 1983, 24 students were seconded to various education ministries, yet the total of graduates from the Social and Education Division for that year was twenty. For succeeding years up to 1986, the number on secondment was often below the overall number of graduates from that particular division even if one included those attached to ministries of health (UNIN Senate Reports July 1983 – June 1984; July 1984 – June 1985; July 1985 – June 1986).

25. UNIN Senate Reports, July – June 1983/84:8, 10; 1984/85:6, 7; 1985/86:6.

26. UNIN Evaluation Team Report, January 1987:34 – 36.

27. Rogerson 1980:678.
Among the first batch of UNIN graduates in 1979 were students who were former teachers, nurses, guerrilla veterans of the liberation war, self-taught individuals, former university students, and matriculants (Duggal 1980:37).

28. Administrator, Namibia Refugee Project, London, 18/07/1985.

29. Interview, Secretary for Primary and Secondary Education, Zimbabwe MOEC, 8/09/1988.

30. Since Namibian trainees were seen to be at the same level as clerks, it is strange that they were included on courses for middle- and high-level personnel.

31. Interview, Deputy Chief Education Officer, Standards Control, Zimbabwe MOEC, 7/09/1988.

32. UNIN Evaluation Team Report, January 1987:36.

33. UNIN Senate Report, July 1983 – June 1984:6.

34. UNIN Evaluation Mission 1985:17.

35. Personal Communication, UNIN Information and Documentation Division, 7/03/1989.

36. UNIN Evaluation Team Report January 1987:13.

37. Askin 1987:13.

38. Personal Communication, Warwick University, Department of Education, English Language Training Course Co-ordinator, 2/07/1990; 12/08/1991.

39. International Conference on Teacher Education, Lusaka, 21 – 27 September 1989:172, 173.

40. International Conference on Teacher Education, Lusaka, 21 – 27 September 1989:180; Personal Communication, Warwick University, Department of Education, English Language Training Course Co-ordinator, 2/07/1990.

41. United Nations Commissioner for Namibia, 14 April 1983:41; 15 September 1983:42, 47; 1 July 1987:44; 24 November 1987:45; 28 September 1988:4; 13 December 1989:53.

42. *ibid.*, 15 September 1983:45; 2 March 1984:56; 15 March 1985:51; 28 September 1988:48.

43. *ibid.*, Appendix IV, 31 December 1980:2; 19 November 1982:57; United Nations Council for Namibia, A/36/24, 1982:110.

44. *ibid.*, 15 September 1983:43; 2 March 1984:53; 15 March 1985:49.

45. *ibid.*, 13 December 1989:58.

46. This programme was originally open to students from the former Portuguese territories as well as South Africans, Namibians, and Zimbabweans (United Nations Secretary General, 6 November 1970; 22 October 1985).

47. No Western-based scholarship body restricted its aid exclusively to SWAPO-endorsed students, but most gave them a degree of preferential treatment, while simultaneously requiring that all applicants met a minimum established academic standard. With UNETPSA, however, SWAPO support of students was strongly considered (Gerhart 1983:25).

48. United Nations Secretary General, 1970 – 1989.

49. Ellis 1983:4.

50. The next Namibian to attend an IIEP training programme was enrolled for the 1992/93 course. He was employed within the Ministry of Education and Culture's regional office at Katima Mulilo and had completed a degree in education at one of the 'black' universities in South Africa. He is the only Namibian since independence to have completed the IIEP course at the time of writing.

51. The NEU was an autonomous body within UNIN with its own Project Management. Its funds, however, were administered by UNIN whose director was NEU's chairperson. The Commonwealth Fund for Technical Co-operation played an important role in planning the Unit (United Nations Council for Namibia, A/37/24 1982:113; Commonwealth Secretary-General 1983:18).

52. By 1984 the Unit also offered courses in community health, child care, nutrition and agriculture (Commonwealth Secretariat, 19/10/1984:3; 1/05/1985:2).

53. It is interesting to compare this staff/pupil ratio of 54:3,700 with those of the ethnic directorates within Namibia and their various target school populations. Out of the 54 NEU staff, there were 31

administrative staff since there were 23 tutors in the field. Administrative staff/student ratios for the NEU in 1986 and some of the larger ethnic directorates in Namibia, including the DNE during 1988 were as follows:

	Staff*	Pupils	Pupil/Staff Ratio
Owambo	2,158	193,219	90:1
Kavango	743	34,563	47:1
Caprivian	375	20,935	56:1
DNE	1,100	42,921	39:1
NEU	311	3,700	119:1**

* These totals include administrative staff employed in schools.
** Figures for 1986

Furthermore, the considerably lower costs of the NEU, approximately $50 per student in 1986, should also be taken into account (NEU 1985:5; NEU Evaluation Report, October 1986:9, 20, 26; Tables 7.4 and 8.2)

54. Interview, Director, International Extension College, Cambridge, 12/11/1985; CCN/RRR Newsletter, 12/04/1990.
55. NEU Evaluation Report, October 1986:12, 26: UNIN Senate Report, July 1985 – August 1986:10.
56. Interview, Permanent Secretary, MOEC, 3/08/1993; Republic of Namibia, March 1993:20.
57. NEU Evaluation Report 1986:16.
58. *ibid.*, 16, 17, 19; UNIN Senate Report, July 1985 – August 1986:10; NEU 1985:7.
59. CCN/RRR Newsletter, 8/09/1989.

The Zimbabwean experience: education and educational administration

11

Zimbabwean education and its administration during colonial rule

Inequality is the very foundation of
Rhodesian society, underpinned and sustained by
the educational system.... Thus, parallel
and complementary to the economic dualism ...
is the existence of a racially segregated
and separate system of education. Not only are
there two separate administrations
and structures; they are also two different systems.
B.T.G. CHIDZERO, 1977

INTRODUCTION

Zimbabwe's colonial past bears many resemblances to that of Namibia's in the sphere of educational provision for its black and white ethnic groups. Since previous works on the colonial period have covered this topic in detail,[1] the focus here is only on certain aspects of the colonial education system from the late nineteenth century until its demise at independence in April 1980. These include:

☐ the development of a dual system of educational provision and administration;[2]

☐ the organisation and staffing patterns of the educational structures by the 1970s; and

☐ the human resource situation at independence.

The aim is twofold: firstly, to highlight the similarities and differences between Zimbabwe's and Namibia's colonial educational experiences; secondly, to throw light on the availability of skilled educational administrators and professionals both from within and outside Zimbabwe at independence, in comparison to those available to an independent Namibia. This analysis provides a background for an appraisal of:

☐ the changes which came about as the post-independence Zimbabwean Government tackled the issue of racial parity in educational staffing; and

☐ the need to expand the educational administrative structure to deal with the policy of increased educational provision.

THE LEGACY OF COLONIAL EDUCATION

THE DEVELOPMENT OF A DUAL SYSTEM OF EDUCATION

The early years

Since the late nineteenth century when Europeans first settled in Rhodesia, education there had been characterised by differences in provision. Although the missionaries at first provided both blacks and whites with education, each group was assigned its own schools and the educational aims for each group were different.

> The education of Africans was intended, from the beginning, to serve two purposes: to facilitate conversions to Christianity; and to give Africans the training needed to fulfil European needs for African labour.... For Europeans its purpose was to inculcate the moral principles on which the Empire was based, to provide an education equivalent to that available in South Africa and to minimise ethnic tensions among the Europeans themselves (particularly those resulting from the Afrikaner defeat in the Anglo-Boer war).[3]

From the 1920s onwards, educational policy for blacks aimed to educate the majority at primary level only, with further education for only a few. The focus was on industrial needs rather than an academic or literary education. Since the government played a greater role in whites' education, as in German South West Africa, whites had access to two different types of schools by 1899: those run by churches or voluntary organisations and schools of no denomination, whose managers were government-appointed. The growth of the latter eventually diminished mission control over white education.

Blacks, in contrast, only had access to mission schools. These schools were less advantaged when it came to government grants. They received only ten shillings per child annually or a maximum grant of £50 per school by the late nineteenth and early twentieth centuries. Moreover, to qualify for these grants, schools had to provide 'industrial training', while white schools received grants without any stipulations attached. White schools' grants covered half the salaries of principals and other teachers, half the cost of school equipment and one Pound quarterly for each pupil who attained high proficiency levels in any subject.[4] By 1916 there was talk of introducing compulsory schooling for whites, but this became legal only in 1930 for children between the ages of six to fifteen. The requirement was extended to coloured and Asian children in 1938 but not to blacks.

Until the late 1920s, all educational administration came under a single Education Department. From 1929, with the establishment of the Department of Native Development, black education was separately administered from that of whites, coloureds and Asians (which all came under one administrative structure), thereby establishing a permanent administrative differentiation between the education of blacks and other ethnic groups.[5]

The 1940s to 1979

From the 1940s until the late 1970s, legislation and the recommendations of various education commissions were based on the premise of a dual society. This meant the further entrenchment of segregation of blacks and whites. During these years, the government also further tightened its control over black education and throughout the 1960s increased its role in black educational provision. The government extended its control over black education by establishing black schools in urban areas, inspecting rural mission schools, and imposing a common curriculum and setting minimum standards.

By the 1970s, a complex system of control had evolved in black education. There were government-run schools as well as schools that fell under various authorities such as African and Rural Councils, Regional Authorities, and missions, all of which were government-aided.[6] In cases where aid was not forthcoming, schools tended to be run by school committees comprising elected representatives of parents within a given community, teachers, and headteachers.

All white schools, with the exception of a few independent schools, were state controlled. In 1977 the largest number of black primary schools (2,096 or 64 per cent) was administered by African Councils, while government schools made up only 3 per cent (100) of the total number of primary schools (see Table 11.1). At secondary level, schools were divided into two categories, namely, academic (F1), which were in the majority, and technical schools (F2). Of the 153 secondary schools, 28 were government, 99 mission and 26 local authority.[7]

Table 11.1   Pupils and Schools by Individual Ethnic
Group, 1977

Ethnic Group	Primary Schools	Pupils	Secondary Schools	Pupils
Black	3,226	855,025	153	47,333
White, Coloured and Asian	168	38,000	43	28,000

Source: Adapted from British Council 1978: 11, 13, 14; Mumbengegwi 1981:9

Of the 168 primary schools for white, coloured and Asian pupils in 1977 (see Table 11.1), 89 per cent were government-administered, compared with the 3 per cent of black primary schools. The remaining white schools were independent. Control of the 43 secondary schools catering for these three groups was as follows: 37 government (86 per cent) and six independent (14 per cent).[8]

The government clearly played a more direct role in the educational provision of coloureds, whites and Asians than in that of blacks. It also made budgetary distinctions between black and white education. As indicated in Table 11.2, government expenditure on white education was thirteen times that for blacks.

Table 11.2   Government Expenditure on Education in
Rhodesian Dollars (Million), 1974/75

Ethnic Group	Pupils	R Dollars (m)	Expenditure per Pupil
Black	863,596	30.1	34.9
White *	69,061	31.8	460

*No separate figures were given for coloured or Asian pupils. It is possible that they have been included in the figure given for white pupils.
Source: Mumbengegwi 1981: 41

The education of whites and blacks served a dual purpose. White education was generally of a very high standard following the pattern of grammar or public schools in the United Kingdom and aiming to produce scholars able to take up positions of leadership in government, commerce, and industry. Black education aimed to produce semi- and unskilled labour for the economy's development. Black students even had a different curriculum and their textbooks were specially written for them or adapted from South African textbooks. In this way education helped to maintain "the existing racial distinctions and therefore prepare black manpower for customary prescribed roles".[9]

The success of this policy was evident in student performance. During the period 1970 – 1978, for every 100 black pupils entering Grade I (the first year of primary school) in 1970, 29 reached Grade 7 and six Form I, and only two proceeded to Form IV. For whites, out of every 100 entering Grade I, virtually every child reached Form IV.[10] The black survival rate within the system by 1974 was clearly much lower than that of whites, with the greatest concentration of black pupils being at the primary level (see Table 11.3). Therefore, even though blacks constituted the majority of the total school population, very few of their cohorts were able to remain within the system and complete the secondary cycle and thus proceed to further training.

Table 11.3   Percentages of Black, White, Coloured and
Asian Pupils in Primary and Secondary
Schools, 1974

Ethnic Group	Percentage	
	Primary School	Secondary School
Black	95.68	4.07*
White	57.87	42.71
Coloured and Asian	61.6	38.4

*This percentage includes F2 non-academic schools.
Source: Adapted from O'Callaghan 1977:90

Disadvantaged as blacks in Zimbabwe were, compared with other ethnic groups, it was alleged that they "have had access to a better quality of education and training than Africans living in countries with a comparable per capita income".[11] At least 90 per cent of blacks sitting the Cambridge 'O' level examinations passed during the period 1975 – 1977.[12] This was a far cry from the matriculation achievements of black Namibians within Namibia.

Another distinction between the two countries was that the liberation struggle in Zimbabwe (which commenced in the mid-1960s) appears to have had a greater negative impact on black education over larger parts of the country and, to some extent, white education, than the war in Namibia had on Namibians' education. This is probably because the Namibian war was largely confined to the northern frontier. During the late 1970s, the war in Zimbabwe was intensified. Schools were forced to close down due to severe damage or because they had fallen into disrepair through lack of occupation or vandalism. Pupils also left school to join the guerrillas or they emigrated along with their parents out of the war zones. Many teachers also departed.

By 1976, 893,175 black Zimbabwean school children and 22,477 teachers had been displaced. As a result, more than half the number of school children in 1976 were without schooling and more than half the black teachers lost their jobs.[13] During the succeeding years, many more schools closed, displacing many more pupils and teachers. In 1978, 1,082 primary and 46 secondary schools were closed. Over 520,000 pupils and almost 13,000 teachers were displaced in 1979 and 7,000 lost their jobs because of the war.[14] Black schools which managed to function did so with fewer staff and limited facilities, which further reduced the number of pupils able to attend school. All this had the effect of considerably eroding the overall quality of black education.

White schooling was also affected by the war in the sense that able-bodied white males under the age of 45 had to spend half the year in the army. This had a disruptive effect on teaching programmes. More serious than this, however, was the growing number of whites emigrating. Between 1973 and the end of 1979, more than 80,000 whites left Rhodesia.[15] Yet despite the net loss of more than 650 white teachers between 1976 and 1978, teacher/pupil ratios were not affected since pupils were also emigrating and white schools closing down.[16]

TERTIARY EDUCATION

Such training comprised teacher, technical and agricultural training, and university education. Black teachers who did not study at university trained separately from white teachers. By 1977 they had access to eleven teacher training colleges, only one of which offered training for secondary school teachers.

In addition to the two main multi-racial technical colleges, there were four smaller technical centres situated around the country providing training solely for blacks. The two major institutions offered a variety of engineering courses, business and management studies, secretarial and clerical studies, and science and technology. The majority of students were white because most skilled jobs were reserved for them. Blacks were virtually ignored by the formal apprenticeship system and only small numbers managed to enter such courses. Between 1961 and 1976, only 575 black apprentices were trained, but in 1976 the number of blacks registered as apprentices rose to 814.[17] Prior to 1976 therefore, most blacks at the two major technical institutions opted to do secretarial and academic studies rather than engineering.

For agricultural training, blacks had access to four agricultural training centres and an agricultural college. There was also a separate agricultural college for whites. Although both colleges had the same entry requirements and students were awarded the same diplomas, whites obtained their diplomas in two years while blacks only graduated in three.

Unlike Namibians, Zimbabweans had access to a local multi-racial university. Namibia's Academy, a tertiary-level institution, started functioning only in 1980 (see Chapter 7), while Zimbabwe's university was established in 1955, initially with a strong British affiliation and degree awards from the University of London and Birmingham University's Medical School respectively until 1970. The university was not entirely autonomous in that the Minister of Education was empowered to approve or disapprove its statutes. In the late 1970s, there were more black full-time students at the university than whites. Many whites went to study at South African universities due to their dislike of the local university's multi-racial policies or because entry qualifications were lower than those in Rhodesia/Zimbabwe. By 1980 the total number of Zimbabwean whites studying at various institutions, including universities in South Africa, reached 5,000.[18]

Although the University of Zimbabwe was multi-racial, enrolment by field of study tended to follow racial lines. Government loans and grants were allocated according to race and a system of job reservation was entrenched. Blacks were awarded bursaries or loans for study only in areas which were not in direct competition to white interests, while whites were supported in whichever fields they chose.[19] As a result, some faculties were almost purely white and others mostly black. Blacks, for example, tended to dominate the Arts and Social Studies faculties and, despite the high rate of achievement among blacks at first degree level, they were in the minority at graduate level. Most graduate black students were enrolled in the Graduate Certificate in Education. In this way the job reservation policies practised against blacks were entrenched, making it difficult for graduates to find employment outside certain occupations.

Until the mid-1970s, black graduates were mostly concentrated in professions like teaching, which was a sure field of employment, as well as in commerce, industry, and the colonial government service in sub-professional posts. From 1968 to 1972, only 3 per cent of black graduates (excepting those in teaching and medicine) entered employment in the public and private sectors, compared with 17 per cent of white graduates. The number of black graduates then rose somewhat between 1973 and 1975. In 1976, 13 per cent of black graduates found jobs with the government and 16 per cent in the private sector. White representation in these sectors dropped by 12 per cent.[20]

THE TEACHING FORCE

As in Namibia, there was a differentiation in pupil/teacher ratios with black Zimbabwean teachers on average having twice as many pupils as white teachers (see Table 11.4).

Table 11.4   Rhodesian/Zimbabwean Teacher/Pupil Ratios
by Ethnic Group, 1975 – 1977

Year	Black			White		
	Pupils	Teachers	Ratio	Pupils	Teachers	Ratio
PRIMARY SCHOOL						
1975	823,863	19,502	42:1	39,613	1,695	23:1
1976	845,162	20,162	42:1	37,897	1,627	23:1
1977	855,025	20,565	42:1	36,129	1,646	22:1
SECONDARY SCHOOL						
1975	39,733	1,576	25:1	29,448	1,807	16:1
1976	43,365	1,767	25:1	28,451	1,741	16:1
1977	47,333	1,850	26:1	26,959	1,674	16:1

Source: Mumbengegwi, 1981:9

Yet white teachers in 1977 still enjoyed average salaries four times higher than those of their black counterparts.[21] Within the black pay structures, however, black teachers earned wages which were double the average black wage in 1977, placing teachers among the highest income earners in this ethnic group.[22] Another similarity to Namibia was the preponderance of women teachers in the lower grades of primary schools while men predominated at all other levels.

The prevailing wage disparities between black and white teachers were chiefly due to the lower overall level of black teacher training compared with that of whites. This was a direct consequence of the structural distortions in the social and educational system which prevented many black pupils from reaching higher levels of education. In consequence, minimum requirements for white teachers to teach in white schools were higher than those needed to teach in black schools. Additionally, few black teachers received the standard three-year teacher training qualification, this being the minimum requirement to teach in white schools. Black teachers also trained separately from whites, except when attending university, and received different qualifications which restricted them to teaching only in black schools.

Notwithstanding these inequalities, black Zimbabwean teachers were on the whole better trained than their Namibian counterparts. Generally speaking, by the late 1970s the proportion of qualified teachers in black schools in Zimbabwe was 88 per cent higher than in most other African countries. This was in part due to the limited job opportunities for educated blacks elsewhere.[23] Even prior to World War II, blacks entering the two-year primary school training had to have completed Standard VI. By 1949 the entry requirement was raised to two years' secondary school. During the 1960s, the period of teacher training itself was increased to three years. For secondary school teachers the entry requirement for the first black Secondary Teacher Training College (established in 1963 at Gwelo, now Gweru) was five Cambridge 'O' levels including English. The training lasted three years.

As in Namibia, however, a major problem during the colonial period was the shortage of teachers. The Secretary for Black Education in 1974 stated that a minimum of 1,000 extra teachers was needed each year to teach the total annual increase of 40,000 pupils in both government and government-aided schools.[24] However, teacher outputs in 1977 and 1980 were below this figure (see Table 11.5).[25] By 1980 the estimated annual pupil increase at primary level alone, an increase of approximately 90,000 pupils, called for a rise of 3,000 new teachers annually. The resultant expansion at secondary level called for approximately 9,000 teachers over a period of ten years.[26]

The war also had a direct impact on the quality of the teaching force. Along with the sharply deteriorating conditions of black education there was a dramatic increase in the number of untrained teachers. By 1980 their number was estimated at nearly 8,000, at least 25 per cent of the total teacher population of 32,154 that year. It was reported that a further 12,000 (37 per cent) were not fully qualified.[27]

Table 11.5 Black Teacher Output, 1977 and 1980

Year	College-Trained Teachers		University-Trained Teachers	Total
	Primary School	Secondary School		
1977	626	177	—	803
1980	700	200	75	975

Source: Adapted from Faruqee 1980: 26; Riddel 1980:21

Although the figures were well below Namibia's 1988 calculation of 64 per cent of undertrained teachers (see Chapter 7), the tendency in Zimbabwe, like Namibia, was for these teachers to be concentrated in the rural areas. This was alarming since over 85 per cent of all primary pupils were situated there.[28] There were no untrained white teachers in white schools, and of those whites teaching in black secondary schools almost all were qualified.

Thus we can see that there were insufficient teachers in the country, especially if universal primary education and secondary school expansion were to become a reality after independence. An independent Zimbabwe was therefore faced with a three-fold problem regarding its teaching force, namely:

☐ It had to prepare for the anticipated explosion in school enrolment after independence;

☐ The estimated 8,000 untrained black teachers had to be exposed to further training;

☐ The inequitable distribution of trained teachers in urban areas had to be overcome.

THE EDUCATION STRUCTURE: ORGANISATION, STAFFING, AND TRAINING PATTERNS

ORGANISATION

There were still two distinct educational administrative structures in Zimbabwe by 1977: the Division of White, Coloured and Asian Education and the Division of Black Education. Two Permanent Secretaries administered these two structures with two separate staffs under one minister. The black structure was responsible for at least 93 per cent of all black pupils enrolled in schools.[29] In 1976 the country's total school population was 954,875, with black pupils totalling 888,527 (93 per cent) and coloureds, Asians, and whites making up 66,348 (7 per cent).[30] The black administrative structure was highly centralised and black parents had little say in the running of the schools in terms of policy or curriculum content. The headquarters had an administrative and professional section each of which was under a Deputy Secretary assisted by Chief Education Officers who were responsible for the staffing and administration of schools. Senior Education Officers and Education Officers staffed the Educational Development Unit, the Educational Measurement Unit, and the Examinations and Secondary Branches. The Educational Development Unit, established as late as 1975, was responsible for developing the school curriculum and worked on syllabus research and innovation in co-operation with Education Officers, teachers, and others.

At the provincial level, there were seven Provincial Education Officers. These each had a Deputy. These officers had administrative functions and provided advisory services to the primary schools in their areas. As of 1976, they were assisted in the latter task by a corps of over 100 supervisors, many of whom were former school managers and primary principals. Each was responsible for approximately 30 primary schools. These supervisors were to provide further professional support to schools. They enabled the separation of professional from purely administrative functions, with administration

317

falling to the various authorities mentioned above, the majority of whom were African Councils.

The white, coloured and Asian administrative structure catered to only 7 per cent of the overall enrolled school population. Like the black structure, it too had administrative and professional sections. Its Visual Aids Division also covered black education, while its other branches resembled those of the black structure. This structure was essentially a duplication of virtually all the administrative functions within the black administrative structure.[31] The White, Coloured and Asian Division was more decentralised than that of the blacks in the sense that principals had more autonomy, and the local parent-teacher associations were involved in daily school activities. The principals and teachers were able to decide on curriculum issues and which board of examiners to use, in order to meet the varying needs of different pupils.

In July 1978 the two separate structures merged into a unified Ministry of Education which was to function at two levels: the head office in the capital and the regional levels. At the end of 1979, there were five regional offices. Such moves were part of a general trend to abandon official policies of discrimination due to mounting international pressure and the escalation of the liberation war.[32] Schools and colleges, however, remained segregated.

STAFFING

Staffing patterns within the Ministry of Education must be viewed within the overall staffing trends prevailing in public administration during the period under discussion. When the public service began to be organised in the late nineteenth century, blacks were unable to join, other than at the lowest level, namely, as janitors, messengers, guards, cooks, gardeners, and labourers. Several factors militated against them taking up top administrative and professional/technical posts (established posts) in the service, but the underlying cause was racial discrimination.

The educational disadvantages suffered by blacks meant that proportionately fewer numbers than whites benefited from further education and professional training. This was especially true in the late nineteenth and early twentieth centuries. As a result, they were automatically excluded from applying for posts which required relatively high qualifications. By the late 1920s, however, more blacks and coloureds were attaining educational qualifications which made them eligible for professional posts within the public service. Even these educated people, however, were barred from gaining access to such posts by the system's ethnically determined employment practices. The 1931 Public Service Act explicitly excluded blacks, coloureds, and Asians from entering posts above the level of manual workers, the so-called non-established posts. It made distinctions between black, coloured and Asian jobs, the lowest being assigned to blacks. This was to protect white skills and it was accompanied by practices of under-categorising and under-utilising black skills. It was alleged that when white applicants for available posts were not forthcoming, these were kept vacant rather than filling them with blacks.[33] As a result, the more highly skilled blacks were usually placed in jobs beneath their capacities.

Finally, in 1961 legislation was passed enabling blacks to serve in established posts for the first time. These, however, were limited to positions dealing essentially with blacks, rather than situations where they would hold supervisory responsibility over white personnel or have direct dealings with a white clientele. These changes were due to rising black nationalism and the need for expansion of a service which could no longer rely on the limited number of available white professionals to fulfil its needs. This amounted to a more subtle form of discrimination. Even if blacks possessed the prerequisite qualifications and training, they were still confronted with subjective obstacles, such as the need to possess suitable character traits, loyalty, and sense of devotion which were not specifically demanded of whites, as well as a one-month induction period.[34] In 1973 the Minister of Public Services said:

> The mere possession of an academic qualification is not in itself a criterion for appointment to any job....

> We have to consider the suitability of the candidates,
> bearing in mind certain factors. Perhaps the most
> important single factor so far as the public service is
> concerned is loyalty to the State .... Secondly, the
> national security.[35]

Furthermore, overt racism was a common characteristic of
the white recruitment and training officers, not to mention
the civil service as a whole.

Government policies and structures hampered black advancement within the service. This was especially true of those
structures employing large numbers of blacks, like education.
For example, black and white teachers were appointed to
separate professional branches, namely, the United African
Teachers' Service and the Schools' Branch of the Public
Service respectively. The two were unequal in status. This
meant that qualified black primary school teachers working
in government schools were not members of the established
public service, unlike their non-black colleagues in the same
schools or elsewhere. Hence they were not allowed automatic
promotion within it.

Whites therefore continued to monopolise the senior administrative, professional, technical, and supervisory grades
within the civil service and dominated the structure as a
whole. In 1978 of the 13,640 established posts in the public
service only 11 per cent were filled by blacks. Concerning the
non-established posts (artisans, junior clerical workers, and
typists), 14 per cent were filled by blacks.[36] By 1980 there was
a further rise in black representation in established posts. Of
the 10,000 established officers in the public service, 3,000 (30
per cent) were black.[37] As far as trends within the educational
structures were concerned, the professional and administrative leadership of the White, Coloured and Asian Division was
predominantly white. Within the Black Division until the
1960s, in line with the policies and legislation mentioned
above, no blacks held middle- or high-level posts. It was only
in the 1970s that they increasingly began to move into more
responsible posts as whites left the service due to military
call-up and emigration. As a result, that decade saw more

blacks filling the Education Officer posts; by the late 1970s one or two had even become Deputy Chiefs within the structure.[38] At the provincial level, at least three of the seven Provincial Education Officers were black, while only two of the seven Deputy Provincial Education Officers were black. When the two Divisions were united in 1978, the former white Secretary for Black Education became Secretary for Education in the reorganised Ministry of Education, while a black was appointed Co-Minister of Education. In June 1979, the first black Minister of Education was appointed.

In 1979 out of a total of 21 senior staff at the then unified Ministry's head office, only one black held a senior-level post as Deputy Chief Education Officer. In the regional offices, out of a total of eighteen senior staff, four blacks served as Deputy Regional Directors, while the remaining nine Deputy Regional Directors were white. Whites therefore continued to dominate all the senior-level posts thereby revealing the extent to which black education remained entrenched in white hands.

TRAINING IN ADMINISTRATION

Most professionals within the Ministry of Education directly involved with purely educational matters had been one-time teachers. They had moved up the promotional path from being heads of schools or departments into inspectorate posts and thereafter into higher-level administrative posts. Generally speaking, there was no formal administration and management training for public servants as a whole at the middle-and higher-levels. When it came to middle-and lower-level staff, however, distinctions were made between blacks and whites within the Ministry of Education, with only the former having to participate in in-service training.

The white staff employed in the educational structures, some of whom had trained abroad, were not exposed to any administrative training after having taken up employment. Yet whites predominated in all the senior posts. They were appointed or promoted directly to their posts since they were considered to be sufficiently qualified. Any learning was to occur on the job.[39] It is doubtful, however, whether white professional staff with teacher training from the University of Zimbabwe had any exposure to specific educational administration courses since the subject was introduced only after independence. One interviewee claimed that, prior to independence, skin colour rather than professional qualifications was the criterion for senior appointments.[40] For the public service as a whole, "access to managerial, executive and administrative occupations (did not) in general demand either high academic, professional or specialised training as an entry qualification to such posts, though such a background would, of course, be desirable in any establishment...."[41]

Within the Division of Black Education, there was more emphasis on training than within the Division of White, Coloured and Asian Education. Such training was targeted at black staff, specifically:

☐ black heads of primary schools, and
☐ the few black professionals within the administrative structure.

Black heads of primary schools, for example, could not be promoted until they had completed three months' training. The Ministry of Education felt it necessary to provide black primary school heads with in-service training because black teachers were generally less qualified than their white counterparts, especially at primary level. The courses for black primary school heads usually covered school administration, the deployment of staff, and drawing up of time-tables. Black heads of high schools did not have to participate in any training since, like whites, they were considered to be sufficiently educated at that level.

The training for black professionals within the administrative structure was directed at black District Education Officers and supervisors. They had to take short courses related to the work they conducted. Generally, compared with their white counterparts, only a very small number of black professionals within the Ministry had trained abroad.[42]

In addition to the training provided to the professional blacks within the Ministry, the lower-level black staff also had to attend general administration courses. These were conducted at the Highlands Training Centre (known after independence as Highlands National Training Centre) which offered courses in personnel procedure, accounting, typing, and secretarial training. At Domboshawa National Training Centre, courses were geared to train people situated in the rural areas for the certificate and diploma in local government. Domboshawa also provided training in such fields as project planning and communication skills. Additionally, there were four provincial training centres: Senya, Esigodini, Alvord, and Rowa. These provided training for staff employed in the rural African Councils. Such training aimed to strengthen the existing structures and was of a more mechanical nature than dealing with policy.

HUMAN RESOURCES WEIGHED AGAINST ADMINISTRATIVE NEEDS

THE INTERNAL SKILLS' SUPPLY

This has to be viewed in terms of the employment trends in the civil service in general, the bastion of the colonial structure.[43] As stated above, whites predominated in that structure. Bearing in mind their monopoly over skilled and professional posts, their emigration, which steadily increased from the mid-1970s onwards, and the compulsory military call-ups were bound to have adverse effects on the civilian economy.[44] Among those leaving was a sizeable net outflow of professional, technical, and related employees, especially men. These included accountants, engineers, teachers, physicians and surgeons, engineering technicians, and physical scientists. There was also a large outflow of administrative employees, a sizeable proportion of which were from managerial grades. This resulted in growing shortages of professional human resources in commerce, industry, and administration.

Though whites had dominated top-level skilled and professional posts, it was not because there were no skilled professional blacks available to fill such posts. Instead, as was pointed out earlier, the policy of under-utilisation or total lack of harnessing educated black potential had resulted in the belief in white indispensability and hence a general breakdown of services with their departure. For example, the reported overall shortage of government executive and administrative officers by the late 1970s was directly attributable to the policy of blocking black promotion in the central state sector rather than a shortage of professional blacks.[45] What this amounted to was a situation in which only half of the country's skilled blacks were using their skills at a time when skills were said to be in short supply. This reality was further borne out by the fact that by July 1981, one year after independence, the public service had a considerably higher representation of blacks in the professional and skilled job categories (see Table 11.6).

Table 11.6   The Percentage Representation of Individual Ethnic Groups in Three Job Categories within the Zimbabwean Public Service, 24 July 1981

Job Category	Black %	Asian/Coloured %	White %
Professional	62	2	36
Skilled	69	6	25
Semi-Skilled	92	3	5

Source: Adapted from National Manpower Survey, Volume III, 1981:172

The small representation of the Asians/coloureds and whites in the semi-skilled categories spelt the continuation of the colonial norms within this job category in all the sectors. Yet the fact that blacks, so shortly after independence, came to outnumber these other three groups in all the job categories proved that there was an available pool of skilled blacks.

The positive effect of the white exodus was that it resulted in a degree of black advancement in selected occupations and sectors in both the public and private domains from 1976 onwards. More blacks were promoted to established and managerial posts, especially in black affairs. As mentioned previously in note 17, there was also a slight rise in the number of black graduates finding employment during this period, thereby again proving the existence of a pool of skilled blacks.

An important difference between Zimbabwe and Namibia, therefore, was that Zimbabwe had an internal supply of suitably qualified blacks who could step into some of the vacancies created by departing whites. Moreover, it also had a sizeable pool of semi-educated blacks who could be trained for responsible work but who had been neglected under the colonial system. Namibia, on the other hand, lacked a sufficient internal supply of both qualified semi-educated blacks to fill vacancies in the event of a large-scale exodus of white professionals.

In Zimbabwe, for example, for three successive years (1975, 1976, and 1977) the percentage pass rate for the total number of black candidates sitting the Cambridge 'O' level examination was 90 per cent. This meant respective totals of 4,466, 4,768, and 5,147 for each of those years. In contrast, out of the total number of black Namibians (excluding those in National Education) enrolled in Standard IX in 1985, only 62 per cent (968) of the original total of 1,556 continued into Standard X the following year.[46] By 1979 the number of black Zimbabwean school leavers from this level, namely, the fourth year of secondary school, had reached 10,000.[47] This meant that Zimbabwe had a potentially larger hidden reservoir of educated people than did Namibia.

The existence of an education structure replete with a Sixth Form education, which provided two years' preparation for university and other tertiary-level education and training, contributed towards the existence — albeit small among blacks compared with other ethnic groups — of potential reserves of middle and upper human resource skills' training. Such a system was lacking in Namibia, even for white pupils.

THE EXTERNAL SKILLS' SUPPLY

The injustices in the historic development of the education system and the dislocation of the war in Zimbabwe forced many to seek education and training outside their country. Those who did not return sought work in their countries of exile. These people represented an important source of skilled human resources to Zimbabwe at independence. There were at least 250,000 Zimbabwean refugees in neighbouring countries by the late 1970s.[48] However, accurate estimates of the total number of Zimbabweans (let alone their field of study) studying or working abroad are hard to obtain.

Two attempts were made prior to independence to conduct such a survey from outside Zimbabwe. The 1979 Commonwealth Secretariat study covered only half the number of black Zimbabweans who had received scholarships since 1965, and the responses from those studying or working abroad were also limited. Data from agencies providing scholarships were said to be underestimates.[49]

The Patriotic Front study of 1978 was also only a partial assessment because its data were based predominantly on statistics provided by the now defunct International University Exchange Fund (IUEF). Any information from other assistance schemes was very incomplete, while many agencies were simply omitted. Not all the aid agencies approached provided complete data, since they did not always keep records of past students nor of the level of studies or the degree of success of the candidates. Moreover, the political situation at the time made many Zimbabweans reluctant to submit any information prior to independence. Therefore, what information materialised from these two studies was mostly fragmentary and uncertain. When the 1981 Zimbabwean National Manpower Survey attempted a similar undertaking, it too was not very successful for reasons similar to those already mentioned.

Chapters 9 and 10 reveal similar shortcomings in the Namibian survey, thereby indicating that such pre-independence surveys in general are mostly speculative and inconclusive. In view of these findings, this section provides only indications of what training and work experiences were available to Zimbabweans prior to independence, especially in as far as these relate to education and educational administration.

Training abroad was facilitated by the assistance of donor agencies and scholarship schemes. By 1979 the Commonwealth Secretariat study estimated that between 6,000 and 8,000 black Zimbabweans were either studying or had completed higher education in various countries of the world.[50]

Teacher education was included in the tertiary education being conducted in the refugee camps in Africa. From 1978 onwards, the liberation movements introduced teacher training courses at Matenje in Mozambique. These included basic teacher education of five months' duration, an advanced teacher training course of twelve months, and a three-month teacher administration course. The basic teacher training course included administration, educational planning, and curriculum development.[51] As far as the administration component of the courses was concerned, the administration within the camps was analysed and theoretical teaching was combined with actual practical application. By 1980 some 700 teachers had participated in such training, the first batch of 49 having graduated in July 1979 at Matenje.[52]

Further contributions to the external skills' reservoir were qualified Zimbabweans with work experience. They were employed in the Secretariat of the liberation movements and served as international civil servants, key executives in the state administrations of a number of countries, and experts in a variety of professional and scientific fields. For example, some exiled Zimbabweans were employed in the Zambian and Canadian public services.[53]

Exiled Zimbabweans with specific experience in educational matters were those people, for example, employed within the Patriotic Front's Department of Education and Culture (established in 1977) and its Research Unit.[54] One of the Unit's functions was to facilitate planning and help resolve educational problems, as well as devising textbooks for the refugee schools and formulating a new curriculum. It was made up of fifteen of the most experienced and competent teachers and was based at Matenje. The Unit also trained its own administrators in supervisory functions.[55]

There appears to have been no organised programme specifically to train Zimbabweans in educational administration. Prior to independence, at least three black Zimbabweans undertook university-level training in educational planning and administration abroad. Two were sponsored by the liberation movements to study at the Institute of Education of the University of London and the International Institute for Educational Planning in Paris respectively; the third studied independently. Only one of the three candidates had actually completed training by 1980. The remainder completed their training later.[56] The only reference made to specific training for future senior civil servants and administrators was in 1978, when the Patriotic Front requested the IUEF to launch a Zimbabwean Manpower Training Programme for such staff. This resulted in 31 students being placed in various institutions in Africa, specifically to study subjects pertinent to their tasks as future public servants. Educational administration training does not appear to have featured in this programme.[57]

OVERVIEW

The years of educational and training disadvantages of most black Zimbabweans and the discriminatory employment policy directed against educated blacks, which deprived them of entry to senior posts, all bore strong parallels to pre-independent Namibia. These tendencies, plus the large number of departing whites pointed towards a potential human resource gap in managerial, executive and administrative occupations in Zimbabwe. However, this was not the case.

Firstly, those occupations mentioned above were not always filled by whites with highly specialised training. Secondly, the country had an internal pool of underutilised graduate or otherwise qualified blacks, in addition to a sizeable reservoir of 'unused' secondary school educated blacks who had the potential for further training. In addition to these internal resources were the several thousand educated and, in some instances, highly experienced one-time exiled Zimbabweans. As such, Zimbabwe appears to have been better off than Namibia in terms of the quality and quantity of its internal skills' supply and the number of externally trained resources.

The extreme educational disadvantages of black Namibians ruled against a similarly well-educated internal supply. Even among the privileged minority white Namibians, it appears that skills were inadequate, hence the strategy of encouraging white South Africans to take up employment in the country. Namibia's external skills' supply also appears to have been far more limited numerically than Zimbabwe's in terms of the number of successful graduates and professionals employed abroad (see for example British Council statistics of overseas students and UNETPSA reports). This was in part due to the smaller population of that country but more so because of the poor educational foundation of many who had been exposed to schooling in Namibia, which required additional time for remedial education. Added to this was the difficulty many Namibians had in getting work experience once they were qualified. The situation was indicative of that country's severe human skills' shortages.

CONCLUSION

Zimbabwe, in contrast to Namibia, had a pool of educated human resources and "a far bigger proportion of people with a wider range of skills than almost any colony on achieving independence (except possibly India)".[58] These realities enabled the new government to embark upon strategies deliberately aimed at overcoming some of the colonial injustices. This it was able to do without fear of a general breakdown in administrative services. How then did the new government go about introducing changes to the educational structure, organisation, and staff?

NOTES

1. O'Callaghan 1977; Chidzero 1977, the British Council 1978; Mumbengegwi 1981; Zvobgo 1986.

2. The emphasis in this chapter is on the differences between the educational provision for blacks and whites. Like the Namibian coloured population, coloureds and Asians in Rhodesia, though not generally as privileged as the white minority, were better off than the majority of blacks. The education of coloureds and Asians appears not to have differed from that of the whites. Furthermore, coloured and Asian education was administered together with that of whites and not separately as in South West Africa/Namibia.

3. O'Callaghan 1977:15.

4. *ibid.*, 16.

5. Although white, coloured and Asian education was administered within one structure, namely, the Ministry of Education's Division of White, Coloured and Asian Education, there were separate state primary and secondary schools for all three groups.

6. African Councils were elected local institutions comprising chiefs and headmen (traditional leaders) and a District Commissioner, all of whom were concerned with the problems of political and administrative control of the rural black population. They enjoyed little or no autonomy, merely operating subject to detailed directives from the District Commissioner, who, in turn, was responsible to higher levels in the hierarchy. These Councils were not accountable to the local black population in any real sense. In terms of education, their role was purely an administrative one. Regional Authorities, which were based on provincial boundaries, predominantly consisted of chiefs and headmen. They were the upper tier of black local government. Rural Councils were made up of white farmers, and schools under their jurisdiction were farm schools.

7. British Council 1978:11,13,14; Mumbengegwi 1981:9.
   The government-run black primary and secondary schools were mostly in urban areas and the same applied to non-government secondary schools but to a lesser extent. Almost all non-government primary schools were situated in the rural areas. This meant that the majority of schools were rural. The Ministry of Education therefore directly controlled only a very small part of the education system and that was almost entirely urban.

8. British Council 1978:14.
   White enrolment at primary level was 100 per cent. Black education, however, was not compulsory, which meant that large numbers of this group's school-age population were not within the system. In 1967, for example, the number of children of primary school age not in school was put at 210,000. With the country's population growth

estimated at 3.6 per cent, this figure was bound to have risen considerably in following years (Mumbengegwi 1981:4, 8, O'Callaghan 1977:46; International Institute for Educational Planning, 11 March 1982:3).

9. O'Callaghan 1977:22.

10. Mumbengegwi 1981:5.

11. Robinson and Shortlidge 1980:3.

12. British Council 1978:14; Atkinson *et al.* 1978:6.

13. Riddell 1980:31,32.
   Many teachers who fled the rural areas during the war grew accustomed to living in urban areas. Some found employment outside of education and were reluctant to return to teaching in rural regions (Robinson and Shortlidge 1980:6).

14. Colclough and Murray 1979:21; Cameron 1980:2; Legum ed. 1981:B985.

15. Stoneman 1981:38.

16. Riddell 1980:32.

17. British Council 1978:16; Faruqee 1981:23.
   Job reservation meant that blacks were excluded from middle and upper echelons in the public service and the private sector, even when they had the necessary qualifications. There was therefore a high level of unemployment among blacks, no matter what their level of education. In 1969 the participation rate for educated blacks in the labour force was estimated as being less than 50 per cent. Towards the end of the 1970s, the situation changed, as moves were afoot to create an internal settlement with more black representation, and also because of the large number of vacancies in skilled jobs caused by departing whites.

18. National Manpower Survey, Volume I, 1981:25.

19. Nine donor agencies were also supporting many Zimbabwean students at the local university as well as in the United Kingdom and other countries (Colclough and Murray 1979:38).

20. *ibid.*, 36.

21. According to the 1959 Native Education Act, black teachers with standard qualifications were entitled to the same remuneration as white teachers with equivalent status. In Namibia, only as of 1978, did black teachers' salaries gradually begin to equate those of whites, there having been no formal legislation, unlike Zimbabwe, to overcome this discrepancy.

22. Riddell 1980:26.

23. *ibid.*, 40.

24. Colclough and Murray 1979:21.

25. The 1979 intake into teacher training colleges was down due to the enforced government regulation that blacks between the ages of

eighteen and 25 were liable for one year's military call-up for the first
time.

26. Faruqee 1980: 26, 28, 39, 42, 43.
27. Mumbengegwi 1981:16; Faruqee 1980:25, 38.
28. Mumbengegwi 1981:17, 18.
29. British Council 1978:22.
30. Whitsun Foundation 1977, Tables 3 and 4.
31. Of note in both divisions was the absence of an Educational Planning
    Unit. Most educational planning was therefore conducted by officers
    within the Ministry of Education on an *ad hoc* basis, although an
    interviewee claims that there was one Planning Officer in the entire
    structure prior to 1980. This meant that political leaders were obliged
    to frame their policies without help from administrative specialists
    and official data. The absence of a planning unit was notable, since
    almost all ministries of education have such a structure able to
    respond to changes by working out alternative strategies to cover the
    medium if not long term. Educational planning is vital to integrate
    educational development into the government's overall develop-
    ment planning.
32. The coalition government of Smith-Muzorewa, formed on the 3
    March 1978, aimed at creating an internal settlement which would
    by-pass the Zimbabwean liberation movements and hopefully attain
    international acceptance. Similar moves occurred in Namibia in
    mid-1985 with the formation of the Transitional Government of
    National Unity and the cosmetic changes made to racial legislation
    from the late 1970s onwards. As with the Zimbabwean coalition, the
    latter did not gain international recognition.
33. Murapa 1984:69.
34. *ibid.*, 66, 67.
35. National Manpower Survey, Volume I, 1981:27.
36. Stoneman 1978:20.
37. Murapa 1984:72.
38. Interview, Minister for Primary and Secondary Education, Zimbabwe
    MOEC, 8/09/1988.
    Even though the Division of White, Asian and Coloured Education
    catered to a much smaller percentage of the overall school popula-
    tion in 1975, it employed 7,494 staff compared with the 1,323 staff
    employed in the Division of Black Education. Of these totals, 3,611
    members of staff (48 per cent) were in established posts within the
    white structure and only 330 (25 per cent) within the black structure.
    This revealed the predominance of professionals within the White
    Division (United Nations Development Programme 1980:240).
39. Interviews, Director of Zimbabwe Institute of Public Administration
    and Management, 5/09/1988; Deputy Secretary for Finance and
    Administration, Higher Education, Zimbabwe MOEC, 6/09/1988.

40. Interview, Deputy Secretary for Higher Institutions, Zimbabwe MOEC, 8/09/1988.

41. National Manpower Survey, Volume I, 1981:26.

42. Interviews, Minister for Primary and Secondary Education, Zimbabwe MOEC, 8/09/1988; Deputy Secretary for Finance and Administration, Higher Education, Zimbabwe MOEC, 6/09/1988; Director of Zimbabwe Institute of Public Administration and Management, 5/09/1988.

43. In all sectors, blacks made up 75 per cent of all the professional, skilled and semi-skilled workers, yet they accounted for only 39 per cent of professional workers, 61 per cent of skilled workers, and 89 per cent of semi-skilled workers. Whites, in contrast, made up only 22 per cent of the total professional, skilled and semi-skilled workers but comprised 57 per cent of the professional group, 35 per cent of the skilled group and a mere 9 per cent of the semi-skilled group (Zvobgo 1986 121, 123; National Manpower Survey, Volume III, 1981:172).

44. White emigration patterns were as follows:
    1975..........10,497
    1976..........14,854
    1977..........16,638
    1978..........18,069
    (Whitsun Foundation 1980:45).

45. Clarke 1978:212.

46. British Council 1978:14; South West Africa Directorate of Development Co-ordination 1985:19 – 22; 1986:18 – 21.

47. Colclough and Murray 1979:28.

48. Zimbabwe Conference on Reconstruction and Development, Harare, 21 – 27 March 1981:25.

49. Colclough and Murray 1979:39, 62, 63.

50. Riddell 1980:33; Colclough and Murray 1979:37; National Manpower Survey, Volume I, 1981:26.

51. Interview, Minister for Primary and Seconary Education, Zimbabwe MOEC, 8/09/1988.
    In addition to the educational administration course offered at Matenje, there existed a small school of administration in Maputo for general administration.

52. Interview, Director of Zimbabwe Foundation for Education with Production, 2/09/1988; Mutumbuka 1980:9; Seminar on Education in Zimbabwe: Past, Present and Future, University of Zimbabwe, 27 August – 7 September 1981:34.

53. Interviews, Secretary for Primary and Secondary Education, Zimbabwe MOEC, 8/09/1988; Minister for Primary and Secondary Education, Zimbabwe MOEC, 8/09/1988.

54. The Patriotic Front was formed in 1976 between the two major Zimbabwean liberation movements, ZAPU and ZANU.
55. Seminar on Education in Zimbabwe: Past, Present and Future, University of Zimbabwe, 27 August – 7 September 1981:25, 26, 32, 34; Nhundu 1981:6; Stoneman 1980:33.
56. Interview, Deputy Secretary for Higher Education Institutions, Zimbabwe MOEC, 8/09/1988.
57. Patriotic Front, Volume I, 1978:30.
58. Stoneman 1978:40.

12

Post-independence educational administration in Zimbabwe

The major tasks of the Government in
resettlement, education, reconstruction and
development will make great demands
on the Public Service. It will be necessary to
expand the Service to discharge this
growing range of tasks, and the African people of
Zimbabwe must be afforded increasing
opportunities of playing their full part
in these developments.
PRESIDENT C.S. BANANA, 1980

INTRODUCTION

A review of the successes and shortcomings of the processes
introduced after independence in April 1980 provides a
clearer insight into the wisdom of adopting similar approaches in Namibia. In addition to discussing the organisational and staffing changes within Zimbabwe's educational
structure, it is necessary to examine:

☐ where educational administrators were drawn from after
independence once the structure expanded; and

☐ the possibility of obstacles in the integration of administrators drawn from inside Zimbabwe with those who had
trained and lived abroad.

This investigation is followed by a review of the training
programmes which persisted or were brought into being after
independence.

THE EDUCATIONAL STRUCTURE

At independence, the Ministry of Education was renamed the Ministry of Education and Culture. The structure of the Ministry did not change much from that prevailing under the colonial system in 1978. It continued to remain centrally controlled and confined to two levels: the head office in Harare and the regional offices.

HEAD OFFICE

In 1980 the head office was administered by the Secretary for Education and Culture who was also the head of the Ministry of Education and Culture. He co-ordinated all four divisions and functions within the Ministry. Under him were four Deputy Secretaries in charge of the four divisions: Education and Services; Professional Staffing and Teacher Training; Administration, Finance and Planning; and Culture. These divisional heads were assisted by Chief Education Officers who all met regularly to discuss ministerial affairs. Further down the hierarchy were the various administrative officers who dealt with the daily running of the Ministry. All matters concerning the curriculum, conditions of service and planning, and teachers' qualifications were dealt with at head office.

THE REGIONAL OFFICES

The organisation, operation and development of education at regional level were the responsibilities of the regional offices. There were six regional offices in 1980, each of which was headed by a Regional Director who operated at the level of Chief Education Officer and who was responsible for co-ordinating all educational matters within a specific region on behalf of the Secretary for Education. The regional offices were not autonomous since they were directly answerable to the head office's four Deputy Secretaries. Their policy decisions not only had to conform with national policy but also had to be formulated in consultation with head office.

Regional Directors held meetings with various responsible authorities including District Councils, churches, farm owners, and other groups involved in running primary and secondary schools. They were assisted by four Deputy Regional Directors (operating at the level of Deputy Chief Education Officer) each of whom was in charge of the following four aspects of the educational system: Education Services and Administration, Primary Education, Secondary Education, and Culture. Below them were the Education Officers who had direct links with primary and secondary schools. The number of Education Officers dealing with primary school matters varied from region to region but was usually between four and six depending on the size of the province. Their tasks were to visit schools regularly and to provide professional advice to principals and their staff. Each Education Officer controlled about 150 schools. They had to submit reports of such visits to the schools, as well as to both regional and head offices.

Linked to each of the regional offices were District Education Officers who were below Education Officers in rank.[1] There were four or five District Education Officers under each Education Officer involved in primary school education. The Education Officers were former primary school principals and school managers who had been promoted to offer professional guidance and assistance to primary school teachers. Their visits to the schools were more regular than those of the Education Officers and they were the regional offices' main contact with schools. They also undertook most of the supervision work. In addition to these tasks, both District Education Officers and Education Officers in the regions (most being staff with extensive experience, having served as teachers or heads of schools for a number of years) were also involved in conducting refresher and orientation courses for primary school teachers.

After 1980 the structure expanded and became more complex. A planning unit was introduced to the head office, a feature which had been conspicuously absent previously. Most expansion occurred at the regional levels. At independence, for example, the number of regional structures increased from five to six and by 1986 had risen to nine.

The government targeted the rural areas because in the past urban areas had been favoured with better facilities, leaving rural populations poorly served despite the fact that the majority of Zimbabweans lived rurally. The growing number of schools, pupils, and teachers placed enormous strains on the administrative structures, especially after free primary schooling was introduced in September 1980. The government's solution was to increase the structures and accord more work and responsibility to the regional offices so as to attain efficiency. This resulted in greater decentralisation and the streamlining of functions to regions and districts giving them more authority. Although educational administration still fell under various authorities such as the state, local government operating through district councils, mission organisations, and private committees, the community was now more active in the domain of administration and educational development. This was an expression of the policy of conferring on the people the right and power to determine their own affairs as part of a democratic process of self-rule.[2]

District councils were able to draw up their own plans for educational development and adapt appropriate strategies based on need factors. The rationale behind district councils' greater involvement in the development of the districts they administered was that they were better placed to identify priority areas for development and to evolve effective strategies for linking educational plans to economic development. It also enabled them to deal with their own problems and seek solutions to them.

Local communities became increasingly involved in the daily activities and decisions regarding future educational developments. Such community participation in educational administration and development occurred through school committees consisting of elected representatives of parents within a community, teachers, and principals. Despite the greater autonomy enjoyed by both local district councils and communities, all major decisions, policies, and programmes for education had to be approved by the higher levels prior to implementation and most major decisions were still taken at the centre.

An example of greater decentralisation in curriculum development was the creation of subject teams and panels at national, regional, district, and school levels. As many teachers as possible were to be involved in curriculum development, thereby facilitating better communication between the curriculum developers and the implementers, that is, the teachers, on all such matters. A more unified approach to educational administration within the Ministry emerged with the establishment in 1983 of the Curriculum Development Unit from the previously separate Primary and Secondary Education Development Units. As a result, curriculum development became more streamlined.

STAFFING POLICIES AND PATTERNS

RIGHTING THE COLONIAL WRONGS

The new government virtually immediately tackled the issue of racial disparity in the public service by adopting a policy of full black participation in government. A constitutional provision dated May 1980, the Presidential Directive, stipulated the following general policy directions to the Public Service Commission so as to accelerate black advancement:[3]

   (a) to recruit staff to all grades of the Public Service in such a manner as will bring about the balanced representation of the various elements which make up the population of Zimbabwe;

   (b) to give more rapid advancement to suitably qualified Africans in appointments and promotions to senior posts in the Public Service;

   (c) in carrying out these directions, to have due regard to the maintenance of a high state of efficiency within the Public Service and the need to satisfy the career aspirations of the existing Public Servants;

   (d) to make an annual report on progress.[4]

Simultaneously, the government also assured all white officers that it would continue to protect their terms of service and that "the impending expansion of the Service will offer them continuing prospects of satisfying careers".[5] Despite such assurances, there was a large-scale white departure from the service for which the government was prepared.

White employees felt that the infusion of blacks into the civil service would block promotions or result in redundancies. Many therefore opted for early retirement in terms of the Incentive Scheme which provided them with certain inducements if they chose to retire before retirement age. Others entered the private sector where salaries were more competitive and some emigrated, many going to South Africa.[6]

The effects of the Presidential Directive on ethnic staffing patterns in the civil service as a whole were dramatic and rapid (see Table 12.1).

Table 12.1   Black Professionals in the Zimbabwean Civil Service, 1980 – 1983

Year	Total Professional Posts	Black Professionals	Blacks as % of Total
1980	10,570	3,368	32
1981	—	—	63
1983	24,300	20,200	83

Source: Adapted from Moyo 1985:7; Maphosa *et al.* 1985:44

In 1980 all 30 Permanent Secretary posts were held by whites. By July 1981, thirteen blacks (43 per cent) were appointed to this category of post, their number rose to 24 (80 per cent) by 1984. Similar patterns were apparent throughout the senior management, professional and technical officer posts, resulting in a situation whereby most top civil servants and middle-ranking personnel were black by 1985. Already by July

1981, the Presidential Directive was showing an impact on the racial balance of the civil service at higher echelons. By 1982 the racial distribution within the structure was sufficiently balanced for the Public Service Commission to announce in its 1983 end-of-year report that normal recruitment, appointment and promotion procedures to senior posts henceforth would be based solely on merit.

The Directive also served to increase the number of women in professional posts. In 1980 there were 3,246 women in such posts. Of these, only 876 were black (27 per cent). In 1983 the number of women in established posts rose to 10,728 of whom 8,851 (83 per cent) were black. Despite this increase, by 1985 women were still in the minority in established posts within the top echelons of the service.[7]

TRENDS WITHIN THE MINISTRY OF EDUCATION AND
CULTURE DURING THE FIRST YEAR OF INDEPENDENCE

The most important changes in the year of independence entailed the expansion of existing job categories and the creation of new services at the head and regional offices to cope with the growing administrative demands.[8] Although no figures are available for the overall staff totals within the entire education structure at independence, the extent of the staff expansion is seen when comparing staff totals of 8,817 and 18,650 for the years 1975 and 1984/85 respectively.[9] As Table 12.2 shows, the rise in the number of staff at senior levels in both the head and regional offices for the period 1979 – 1986 was not considerable. Expansion within the Ministry as a whole therefore was more at middle- and lower-levels, especially at regional levels.

Notwithstanding the fact that there were not many white departures in 1980, from 1981 onwards, there was a growing tendency towards massive white and minimal black retirement. In 1981 alone, 43 senior whites retired compared with three senior blacks (this figure includes those holding senior posts at the head and regional offices, as well as heads of schools, while teachers were excluded from these figures). It was estimated that in total, only about 20 blacks had left the

Table 12.2 The Number of Senior Staff at the Head and
Regional Offices, Ministry of Education and
Culture, 1979 – 1986

Year	Head Office	Regional Office
1979	21	18
1980	31	25
1981	—	23
1982	26	26
1983	28	26
1984	22	22
1985	29	21
1986	28	21*

* By that year there were nine regional offices.
Source: Secretary for Education, 1980 – 1987

educational administrative structure since independence,
some of them receiving promotion to other sectors. For
example, in 1980 two former black staff from the regions, one
Deputy Regional Director and one Education Officer, were
promoted to the posts of Secretary and Deputy Secretary
respectively in other ministries. The number of white retirements tapered off by 1984, so much so that by 1985 there were
no retirements with only three in 1986.[10]

However, white departures resulted in the drastic decline
in the overall number of whites in the educational structure.
Of the 28 senior posts at head office in 1986, whites occupied
only three, while at the regional level, out of the total of 21
senior staff the number of whites had dropped to three. Out
of the white head office staff total of about 400 in 1980,
roughly ten remained by 1988.[11]

At school level, already by 1980 the lists of white retirements
at senior- and headship-levels were extensive. These only

began to decrease in 1985. Losses to the country's teaching force as a whole were great. In 1982 alone, 500 teachers and heads in government schools retired or resigned, the majority of the whites having opted for early retirement in terms of the Incentive Scheme.[12]

There was also a drain of qualified and experienced black and white teachers (especially black secondary teachers) to other ministries and the commercial and industrial sectors. Since teaching had been one of the few areas available to black professionals during the colonial period, the opening of new opportunities in other sectors was bound to attract staff away from teaching, as well as the more competitive salaries of the private sector.

It was alleged that many whites in the administrative structures held their posts in the colonial education structure on the basis of colour alone rather than qualifications. Many were in fact less qualified than some blacks. Therefore, at independence the professionally more vulnerable whites tended to move out first. Most of those who left came from teaching backgrounds and may not have had any training in administration.

Although those whites who left did so of their own volition rather than having been pushed out of the system, the overall thrust for promotion and personnel development was clearly in line with a policy of affirmative action. This was seen in the process whereby, as existing posts were increased or new ones created, the tendency was to select blacks rather than whites. White departures therefore helped to accelerate the process of recruiting more blacks, as did the government's policy of affirmative action, when it came to filling new posts or vacancies.

PROFESSIONAL STAFF COMPOSITION

Educational administrators within the post-independence structure came predominantly from three sources:

☐ the educational administrators serving within the colonial system;

343

☐ practising Zimbabwean teachers living within the country and graduates of the University of Zimbabwe and universities abroad who had not been exiles; and

☐ Zimbabwean exiles.

Little change was observed among those educational administrators who had served in lower-level posts. As mentioned previously, black Zimbabweans in the old system had predominated at such levels in the public service even though some were highly qualified. At independence they continued to hold these posts. However, as whites began to leave the system, there were many blacks within the structure who qualified for the vacant posts. Most of the blacks who held responsible posts within the old educational structure's head office had trained in education at the University of Zimbabwe. Therefore, some of the old administrators were promoted into these posts. They were an obvious choice because of their familiarity with the daily functioning of the structure, but their promotion was not always automatic.

Party loyalty and political activity were important criteria for senior post selection. In fact, within the first few years of independence, it was alleged that appointments were made according to political ideology rather than on the basis of merit. Generally, all former black administrators from the old system who had not been active in the struggle were initially left in their old posts and did not receive promotion. Only after the changes had begun to stabilise were they moved on to other posts. The majority of lower-level administrative posts were therefore filled by those who had served within the old structure. On the whole, very few blacks left the Ministry. Those who did claimed that they did not receive promotion because they were allegedly lacking in party loyalty despite working well.[13]

Candidates for middle-, higher-level and decision-making posts came from among Zimbabweans serving outside the educational administrative structure. They had often participated actively in the struggle both within the country and from abroad. Black Zimbabweans moving into high positions in government were usually university educated. The first and largest choice for high-level posts was made from among politically active Zimbabweans living in the country. These 'domestic' administrators were selected from among principals and teachers at teacher training colleges. One author asserts that nearly half of the promotion appointments to the post of Education Officer were made from among lecturers at teacher training colleges.[14] This obviously affected the quality of the Zimbabwean teacher training programme. Virtually all the 'domestic' administrators had an educational background.

Zimbabwean exiles were the next group considered for educational administration posts. Qualifications and experience were the major criteria. The exiles comprised people in the educational field and those with other higher qualifications.[15]

Concerning the employment of new recruits from outside the public service, a strategy was adopted whereby ministers or ministries with senior vacancies to fill had to inform the Public Service Commission of these vacancies. They had to furnish the name of the candidate whom they wanted to interview for the post. The Commission then conducted the interview and informed the ministry of the candidate's suitability. Thereafter, the Commission would submit its recommendation to the Prime Minister for approval if the appointment was for an Assistant Secretary or equivalent or higher posting.

Alternatively, the Commission also kept records of candidates who had responded to advertisements it had placed in prominent international journals and newspapers, appealing to Zimbabweans to return home and help reconstruct the country. At least 18,000 people responded.[16] After having interviewed the selected applicants, the Commission then referred them to various ministers for comments. Hence ministries with vacancies could either approach the Commission with a nomination, or they could select one of the candidates referred to them by the Commission. Whatever the process, all candidates had to undergo appraisal by the

Public Service Commission in addition to the ministry where they were to work, while those recommended for more senior positions also had to have the Prime Minister's approval.

A positive feature of the Ministry's selection process in general after independence was its emphasis that most staff employed within its administration be drawn from an educational background. Only in departments which did not specifically require educationists, namely, Administration and Finance, were other professionals selected. These included statisticians, accountants, and so forth. Within the old structure this had not always been the case, especially at regional levels where it was alleged that the District Commissioners who were involved with school administration did not necessarily come from education backgrounds.[17]

THE TEACHING FORCE: SOURCE OF NEW CIVIL SERVANTS

The trend in most developing countries at independence showed a heavy dependence on the services of former teachers or people with teaching qualifications to staff other sectors. Zimbabwe proved no different. Since independence, "many new civil servants have been appointed from among the rank and file of the teachers".[18] The overall impact of this departure of teachers to other sectors is difficult to assess. Already in 1980, the education system was suffering from shortages of trained primary and secondary teachers. The situation was further exacerbated by the increased enrolment of pupils at both primary and secondary levels as of 1980, which, in turn, resulted in primary school and untrained teachers being recruited into the new secondary schools, while unemployed school leavers provided a major source of recruitment for primary schools. As a result, there was a rise in the proportion of underqualified and untrained teachers, the former comprising 25 per cent (8,000) of the 1980 teacher totals compared with three per cent (500) in 1979.[19] This highlighted the need for even more trained teachers. Moreover, the output of locally trained teachers in 1982 proved inadequate to meet these needs.

The government addressed the problem of teacher short-ages almost immediately by employing teachers from the United Kingdom, Canada, Australia, Mauritius, and Scandinavian countries, especially in the fields of mathematics and science for rural secondary schools. Between independence and late 1982, nearly 700 secondary teachers had been recruited from abroad. Even though a large proportion of these teachers had previous experience, a fair number had not. Yet it was reported that they were making a satisfactory contribution to education in Zimbabwe. Overseas teachers were twice as expensive as local teachers, but the Zimbabwean Government paid them according to its local salary scales, while the donor countries supplemented their salaries.[20]

Teacher training was expanded. The Zimbabwe Integrated Teacher Education Course (ZINTEC), introduced in January 1981, aimed at providing over 2,000 primary teachers a year. The ZINTEC training was four years long with emphasis on learning on-the-job. Students therefore spent at least two years of their training period actually engaged in practical teaching. During the entire four-year period they received a salary. The programme was very cost-effective, while it also served to release more semi-qualified teachers to the rural schools which were poorly staffed. During the period of practical teaching, trainees continued their studies by distance education coupled with field supervision by tutors and attendance at district and regional seminars. Enrolments at teacher training colleges (excluding ZINTEC colleges) also increased considerably from 2,249 in 1979 to 4,376 in 1983 for primary-level training, and 338 in 1979 to 2,505 in 1983 for secondary school teachers.[21]

EXPATRIATE POLICY

Zimbabwean policy towards expatriates was extremely cautious compared with other Sub-Saharan countries where, in the 1960s, over three-quarters of the cadre of trained human resources were foreigners dominating the senior executive and technical jobs in government so that by 1980 "some post-independent African countries had ... more expatriates than they had four years after independence".[22] The Zimbabwean Government viewed expatriate employment as an 'unfortunate' short-term solution. Foreigners were therefore carefully selected according to their qualifications and experience in order to fulfil clearly defined needs as well as to transfer skills to Zimbabwean counterparts as part of their contracts. The government stipulated that the roles of recruited foreign experts were not to be executive but advisory. Strict control was therefore maintained over foreign personnel recruitment by the Inter-Ministerial Manpower Planning Committee on Foreign Recruitment which was situated within the Ministry of Manpower Planning and Development.

The Ministry of Education and Culture was especially particular with regard to foreign recruitment within its administrative structures. No expatriates were permitted to serve in administrative or decision-making posts within the Ministry. The few that were there merely fulfilled an advisory function and even this was on a short-term basis. This policy was strictly adhered to despite the reported shortages of trained people in the Ministry even by the late 1980s. Zimbabwe therefore avoided the undesirable situation of having foreigners in prominent posts and playing a role in policy formulation. This practice remained essentially a prerogative of Zimbabweans.

The attitude towards expatriate teachers was more flexible, although they were not permitted to be heads of departments or principals. Expatriates were also permitted to take up posts as university lecturers and research associates.

Expatriate teachers (396) and those in university posts (seventeen) made up 45 per cent of the 914 expatriate workers in professional, technical and related workers' posts in 1982.[23] They constituted the largest group of foreigners in this category. The number of foreign teachers, however, had drastically declined by 1985 to 185 (14 per cent of the overall expatriate total of 1,307).[24] This was because of the increased supply of trained teachers from local institutions and the combined use of untrained teachers and ZINTEC trainees in schools. The number of those in university teaching and research posts rose to 129 by 1985.[25]

THE OUTCOME OF CHANGE

The government, being aware of the likelihood of a massive white departure from the public service due to its affirmative action policies, devised a scheme to cushion the effects of such an exodus on its administrative service. In 1980 it set aside one million Zimbabwean Dollars to create additional/parallel posts at various levels in the service where there were no vacancies in some of the key established posts. These were the so-called Presidential Directive (PD) posts which were to be filled by blacks. The occupants of such posts would then closely observe the work of the person holding the specific post, normally a white, and as soon as the incumbent vacated the post, the PD staff member would take over, the PD post becoming obsolete. This scheme aimed at blending experienced staff at senior and middle levels with new recruits who were unfamiliar with its procedures.

PD posts did not exist for long since whites left fairly quickly. Only 100,000 Zimbabwean Dollars of the total amount set aside for this scheme were actually used and it did not result in the displacement of any serving officers.[26] Within the Ministry of Education and Culture, PD post holders, once they were familiar with the procedures and even before the departure of their white counterparts, began to exercise more power.[27]

The inflow of new black staff into the public service as a whole at all levels was not without drawbacks. Many of the newcomers, though academically well-qualified (in some cases more so than the whites they were replacing), lacked the concomitant administrative experience and training.[28] Bearing in mind that "a government's effectiveness and efficient performance depends on the existence of a pool of experienced public servants", the lack thereof meant that it could suffer serious setbacks in terms of efficient performance and continuity.[29]

Although most replacements for vacant white posts in the Ministry of Education and Culture's head office came from blacks within the Ministry itself (the majority of people within the Ministry consisting of those drawn from inside), many senior, decision-making posts were occupied by Zimbabweans from abroad who were not familiar with the daily functioning of the structure. They therefore took time to adapt.

With these short-comings in mind, the Public Service Commission in 1982 set about examining the performance of all officers appointed under the Presidential Directive who had been serving for a year, in order to establish whether they were settled and suited to their jobs and to make the necessary adjustments if this were not the case. Since thousands had been appointed to the public service, it was possible for misallocations to have occurred, as well as under- and over-grading. In total, this checking system resulted in no more than ten to fifteen people being downgraded or asked to leave.[30]

Blacks who were promoted from within the system, despite their familiarity with the procedures, lacked the concomitant experience needed for management and decision-making posts. This was due to the former practice of deliberately keeping blacks out of such posts. As one author explains, "the newly appointed black educational administrators recruited from the rank and file of teachers and college lecturers, were inexperienced in translating policy for purposes of implementation in schools".[31]

Even black principals had no experience in taking independent decisions or of being innovative. They were used to carrying out instructions and directives from school superintendents. These had come in the form of circulars. At independence, expected reforms were announced at political rallies by politicians and reached some teachers via television and radio. It was up to them to try to translate these policies at school level.

The initial preference shown in the selection process by the Ministry of Education and Culture towards those with a sound political ideology and those who had been activists proved detrimental to the system's efficiency. By the mid-1980s, certain individuals were not coping.[32] As a result, the concept of merit gradually came more into play rather than 'sound' political ideology. The structure took some years to recover lost ground because of all these factors, but by the latter part of the decade the problems had generally been overcome.

As far as the meshing of the different groups of educational administrators was concerned, this was not without difficulties. There was no problem between Zimbabwean blacks who had lived outside the country and those living within it. But there was resentment from the old group of administrators who felt that many people who were juniors and lacking experience were getting promotion. Political ideology aside, there was also bound to be a clash of ideas and approaches between these two groups.[33]

On an ethnic level, during the first two years of independence, relationships between blacks and whites at all levels within the public service were characterised by tension and mutual suspicion. In fact, the departure of some whites was directly attributed to "the aggressive and vengeance-seeking attitudes of some black civil servants...."[34]

Many former white civil servants were inculcated with strong racist and political attitudes diametrically opposed to the new government's policies. The hard-liners of this group were among the first to leave the service. Those who did not leave immediately, but whose attitudes were unreconstructed, had the potential to obstruct changes in their bid to maintain the former status quo. Within the Ministry of Education and Culture, this problem was overcome by no longer involving whites in policy making. Instead, they were left more routine work where they could not cause major obstructions. This too was an incentive for whites to leave, especially those who had formerly occupied responsible posts. These tendencies, together with the concept of PD posts, resulted in the phasing out of whites.

Whites who were considered to be doing a good job were encouraged to stay on. As we have seen above, however, their number was few. By 1983 there were only 5,000 whites within the entire public service structure. They served the government loyally, while many in top echelon posts stayed on until suitable replacements had been found.[35]

STAFF TRAINING

THE NEED TO TRAIN

After independence, the government changed from a regulatory law and order role to a development-oriented one. As a result the public service, being the major instrument used to translate government policy, was bound to have to undergo reorientation. Its new role was not only to ensure continuity of service provision but also to implement changes in line with the government's new policies. Such changes were evident in the expansion of the overall system and its restructuring. These trends were manifested in the moves towards decentralisation, the development of local authorities, the creation of more unified administrative structures, and the co-ordination of the activities of central government ministries and local authorities at different levels. Such alterations resulted, as was shown with the Ministry of Education and Culture, in an expansion of the structure as a result of the parallel increase in the volume of services and their extension to new areas, as well as the accompanying growth of staff.

The public service staff constituted the most vital elements in the smooth functioning of the system as a whole and the implementation of changes. For these functions to be carried out effectively, it was necessary to have an increase in well-trained, efficient and disciplined civil servants. At independence, however, there were two major problems regarding the public service's staff. The high turnover of skilled civil servants leaving the system at all levels shortly after independence to join the private sector deprived it of an important group characterised by experience and expertise. Despite this loss being accompanied by replacements and rapid growth in overall staff totals, the situation was not one of simply replacing departing staff to ensure continuity and the filling of new posts, as the structures expanded, with well-educated replacements.

As mentioned, many of the newcomers, though academically well-qualified, lacked administrative experience and training. Additionally, the old staff who remained on required reorientation to familiarise them with the government's new objectives. The situation therefore was one in which the new role of government and the expansion of the service increased the need for training that would equip staff with skills in the art and practice of management, as well as orienting them to the ideological perspective of the new government. Additionally, adequate training was another alternative to the expense of employing expatriates.

THE TYPES OF TRAINING OFFERED

The immediate post-independence period was characterised by earnest governmental efforts in the sphere of public service staff training programmes. These aimed not only at equipping personnel with administrative skills but also at imbuing both the old and new civil servants with the government's socialist ideology. The first of such training programmes, which was for Permanent Secretaries, took place in 1980. The structure assigned to oversee such training of an in-service nature was the Ministry of Public Service through its Training and Management Bureau (TMB) which was created at independence. The Ministry of Public Service was responsible for all human resource matters pertaining to the public service. The TMB had two units responsible for training, namely, the Rural Development Training Branch and the Administrative and Management Training Branch.

Three specific types of training existed in the post-independence period:

☐ specialised technical and professional training;
☐ rural development-oriented training;
☐ administrative and managerial training.

Although the first type of training was not necessarily government-run, the latter two fell directly within the orbit of the TMB's two units, the Rural Development Training Branch and the Administration and Management Training Branch. Many of the courses offered by the TMB were compulsory for promotion and advancement.

Specialised technical and professional training

Such training was normally of the pre-service variety, provided through various professional and vocational institutions run by the different ministries and the University of Zimbabwe, as was the case prior to 1980. Ministries with large volumes of training included Education, Agriculture, and Health. The Ministry of Education and Culture, for example, ran eleven primary and three secondary teacher training colleges. At university-level, in addition to the existing education courses, the Faculty of Education in 1982 introduced a Masters degree in educational administration and in 1985 a B Ed degree and diploma in this subject.

The Masters degree was designed to meet the needs of those working in the educational system at all levels, especially teachers, heads, lecturers at teacher training colleges, inspectors, administrators, graduates involved in adult education, and those aspiring to such posts. A few of the Ministry of Education and Culture's top-level staff were sent to the local university for further studies, presumably in areas such as educational administration.

A large proportion of specialised technical and professional training also occurred as in-service training run by individual ministries. In 1984, for example, there were training programmes for Education Officers, District Education Officers, and Heads of District Council schools. Officials of local government and town planning responsible for education also attended training programmes which aimed to:

> ◻ increase understanding of and respect for the roles played by the Ministry of Education and Ministry of local government and Town Planning in the running of District Council Schools;

☐ find ways and means of simplifying the administrative systems and routines with a view to making
them more efficient.[36]

The courses were geared towards staff at head office as well
as those at regional and provincial levels, and at district levels
where principals and District Council officials participated.
Professionals from head office were sent to run education-
specific courses in the regions as well.

Another example of training organised by the Ministry of
Education and Culture was that provided to middle- and
upper-level administrative staff, most of whom were already
university-educated. This training took the form of short-term
observational visits abroad and occurred on a large scale.
Training of this sort appears to have been one of the new
trends to emerge in the in-service training after 1980.

Rural development-oriented training

In 1981 the TMB established its Rural Development Training
Branch to develop and deliver in-service rural development-
oriented training programmes in common core areas for all
public servants involved in rural development. Its activities
were conducted at the Domboshawa National Training
Centre (which existed before independence), four provincial
training centres, and two district centres. The target group
was estimated to be between 7 – 8,000.[37] One of the four
certificate courses offered at Domboshawa was the twelve-
month course in local government for executive officers from
district councils. Generally speaking, both Domboshawa and
the provincial centres were for lower-level administrators.

Administrative and managerial training

The TMB's Administrative and Management Training
Branch ran courses and seminars for middle- and senior-level
managers in government as well as regular courses for lower-
level staff. The training covered areas such as general administration, personnel and financial administration, and
supervision and management. Since these skills were com-

mon to all the ministries, the latter tended to rely heavily on the TMB to provide such generalised administrative training rather than providing it themselves. Such training occurred at two locations each of which catered to a different category of staff.

These training centres consisted of a small unit of the TMB's head office and the Highlands' Public Service Training Centre near Harare. The unit at head office, for example, mounted short courses and workshops for middle and senior managers in government. Between 1981 and 1984, 1,255 people participated in such workshops. Highlands was the only training centre specialising in civil service administration training for lower-level public servants. The size of the target groups for administrative and management training for staff from all levels was high, in 1985 totalling 4,938.[38]

From 1981 the then Federal Republic of Germany, through the German Foundation for International Development (DSE), played an important role in participating in and organising workshops and seminars for middle- and senior-level management officials within the public service. In 1982 an agreement was reached whereby the DSE, through its Public Administration Promotion Centre (ZOV), was to assist with the advanced training of all middle-level management officials of Zimbabwe's ministerial administration. This formed part of the Zimbabwean Government's ambition to expose all its senior officials to training geared towards meeting the requirements of the country's future development tasks.

The outcome of these arrangements was the organisation by the TMB of a series of two week-long workshops from September 1982 through to March 1983 for assistant secretaries and chief executive officers from all the ministries. In total, 241 officials attended the workshops where they were familiarised with modern administration procedures; management methods; techniques of decision-making and problem solving; and the administrative structures needed for the planning and implementation of government policies, "as well as with the principles and framework conditions required for taking administrative action in accordance with the legal standards and political decisions taken by the government".[39] The training was conducted by a combination of high-ranking Zimbabwean administrative officials and lecturers from the local university, as well as by two German administration experts.

Zimbabwe Institute of Public Administration and Management (ZIPAM)

Founded in 1983, this institute's first training activities commenced in 1985/86. It was hoped that ZIPAM would provide a more regular short-term management training programme, in addition to the TMB's training in public administration and management, which was mostly of a crash-course nature with no regular management training programme. The need for this was particularly great in view of the appointment of academically well-qualified but inexperienced newcomers to management posts in the public service. It has four divisions, namely: Local Government Studies, Financial Management, Development Planning and Management, and Development Administration and Management.

ZIPAM's target group was 2,000 middle- and senior-level public servants from ministries, parastatals, urban and rural authorities whom it was to equip "with management skills, attitudes and knowledge that enable them to be efficient and effective in performing their tasks".[40] This group included Permanent and Deputy Secretaries as well as Under and Assistant Secretaries. ZIPAM has also run courses in auditing for groups of people below their usual target group simply because this was not offered elsewhere. Its trainers were mostly locals who came from the various ministries, since its policy was not to use expatriate trainers even though difficulties were experienced in recruiting professional staff.

A CRITIQUE OF TRAINING

ZIPAM's courses were felt not to have had an impact according to two senior-placed interviewees, one of whom had attended one of the courses offered. Although satisfactory for middle-level staff, the training lacked intellectual depth and know-how appropriate to more senior staff. Its personnel were said to be too few and inexperienced and reference was made to constraints in its finances and training facilities. The institute was said to be lacking the 'correct' ideological orientation.[41] Since ZIPAM's training was of a general administrative nature, it is not surprising that those involved in a specific area such as educational administration might find its courses limited in scope, especially the more senior-level staff.

As far as the combined DSE/TMB training programmes were concerned, the reports were encouraging. In addition to familiarising the participants with the development policy objectives of the government of Zimbabwe and the administrative structures and procedures required for the implementation of these objectives, information was, above all, provided on the functional conditions on which the efficiency of an administration depends. The participants gained a better understanding of the importance of formalised working processes. At the same time they were given a better insight into those forms of decentralisation which ensure that the administration system is as citizen-oriented as possible.

Starting in 1980, within a space of four months, virtually all the government's senior officers, who totalled over 200, had participated in short-term training programmes, including the Prime Minister. This was in accordance with the government's firm conviction that reorientation and training should start with the senior government personnel, especially in view of the unique problems of transition in Zimbabwe and its mix of white and black officers. In short, this was to be a top-down training process. An external evaluation of this series of advanced training programmes reported that the participants, "many of whom had never attended such programmes, were overwhelmingly positive about their training experience".[42] A less favourable review came from the 1985 joint SIDA/TMB report on Public Service training, which revealed that administrative and management training for middle- and top-level personnel in general was weak.[43]

Interviews conducted within the Ministry of Education and Culture regarding administrative training programmes in general did not reveal positive reports. Such training was said to be not very effective and only of use to personnel with basic qualifications who merely needed a refresher course. Moreover, very little of what was learnt at the workshops was actually implemented. It was alleged that even competent staff who were not in need of training were included in training programmes, resulting in a waste of man-hours and money. The tendency was that workshops were used to reward people who were thought to be good at their jobs and hence did not address themselves to staff who were in need of training. Furthermore, workshop organisation was said to be poor and recipients did not participate in the process of deciding their actual needs. This highlighted a failure to identify true needs and the selection of staff who were in need of training. 'Good ideas' rather than careful needs' analysis prevailed when it came to the selection of the type of courses to be offered for staff training.

Although training was to have a dual function, providing both administrative and management training and an ideological orientation, there were never any 're-education' programmes. One reason was that the prolonged liberation struggle had so heightened political consciousness and activism that most people were familiar with the new government's programmes.

Another problem related to training was the lack of trainers. At Highlands, for example, there were only nineteen trainers in post out of an establishment of 28. In fact, lack of staff was said to be the TMB's main constraint. This placed a limit on the TMB's ability to expand training which was needed to cope with the backlog of candidates due to the rapid expansion of the service, in addition to the high turnover rate. The situation, in turn, highlighted the need to train officer cadres.

CONCLUSION

Two important features stand out in terms of post-independence trends in the Zimbabwean Ministry of Education and Culture: firstly, the speedy process of affirmative action and staff increases following independence; and secondly, the rapid expansion of the administrative structure, especially at regional levels. The latter came about as a result of the need to redress the imbalances of the colonial education system. The former policy was realised because Zimbabwe was fortunate in having a large pool of educated people. This meant that it could confidently adopt a policy of affirmative action without the threat of a collapse to its administrative structures. It had the capacity to fill empty posts left by departing whites, as well as those which were newly created as a result of the need to expand the public service.

The problems of meshing the old and new groups of administrators within the structure turned out to be minimal. Most whites left the educational administrative structures, yet the few who remained proved themselves on the whole to be loyal and good workers.

The fact that the government was able successfully to achieve some of its post-independence goals, the massive expansion of educational provision being the most impressive, was in itself proof that the administrative structure was competent to cope with the new demands. The Public Service Commission's system of checking on the newly appointed recruits to the service's vacant and newly created posts helped to ensure staff suitability which in turn facilitated the smooth running of the system overall. Administrative training for staff at all levels was widely acclaimed in the initial stages by external evaluation reports but, judging from the opinions of the various interviewees in the late 1980s and an official 1985 report, it appeared to be in need of much attention if it were to obtain the desired results. The numerical strength and suitability of trainers are important issues which need to be addressed, in addition to a serious review of staff needs and the adaptation of training to such needs.

It is important to relate all the Zimbabwean experience to the changes currently occurring in Namibia. Bearing in mind some of the differences between the two countries and how these play a role in defining certain options available to Namibia in its post-independence period, Zimbabwe's successes and shortcomings can provide a guideline of sorts as to how Namibia could proceed in its attempt to respond to its new educational challenges.

NOTES

1. In total there were 56 Districts in the six regions. The arm of the central government at this level was the district council which fell under the Ministry of Local Government, Urban and Rural Development. After 1980, the role of local government had become more prominent, especially in the rural areas. Each district council had an education department which was the policy-making organ determining the pattern of educational development, organisation, and administration. All this occurred under the supervision of the District Administrator who was appointed by the central government to monitor council affairs. This person was the link between local and central government. The District Administrator was the district council's chief executive officer and was assisted by the council's Education Executive Officer in co-ordinating and implementing all development programmes including education.

2. Zvobgo 1987:335.

3. The Public Service Commission was responsible for regulating and controlling the general organisation of the public service, administrative and managerial training, as well as rural development-oriented training.

4. Cameron *et al* 1980, Appendix A.

5. Mawande 1983:297, quoting the Presidential Directive of 22 May 1980:297.

6. One interviewee claims that the private sector actually created jobs for whites moving from the public service, while another author states that it became the *laager* for whites (Interview, Director of the Zimbabwe Institute of Development Studies, 1/09/1988; Murapa 1984:73).

7. *ibid.*, 73; Moyo 1985:9.

8. Between 1981 and 1984 the public service as a whole expanded by 50 per cent. The greatest expansion occurred in the education and health sectors. In 1985 these represented about 60 per cent of the total number of established/professional posts and 40 per cent of the overall number of public service posts. (The fiscal provision for education represented 14.4 per cent of the total national budget of 1981/82, making it the largest single item of government expenditure. This pattern was evident in 1988, making Zimbabwe's expenditure on education among the highest in the world at 22 per cent of its national budget). The overall number of black employees in the public service as a whole increased from 29,538 in 1980 to 51,635 by 1982 (Maphosa *et al* 1985:(i), 44; Mawande 1983:301; Seminar on Education in Zimbabwe, 27 August – 7 September 1981:8; Interview, Secretary for Primary and Secondary Education, Zimbabwe MOEC, 8/09/1988; World Bank 1990:198).

9. United Nations Development Programme 1980:240; Maphosa *et al.* 1985:4.

10. Secretary for Education 1983; 1984; 1985; 1986; 1987.

11. Interviews, Deputy Secretary for Policy and Planning, Higher Education, Zimbabwe MOEC, 6/09/1988; Secretary for Education 1987:37, 38.

12. Secretary for Education 1980; 1982; 1983; 1984; 1985; 1986; 1987.

13. Interviews, Deputy Secretary for Higher Institutions, Zimbabwe MOEC, 8/09/1988; Deputy Secretary for Finance and Administration, Higher Education, Zimbabwe MOEC, 6/09/1988; Deputy Secretary for Policy and Planning, Higher Education, Zimbabwe MOEC, 6/09/1988.

14. Zvobgo 1986:84, 105.

15. Regarding Zimbabweans trained abroad, those with Western qualifications were preferred over those who had trained in East-bloc countries. No Zimbabweans, it was claimed, had trained in educational fields in the East-bloc countries. The majority of the new black civil servants allegedly had been educated in schools and universities in the United Kingdom, the United States, and other Western countries (Director of the Zimbabwe Institute of Development Studies, 1/09/1988; Director of the Zimbabwe Institute of Public Administration and Management, 5/09/1988; Deputy Secretary for Policy and Planning, Higher Education, Zimbabwe MOEC, 6/09/1988; Murapa 1983:204).

16. Mawande 1983:299, 300.

17. Interviews, Secretary for Primary and Secondary Education, Zimbabwe MOEC, 8/09/1988; Deputy Secretary for Higher Institutions, Zimbabwe MOEC, 8/09/1988; Deputy Secretary for Finance and Administration, Higher Education, Zimbabwe MOEC, 6/09/1988.

18. Mumbengegwi 1981:36.

19. Faruqee 1981:38; Maravanyika 1986:206; 207.

20. Robinson and Shortlidge 1980:7; Secretary for Education 1984:8; Zvobgo 1986:75.

21. Government of Zimbabwe 1984:12, 16; Ministry of Labour, Manpower Planning and Social Welfare 1985:51; Secretary for Education 1984:6.

22. Government of Zimbabwe Manpower Information Services Volume 2, No. 3, October 1982:2.

23. Central Statistical Office 1985:49.

24. The Annual Review of Manpower lists the number of approved expatriate personnel serving as secondary school teachers in 1984 as totalling 248. Yet the Annual Report of the Secretary for Education for that year stated that "there were 1,333 expatriate teachers serving in both government and aided schools — almost entirely in the secondary sector". This discrepancy could have arisen simply because

not all teachers employed were actually approved (Ministry of Labour, Manpower Planning and Social Welfare, 1985:33; Secretary for Education 191985:9).

25. Ministry of Labour, Manpower Planning and Social Welfare 1985:33.

26. Murapa 1984:77; Mawande 1983:298.

27. As more blacks began to occupy higher-level posts, greater trust was shown towards their subordinates, whereas in the old system there had been a reluctance to delegate tasks. This helped to improve efficiency (Interview, Deputy Secretary for Finance and Administration, Higher Education, Zimbabwe MOEC, 6/09/1988).

28. At independence, most exiled intellectuals and researchers returned to Zimbabwe to take up government jobs. Many academics too ended their careers in universities to go to state employment (Raftopoulos 1988:5, 7).

29. Murapa 1984:77.
    There were reports that new staff applying for jobs within the Ministry of Education and Culture, who had previously worked within the refugee camps and who were therefore experienced but who did not necessarily have advanced degrees and diplomas, might have been overlooked in favour of those who did. This reveals the potential competition between Zimbabweans with experience abroad and those without such experience. One source alleged that though ex-combatants, for example, were not given special entry into the Ministry, a certain number of places were set aside for them (Seminar on Education in Zimbabwe: Past, Present and Future, University of Zimbabwe, 27 August – 7 September 1981:33; Interview, Minister for Primary and Secondary Education, Zimbabwe MOEC, 8/09/1988).

30. Mawande 1983:303.

31. Maravanyika 1986:207.

32. Interview, Deputy Secretary for Policy and Planning, Higher Education, Zimbabwe MOEC, 6/09/1988.

33. This is a common problem among people trained abroad who return to jobs in their country of origin with new insights and skills which are difficult to apply in the job setting where old methods prevail (see Chapter 2).

34. Murapa 1984:77.

35. Mawande 1983:301.

36. Secretary for Education 1985:25.

37. The government planned on eventually establishing a total of 30 district training centres which, unlike the provincial centres, were not only to be open to public servants but the general public as well. All of the TMB training facilities were available for use by the various ministries for their own specialist in-service training programmes.

38. Maphosa *et al.* 1985:25, 51, Appendix 12.

39. German Foundation for International Development 1983:3 – 5.

40. ZIPAM undated:3, 4.
41. Interviews, Deputy Secretary for Higher Institutions, Zimbabwe MOEC, 8/09/1988; Deputy Secretary for Finance and Administration, Higher Education, Zimbabwe MOEC, 6/09/1988; Deputy Secretary for Policy and Planning, Higher Education, Zimbabwe MOEC, 6/09/1988; Maphosa *et al* 1985:51.
42. Paul 1983:28.
43. Maphosa *et al* 1985:55.

Namibia: assessments and post-independence developments

13

Administration in Namibia: where to now?

The fact that many attempts to achieve
ideals have failed does not vitiate either the ideals
or the desire to achieve them. What is needed are
better ways of getting there.
R.S. ADAMS,1983

INTRODUCTION AND RATIONALE

Educational administration *per se* is a field of study which has
only recently begun to command attention in the international arena. In Namibia, as in most African countries, the
training of prospective educational administrators and those
in service has been neglected. Although it is not surprising
that there has been no serious attempt to examine this important aspect of the country's educational system, the absence of knowledge about educational administration in
Namibia is disturbing, in view of the central role administration plays in the process of educational continuity and innovation.

Furthermore, colonial Namibia's educational administrative structure exhibited certain tendencies that put in doubt
its ability to provide such continuity and change at independence. Most obvious was the predominance of whites in
virtually all the educational administrative structures. If there
had been a massive white exodus as had occurred in Zimbabwe, then the whole functioning of the system would have
been threatened. The relatively small number of highly educated blacks and coloureds and the deliberate barring of
these groups from access to the decision-making levels raised

doubts as to their capacity to replace departing whites. Although the country had recourse to Namibians trained and living abroad, it was not certain whether there were sufficient with educational administrative experience and training to fill the gap caused by a large white departure. This section:

☐ summarises the major findings of the research and discusses the implications for an independent Namibia;

☐ evaluates the Zimbabwean post-independence strategies in terms of how practical their application might be for Namibia;

☐ examines the trends in Namibia's civil service immediately prior to independence;

☐ describes the changes which have come about in educational administration after independence; and

☐ makes proposals for future action regarding Namibia's educational administration.

RESEARCH FINDINGS

EDUCATIONAL ADMINISTRATION IN NAMIBIA

During the period of German occupation, the country's relatively small indigenous population received schooling that differed from that of the small white settler community. The colonial government's role in education was limited to the white population, the missionaries having total control over coloured and black education. This was in marked contrast to the active role played by the colonial government of German East Africa in the education of the indigenous population. The latter also had access to administrative posts within the government, unlike the local peoples in SWA who were only allowed to serve in menial jobs within such structures.

This pattern of differentiation in educational provision between whites and the blacks and coloureds characterised the entire period of colonial occupation by Germany and South Africa. A marked difference between the German and South African occupations was that South Africa played a greater role in black and coloured education through the

Department of Education in Windhoek, while retaining the missions' services as educational providers. During the late 1950s, a separate branch of administration for black education was established within the Department of Education in Windhoek, white and coloured education being administered together. From this period onwards, the missions' role in education was gradually reduced.

The 1960s saw the onset of vital changes in administrative control. This was the period when separate educational administration for all three ethnic groups was realised. In addition to separating the administration of education, control was shifted to three ethnically-defined administrative bodies in South Africa, all of which had separate regional offices in Namibia. Educational administration was made yet more complex by the creation during the early 1970s of separate ethnic 'homelands', each responsible for administering its own education system. These authorities had little capacity to act independently, and major decisions concerning education still emanated from South Africa via its Department of Education and Training (for blacks), the Department of Coloured Affairs and the Department of Education (for whites) through their respective Windhoek-based offices.

During 1979 an attempt was made to amalgamate the three regional offices into one structure. The intention was to shift control of education from South Africa to Windhoek in line with South Africa's overall aim of creating an 'independent' government in Namibia. As a result the Directorate of National Education came into being that year.

By 1980 the Directorate of National Education was converted into the Department of National Education (DNE). The establishment that same year of ten so-called representative authorities out of the country's eleven ethnically-defined groups resulted in each of these authorities creating its own Directorate of Education and Culture. This meant that the country had ten ethnically run educational administrations as well as the centrally run DNE. The latter continued to remain heavily reliant on educational bodies in South Africa and policy still emanated from there. In turn, the ethnic Directorates of Education and Culture, other than that of the whites, sought much assistance from the Department of National Education which, among other things, provided professional services to them at primary and secondary school level on request. In reality, very little had changed and South Africa still enjoyed the final say in the more fundamental issues of education.

EDUCATIONAL ADMINISTRATORS

The inequitable educational provision among the country's three main ethnic groups had extremely detrimental results for the skilled human resource output. Most skills were concentrated among the minority whites who were insufficient to satisfy all the sectors' professional needs. White South Africans were imported into Namibia to fill the gaps. Moreover, the few coloureds and blacks who possessed requisite skills were deliberately barred from appropriate positions of responsibility within the South African controlled, white-run administrative structures. Most highly educated blacks and coloureds were therefore confined to the teaching profession, nursing or the religious ministry.

By the 1980s, teachers constituted the largest group of educated blacks and coloureds. The majority of black teachers, however, were under- or unqualified. In secondary schools the situation was particularly acute. There were not enough teachers to cope with the demands of the growing school population. These realities were alarming especially in view of the likelihood of massive expansion in schooling provision after independence. Furthermore, as new job opportunities opened to educated blacks and coloureds in the post-independence period, there was the possibility that teachers would be lured away from their former professions. The poorer the level of black teachers' qualifications, the shallower the pool of potential educational administrators.

As a result of the discrimination practised against coloureds and blacks in terms of educational provision and job opportunities, whites enjoyed a monopoly over all the middle- and top-level posts in the educational administrative structures. It was during the 1970s, however, that a slight variation in this pattern came about. As a result of the policy of creating ethnic 'homelands' throughout the 1970s, blacks and coloureds gained a greater measure of representation within their own ethnic administrative structures. Coloureds in particular began to enjoy more upward mobility, even outside their own ethnic administrations. However, even within the 'homeland' educational administrations, whites held most of the decision-making positions. Furthermore, the majority of the middle- and high-ranking posts within the country's educational structures were occupied by South Africans seconded to Namibia. This process continued well into the following decade.

Within the DNE, ethnically determined staffing patterns persisted throughout the 1980s. White Afrikaner males, many of whom were South Africans, dominated the top rungs of the structure as well as most of the professional posts. Only a small number of coloureds and even fewer blacks filled professional posts. Professional blacks were mostly confined to inspectorate roles or they served as subject advisors for African languages or as African language assistants. Generally speaking, the majority of coloureds and blacks were allocated the jobs of typists, clerks, messengers, workspersons, and cleaners. Further discrimination was evidenced in the ranking of women within the DNE. Where women did have access to professional posts, they tended mostly to be white.

Similar trends were evident within the ten ethnic Directorates of Education and Culture where white males continued to monopolise the top-level posts during the 1980s. The only exception to this pattern was the Owambo Directorate of Education and Culture. It boasted an all-black top- and middle-level structure in which whites were confined to the clerical posts. The best black and white mix within these directorates occurred among the inspectors and subject advisors. Women were virtually absent from professional posts within these structures. The Coloured and Rehoboth Government's Directorates also enjoyed better representation of their own groups among the professional and top-level categories, though it was alleged that many coloureds were South Africans rather than Namibians. Generally speaking, the 1980s were marked by a greater representation of black professionals within ethnic educational structures than had been the case in the late 1970s.

Despite these improvements, some alarming factors concerning the staff could not be ignored. Even within the DNE, reference was made in the annual report of 1988 to the serious shortage of staff. This situation was especially severe within the black ethnic directorates where serving educational administrative staff lacked the qualifications and experience necessary for effective work. For example, many inspectors and subject advisers (except possibly in the White Directorate) were not trained to perform those functions properly. Such obstacles prevented most of the ethnic structures from developing the complexity needed to control their education systems fully, autonomously and, above all, efficiently.

The use of training to compensate for these problems seems to have been much neglected. Although the Central Personnel Institute (CPI) ran short administrative training courses for lower-level staff and some middle-level staff at the DNE and the directorates, these were not specific to educational administration. The DNE did not subject its own head office staff to regular administrative training. (DNE training consisted of a one-week principals' course, compulsory for all heads serving in its schools and also available to the ethnic directorates. Subject advisers and inspectors from the DNE and the ethnic directorates provided somewhat more regular training to teachers. The White Directorate was the exception, providing education-specific management training for its top- and middle-level staff serving at head office and school heads.) Long courses in educational administration were not available anywhere within the country. The subject was offered as a component of some of the Academy's teacher training courses but was not always compulsory. Education staff were not particularly encouraged to undertake such training in South Africa or elsewhere.

NAMIBIANS TRAINED ABROAD

By far the largest number of Namibians who trained abroad in education under the auspices of SWAPO or with assistance from the Commonwealth Secretariat underwent primary teacher training and English language teacher training. Such training devoted minimal attention to educational administration either as a course of instruction or as a part of the teacher training programmes. Although the Commonwealth Secretariat sponsored ten Namibians from SWAPO's Department of Education and Culture to train in educational planning in India, these were short diploma courses that were not specifically adapted to Namibians' needs. Most Namibians attending such training were not graduates, and this placed them at a considerable disadvantage compared with other candidates. In general, the overall performance of Namibians on sponsored tertiary-level training was not always encouraging, largely because of the severe educational handicaps many had suffered under the apartheid system of education.

Data on Namibians sponsored for training abroad are too fragmented to allow even a rough estimate of the number enrolled in educational administration. A similar problem emerged in trying to identify the field of study of Namibians on UN scholarships. However, where these were discernible, for example, with the UNETPSA statistics, the output in educational administration was negligible. Even on completion of their training, Namibians did not always have easy access to employment in structures applicable to their areas of training, unlike other students returning to their own countries. This meant that many who had acquired theoretical knowledge did not have concomitant experience in the field. There were Namibians with appropriate experience by virtue of their work with the SWAPO Department of Education and Culture, the NEU, UNIN, and the various refugee schools. Although managerial posts in such organisations were relatively few, some of them, such as the NEU and SWAPO's INSET programme, reported being short of suitable administrative staff. Moreover, exiled educationists who might have had the practical experience appear to have been lacking in the theoretical background of educational administration.

Research into the UN training programmes for Namibians gave a clearer picture of educational administration training, if only because of the lack of emphasis on this area. Public administration and public enterprise management took precedence. UNIN offered courses in educational administration to students in its Social and Education Division. Although the graduates from this division constituted the largest number of trainees by 1989, their professional calibre was questionable. Far from being trained for middle-level employment as educational officers, they were considered better-suited for clerical posts. The only other course in educational administration for Namibians was that of the IIEP which was geared towards trainees from all over the world already serving in middle-level posts within ministries of education. At least four Namibians participated in this programme, but most were reported too ill-equipped to benefit from it. The small number of Namibians participating in such a course in itself was an indication of the absence of suitably trained professionals outside the country.

IMPLICATIONS OF THE RESEARCH FINDINGS

It is clear from the empirical evidence that Namibia had an inadequate supply of trained and qualified administrators staffing its educational administrative structures, especially within the black ethnic directorates. This problem was exacerbated by the top-heavy and cumbersome administrative structure of the ethnically divided educational organisation with its eleven directorates to oversee the education of the country's relatively small school-going population. The ability and, in some instances, the willingness of the serving administrators, many of whom were white South Africans, to rise to the educational challenges accompanying independence was problematic. Their experience had been wholly within the apartheid structure to which a high proportion had been ideologically committed. Furthermore, the quality of the teaching force, especially black teachers, and the prevailing shortages of teachers in the country as a whole, lessened the available pool from which to select future educational administrators.

Exiled Namibian teachers, many of whom participated in the training programmes for teachers run by SWAPO, were unlikely to make much impression on teacher shortages in Namibia after independence, let alone that of educational administrators, especially as the refugee school populations returned and added to the growing ranks of the school-going population. Many of the children who returned from the refugee camps in Zambia were sent to their home villages in the north of Namibia, the very area where educational facilities were most stretched and where teacher shortages and administrative difficulties abound. The number of Namibian exiles trained specifically in educational administration, as well as those with experience in this field, are not significant in relation to national needs. The formerly exiled Namibians could not be relied upon to fill the vacancies in the event of large-scale white departures, especially top-level management/executive posts.

These findings highlight the short-sightedness of certain scholarship and training programmes in determining areas of human resource needs. In view of UNESCO's pivotal role in emphasising the importance of educational administration (see Chapter Two) and the UN's active participation in assisting with the development of Namibia's education-related human resources, it is surprising and disappointing that a specific training programme for educational administrators on the lines of the public enterprise management course was never devised. The lack of emphasis on educational administration training in the early UN programmes could be excused by the fact that training educational administrators *per se* was gaining momentum outside North America only in the 1970s, the decade when UN training programmes specifically for Namibians were launched; but even in the 1980s no concerted effort was made to emphasise such training, either as a separate area of study or even as a component of the many teacher training programmes for Namibians.

As a result, Namibia was short of expertise in the very sector that would have to bring about and implement fundamental change, and the government's ability to achieve rapid affirmative action in the management of the national education was compromised. In view of these realities, what light could the Zimbabwean paradigm cast on the problem of how best to tackle the issues at hand?

INSIGHTS FROM ZIMBABWE

Despite Zimbabwe's resemblances to Namibia, there were some fundamental differences between the two countries. Although black Zimbabwean pupils were discriminated against, their education was said to be among the best in Africa. They had access since the 1950s to a local university. Black Zimbabwean teachers were also better trained than their Namibian counterparts. The proportion of qualified teachers in black schools there was said to be 88 per cent higher than in most African countries. The proportion of under- or unqualified Namibian teachers was the same. As in Namibia, teaching was one of the few fields open to educated Zimbabweans. Concomitantly, most black university graduates were concentrated in that discipline. As a result, Zimbabwe did not suffer from an acute internal shortage of skilled black professionals. The dominance of whites in all top-level skilled and professional posts had been due largely to the Rhodesian policy of job discrimination. As a result, a great deal of black potential remained un- or underutilised. Proof of the existence of this unused source was that as soon as whites began leaving the country, well-qualified blacks were promoted to more responsible posts.

In addition to an internal skills' supply, Zimbabwe also had recourse to its large pool of externally trained and skilled professionals, some of whom were also highly experienced. Zimbabwe was therefore better off than Namibia in terms of the quality and quantity of its internal and external skills' supply. Nevertheless, it was impossible to ascertain how many of these had been trained in educational administration.

At independence, the government embarked immediately on a programme of affirmative action, secure in the knowledge that the country had a large pool of skilled resources to rely on. Such a move was important, not only in terms of righting colonial wrongs but also for practical reasons. The successful implementation of government policies was greatly dependent upon a supportive administrative structure. It was doubtful whether such support would be forthcoming from the white civil servants who in the past had been the instigators and supporters of the colonial injustices and who monopolised the senior administrative, professional, technical, and supervisory grades within the civil service. Overall, white insecurity and the government's scheme of early retirement resulted in massive departures which, in turn, facilitated the task of affirmative action. The effects of this policy were dramatic and rapid. As early as 1981, white departures within the Ministry of Education had resulted in a drastic decline in their number.

The first and largest selection of blacks for high-level posts in education was made from among politically active Zimbabwean educationists living in the country. Zimbabwean exiles, both from education and other fields, were next in the selection line. Black Zimbabweans who had served under the old system continued to hold their posts. Those who had not been active in the struggle, in particular, were initially left in their old jobs and some, because of their familiarity with the system, were promoted to the posts vacated by whites. Nevertheless, party loyalty and political activity were important criteria for senior post selection. As it turned out, this was detrimental to the system's efficiency since many of the newcomers lacked appropriate administrative experience and specific training despite often possessing good academic qualifications. 'Sound' political ideology was gradually replaced by merit criteria, but it took the administration at least eight years to recover lost ground. Much tension and mutual suspicion between blacks and whites prevailed within the public service, especially during the first two years of independence. Whites were deliberately excluded from decision-making posts, yet another factor which prompted many to leave.

Independence also brought about the expansion of educational administrative structures both at head office and in the regions, resulting in more complex organisations. Unlike Namibia, the two separate administrative structures for blacks and for whites, coloureds, and Asians had been merged during the latter years of colonial rule into a unified Ministry of Education with a head office and five regional offices. After independence, new posts were created both at head office and in the regions. The number of regional offices was increased to six in 1980 and by 1987 had risen to nine. Of note is that during the colonial period, the Zimbabwean head office structure had fewer staff than Namibia's DNE despite the greater number of school-going pupils in Zimbabwe. There was therefore good cause to expand the administrative structures, especially those at regional level where most of the population and schools were concentrated. As a result, the government targeted much of its attention on the rural areas.

In line with trends in most developing countries at independence, Zimbabwe's teaching force became a pool from which many new civil servants were selected. Although the actual impact of this departure of teachers to other sectors is difficult to assess, it was an important factor for Namibia to bear in mind, especially in view of its severe teacher shortages. Already by 1980, Zimbabwe was suffering from a shortage of trained teachers. This was not helped by the vastly increased pupil enrolment of the succeeding years. Teachers from abroad were recruited to overcome the shortages. They made up the largest group of expatriate workers. Expatriates were not permitted to take on executive positions and foreign teachers were not allowed to be heads of departments or principals. The Ministry of Education was particularly cautious in employing expatriates solely in an advisory capacity for only short periods, notwithstanding the shortage of trained professionals in the Ministry by the late 1980s.

Bearing in mind the huge changes that occurred in Zimbabwe, we shall now review the situation in Namibia's civil service just prior to independence and the trends which followed thereafter.

NAMIBIA'S WHITE CIVIL SERVANTS AND THE ISSUE OF INDEPENDENCE

Namibia's white population was more than twice as large as that of pre-independence Zimbabwe (which had over eight times the total population of Namibia). They played a more important role than whites in any other African country except South Africa, as was evident from the number of whites employed in the public service.[1]

In 1979 at least 50,000 white Afrikaners were employed as public servants or were members of such employees' families. The official report quoting this figure stated that "after independence, these public servants will have to decide whether to join a new Namibian public service, or to remain in the country on a temporary secondment, or to return home".[2] With the formation of the ethnic directorates in 1979 (see Chapter 6) 7,200 posts were created. Of these, 3,000 (42 per cent) were filled by South African officials.[3] The heavy reliance on white South Africans was both a control mechanism and a reflection of the inadequate number of white Namibians to fill such posts. A study done in the early 1980s alleged that the bulk of white civil servants were supporters of the conservative National Party of South West Africa and, as such, favoured close ties with South Africa and possibly also actively maintained options in South Africa.[4] They were also said to have had a total antipathy towards SWAPO.

After the establishment of Namibia's own Government Service on 1 July 1980 in accordance with the provisions of the Government Service Act, No. 2 of 1980, seconded South Africans were given the choice to return to South Africa or to provide their services as seconded officials in the Namibian Government Service for a term of three years. These seconded staff, although given housing and a secondment allowance, were not eligible for promotion and were to be systematically replaced by suitable local staff as these became available. By July 1980, 3,464 seconded South African civil servants were in the employ of the Namibian Government Service, comprising the Central Government departments and the ethnic administrations. The figure constituted roughly 9 per cent of the 37,750 staff employed by the Government Service. No figures are available indicating the number of South Africans who decided to join the public service outright.[5]

Between 1980 and 1987, 3,147 of the seconded officials either joined the Government Service or returned to South Africa. The number of declared seconded officials in the Government Service by 1987 had dropped to 216 (0.48 per cent of the 44,758 Government Service) of which 158 were at Central Government level and 58 within the various ethnic administrations. Impressive though these reductions may appear, a number of factors must be considered. The actual number of seconded officials was not high comparatively speaking, but many were employed in top-level posts. Moreover, the Government Service Commission's 1980 – 1987 report stated that for certain categories of trained personnel it would continue relying heavily on the South African Public Service's resources.[6] Most importantly, the bulk of white South African public servants evidently joined the Government Service on permanent terms.

By the mid-1980s, the Government Service, agriculture, and the mining industry were the three largest employers in the country. In 1990 civil servants alone made up 40 per cent of the workers in the formal sector.[7] The UNIN study of 1986 estimated Namibia's public service's strength to be around 55,000 in 1985 of whom a little over 18,000 (33 per cent) were said to be white, including teachers. The official Government Service staff total for 1985 was given as 41,974.[8] The UNIN figure for white employees represented a considerable drop over the official 1979 figure of 50,000 but it reflected the decline in the white population during the early 1980s.

In spite of the significant numerical decline in white civil servants and the assertion by Simon that blacks and coloureds were gradually outnumbering whites in the civil service, within educational administration (which most likely mirrored the trends in other government departments and ethnic administrations) whites still dominated all the top and middle professional posts within the Department of National Education and many of the ethnic Directorates of Education and Culture.[9] Whites therefore continued to be the very backbone of the Central Government structure while simultaneously wielding much power within the ethnic administrations' educational administrations. Unlike Zimbabwe, if these whites had chosen to leave Namibia the entire administrative system would have collapsed, simply because there were not sufficient blacks with the experience or training to take over from them.

Even by the late 1980s, all signs pointed to the likelihood of white professionals leaving Namibia after independence. We have already mentioned the existence of 30 per cent vacancies in the public sector by the early 1980s (see page 270, Chapter 10) and the difficulties encountered in filling posts, especially higher-level ones, in part due to the white exodus and the lure of higher salaries elsewhere. At that time skilled and semi-skilled whites were leaving Namibia at a steady pace, but it is unknown whether the majority of the departing whites were South Africans or white Namibians. In the circumstances, UNIN's 1978 prediction that 75 per cent or more of white personnel would leave once independence was attained could not be discounted.[10] The South African Reserve Bank by mid-April 1989 confirmed a considerable flight of capital, mostly among small investors. This may have reflected precautionary transfers by whites including money for medical and educational use by white South Africans fearful of the prospect of declining standards in Namibia.

After the SWAPO election victory in November 1989 a very different picture began to emerge. There were no signs of a large-scale white exodus either immediately after the election results or in the subsequent months. This could have been due to the success of the constitutional negotiations and the care taken by SWAPO to allay the fears of whites by stating that it would stand by its policy of national reconciliation. The main aim behind such a policy was to convince businesses and South African civil servants to remain in order to maintain a stable economy and avoid disruption of services. Also, in view of political and economic developments in South Africa, it may no longer have been seen as a greener pasture. Even hard-core white right-wing groups were adopting a wait-and-see approach, while the overall feelings among whites appears to have been "that so long as the government doesn't interfere with out standard of living, we will co-operate with the new government".[11]

White public servants were watchful. The Namibian Government Service *per se* was considered even by its own staff to be "too large and expensive for the country", while a top-ranking member of staff within National Education referred to the educational administrative structure as "absurd and overly expensive".[12] The Government Service Staff Association (GSSA) anticipated that the new government might resort to restructuring the format, size, and composition of the Government Service and thus create numerous redundancies. Many civil servants expressed the concern that a SWAPO Government would lower whites' salaries and place blacks prematurely in senior posts without appropriate training.

By the late 1980s, therefore, the white civil servants were not on the brink of mass departure, but they were imbued with fear and mistrust. Their reliability and loyalty towards the new government was doubtful. In mid-1989 a local newspaper published the leaked minutes of a National Security Council meeting dated September 1988, referring to a plan by the former interim government Cabinet, police, army chiefs, and top civil servants to prevent a SWAPO victory in the 435-election.[13] The fact that many civil servants were South Africans meant that their allegiance to Namibia was questionable.

These drawbacks aside, the dire shortage of black and coloured professionals to step into potential vacant white posts dictated that these experienced whites were the very people needed to ensure the continuity of certain essential services so as to avoid total collapse of the administrative structure in its day-to-day functioning. *The Namibian* news-paper summed up the situation as follows:

> One of the most crucial aspects of the new constitu-tional dispensation is the civil service. These men and women are very important to the well-being and smooth and efficient functioning of the country as a whole. We are all aware of the dangers of instability in the civil service — it is an area where there should be a maximum of stability; and yet at the same time it is an area which necessitates much change. A healthy balance will have to be found between the old and the new....[14]

A pragmatic approach dictated that the requirement for continuity of services should take precedence over the im-plementation of immediate change. However, if the govern-ment wished to retain the services of whites it would have to set about placating their fears. In Zimbabwe, even though the government had assured white civil servants of continued employment, it did little to actively encourage them to stay on. As we have seen, it could do this because it had enough skilled persons to step into vacated posts, unlike independent Namibia. The SWAPO-dominated government opted for an approach suited to its own realities.

POST-INDEPENDENCE STRUCTURAL AND STAFFING TRENDS IN EDUCATIONAL ADMINISTRATION

THE EDUCATIONAL ADMINISTRATIVE STRUCTURE

In a document issued by the Ministry of Education, Culture, Youth and Sport (MECYS) in July 1990 it was stated that:

> restructuring and rationalisation of the educational services is a priority for the Government. In this regard the Government is determined to unify the various educational entities and create a common system of educational administration for all. This process will be accomplished on the principle of a unified central administration and decentralization of services.[15]

One year after independence these proposals had resulted in the absorption of the DNE and the separate ethnic Directorates of Education and Culture into a a single ministry with its head office in Windhoek and six regional offices: Windhoek, Keetmanshoop, Khorixas, Rundu, Ondangwa, and Katima Mulilo.

The reorganisation process effectively amounted to both the unification and integration of the former structures as well as decentralisation through the creation of regions. Such changes reduced the number of administrative structures from eleven to seven and helped to overcome the duplication of functions that occurred in the the colonial system.

However, the current structure of the Ministry of Education and Culture (MOEC) is extremely complex, more so even than the comparable Zimbabwean organisation which caters for the needs of a larger population. The Namibian Ministry has six departments and sixteen directorates at head office alone. In line with the government's determination to rationalise all of its ministries, the MOEC plans to adopt a new structure by April 1994. Huge expansion of the civil service after independence and the concomitant costs to the government are among the reasons for this decision. The new structure will consist of two departments:

☐ Formal Education Programmes; and
☐ Adult and Continuing Education, Libraries, Arts and Culture.

The number of directorates will be reduced to ten. Overall responsibility for the management of the Ministry will rest with an Executive Management Team (EMT) comprising the Permanent Secretary, two Under Secretaries, the Director of Planning and Development, and the Director of General Services.

There will be seven regional offices once Ondangwa I and II come into existence. The regional offices will function as regional outposts or directorates of the Ministry. They are to report to the EMT at head office through the office of the Permanent Secretary. As in Zimbabwe, the tasks of the regional office appear to be confined to the co-ordination of all educational matters within their regions. Furthermore, they will have autonomy over personnel and accounting functions.

The seven regional offices will have similar organisational structures with some variations. For example, Katima Mulilo, Khorixas, Windhoek, and Keetmanshoop each have additional District Education Offices. Rundu has a Culture Centre section, while Keetmanshoop has the Rehoboth Museum.[16]

The establishment of the National Institute for Educational Development (NIED) early in 1991 was an important innovation in ministerial organisation. While this department is part of the MOEC (in the new structure it will become one of the ten directorates), it is expected to occupy new premises at Okahandja from 1994 and is to be responsible for curriculum development, learning materials design, teacher training programmes, language research and development, and language policy formulation. Its role also involves providing in-service training for inspectors and pedagogical advisors. Essentially, NIED performs a service for the formal education system. Eventually it will become a semi-autonomous body with its own Board of Governors. NIED's existence will enable functions previously undertaken in South Africa to be carried out in Namibia itself. The move towards a more rationalised structure and the development of a directorate like NIED to attain the 'Namibianisation' of educational content, training, and so forth, are necessary strategies for change. These strategies should enable the Ministry to better achieve its stated goals of access, equity, quality, and efficiency. However, as Turner points out, "the most important aspect of the Ministry of Education will not be its mode of organisation but the quality of staff who are recruited to it".[17]

STAFFING

Namibia's constitution, in addition to confirming its support for a policy of affirmative action for those previously disadvantaged by past discriminatory laws or practices, pronounced that "any person holding office under any law in force on the date of Independence shall continue to hold such office unless and until he or she resigns or is retired, transferred or removed from office in accordance with law".[18]

President Sam Nujoma, in a proclamation dated 22 March 1990, urged all civil servants to remain in their posts. To encourage acting officials to stay on, directors and departmental heads were awarded salary increments. This was in stark contrast to Zimbabwe's Presidential Directive and Incentive Scheme which actively encouraged affirmative action and resulted in rapid white departures.[19] It appears that the Namibian Government has embarked upon the road of "change with continuity" (to cite the title of a 1990 policy review by the Minister of Education). Zimbabwe, perhaps because of its security in terms of human resources, gave priority to rapid change.

In Namibia most ministerial and permanent secretary posts are held by black Namibians, while white males, even some South Africans, continue to dominate other top posts. In education the tendency has been to incorporate most staff from the former DNE and the White Directorate of Education and Culture, as well as a few members from the other ethnic directorates and some former exiles, into the new Ministry of Education. Whites therefore continue to occupy many vital decision-making, professional and executive posts. Furthermore, shortly after independence, only a small number of teachers, mostly at middle-management level and principals, left schools to take up posts in the MOEC and other ministries. Although they numbered amongst the country's best-qualified teachers, they did not represent a huge drain from this profession.[20]

The retention of many former colonial administrators has a parallel in the Malawian situation where at independence in 1964, the number of trained Malawians were insufficient to administer all the government services. As a result, qualified expatriates were permitted to hold their posts until Malawians were competent to replace them. As late as 1970 the expatriates, who were mostly British subjects, made up the majority of the country's specialists in the civil service. Because they were in a position to influence and in many cases control the personal advancement of Malawians, blacks, even though they were the majority in the civil service, remained second class officers in their own government, resulting in much resentment.[21]

Potential problems

The retention of civil servants from the old regime was in no way an obstacle to recruiting new Namibian staff. Many appointments were made in the years following independence, as functions expanded and new departments were created. Staff expansion in the MOEC, especially at management level, was also a direct outcome of the application of a rigorous policy of affirmative action.[22] Overall, the Namibian civil service grew from an estimated 55,000 posts in 1989 to 60,892 (excluding defence) by early 1991. At least 14,000 staff were affirmative action appointments. By 1993 the number of public servants had swollen to around 70,000 despite the call by the Prime Minister in 1991 to rationalise. The MOEC experienced such rapid expansion in staff terms that, one year into independence, it alone employed about 56 per cent of the entire public service, including teachers. Most new appointments occurred at management level in both the head and regional offices due to the creation of new posts. The salaries of all the officials in the educational structures took up at least 83 per cent of the entire educational budget, an added incentive to rationalise.[23]

There was another dimension to the issue of rationalisation. The expansion of educational provision called for more middle-level skills, especially teacher trainers, subject advisers, and a larger inspectorate, to name but a few. Such needs ruled out the possibility of cutting back on staff within the MOEC, especially at regional and district levels, where the need to improve provision was greatest. Moreover, it was unlikely that excess white staff from the Windhoek region would be happy to relocate to areas of greater need. For example, shortly after independence the Ministry inherited 90 subject advisers from the former DNE and the various ethnic directorates. Of this total only 30 accepted relocation and transfers. By 1992 most of the remaining 57 Windhoek-based subject advisers refused to transfer to areas of greater need, despite having little work due to the greater concentration of qualifed teachers in that region. As a result, 40 were presented with redundancy packages.[24]

Rationalisation is due to occur within the period 31 March 1993 to 31 March 1994. The MOEC, which currently has 2,419 posts, hopes to reduce the number to 1,753. This would result in a national saving of R29,410,475 per year compared with the present R85,777,745 annual recurrent cost.[25] The reduction in the number of some posts and the creation of new ones, as a result of the proposed restructuring of the MOEC, means that certain staff will be faced with either accepting the proposed retirement packages or applying for new posts. At the time of writing no details were available as to which staff members would be offered such packages and what the terms would be. This has again resulted in widespread uncertainty, especially amongst the more senior members of staff who feel these changes might force many of them to leave.

The current situation is one in which many managers and middle-level professionals (former heads of departments, inspectors, and subject advisers), who had maintained and implemented the previous inequalities, have to interpret and apply policy decisions concerning the efficient expansion and equalisation of educational opportunities. Additionally, though many members of staff in the DNE and the White Directorate of Education were well-qualified and well-versed in the apartheid system of education, they were "not necessarily in touch with the best modern international practice".[26] This raised doubts about the level of their commitment and ability to implement change.

Such doubts were particularly pronounced in respect of the former ethnic directorates. As shown in Chapter 8, most of these suffered from skilled staff shortages. Well-qualified staff in the ethnic directorates, some of whom had studied abroad, were too few to make a great impact. The ethnic administrations were also afflicted by severe mismanagement, inefficiency, and corruption, as highlighted in the Thirion

Commission Report. It is uncertain whether those guilty of misdemeanours were actually dismissed.

Although there has never been a conscious attempt to block change, there have been reports of obstruction or delaying tactics emanating from two distinct groups. On the one hand, this has been observed among some of the elites in the structure, many of whom are white, who feel threatened by innovation and their perception of falling standards. They, for example, have pushed for piecemeal rather than immediate integration of black, coloured and white schools and the gradual introduction of English as the medium of instruction. The second group are those officials who obstruct unknowingly simply because they do not have the necessary expertise to implement changes. These include some of the later appointees who have the necessary paper qualifications but lack managerial work experience. As a result, they are unable to perform their tasks professionally. Among the former staff members are those who tend to adhere to the old, inefficient methods rather than adopt new approaches.[27]

Another problem regarding staff is directly related to whites' perceptions of blacks. From the 1988 interviews conducted in Windhoek among a wide range of staff within the DNE and certain ethnic directorates based in Windhoek, we gained the impression that white officials still saw blacks as incompetent and unable to manage affairs without a guiding white hand.

Added to the racial dimension of the potential problem was the common tendency for old staff to feel professionally threatened by the modern skills and techniques of new recruits. The potential for friction based both on race and resentment by serving staff at the appointment of new, inexperienced, yet educated recruits to senior posts, as in Zimbabwe, was a potential problem to Namibia. After independence, there were reports of poor communication between former staff and the new appointees due largely to old patterns of mistrust. This called for a huge adaptation on both sides. By 1993 a better understanding prevailed, though there was still need for better communication.[28]

Expatriates

Finally, the role of expatriates cannot be ignored. Since Namibia suffers from a shortage of skilled educational professionals, especially in highly specialised areas such as planning and policy analysis, it is clear that expatriates are needed to assist the Ministry to fulfil these functions until such time as Namibians themselves can confidently take over those roles. At present there are about 25 expatriates in the MOEC.[29] Although they are employed essentially as consultants and advisors, there are those who have been placed in senior management and who play an active role in policy-making. This has resulted in some resentment, especially among the Ministry's established senior-level staff. They claim that certain of these foreigners have better access to the Minister than they have. They also allege that the expatriates tend to gravitate more towards the newly appointed staff and that they are dismissive of the capabilities of the established staff. This could be due to the old feelings of suspicion and fears of being professionally threatened by innovative approaches.

It was also reported that although certain expatriates make a concerted and successful effort to work together with all staff in the Ministry, others operate independently. There is no clearly defined policy addressing this matter at present despite it being generally understood that one of the desired tasks of an expatriate is to train a local counterpart. As a result, training occurs only in some instances.[30] This is a serious problem, particularly since some of the foreign professionals have long-term contracts and occupy sensitive posts.[31] It is vital that Namibians work closely together with expatriates and receive regular on-the-job training in order to replace foreign skills at the earliest opportunity.

The present situation is not a favourable one since it could increase the Ministry's dependence on foreign expertise while ignoring the development of local professionals, including qualified and experienced persons, to fill such posts. In short, it can exaggerate and aggravate the problem of a lack of management expertise and result in a form of neo-colonialism. For this reason, lessons should be learned from

Zimbabwe's example of allowing expatriates to serve strictly in advisory posts for short terms. There should also be an ongoing review of individual expatriate performance to ensure that they are training their Namibian counterparts.

DIRECTIONS FOR FURTHER ACTION AND RESEARCH

While this research has contributed to a firmer understanding of some of the realities involved in Namibia's independence process insofar as these relate to educational administration, much remains to be done in order to ensure that the process of educational reform has a greater chance of succeeding. Bearing in mind that success is very much dependent upon the professional competencies of the educational administrators, we shall devote this final section to discussing issues concerning their training. This entails examining the role of the Office of the Prime Minister in training civil servants. We will also make proposals regarding the following:

☐ conducting research into training needs;
☐ the establishment of specific educational administration training programmmes;
☐ training trainers; and
☐ compiling country-specific and relevant course materials.

THE OFFICE OF THE PRIME MINISTER

The Namibian Government has always recognised the importance of training to develop the skills and hence the performance of its civil service personnel. Shortly after independence, the Office of the Prime Minister, which was responsible for managing the entire public sector and transforming Namibia's former civil service, was intent on establishing "the necessary institutional mechanisms and capability that would foster and sustain an efficient public service".[32] Consequently, the CPI was abolished in late 1990 and its staff were assigned to two new institutions (separate but functionally interrelated) whose mandate is to deal with different aspects of the public service. The institutions are:

☐ the Secretariat of the Public Service Commission; and
☐ the Public Service Personnel Management Directorate, now called the Directorate of Human Resources Management and Development (DHRMD).

The Secretariat's role is to provide direct technical and administrative support to the Public Service Commission. The Public Service Commission, in turn, is an independent and impartial advisory body to the government on public service matters, primary among these being staff appointments.

Within the DHRMD is the Division of Training Policies and Co-ordination. It is responsible for providing short-term, on-the-job training and co-ordinating, evaluating, and monitoring all short-term in-service training both in Namibia and abroad for public servants from the level of Permanent Secretary downwards.[33]

Among the topics covered in the Division's short-term courses are: supervision, management induction, generic administrative processes, communication, personnel evaluation, to name but some. As examples of former CPI programmes and those of ZIPAM have revealed, administrative training of this sort is too generalised to provide any great benefit to staff in the MOEC. Many education staff require administrative training which is education-specific. This highlights the need for government to seriously set about addressing Namibia's lack of professionals trained specifically in educational administration.

Certain short-term training in education-specific subjects has occurred abroad. Most of this training was directed towards management-level staff in areas like examinations, planning, school mapping, curriculum assessment, and so on. One candidate interviewed, felt that knowledge gained from such training was not shared once candidates returned to their desks nor was there any feedback on the courses.[34] These problems must be addressed if there is to be a successful filtering down process following such courses. Courses should also be evaluated to gauge their usefulness. The draft policy for public service training has made certain recommendations regarding reports on and evaluations of local short courses presented by institutions outside the public service and any training abroad. The draft policy stresses that "information sharing on the knowledge/skills obtained, must be conducted by the person who attended the training, to others who might benefit from the training received".[35]

One of the stipulations embodied in the training policy of the Namibian public service is that each ministry should develop among its personnel "substantive staff expertise in training and staff development, orientated towards the particular needs of the ministry".[36] To date the MOEC does not have its own formalised in-service training programmes for staff despite the Minister of Education having stressed the need for in-house staff training. However, the Ministry established a Training Committee in 1992, each ministry being required to establish a similar committee. The tasks of these committees include:

☐ holding monthly meetings;
☐ assessing training and identifying training needs of officials;
☐ presenting training or having it presented;
☐ controlling ministerial training programmes;
☐ regularly reviewing and evaluating existing training programmes;
☐ following up on reports by officials who have undergone training abroad; and
☐ generally performing all functions related to training issues.[37]

It is planned that each ministerial training committee will have a training officer from the Office of the Prime Minister to better co-ordinate each ministry's training functions and assist in identifying any problems. To realise this there is a need for at least twenty trainers. At present the Training Policies and Co-ordination Division only has eleven staff members, two of whom are on study leave. This small staff has to cater to the training needs of the entire Namibian civil service.[38]

The implementation of the government's public service training policy is very much in the formative stages. One of the major obstacles to its realisation is the shortage of professional trainers in the individual ministries and the Office of the Prime Minister. Despite these shortcomings, however, it is very encouraging that such a policy has been formulated and that serious moves are afoot to implement the policy. It appears that in Namibia far more attention and recognition is being given to the issue of regular training than was the case in Zimbabwe. However, attention must, in some instances, focus more on the specific training needs of each ministry's staff.

RESEARCH INTO TRAINING NEEDS

Action cannot be accomplished without meticulous and thorough research. For example, to ensure that training does not occur in a vacuum, Namibia's reform process should be studied carefully, the better to ascertain what precise professional skills are needed. This calls for undertaking a national inventory of available expertise and a needs' assessment of the country's requirements. Such an investigation would not only help identify the priority personnel for training but also those capable of providing the training. From this research, for example, it is clear that special attention should be directed to training staff working in the regional offices and to building up a pool of well-trained professionals to serve there. The greatest burden in terms of righting the colonial wrongs will fall upon staff in these very offices, and for this reason it is vital that they are suitably prepared for such challenges. Additionally, because of the prevailing dearth of administrators in the regions, serious thought should be given to the principle whereby the structures of promotion and career development at regional level are such as to attract and retain highly qualified people. As pointed out in Chapter 2, in many countries in Africa the trend is for the well-educated staff at local levels to move to central administration.

EDUCATIONAL ADMINISTRATION TRAINING

As we know, many of the staff from Namibia's former colonial structures were absorbed into the MOEC and most of them, on the basis of this research, do not have qualifications or experience suitable to enable them to provide training in educational administration. It follows that there is a serious need to look elsewhere for such trainers. A first option is UNAM.

UNAM's Faculty of Education could play an active role in the provision of both in-service and induction training of educational administrators. The former would be geared towards improving the professional knowledge of serving administrators, while the latter would help to build up a pool of trained professionals able to move into the structure. Such training would better equip Namibian administrators for the tasks of reform, as well as increase the number of black and coloured administrators, thereby enabling the policy of affirmative action to be applied without having to resort to recruiting underqualified or unsuitable staff. But since UNAM is currently undergoing much change (see Chapter 7), establishing in-service and induction courses for educational administrators there may take some time.[39]

In setting up educational administration training programmes within Namibia, assistance could be sought from the International Institute for Educational Planning, the Commonwealth Secretariat, and UNESCO's Regional Office for Education in Africa (BREDA), all of which have experience in running educational administrator training programmes. Namibians could also be sent to selected African or other countries for specialised training or attachment.

TRAINING TRAINERS

Potential trainers should be selected from the most qualified and experienced of Namibia's educational administrators or lecturers at the University, who should then undergo a specialised training of trainers' course in educational administration. The UNESCO/SIDA project for training trainers in educational management, based in Kenya and co-ordinated by a Namibian, is an example of the training available in the region for potential trainers. In the interim, suitable trainers could be recruited from outside Namibia as a short-term solution. The Training Policies and Co-ordination Division of the Office of the Prime Minister also hopes to conduct training courses for trainers in future.

COUNTRY-SPECIFIC AND RELEVANT COURSE MATERIALS

Relevant course materials are needed for local training in educational administration programmes. The content and quality of a training programme are as important as the staff at whom such training is targeted. The mere attainment of formal qualifications will not suffice. It is essential that training be country-specific and relevant. The drawing up of pertinent case studies, a common feature of most management training, is a vital component for such training courses. Another important factor to bear in mind when drawing up training programmes is that the educational demands and needs in the post-independence era differ from those of the colonial period. Training in the new era will have to prepare staff for their roles as innovators and not merely custodians of the old system.

In devising the training programmes, allowance must be made for local conditions, perceptions, and values. Training should reflect and contribute to the formation of a new post-apartheid social and organisational system. This calls for an in-depth analysis of specific national and local conditions. Such analysis requires familiarity with the Namibian cultures, the people's expectations of the way in which authority is and should be exercised in the educational system, and the nature of social participation in educational development. It also calls for thorough investigation into the nature and demands of educational administration at district level and into such fundamental topics as the organisation of schools, financial administration, and the concept of professionalism in education. As much of such research as possible should be undertaken by Namibian specialists from the Ministry of Education, the teachers' colleges, and the new national University, working collaboratively, where necessary, with support from out-side specialists.

CONCLUSION

It is essential to remember that "not all the objectives of government, no matter how noble, can possibly be achieved within the first four or five years of independence".[40] Change takes time, and Namibia will stand a better chance of attaining many of its educational goals by recognising the indispens-able potential contribution of its educational administrators to the success of the reform process. Failure to do so might well reproduce the disappointments experienced by other African countries which ignored the professional needs of the administrative personnel on whom they relied to implement educational reform.

NOTES

1. Thomas 1983:49.
2. AGN 2 1982:12.
3. Government Service Commission *et al* 1987:8.
4. Thomas 1983:74.
5. Government Service Commission *et al* 1987:33, 43, 94.
6. *ibid.*, 20, 43, 44.
7. Department of Governmental Affairs 1986:4; CCN/RRR, Newsletter, 16/02/1990.
8. UNIN 1986:800; Government Service Commission *et al* 1987:94.
9. Simon 1983:402.
10. UNIN 1978:4.
11. CCN/RRR Newsletter, 3/02/1989.
12. The Namibian, 23/06/1989; Interview, Head of Formal Education, DNE, 11/11/1988.
13. The Namibian, 9/06/1989.
14. The Namibian, 6/04/1990.
15. MECYS, July 1990:9.
    In February 1991 the government announced the creation of a separate Ministry of Youth and Sport, and MECYS became the Ministry of Education and Culture (MOEC) (The Namibian, 22/02/1991).
16. Government of the Republic of Namibia, March 1993:26, 29, 64 – 82.
17. Turner 1990:138.
18. Republic of Namibia Articles 23 and 141, 1990:14, 15, 70.
19. Interestingly, it was prior to independence that a special pension fund for white civil servants was established, allowing annuities to be paid in South Africa in view of the uncertainty surrounding white civil servants' future under a SWAPO Government. According to the Minister of Education, some white officials in his Ministry had already taken out such pensions, but he was willing to take a lenient view and allow them to remain (Interview, Minister of Education, MOEC, 8/11/1990).
20. Interview, Deputy Minister, MOEC, 5/08/1993.
21. Richardson 1970.
22. From the level of Deputy Directors to Permanent Secretaries, the number of posts grew from nineteen (prior to independence) to 72 thereafter (Interview, Chief Education Planner, MOEC, 2/08/1993).
23. Interviews, Director of Planning, MOEC, 11/09/1991; Chief Educational Planner, MOEC, 2/09/1993; The Namibian, 23/06/1989; 8/02/1991; 23/08/1991.
24. The Namibian, 3/11/1992.
25. Government of the Republic of Namibia, March 1993:1.
26. Turner 1990:16.

27. Interviews, Director of Planning, MOEC, 11/09/1991; Under Secretary, Formal Education, MOEC, 2/09/1993; Director of Administration and Logistics, MOEC, 4/08/1993.

28. Interview, Director of Administration and Logistics, MOEC, 4/08/1993.

29. *ibid.*

30. Interviews, Deputy Minister, MOEC, 5/08/1993; Chief Education Planner, MOEC, 4/08/1993.

31. For example, foreign aid co-ordination within the MOEC is in the hands of an expatriate who, though on this Ministry's payrole, is simultaneously sponsored by a major foreign donor (Interview, Deputy Minister, MOEC, 2/08/1993).

32. Republic of Namibia 1991:11.

33. The maximum duration of short-term courses is three to five months. Training which is longer than nine months is classified under the governmental bursary scheme and referred to the MOEC which manages these bursaries. The scheme focuses entirely on training for the public service. From March 1993 this scheme was frozen, pending clarification of whether it will continue to be run by the MOEC or by the Office of the Prime Minister and whether it will cater to students on a national basis rather than just to the civil service (Interviews, Permanent Secretary, MOEC, 3/08/1993; Director of Administration and Logistics, MOEC, 4/08/1993).

34. Interview, Under Secretary, Formal Education, MOEC, 3/09/1993.

35. Republic of Namibia, Office of the Prime Minister, undated:13.

36. *ibid.*, 9.

37. *ibid.*, 10.

38. Interviews, Director and Deputy Chief of Training, Training Policies and Co-ordination Division, Directorate of Human Resources, Management and Development, Office of the Prime Minister, 6/08/1993.

39. The newly established Centre for Public Service Training (CPST) at UNAM is geared towards strengthening professionalism in an administrative environment. Its courses focus on financial management and policy analysis and are complementary to those offered by the Office of the Prime Minister. Since they are broad-based, they do not address the specific professional needs of the MOEC.

40. Zvobgo 1986:52.

APPENDIX A:

Ethnic distribution of posts within the Department of National Education, 1988

All top management posts, namely, those of secretary and director of each of the four directorates were white Afrikaners, three of whom were South Africans who had lived for more than ten years in Namibia. The remaining director was a Namibian. The heads of the two education directorates, Educational Control and Educational Auxiliary Services had teaching backgrounds.[1]

The heads of the nine divisions within the DNE's four directorates were all whites, with the exception of the head of the Formal Education Division who was a coloured Namibian. It was only in posts within the subdivisions, namely, middle-level professional to low-level posts, that there was a better ethnic mix. For example, within the subdivision Inspection (of the Formal Education Division), half the staff were black inspectors and the other half whites, the majority of whom were originally South Africans.[2] Within the Subject Advisory Services' Subdivision, all eight senior subject advisers were white South Africans as was the head subject adviser. Among the 54 subject advisers within the seventeen Subject Sections, there were only three blacks. Most of the white subject advisers were South African. There were also some coloureds, but it is less easy to distinguish them from the whites because many of them had Afrikaans-sounding names.[3]

The Non-Formal Education Division had only one black inspector, the remaining staff being white. Whites predominated in all the professional posts and the only black was a secretary serving in the Teachers' Centre Subdivision.

The Directorate of Auxiliary Services employed ten black professionals, nine of whom were language assistants in the Language Curriculum Subdivision and one of whom was an educational planner for technical and vocational education within the Diverse Subjects Curricula Subdivision.

The coloureds and blacks serving within the Directorate of Culture occupied clerical and unskilled positions. Three sections of this directorate had three coloured professionals, all of whom came from Rehoboth: an archivist, a language practitioner, and a museum technician. There appeared to be two black technical assistants. Most professional posts in this directorate were held by whites, including many South Africans who occupied a third of the division's 89 posts.[4]

The Directorate of General Services followed the pattern of having the greatest concentration of blacks and coloureds in secretarial, clerical, and lower-level jobs. Two blacks were employed as Senior Assistant Personnel Officials within the Personnel Service Division and there were two black assistant accountants within the Creditors' Section.

NOTES

1. Interview, Head, Formal Education Division, DNE, 6/10/1988.
2. *ibid.*
3. Interview, Head of Formal Education Division, DNE, 11/10/1988.
4. DNE, Telefoon-en Kodelys, 1/01/1987; Interview, Director of Culture, DNE, 17/10/1988.

Ethnic distribution of posts within the ten directorates, 1988

THE OWAMBO DIRECTORATE OF EDUCATION AND CULTURE

Unfortunately, all attempts at obtaining up-to-date information from the Owambo Directorate met with failure. The director's excuse was that the pertinent correspondence could not be traced because of the lack of a central filing system. Other excuses proffered by the member of staff who initially offered to send the information were that the details had been sent on three occasions but had gone missing in the post. In 1988 this was the only ethnic directorate headed by a local black Namibian. The staffing trends prevailing there appeared to differ somewhat from those in other black directorates. In 1986 there was a white educational planner, the educational adviser was black and other top-level posts were occupied by blacks.[1] By 1988 the top structure was composed entirely of local blacks while all the inspectors were black. There appears to have been no white professionals; instead whites were confined more to clerical posts.

THE KAVANGO DIRECTORATE OF EDUCATION AND CULTURE

This directorate was headed by a white Afrikaner from Namibia. In 1976 he had been a senior educational planner in the Windhoek head office branch of the South African Department of Education and Training. The inspectorate was headed by a black Namibian and all serving inspectors were black except for one white South African. At least three of the inspectors' posts were vacant by the end of 1988. The remaining professional posts (head cultural official and librarian) were filled by white South Africans, while the language practitioners were all black Namibians. Vacancies were listed for the two cultural officials. The lower-level posts were filled by black Namibians.[2]

CAPRIVIAN DIRECTORATE OF EDUCATION AND CULTURE

A white South African with many years of experience in Namibia headed this educational structure. Here the majority of professional staff, namely, subject advisers and inspectors were all black except for one inspector of technical education, a white South African who had spent many years in Namibia, and one white Namibian educational planner. The Cultural Officer was a black Namibian. The lower-level posts were occupied predominantly by black Namibians, but the typist was a white Namibian woman.[3] By 1989 the former black head inspector had been made director of this ethnic directorate.[4]

THE DAMARA DIRECTORATE OF EDUCATION AND CULTURE

An Afrikaner Namibian headed this directorate. One of the two inspectors was a white Namibian and the other a local black. The subject advisers, headed by an Afrikaner Namibian, comprised local blacks, local whites, and South African whites, with the latter predominating. One of the local black subject advisers was a woman. No information was forthcoming on the origins of the cultural officers and language practitioners.[5]

HERERO DIRECTORATE OF EDUCATION AND CULTURE

This educational structure was headed by a white Namibian. All its inspectors were whites (no information was available as to whether they were South Africans or locals). Within the Subject Advisory Services' Division, the senior subject adviser was a white Afrikaner, while out of the remaining eighteen, only two were black, one of whom was a woman. The senior assistant cultural official was a local black, while all the lower-level posts were occupied by black Namibians.[6]

THE TSWANA DIRECTORATE OF EDUCATION AND CULTURE

A white Afrikaner inspector was in charge of administering the Tswanas' two schools. Within this very basic structure, lower-level posts were occupied by local Tswanas.[7]

THE NAMA DIRECTORATE OF EDUCATION AND CULTURE

The director of this directorate was a white South African as was its head inspector, the educational planner, and the school psychologist. Of the four inspectors, one was a white South African; the remaining three were local Namibians of whom only one was black. The majority of subject advisers were white South Africans, four being women. There was only one Nama within this professional category and he was the senior subject adviser.[8]

407

COLOURED DIRECTORATE OF EDUCATION AND CULTURE

No information was forthcoming on the ethnic occupational pattern in this directorate, but its director was coloured. However, it has been alleged that the Coloured Representative Authority *per se* "consists almost entirely of persons who are not Namibians, but persons with residential permits only", which presumably means that they were from South Africa.[9]

THE REHOBOTH BASTER DIRECTORATE OF EDUCATION AND CULTURE

Their deputy director was a Baster. At the time of communication with this directorate in early 1989, only two inspectors were employed, both of whom were Namibians, one white and one coloured. There were eight subject advisers: five Basters, two whites (a Namibian and an American), and one South African coloured. It appears that the latter also doubled up as the educational planner.[10]

WHITE DIRECTORATE OF EDUCATION AND CULTURE

Within this organisation, all top- and middle-level posts were occupied predominantly by white Afrikaners as were the clerical posts. The more menial occupations (cleaners and messengers) were occupied by black and coloured staff. The small minority of female educational professionals were confined to subject advisers, but most women were in clerical and secretarial jobs. Staff qualifications were much higher than in many of the other ethnic directorates. Inspectors, planners, subject advisers, and psychologists were solely advisory personnel whose role was to increase the effectiveness of schools.[11]

Teachers in this directorate could be promoted along two lines, either through management or through subject speciality. The latter was as follows: teacher to senior teacher to principal to subject adviser to inspector of a specific subject. Managers were drawn from heads of schools who had experience in administration and management. But teachers were also able to move to higher salary levels by remaining in the classroom. This meant the system did not lose a good teacher who might not necessarily be a good manager.[12]

NOTES

1. Interview, Head Subject Adviser, Formal Education Division, DNE, 4/11/1988.
2. Personal Communication, the Director, Kavango Directorate of Education and Culture, 18/11/1988.
3. Personal Communication, Educational Planner, Caprivian Directorate of Education and Culture, 18/10/1988.
4. International Conference on Teacher Education for Namibia, Lusaka, 21 – 27 September 1989:54.
5. Personal Communication, Inspector, Damara Directorate of Education and Culture, 6/02/1989.
6. Interview, Deputy Director, Herero Directorate of Education and Culture, 17/10/1988.
7. Personal Communication, Inspector, Tswana Directorate of Education and Culture, October 1988.
8. Personal Communication, Head Inspector, Nama Directorate of Education and Culture, 11/11/1988.
9. The Worker, No. 3, February – March 1988:3; Interview, Director, Educational Control, 12/10/1988.
10. Interview, Director of Educational Control, DNE, 12/10/1988; Personal Communication, Inspector of Education, Rehoboth Baster Directorate of Education and Culture, April 1989.
11. Interview, Director, White Directorate of Education and Culture, 20/10/1988.
12. *ibid.*

SELECT BIBLIOGRAPHY

SOUTH WEST AFRICA/NAMIBIA AND GERMAN EAST AFRICA

BOOKS

Amukugo, E.M. *Education and Politics in Namibia: Past Trends and Future Prospects.* Windhoek: New Namibia Books, 1993.

Bley, H. *South West Africa under German Rule 1894 – 1914.* London: Heinemann Educational Books Ltd., 1971.

Catholic Institute for International Relations. *Mines and Independence.* London: CIIR, 1983.

_____. *Namibia in the 1980s.* London: CIIR, 1986.

Cranmer, D.J., and Woolston, V.A. *Southern Africa. A Study of the Educational Systems of Botswana, Lesotho, South Africa, South West Africa/Namibia and Swaziland with an Addendum on Zimbabwe-Rhodesia: A Guide to the Academic Placement of Students in Educational Institutions of the United States.* Washington D.C.: American Association of Collegiate Registrars and Admissions Officers, 1980.

De Vries, L.J. *Mission and Colonialism in Namibia.* Johannesburg: Ravan Press, 1978.

Drechsler, H. *Let Us Die Fighting: The Struggle of the Herero and Nama against German Imperialism (1884 – 1915).* London: Zed Press, 1980.

Du Pisani, A. *SWA/Namibia: The Politics of Continuity and Change.* Johannesburg: Jonathan Ball Publishers, 1986.

Ellis, J. *Education, Repression & Liberation: Namibia.* London: Catholic Institute for International Relations, 1984.

First, R. *South West Africa.* Harmondsworth, Middlesex: Penguin Books Limited, 1963.

Fraenkel, P., and Murray, R. *The Namibians.* London: Minority Rights Group Ltd., 1985.

Goldblatt, I. *The History of South West Africa from the Beginning of the Nineteenth Century.* Cape Town, Johannesburg: Juta and Company Limited, 1971.

Groves, C.P. *The Planting of Christianity in Africa: Volume 3 (1878 – 1914).* London: Butterworth Press, 1955.

König, B. *The Ravages of War.* London: IDAF Publications Ltd., 1983.

Iliffe, J. *Tanganyika under German Rule 1905 – 1912.* Cambridge: Cambridge University Press, 1969.

International Defence and Aid Fund for Southern Africa. *Namibia the Facts.* London: IDAFSA, 1980.

_____. *Namibia the Facts.* London: IDAFSA, 1989.

411

Katholische Mission. *Geschichte der Katholische Mission in Südwestafrika 1896 – 1946: Festschrift zum Fünfzigjährigen Bestehen der Katholischen Mission in Südwestafrika.* Windhoek: John Meinert Ltd., 1946.

Katjavivi, P. *A History of Resistance in Namibia.* London: James Curry Ltd, 1989.

Legum, C., ed. *Africa Contemporary Record: Annual Survey and Documents.* Volumes 11 – 20. New York: Africana Publishing Company, 1980, 1981, 1984, 1985, 1987, 1989.

Lenz, G. *Die Regierungsschulen in den Deutschen Schutzgebieten.* Darmstadt: Neuen Gymnasium Darmstadt, 1900.

Majeke, N. *The Role of the Missionaries in Conquest.* Johannesburg: Society of Young Africa, 1952.

Mbamba, A.M. *Primary Education for an Independent Namibia: Planning in a Situation of Uncertainty and Instability.* Stockholm: Almqvist & Wiksell International, 1982.

Melber, H. *Schule und Kolonialismus: Das Formale Erziehungswesen Namibias.* Hamburg: Institut für Afrika-Kunde, 1979.

Moritz, E. *Das Schulwesen in Deutsch-Südwestafrika.* Berlin: Dietrich Reimer (Ernst Vohsen), 1914.

O'Callaghan, M. *Namibia: The Effects of Apartheid on Culture and Education.* Paris: UNESCO, 1977.

Paul, P.C. *Die Mission in Unsern Kolonien: Drittes Heft.* Dresden: Verlag von C. Ludwig Ungelent, 1905.

Pütz, J., Von Egidy, H., and Caplan, P. *Political Who's Who of Namibia. Namibia Series Volume 1.* Windhoek: The Magus Company, 1987.

Rhenisch Mission. *Schulordnung: Bereich der Hererokonferenz.* Gütersloh: C. Bertelsmann, 1910.

Rudin, H.R. *Germans in the Cameroons 1884 – 1914: A Case Study in Modern Imperialism.* London: Jonathan Cape, 1938.

Schlunk, M. (a) *Die Schülen für Eingeborene in den Deutschen Schutzbebieten am 1 Juni 1911.* Hamburg: Abhandl. d. Hamburg. Kol.-Instituts., 1914.

_____. (b) *Das Schulwesen in den Deutschen Schutzgebieten.* Hamburg: L. Friedrichsen and Co., 1914.

Schmidlin, J. *Die Katholischen Missionen in den Deutschen Schutzgebieten.* Munster: Aschendorffische Verlagsbuchhandlung, 1913.

Segal, R., and First, R., eds. *South West Africa: A Travesty of Trust.* London: André Deutsch Ltd., 1967.

Smith, S. *Namibia: A Violation of Trust.* Oxford: Oxfam, 1986.

South African Institute of Race Relations (SAIRR). *Survey of Race Relations in South Africa 1977, 1978, 1979, 1980, 1981, 1982, 1983.* Johannesburg: South African Institute of Race Relations, 1978, 1979, 1980, 1981, 1982, 1983, 1984.

SWAPO Department of Information and Publicity. *To be Born a Nation: The Liberation Struggle for Namibia.* London: Zed Press, 1981.

Thomas, W.H. *Economic Development in Namibia: Towards Acceptable Development Strategies for Independent Namibia.* Munich: Kaiser Grünewald Verlag, 1978.

Tötemeyer, G. *South West Africa/Namibia: Facts, Attitudes, Assessment, and Prospects.* Randburg: Fokus Suid Publishers, 1977.

_____. *Namibia Old and New: Traditional and Modern Leaders in Ovamboland.* London: Hurst and Company, 1978.

Wellington, J.H. *South West Africa and its Human Issues.* Oxford: Clarendon Press, 1967.

Wright, M. *German Missions in Tanganyika 1891 – 1941: Lutherans and Moravians in the Southern Highlands.* Oxford: Clarendon Press, 1971.

OFFICIAL PUBLICATIONS AND REPORTS

Administration of South West Africa. *Report of the Commission of Inquiry into Non-European Education in South West Africa (The Van Zyl Commission) Part I: Native Education.* Windhoek: Windhoek Government Printer, November 1958.

_____. *Report of the Commission of Inquiry into Non-European Education in South West Africa (The Van Zyl Commission) Part II: Coloured Education.* Windhoek: Windhoek Government Printer, November 1958.

Administration of South West Africa/Namibia. 'Department of Education Memorandum of the Education Policy adopted with Reference to the Reports of Commissions of Enquiry regarding European and Non-European Education appointed in 1956 and 1958, respectively', undated.

_____. *Academy for Tertiary Education Act, No. 13 of 1980.* Official Gazette Extraordinary of South West Africa, No. 4223. Windhoek: Suidwes-Drukkery Beperk, 14 July 1980.

_____. *National Education Act, No. 30 of 1980.* Official Gazette Extraordinary of South West Africa, No. 4358. Windhoek: Suidwes-Drukkery Beperk, 31 December 1980.

Administrasie vir Kavangos. *Jaarverslag 1 April 1986 – 31 Maart 1987.* Kavango: Administrasie vir Kavangos, 1987.

Administration for Ovambos. *Annual Report 1985/1986.* Owambo: Administration for Ovambos, 1986.

Administration for Whites. *1986 Annual Report.* Windhoek: Administration for Whites, 1986.

_____. *1987 Annual Report.* Windhoek: Administration for Whites, 1987.

Administrator-General for South West Africa. *General Provisions Applicable in Respect of Representative Authorities Established for Population Groups.* No. AG. 8, 1980. Official Gazette Extraordinary of South West Africa, No. 4127. Windhoek: Suidwes-Drukkery Beperk, 24 April 1980.

_____. *Amendment of the Government Service Act, 1980, and Provision for Matters Connected Therewith.* No. AG. 39, 1984. Official Gazette Extraordinary of South West Africa, No. 4983. Windhoek: Suidwes-Drukkery Beperk, 30 November 1984.

_____. *Academy for Tertiary Education Act, No. 13 of 1980.* Promulgation of Act of National Assembly. No. AG. 89, 1980. Official Gazette Extraordinary of South West Africa, No. 4223. Windhoek: Suidwes-Drukkery Beperk, 14 July 1980.

_____. *Commencement of the Academy Act No. 9 of 1985.* No. AG. 44, 1985. Official Gazette Extraordinary of South West Africa, No. 5123. Windhoek: Suidwes-Drukkery Beperk, 1 November 1985.

_____. *Proclamation No. AG. 8 Representative Authorities Proclamation, 1980.* Official Gazette Extraordinary of South West Africa, No. 4127. Windhoek: Suidwes-Drukkery Beperk, 24 April 1980.

Advieskomitee vir Geesteswetenskaplike Navorsing in SWA/Namibië (AGN). *Ondersoek na die Onderwys in SWA/Namibië: Verslag oor Demografie en Onderwysstatistiek vir SWA/Namibië (Verslag AGN 2).* Windhoek: Advieskomitee vir Geesteswetenskaplike Navorsing in SWA/Namibië, 1982.

_____. *Ondersoek na die Onderwys in SWA/Namibië: Verslag van die Navorsingsprojekkomitee: Onderwysstelselbeplanning (Verslag AGN 5).* Windhoek: Advieskomitee vir Geesteswetenskaplike Navorsing in SWA/Namibië, 1983.

Angula, N. *The National Integrated Education System for Emergent Namibia.* Windhoek: Namibia Education & Training Trust Fund, 1990.

Authority of South West Africa. *The Education Ordinance No. 27 of 1962.* Official Gazette Extraordinary of South West Africa, No. 2413. Windhoek: Windhoek Government Printer, 4 July 1962.

Department of National Education (DNE). *Annual Reports* 1980 – 1988. Windhoek: Department of National Education, 1981, 1982, 1983, 1984, 1985, 1986, 1987, 1988.

_____. 'Tenth Schoolday Statistics – 1988'. Windhoek: undated.

_____. 'Telefoon-en Kodelys'. Windhoek: 1/01/1987.

Education Committee. 'Recommendations for a National Education Policy Objectives and Strategies'. Windhoek, 1985.

Government of the Republic of Namibia. *Rationalization of the Structure of the Ministry of Education and Culture.* Windhoek: Ministry of Education and Culture, March 1993.

Government Service Commission and the Central Personnel Institution. *Annual Report 1980 – 1987.* Windhoek: Windhoek Printers & Publishers (Pty) Ltd., 1987.

_____. *Annual Report 1987/88.* Windhoek: Ultra Press, 1988.

Ministry of Education, Culture, Youth and Sport (MECYS). *Education in Transition: Nurturing our Future. A Transitional Policy Guide-Line Statement on Education and Training in the Republic of Namibia.* Windhoek: Ministry of Education, Culture, Youth and Sport, July 1990.

_____. *Change with Continuity: Education Reform Directive: 1990. A Policy Statement of the Ministry of Education, Culture, Youth and Sport.* Windhoek: Ministry of Education, Culture, Youth and Sport, 28 November 1990.

Regering van Rehoboth. *Jaarverslag vir die Tydperk 1 April 1986 tot 31 Maart 1987*. Rehoboth: Regering van Rehoboth, 1987.

Representative Authority of the Coloureds. *Annual Report 1980/81*. Windhoek: Administration for Coloureds, 1981.

Republic of Namibia. *The Constitution of the Republic of Namibia*. Windhoek: Government Gazette of the Republic of Namibia, No. 2, 21 March 1990.

_____. *White Paper on National and Sectional Policies*. Windhoek: Government of the Republic of Namibia, March 1991.

_____. *The Broad Curriculum for the Basic Education Teacher Diploma*. Windhoek: Ministry of Education and Culture, October 1992.

_____. *Rationalization of the Public Service Part III*. Windhoek: Office of the Prime Minister, November 1992.

_____. *Transitional National Development Plan 1991/92 – 1993/94*. Windhoek: National Planning Commission, March 1993.

Republic of South Africa. *Report of the Commission of Enquiry into South West Africa Affairs 1962 – 1963 (The Odendaal Commission)*. R.P. No. 12/1964. Pretoria: Pretoria Government Printer, 1964.

Secretary of the National Assembly of South West Africa. *National Education Act, No. 30 of 1980*. Promulgation of Act of National Assembly, No. AG. 196, 1980. Official Gazette Extraordinary of South West Africa, No. 4358. Windhoek: Suidwes-Drukkery Beperk, 31 December 1980.

South West Africa Administration, Education Department. *Memorandum of Education Policy Adopted with Reference to Reports of Commissions of Enquiry Regarding European and Non-European Education Appointed in 1956 and 1958 Respectively*. Windhoek: undated.

South West Africa Department of Economic Affairs. *Report 02 – 04 Statistics of Schools 1985 to 1988*. Windhoek: Department of Economic Affairs, undated.

_____. *Report 02 – 05: Statistics of Schools 1986 to 1989*. Windhoek: Department of Economic Affairs, undated.

South West Africa Survey 1967. Pretoria: Department of Foreign Affairs, March 1967.

Von Kleist, K.E.B. *Investigation into Education in SWA/Namibia: The Economic Effectiveness of the Education System of South West Africa/Namibia (Report ACHSR 6)*. Windhoek: Advisory Committee for Human Sciences Research in SWA/Namibia, 1985.

OTHER OFFICIAL PUBLICATIONS

Great Britain, Parliament. *Parliamentary Papers*. Cmd. 1428, 'Report on Tanganyika Territories Covering the Period from the Conclusion of the Armistice to the End of 1920'.

United Kingdom, Parliament. *Parliamentary Blue Book*. CD 9146, 'Report on the Natives of South-West Africa and their Treatment by Germany'. London: His Majesty's Stationery Office, 1918.

415

ARTICLES, CONFERENCES, PUBLICATIONS, REPORTS AND
SEMINARS

Abrahams, K. 'Whither Education in Namibia?'. *The Namibian Review*, No.
29 (July – August 1983), 19 – 26.

The Academy for Tertiary Education. *Annual Report by the Rector of the
Academy*. Windhoek: Academy, 1984.

_____. *Academy News 1980 – 1985*. Windhoek: Academy, 1985.

_____. *Policy Statement of the Academy*. Windhoek: Academy, 1985.

_____. *Sensusopname*. Windhoek, 4 Junie 1986.

_____. *Academy Annual Report 1987*. Windhoek: Academy, 1987.

_____. *Yearbook 1988, Part 1 General Information and Regulations*. Wind-
hoek: Academy, 1987.

_____. *Yearbook 1988, Part 2 Faculty of Economics and Management Science*.
Windhoek: Academy, 1987.

_____. *Yearbook 1988, Part 5 Faculty of Education*. Windhoek: Academy,
1987.

_____. *Yearbook 1989, Part 8 Technikon Training*. Windhoek: Academy,
1988.

_____. *Yearbook 1989, Part 10 Distance Teaching*. Windhoek: Academy,
1988.

_____. *Jaarboek 1990, Deel 5 Fakulteit Opvoedkunde*. Windhoek: Academy,
1989.

_____. *Yearbook 1993, Part 5 Faculty of Education*. Windhoek: Academy,
1992.

Adams Jr., S.C. *Zimbabwe Namibia: Anticipation of Economic and Humanitarian
Needs. Transition Problems of Developing Nations in Southern Africa*. Wash-
ington: African-American Scholars Council Inc. and the Agency for
International Development, 15 March 1977.

Afrikaans-Duitse Kultuurunie (SWA). 'The Educational System in
SWA/Namibia'. *Information* 4 (15 December 1987), 3 – 6.

Ankama, I. *United Nations Vocational Training Centre for Namibia, Sumbe,
People's Republic of Angola*. Paper presented at an International Extension College and World University Service (UK) conference. Dartington: 29 March – 1 April 1985.

Askin, S. 'UN Institute for Namibia'. *MOTO*, No. 60 (November 1987), 13.

Catholic Institute for International Relations (CIIR). *Profile Namibia*. London: CIIR, 1989.

Centre d'Information sur le Mozambique et l'Afrique Australe (CIDMA).
Towards Namibian Independence: Prospects for Development and Assistance.
Ottawa: Inter-Agency Working Group on Southern Africa of CIDMA,
1984.

Chase, N. 'People's Education in Namibia'. *Namibia in Perspective*, pp. 143
– 150. Edited by G. Tötemeyer, V. Kandetu, and W. Werner. Windhoek:
Council of Churches in Namibia, 1987.

Collett, S. 'The Human Factor in the Economic Development of Namibia'. *Optima* 28, No. 4 (January 1980), 191 – 219.

Commonwealth Secretariat. *Notes on the Commonwealth. The Fellowships and Training Programme.* London: January 1987.

_____. *Sharing Experiences on the Organisation and Management of Ministries of Education: The Namibian Case.* Report of a seminar held in Windhoek, Namibia: 21 – 25 January 1991.

Commonwealth Secretariat, and SWAPO of Namibia. *English Language Programme for Namibians.* Seminar, Lusaka: 19 – 27 October 1987.

Commonwealth Secretary-General. *Report of the Commonwealth Secretary-General.* London: Commonwealth Secretariat, 1981.

_____. *Report of the Commonwealth Secretary-General.* London: Commonwealth Secretariat, 1983.

Concordia College Trust. *Concordia.* Windhoek: John Meinert Pty. Ltd., undated.

Consolidated Diamond Mines. *CDM Bursary Scheme: Guidelines for Applicants.* Oranjemund: CDM (Pty.) Ltd., undated.

Department of Governmental Affairs. *Namibia/SWA Facts and Figures.* Windhoek: Service Division of Liaison Services Department of Governmental Affairs, 1986.

_____. *SWA/Namibia Today.* Windhoek: Liaison Services Department of Governmental Affairs, 1988.

Dodds, T., and Inquai, S. *Education in Exile: The Educational Needs of Refugees.* Cambridge: International Extension College, 1983.

Doyle, M.V. 'Adult Literacy Education in Namibia'. *Community Development Journal,* 14, No.2 (1979), 91 – 97.

Duggal, N.K., ed. *UNIN News. Special Issue.* Lusaka: UNIN, 1980.

Ellis, J. 'Education'. Paper presented at the Catholic Institute for International Relations *Seminar on the Economic Future of Namibia.* London: 18 February 1983.

First, R. 'Namibia (South West Africa)'. *Africa South of the Sahara,* pp. 604 – 614. London: Europa Publications Limited, 1983.

Foundation for Education with Production. *Education and Culture for Liberation in Southern Africa.* Botswana: Gaborone Printing Works, 1981.

Gerhart, G.M. *A Survey of Educational Assistance to Refugees from South Africa and Namibia.* New York: Ford Foundation, 4 January 1983.

Group on Educational Assistance to Refugees (GEAR). *The Forgotten Overseas Students: Towards a Policy for Refugees.* London: Group on Educational Assistance to Refugees, January 1986.

Geingob, G.H. 'Experiences as a Student and as a Teacher'. *South West Africa: Travesty of Trust,* pp. 213 – 221. Edited by R. Segal and R. First. London: André Deutsch Ltd., 1967.

Heese, C.P. 'Das Erziehungswesen in Südwestafrika unter der Deutschen Regierung bis 1915'. *SWA Annual,* pp. 127 – 135. Edited by J. Fischer and P. Meinert. Windhoek: John Meinert Ltd., 1986.

Hirji, K.F. 'Colonial Ideological Apparatuses in Tanganyika under the Germans'. *Tanzania under Colonial Rule*, pp. 192 – 235. Edited by M.H.Y. Kaniki. London: Longman Group Limited, 1979.

Hoeflich, K.F. 'Das Deutsche Sprach- und Schulproblem in S.W.A'. *Festschrift Dr H.C.H. Vedder: Ein Leben für Südwestafrika*, pp. 111 – 136. Edited by D.W. Drascher and H.J. Rust. Windhoek: S.W.A. Wissenschaftliche Gesellschaft, 1961.

Hornsby, G. 'German Educational Achievement in East Africa'. *Tanganyika Notes and Records* 62 (March 1964), 83 – 90.

Institute of International Education. *Profiles: Detailed Analysis for the Foreign Student Population 1985/86*. New York: Institute of International Education, 1988.

International Conference on Teacher Education. *International Conference on Teacher Education for Namibia. Volume 1: Research Papers & Teacher Training Reviews*. Lusaka: 21 – 27 September 1989.

International Extension College. *Evaluation Report on the Namibian Extension Unit*. Cambridge: International Extension College, October 1986.

International Extension College and World University Service. *Preliminary Report on a Workshop on Education for Refugees*. Dartington: 29 March – 1 April 1985.

Joint Committee on Southern African Scholarships. *Southern African Scholarship Schemes: A Manual on their Establishment*. London: Joint Committee on Southern African Scholarships, *circa* 1979.

Kalenga, L.H. *Seminar to Study Strategies, Techniques, Methods and Content Towards Establishment of a National Literacy Programme for an Independent Namibia*. Lusaka: SWAPO Department of Education and Culture, 17 – 24 May 1978.

Kennedy McGill, M.K. 'Education Policy and Results'. *South West Africa: Travesty of Trust*, pp. 194 – 212. Edited by R. Segal and R. First. London: André Deutsch Ltd., 1967.

Lachenmann, G. *Namibia: Sektorstudie Bildungswesen*. Berlin: Deutsches Institut für Entwicklungspolitik, 1979.

Lawuo, Z.E. 'The Beginnings and Development of Western Education in Tanganyika — the German Period'. *The Educational Process: Theory and Practice, with a Focus on Tanzania and other Countries*, pp. 42 – 64. Edited by A.G.M. Ishumi and G.R.V. Mmari. Dar Es Salaam: University of Dar Es Salaam, 1978.

Leistner, E., Esterhuysen, P., and Malan, T. *Namibia/SWA Prospectus*. Pretoria: Africa Institute of South Africa, 1980.

Leu, C.A. 'Colonial Education and African Resistance in Namibia'. *Independence Without Freedom: the Political Economy of Colonial Education in Southern Africa*, pp. 152 – 171. Edited by A.T. Mugomba and M. Nyaggah. Santa Barbara and Oxford: ABC-Clio Inc. and Clio Press, 1977.

Mbamba, A.M. *The Namibia Education and Health Centres. A Study of SWAPO Schools among Namibian Refugees in Zambia and Angola.* Stockholm: Institute of International Education, University of Stockholm, November 1979.

_____. *A Diagnostic Analysis of the Education System in Namibia.* Paris: International Institute for Educational Planning, Occasional Papers, No. 58, 1981.

Mbuende, E.A. *Teacher Education for an Independent Namibia: Problems and Prospects.* Pedagogical Reports 17. Lund: Department of Education, University of Lund, 1987.

Melber, H. 'New Tendencies of an Old System: Neo-Colonial Adjustment within Namibia's System of Formal Education'. Paper presented at the conference *Namibia 1884 – 1984: 100 Years of Foreign Occupation, 100 Years of Struggle.* London: 10 – 13 September 1984.

_____. 'Educational Reform — Unto What End?'. *Namibia in Perspective,* pp. 128 – 142. Edited by G. Tötemeyer, V. Kandetu and W. Werner. Windhoek: Council of Churches in Namibia, 1987.

Milk, O. 'Das Augustineum'. *Ein Leben für Südwestafrika: Festschrift Dr H.C.H. Vedder,* pp. 23 – 34. Edited by D.W. Drascher and H.J. Rust. Windhoek: S.W.A. Wissenschaftliche Gesellschaft, 1961.

Morgan, W. 'German Educational Policy: The School System in the German Colonies'. *Traditions of African Education,* pp. 27 – 50. Edited by D.G. Scanlon. New York: Bureau of Publications, Teachers College, Columbia University, 1964.

Murray, R., Morris, J., Dugard, J., and Rubin, N. *The Role of Foreign Firms in Namibia. Studies on External Investment and Black Workers' Conditions in Namibia.* Uppsala: Africa Publications Trust, 1974.

Muundjua, F. 'Education in Namibia: The Way I See It'. *Namibia Educational Forum Publications,* No. 1 (10 December 1983), 3 – 9.

Namibia Extension Unit. *Namibian Extension Unit.* Lusaka: Namibian Extension Unit, January 1985.

Namibia Foundation. 'Brave Battle for Better Education'. *Namibia Brief,* No. 10 (Second Quarter 1988).

Namibia Office. *Namibia Digest,* No. 2 (July 1986). London: Namibia Office and Strategy Network International Limited, 1986.

_____. *Namibia Digest,* No. 3 (October 1986). London: Namibia Office and Strategy Network International Limited, 1986.

_____. *Namibia Now,* No. 5 (May – July 1986). London: Namibia Office and Strategy Network International Limited, 1986.

Namibia Vocational School, TVIND, Denmark. Denmark: undated.

Nangoloh, P.Y. 'The United Nations. International Double Standards and the Collusion to Promote Elitism in Namibia'. *Namibia Digest,* No. 3 (October 1986), 2 – 6.

Ongwediva — the New Training Centre. SWA Annual 1979, p. 96. Windhoek: John Meinert Ltd., 1979.

Overseas Development Institute (ODI). 'Economic Prospects for Namibia', Briefing Paper. London: August 1989.

Rector of the Academy. *The Annual Report by the Rector of the Academy.* Windhoek: The Academy, 1983.

Rogerson, C.M. 'A Future 'University of Namibia'?: the Role of the United Nations Institute for Namibia'. *The Journal of Modern African Studies* 18, No. 4 (1980), 675 – 683.

Rössing Uranium Limited. *The Rössing Foundation.* Windhoek: Rössing Uranium Limited, *circa* 1983.

————. *The Rössing Fact Book.* Windhoek: Rössing Uranium Limited, 1985.

Rubin, N. *Labour and Discrimination in Namibia.* Geneva: International Labour Office, Geneva 1977.

Sano, H-O., Koponen, J., Tostensen, A., and Stanbridge, R. *Namibia and the Nordic Countries.* Uppsala: Scandinavian Institute of African Studies, 1981.

Selle, R. '1980 – 1985 The First Five Years'. *Academy News*, No. 1 (*circa* 1985), 6 – 8.

Simon, D. *Independent Namibia One Year On.* Conflict Studies 239. London: the Research Institute for the Study of Conflict and Terrorism, March 1991.

Smith, A. 'The Missionary Contribution to Education'. *Tanganyika Notes and Records*, No. 60 (March 1963), 91 – 109.

Smythe, M.M. *Namibia, Anticipation of Economic and Humanitarian Needs: The Education of Refugees in Zimbabwe and Namibia.* Washington: Agency for International Development, 20 January 1977.

South African Barometer. 'Namibia Focus', *Journal of Current Affairs Statistics.* Special Edition: Namibia. Johannesburg: Hoopoe Publications, 1989.

South African Department of Labour. *Manpower Survey No. 12.* Pretoria: Department of Labour, 29 April 1977.

SWA/Namibia Information Service. *SWA/Namibia Today.* Windhoek: South West Africa Information Service, 1981.

————. *On Record.* The SWA/Namibia News Magazine. Windhoek: South West Africa Information Service, 7 October 1987.

Spray, P. 'Namibia (South West Africa)'. *Africa South of the Sahara*, pp. 722 – 738. London: Europa Publications Limited, 1987.

Swedish International Development Authority (SIDA). (a) *Sweden and Development Co-operation in Southern Africa.* Sweden: SIDA, undated.

————. (b) *Sweden and the Southern African Development Coordination Conference.* Sweden: SIDA, undated.

Thomas, W.H. 'The Economy in Transition to Independence'. *Namibia: Political and Economic Prospects*, pp. 41 – 92. Edited by R.I. Rotberg. Cape Town: David Philip, 1983.

Tjitendero, M.P. *Education Policy Planning for Independent Namibia.* Lusaka: United Nations Institute for Namibia, 1980.

Turner, J.D. *Education in Namibia.* Report of a Consultancy for the Ministry of Education, Culture and Sport, Windhoek: 25 March – 6 April 1990.

University of Namibia. *UNAM Forum,* No. 2 (May/June 1993), 5.

Visser, J.A. *The South African Defence Force's Contribution to the Development of South West Africa.* Johannesburg: Military Information Bureau, South African Defence Forces, 1984.

Williams, P.R.C. *A Policy for Overseas Students: Analysis, Options, Proposals.* London: Overseas Student Trust, 1982.

_____. *They Came to Train: An Evaluation of Technical Co-operation Training in Britain.* London: Overseas Development Organisation, 1985.

The Worker. No. 3 (February – March 1988), Windhoek.

World University Service (WUS) (UK). *Seminar on Education for Namibians in the UK.* Report and background papers. London: WUS, 7 June 1982.

_____. *Divided Campuses: Universities in South Africa.* London: World University Service and the Association of University Teachers, May 1986.

WUS and British Defence and Aid Fund for Southern Africa. *Briefing Paper. Namibia: Education in Conflict.* London: World University Service and British Defence and Aid Fund for Southern Africa, 1987.

UNPUBLISHED MATERIAL AND REPORTS

Buitendacht, A.J.H. 'The Academy: A Model for Tertiary and out of School Education in a Third World Environment', Windhoek: Academy, undated.

Commonwealth Secretariat. 'Statement by T. Dormer on behalf of the Commonwealth Secretariat to the Second International Conference on Assistance to Refugees in Africa'. Geneva: 10 July 1984.

_____. 'Statement by T. Dormer of the Commonwealth Secretariat to an informal session of the UNETPSA Advisory Committee'. New York: 19 October 1984.

_____. 'Statement by T. Dormer of the Commonwealth Secretariat to the Forty-Seventh Meeting of the Advisory Committee on UNETPSA', Conference Room 5, United Nations. New York: 1 May 1985.

_____. 'Statement by T. Dormer of the Commonwealth Secretariat to the Fiftieth Meeting of the Advisory Committee on UNETPSA', Conference Room 5, United Nations. New York: 4 October 1985.

_____. 'Statement by T. Dormer of the Commonwealth Secretariat to the Fifty-Second Meeting of the Advisory Committee on UNETPSA'. Conference Room 5, United Nations. New York: 8 October 1986.

_____. 'Enhanced Commonwealth Programme of Technical Assistance for Namibia'. London: 24 January 1990.

Ellis, J. 'Basic Adult Education in Namibia after Independence'. M Ed dissertation, University of Manchester, 1981.

Harlech-Jones, B. 'Education in Namibia, 1919 – 1960: The Role of the Administration of South West Africa and the Contribution of the Mission Societies and Local Communities'. Windhoek: *circa* 1983. (Photocopy).

Katzao, J.J. 'Formal Education in Namibia with Special Attention to German and South African Influence up to 1980 and the Implications for Future Development'. M Ed dissertation, University of Wales, 1980.

Kazapua, J.N. 'A Critical Analysis of the Educational System in Namibia'. M Ed dissertation, University of London, Institute of Education, 1984.

Mukendwa, M.J. 'Educational Wastage in Namibia: Extent and Possible Causes and Cures'. Diploma in Educational Planning, University of London, Institute of Education, 1985.

_____. 'Curriculum Planning and Development in Namibia: Strategies and Implications for the Future'. M Ed dissertation, University of London, Institute of Education, 1986.

Noble, J. 'Education in Namibia'. M Ed dissertation, University of Nairobi, 1977.

Nowack, K. 'Erziehungsanstalt für Halbweise Kinder'. *Rhenish Mission File 1904 – 1909 and 1910 – 1915.*

Olp, J. 'Referate bei den Missionarskonferenzen im Hereroland 1899 – 1910'. *Rhenish Mission File CK2B.*

Presidential Commission. 'Higher Education in Namibia. Report of a Presidential Commission under the Chairmanship of Professor J.D. Turner'. September 1991.

Republic of Namibia. 'Training Policy of the Public Service of Namibia'. Windhoek: Office of the Prime Minister, Directorate of Human Resources Management and Development, undated. (Draft.)

Rössing Foundation. 'Report for the Period 1st January to 31st December 1987'. Windhoek: Rössing Foundation, 1987.

_____. 'Report of Activities May 1988'. Windhoek: Rössing Foundation, 1988.

Simon, D. 'Aspects of Urban Change in Windhoek, Namibia, During the Transition to Independence'. D Phil dissertation, University of Oxford, 1983.

South West Africa Government Service. 'Bursaries 1989'. Windhoek: SWA Government Service, 1989.

Takala, T., Bennett, B., Järvinen, H., Kann, U., Lasonen, J., Takala, E., and Torvinen, L. 'Report of the FINNIDA Education Sector Project Identification Mission to Namibia'. March 1991.

Thirion Commission. 'Commission of Inquiry into Alleged Irregularities and Misapplication of Property in Representative Authorities and the Central Authority of South West Africa'. Eerste Tussentydse Verslag Volume I and Seventh Interim Report Volume I Part I. Windhoek: 1983.

Tjitendero, M.P. 'Examination of an Alternative: A Look at the Primary and Secondary Education in Namibia'. D Ed dissertation, University of Massachusetts, 1977.

West, R. *et al.* 'A Proposal for Improved Teaching through In-Service Training'. Windhoek: 1988.

UNITED NATIONS

United Nations. *A Trust Betrayed: Namibia.* New York: United Nations, 1981.

_____. *Namibia: A Unique UN Responsibility.* New York: United Nations, April 1983.

_____. *Basic Facts.* New York: United Nations, 1985.

_____. *Demographic Yearbook.* Department of International Economic and Social Affairs Statistical Office. New York: United Nations, 1987.

United Nations Commissioner for Namibia. *Nationhood Programme for Namibia and Educational, Social and Relief Activities under the United Nations Fund for Namibia.* Progress Report of the United Nations Commissioner for Namibia, Conference Room Paper No. 282. New York: 31 December 1980.

_____. _____. _____, Conference Room Paper No. 195/80. New York: 30 April 1980.

_____. _____. _____, Conference Room Paper No. 355. New York: 26 January 1982.

_____. _____. _____, Conference Room Paper 1982/14. New York: 5 May 1982.

_____. _____. _____, Conference Room Paper No. 1983/14. New York: 5 May 1982.

_____. _____. _____, A/AC.131/1982/CRP.5. New York: 19 November 1982.

_____. _____. _____, A/AC.131/1983/CRP.20. New York: 14 April 1983.

_____. _____. _____, A/AC.131/1983/CRP.48. New York: 15 September 1983.

_____. _____. _____, A/AC.131/1984/CRP.6. New York: 2 March 1984.

_____. _____. _____, A/AC.131/1985/CRP.15. New York: 15 March 1985.

_____. _____. _____, A/AC.131/1986/CRP.16. New York: 13 May 1986.

_____. _____. _____, A/AC.131/1986/CRP.84. New York: 31 December 1986.

_____. _____. _____, A/AC.131/1987/CRP.47. New York: 1 July 1987.

_____. _____. _____, A/AC.131/1987/CRP.60. New York: 24 November 1987.

_____. _____. _____, A/AC.131/1988/CRP.18. New York: 28 September 1988.

_____. _____. _____, A/AC.131/1989/CRP.19. New York: 17 March 1989.

_____. _____. _____, A/AC.131/303. New York: 31 May 1989.

_____. _____. _____, A/AC.131/1989/CRP.36. New York: 13 December 1989.

United Nations Council for Namibia. *General Assembly Official Records: 32 Session Supplement No. 24 (A/32/24).* New York: United Nations, 1977.

_____. _____: *33 Session Supplement No. 24 (A/33/24).* New York: United Nations, 1978.

_____. _____: *34 Session Supplement No. 24 (A/34/24).* New York: United Nations, 1979.

_____. _____: *35 Session Supplement No. 24 (A/35/24).* New York: United Nations, 1980.

_____. _____: *36 Session Supplement No. 24 (A/36/24).* New York: United Nations, 1982.

_____. _____: *37 Session (A/37/24) (Part I).* New York: United Nations, 1982.

_____. _____: *38 Session Supplement No. 24 (A/38/24).* New York: United Nations, 1983.

_____. _____: *39 Session Supplement No. 24 (A/39/24).* New York: United Nations, 1985.

_____. _____: *40 Session Supplement No. 24 (A/40/24).* New York: United Nations, 1986.

_____. *General Assembly: Report of the United Nations Council for Namibia (A/41/24).* New York: United Nations, 26 October 1986.

_____. *General Assembly: Report of the United Nations Council for Namibia (A/42/24) (Part I).* New York: United Nations, 15 October 1987.

_____. *General Assembly: Report of the United Nations Council for Namibia (A/42/24) (Part II).* New York: United Nations, 19 October 1987.

_____. (a) *Nationhood Programme for Namibia.* New York: United Nations Council for Namibia, 1981.

_____. (b) 'Social Conditions in Namibia'. Report to *The International Conference in Support of the Struggle of the Namibian People for Independence.* UNESCO, Paris: 25 – 29 April 1983.

_____. (c) *Statement by the Representative of the United Nations Council for Namibia at the 39 Session of UNESCO's International Conference on Education.* Geneva: 16 – 25 October 1984.

United Nations Department of Political Affairs. *Decolonization.* New York: United Nations Department of Political Affairs, Trusteeship and Decolonization, December 1977.

United Nations Development Programme. *Report of the Evaluation Mission on NAM/82/005, Assistance to the United Nations Institute for Namibia.* UNDP, April 1985.

424

United Nations Economic Commission for Africa (UNECA). *Africa Statistical Yearbook 1983*. Addis Ababa: United Nations Economic Commission for Africa, 1986.

United Nations Educational, Scientific and Cultural Organization. *UNESCO Questionnaire on Statistics of Education at the Third Level*. Paris: UNESCO Office of Statistics, 1985/1986.

_____. *Apartheid: Its Effects on Education, Science, Culture and Information*. Paris: UNESCO Press, 1972.

_____. *Statistics of Students Abroad, No. 27, 1974 – 78*. Paris: UNESCO Division of Statistics on Education, 1982.

_____. *1987 Statistical Yearbook*. Paris: UNESCO, 1987.

_____. *In-Service Teacher Education for Namibia: Report and Proposals*. UNESCO Mission in Collaboration with the United Nations Development Programme, 20 May – 3 August 1990.

United Nations Secretary-General. *United Nations Educational and Training Programme for Southern Africa*. Report of the Secretary-General, A/8151. New York: 6 November 1970.

_____. _____. _____, A/8485. New York: 29 October 1971.

_____. _____. _____, A/8850. New York: 25 October 1972.

_____. _____. _____, A/9240. New York: 21 November 1973.

_____. _____. _____, A/9845. New York: 25 November 1974.

_____. _____. _____, A/10331. New York: 7 November 1975.

_____. _____. _____, A/31/268. New York: 26 October 1976.

_____. _____. _____, A/32/283. New York: 1 November 1977.

_____. _____. _____, A/33/297. New York: 2 November 1978.

_____. _____. _____, A/34/571. New York: 22 October 1979.

_____. _____. _____, A/35/525. New York: 10 October 1980.

_____. _____. _____, A/36/147. New York: 6 October 1981.

_____. _____. _____, A/37/436. New York: 23 September 1982.

_____. _____. _____, A/38/469. New York: 19 October 1983.

_____. _____. _____, A/39/351. New York: 23 October 1984.

_____. _____. _____, A/40/781. New York: 22 October 1985.

_____. _____. _____, A/41/678. New York: 8 October 1986.

_____. _____. _____, A/42/628. New York: 9 October 1987.

_____. _____. _____, A/43/681. New York: 5 October 1988.

_____. _____. _____, A/44/557. New York: 28 September 1989.

United Nations Fund for Namibia. *Report of the Committee on the United Nations Fund for Namibia: Draft Report of the First Group of Projects and on the Administration and Management of the Programme*. Conference Room Paper 112. New York: 6 February 1979.

United Nations Inter-Agency Mission. *Report of the UN Inter-Agency Missions to the People's Republic of Congo on the Namibia Secondary Technical School*. Loudima, Congo: 20 April – 10 May 1982.

United Nations Institute for Namibia (UNIN).*Manpower Estimates and Development Implications for Namibia*. Namibia Study Series, No. 1. Based on the work of R.H. Green. Lusaka: United Nations Institute for Namibia, 1978.

_____. *Constitutional Options for Namibia: A Historical Perspective.* Namibia Study Series, No. 2. Based on the work of M.D. Bomani and C. Ushewokunze. Lusaka: United Nations Institute for Namibia, 1979.

_____. *Toward a Language Policy for Namibia. English as the Official Language: Perspectives and Strategies.* Namibia Study Series, No. 4. Based on the work of R. Chamberlain, A. Diallo, and E.J. John. Lusaka: United Nations Institute for Namibia, 1981.

_____. *Education Policy for Independent Namibia: Some Fundamental Considerations.* Namibia Study Series, No. 8. Based on the work of M. P. Tjitendero. Lusaka: United Nations Institute for Namibia, 1984.

_____. *Namibia: Perspectives for National Reconstruction and Development.* Lusaka: United Nations Institute for Namibia, 1986.

_____. 'Planning for Namibian Independence: Manpower Development Strategies'. Report to *The International Conference in Support of the Struggle of the Namibian People for Independence.* UNESCO, Paris: 25 – 29 April 1983.

_____. *Report of the Evaluation Team on the Training and Research Activities of the Institute to the Senate.* Lusaka: November 1981.

_____. _____. Lusaka: January 1987.

_____. *Report of the Senate of the UNIN to the UN Council for Namibia and the Secretary-General of the United Nations, January – December 1978.* Lusaka: United Nations Institute for Namibia, 1978.

_____. _____, *January – December 1979.* Lusaka: UNIN, 1979.

_____. _____, *July 1983 – June 1984.* Lusaka: UNIN, 1984.

_____. _____, *July 1984 – June 1985.* Lusaka: UNIN, 1985.

_____. _____, *July 1985 – August 1986.* Lusaka: UNIN, 1986.

_____. *UNIN Development Studies and Management Secondment Programme.* Lusaka: UNIN, 1985.

_____. *UNIN in Brief.* Lusaka: United Nations Institute for Namibia, undated.

_____. *UNIN Prospectus 1981/82.* Lusaka: United Nations Institute for Namibia, 1981.

_____. *UNIN Prospectus 1985/86.* Lusaka: United Nations Institute for Namibia, 1985.

PARTY DOCUMENTS

Swapo. *Constitution of the South West Africa People's Organisation.* Lusaka: SWAPO Department of Information and Publicity, 1981.

_____. *Education for All: National Integrated Educational System for Emergent Namibia.* A Handbook of the Educational Programme of SWAPO of Namibia. Luanda: SWAPO Department of Information and Publicity, 1984.

_____. *Information on SWAPO: An Historical Profile.* Lusaka: SWAPO Department of Information and Publicity, 1978.

_____. *Information on the People's Resistance 1976 – 1977.* Lusaka: SWAPO Department of Information and Publicity, 1978.

_____. 'Namibia Secondary Technical School, Loudima, People's Republic of Congo'. Architect's Brief. Loudima: 1982.

_____. *Political Programme of the South West Africa People's Organisation.* Lusaka: SWAPO Department of Information and Publicity, 1981.

_____. 'Preliminary Perspectives into Emergent Educational System for Namibia'. Lusaka: SWAPO Department of Education and Culture, May 1982.

NEWSPAPERS

Council of Churches in Namibia and the Repatriation Resettlement and Reconstruction (CCN/RRR) Weekly Newsletter

The Daily Telegraph (London)

The Financial Times (London)

The Guardian (London)

The Independent (London)

The Namibian

The Times (London)

The Times Educational Supplement (London)

The Weekly Mail (South Africa)

ZIMBABWE

BOOKS

Chung, F., and Ngara, E. *Socialism, Education and Development: A Challenge to Zimbabwe.* Harare: Zimbabwe Publishing House (Pty) Ltd., 1985.

Colclough, C., and Murray, R. *The Immediate Manpower and Training Needs of an Independent Zimbabwe.* London: Commonwealth Secretariat, 1979.

Government of Zimbabwe. *National Manpower Survey.* Volumes I, II and III. Harare: Ministry of Manpower, Planning and Development, 1981.

_____. *Annual Review of Manpower 1983.* Volume I. Harare: Ministry of Labour, Manpower Planning and Social Welfare, 1983.

_____. *Annual Review of Manpower 1984.* Harare: Ministry of Labour, Manpower Planning and Social Welfare, 1984.

_____. *Annual Review of Manpower 1985.* Harare: Ministry of Labour, Manpower Planning and Social Welfare, 1985.

_____. *Manpower Information Services.* Vol. I (January 1981).

_____. _____. Vol. 1, No. 2 (November 1981).

_____. _____. Vol. 2, Nos. 1 and 2 (May/June 1982).

_____. _____. Vol. 2, No.3 (October 1982).

_____. _____. Vol. 3, No. 1 (June 1983).

_____. _____. Vol. 3, No. 2 (November 1983).

_____. *Statistical Year-book 1985 of Zimbabwe.* Harare: Central Statistical Office, 1985.

_____. *Statistical Year-book 1987 of Zimbabwe.* Harare: Central Statistical Office, 1987.

O'Callaghan, M. *Southern Rhodesia: the Effects of a Conquest Society on Education, Culture and Information.* Paris: UNESCO, 1977.

Republic of Zimbabwe. *Transitional National Development Plan 1982/1983 – 1984/85.* Volumes I and II. Harare: Government Printer, November 1982 and May 1983.

Riddell, R. *From Rhodesia to Zimbabwe: Education for Employment.* London: Catholic Institute for International Relations, 1980.

Stoneman, C. *From Rhodesia to Zimbabwe: Skilled Labour and Future Needs.* London: Catholic Institute for International Relations, 1978.

_____., ed. *Zimbabwe's Inheritance.* London: College Press and Macmillan Press, 1981.

United Nations Development Programme. *Zimbabwe: Towards a New Order: An Economic and Social Survey.* UNDP/UNCTAD Project PAF/78/010. New York: United Nations, 1980.

Whitsun Foundation. *A Programme for National Development. Data Bank: Education and Training.* Project 1.05. Salisbury: Whitsun Foundation, 1977.

_____. *Manpower Inventory Study of Zimbabwe, 1980.* Part I, Manpower Data Bank of Zimbabwe, Vol. I. Harare: Whitsun Foundation, April 1980.

Zvobgo, R. *Transforming Education: The Zimbabwean Experience.* Harare: The College Press, 1986.

ARTICLES, CONFERENCES, PUBLICATIONS, REPORTS AND SEMINARS

Atkinson, N.D. (a) 'Racial Integration in Zimbabwean Schools'. Harare: University of Zimbabwe, Faculty of Education, 1980.

_____. (b) 'Zimbabwe's Educational Resources'. Harare: University of Zimbabwe, Faculty of Education, 1980.

_____. _____. Harare: University of Zimbabwe, Faculty of Education, 1983.

_____., *et al.* 'Report of an Investigation into the Possibilities for Educational Development in Rhodesia-Zimbabwe after a Political Settlement'. Salisbury: University of Rhodesia, Faculty of Education, April 1978.

British Council. *Education Profile Rhodesia.* London: The British Council, October 1978.

Broby, M.L. 'Can Rhodesia Survive an Exodus of Skilled White Manpower'. Salisbury: University of Rhodesia, 1978.

Cameron, J., Adams, S., and Ntiro, S. 'Zimbabwe: Reorganization of the Ministry of Education and Culture, and Allied Matters'. Harare: 10 July 1980 – 23 August 1980.

Chidzero, B.T.G. *Education and the Challenge of Independence.* Geneva: International University Exchange Fund, August 1977.

Clarke, D.G. *The Patterns of White Emigration/Immigration and their Effects on the Zimbabwean Economy.* Patriotic Front Seminar, Paper No. 8. Dar-es-Salaam: 5 – 9 November 1978.

Davies, R. *External Zimbabwean Manpower Supplies: A Partial Assessment Based upon IUEF Data.* Patriotic Front Seminar, Paper No. 7. Dar es Salaam: 5 – 9 November 1978.

Dube, K.L. 'Educational System in Colonial Zimbabwe'. *Zimbabwe: Towards a New Order: An Economic and Social Survey,* Volume II, Working Papers pp. 315 – 340. New York: United Nations, 1980.

Faruqee, R. *Social Infrastructure and Services in Zimbabwe.* World Bank Staff Working Paper No. 495. Washington: The World Bank, 1981.

Foley, G. 'The Zimbabwean Political Economy and Education, 1980 – 1982'. Henderson Seminar, Vol. 3, No. 2, Paper No. 52. Harare: University of Zimbabwe, Department of History, August 1982.

Gillespie, R.R. and Collins, C.B. 'Education in Zimbabwe', *Education and Society,* Vol. 3, No. 2 – Vol. 4, No. 1 (1986), 62 – 68.

Government of Zimbabwe. *Zimbabwe Conference on Reconstruction and Development (ZIMCORD).* Harare: 23 – 27 March 1981.

_____. *Education in Zimbabwe – Past, Present and Future.* A selection of papers from a seminar sponsored by the Ministry of Education and Culture and the Dag Hammerskjold Foundation, University of Zimbabwe. Harare: 27 August – 7 September 1981.

_____. *National Report: Zimbabwe. Development of Education: 1981 – 1983.* Report for presentation at the Thirty-Ninth Session of the International Conference on Education. Geneva: October 1984.

_____. *National Report: Zimbabwe. Development of Education: 1984 – 1986.* Report for presentation at the Fortieth Session of the International Conference on Education. Geneva: 1986.

_____. *National Report: Zimbabwe. Development of Education: 1984 – 1987.* Report for presentation at the UNESCO General Conference, Twenty-Fourth Session. Paris: October – November 1987.

_____. *Zimbabwe: Review of Education 1959 – 1979 Current Problems and Prospects for the Next 20 Years.* Country Paper Prepared for MINEDAF V Conference of Ministers of Education and those Responsible for Economic Planning of African Member States on Education Policy and Co-operation. Harare: 28 June – 3 July 1982.

International Institute for Educational Planning. *Report of Pilot Study, Education in Zimbabwe: Sector Analysis.* IIEP/Prg.RG/82.067. Paris: IIEP, 11 March 1982.

Mandaza, I. 'Education in Zimbabwe: The Colonial Framework and the Response of the National Liberation Movement'. *Zimbabwe: Towards a New Order: An Economic and Social Survey*, Volume II Working Papers pp. 341 – 400. New York: United Nations, 1980.

Maphosa, N., Manuimo, E., Andersson, G., Larsson, K-A., and Oden, B. *Public Service Training Needs and Resources in Zimbabwe.* Swedish International Development Authority, Education Division Documents, No. 23. Stockholm: SIDA, May 1985.

Maravanyika, O.E. 'School Management and Nation Building in a Newly Independent State'. *World Yearbook of Education 1986: The Management of Schools*, pp. 199 – 210. Edited by E. Hoyle and A. McMahon. London: Kogan and Page, 1986.

Mawande, N.K. 'Senior Recruitment in the Public Service'. *Report on Development Administration and Management: Training Workshops for Assistant Secretaries and Chief Executive Officers from the Government of Zimbabwe, Organised by the Government of Zimbabwe, Ministry of the Public Service, Management Training Bureau and the German Foundation for International Development Public Administration Promotion Centre*, pp. 293 – 303. Harare: German Foundation for International Development, 20 September 1982 – 18 March 1983.

Moyo, N.P. 'The Economic Crisis and Recent Trends in Public Sector Employment and Pay in Zimbabwe'. *Conference on Economic Policies and Planning under Crisis Conditions in Developing Countries*, Paper No. 24. Harare: University of Zimbabwe, Department of Economics, 2 – 5 September 1985.

Mumbengegwi, S.C. *Zimbabwe: A Diagnosis of an Educational System in Rapid Change.* IIEP/TP.81/2. Paris: International Institute for Educational Planning, 23 June 1981.

Murapa, R. 'Political Neutrality and the Public Service'. *Report on Development Administration and Management: Training Workshops for Assistant Secretaries and Chief Executive Officers from the Government of Zimbabwe, Organised by the Government of Zimbabwe, Ministry of the Public Service, Management Training Bureau and the German Foundation for International Development Public Administration Promotion Centre*, pp. 193 – 205. Harare: German Foundation for International Development, 20 September 1982 – 18 March 1983.

_____. 'Race and the Public Service in Zimbabwe: 1890 – 1983'. *The Political Economy of Zimbabwe*, pp. 55 – 80. Edited by M.G. Schatzberg. New York: Praeger Publishers, 1984.

Mutumbuka, Z. 'Zimbabwe's Educational Challenge'. *Africa Currents*, No. 19/20 (Spring/Summer 1980), 5 – 9.

_____. 'News Notes: Seminar on Education in Zimbabwe: Past, Present and Future'. *Development Dialogue*, Nos. 1 – 2 (1982), 165 – 174.

Nhundu, J.T. 'Education System in Zimbabwe Refugee Schools in Mozambique'. Report to the *Seminar on Education in Zimbabwe – Past, Present and Future,* University of Zimbabwe. Harare: 27 August – 7 September 1981.

Patriotic Front. *Zimbabwe Manpower Survey.* Volumes I and II. Patriotic Front Seminar, Dar-es-Salaam 5 – 9 November 1978. Geneva: International University Exchange Fund, 1978.

Raftopoulos, B. (a) 'Human Resource Development and the Problem of Labour Utilisation'. *Zimbabwe: The Political Economy of Transition 1980 – 1986,* pp. 275 – 317. Edited by I. Mandaza. Harare: Jongwe Press, 1987.

_____. (b) 'Problems in Education, Training and Employment since 1980'. *Teachers' Forum,* Vol. 15, No. 11 (November 1987), 27 – 30.

_____. *Problems in Research in a Post-Colonial State: The Case of Zimbabwe.* Zimbabwe Institute of Development Studies, Paper No. 9. Harare: ZIDS, March 1988.

Republic of Zimbabwe. 'National Report on Education in Zimbabwe' at the UNESCO General Conference, Twenty-Fourth Session. Paris: October – November 1987.

Robinson, B. and Shortlidge, R.L., Jr. *Draft Preliminary Report of Education and Training in Zimbabwe.* Washington: United States Agency for International Development, 21 November 1980.

Secretary for Education. *Annual Report of the Secretary for Education for the Year Ended 31 December 1979.* Salisbury: Government Printer, 1980.

_____. *Annual Report of the Secretary for Education for the Year Ended 31 December 1980.* Harare: Government Printer, 1982.

_____. *Annual Report of the Secretary for Education for the Year Ended 31 December 1981.* Harare: Government Printer, 1983.

_____. *Annual Report of the Secretary for Education for the Year Ended 31 December 1982.* Harare: Government Printer, 1984.

_____. *Annual Report of the Secretary for Education for the Year Ended 31 December 1983.* Harare: Government Printer, 1984.

_____. *Annual Report of the Secretary for Education for the Year Ended 31 December 1984.* Harare: Government Printer, 1985.

_____. *Annual Report of the Secretary for Education for the Year Ended 31 December 1985.* Harare: Government Printer, 1986.

_____. *Annual Report of the Secretary for Education for the Year Ended 31 December 1986.* Harare: Government Printer, 1987.

Shamuyarira, N. 'Educational and Social Transformation in Zimbabwe', *Development Dialogue,* No. 2 (1978), 58 – 72.

University of Zimbabwe. *Prospectus 1987.* Harare: University of Zimbabwe, 1987.

Zimbabwe Institute of Public Administration and Management. *ZIPAM's Mission.* Harare: ZIPAM, undated.

Zvobgo, R. 'Education and the Challenge of Independence'. *Zimbabwe: The Political Economy of Transition 1980 – 1986,* pp. 319 – 354. Edited by I. Mandaza. Harare: Jongwe Press, 1987.

EDUCATIONAL AND PUBLIC ADMINISTRATION

BOOKS

Baron, G. *et al.* eds. *Educational Administration: International Perspectives.* United States: Rand Mc Nally, 1969.

Campbell, R.F., Corbally, J.E., and Nystrand, R.O. *Introduction to Educational Administration.* Newton, Massachusetts, Allyn and Bacon Inc., 1983.

Cohen, L., and Manion, L. *Research Methods in Education.* London: Croom Helm, 1986.

Coombs, P.H. *The World Educational Crisis: A Systems Analysis.* Oxford: Oxford University Press, 1968.

_____. *The World Crisis in Education: The View from the Eighties.* Oxford: Oxford University Press, 1985.

Friesen, D., Farine, A., and Collins Meek, J. *Educational Administration: A Comparative View.* Edmonton, Canada: Department of Educational Administration, University of Alberta, 1980.

Gant, G.F. *Development Administration: Concepts, Goals and Methods.* Wisconsin: University of Wisconsin Press, 1979.

Glatter, R. *Management Development for the Education Profession.* London: George G. Harrap and Co. Ltd., 1972.

Guruge, A.W.P. *A Functional Analysis of Educational Administration in Relation to Educational Planning.* Paris: International Institute for Educational Planning, 1969.

Haag, D. *The Right to Education: What Kind of Management?* Paris: UNESCO, 1982.

Hatchard, D.B. *The Theory Problem in Educational Administration.* Australia: Institute for Higher Education, Armidale, 1980.

Hughes, M., ed. *Administering Education: International Challenge.* London: The Athlone Press of the University of London, 1975.

_____. *Leadership in the Management of Education: A Handbook for Educational Supervisors.* London: Education Division, Commonwealth Secretariat, 1981.

Husen, T., and Postlethwaite, T.N., eds. *International Encyclopaedia of Education* Volume 6. Oxford: Pergamon Press, 1985.

Makulu, H.F. *Education, Development and Nation-building in Independent Africa.* London: SCM Press, 1971.

Mathur, H.M. *Administering Development in the Third World.* New Delhi: Sage Publications, 1986.

Miklos, E. *Training in Common for Education, Public and Business Administrators.* Columbus, Ohio: University Council for Educational Administration, 1972.

Musaazi, J.C.S. *The Theory and Practice of Educational Administration.* Nigeria: The Macmillan Press Ltd., 1982.

Reilly, W. *Training Administrators for Development: An Introduction to Public Servants and Government Training Officers.* London: Heinemann, 1979.

Rodwell, S. (a) *Training Third World Educational Administrators: Methods and Materials. A Guide to the Literature.* London: University of London Institute of Education, 1986.

_____. (b) *Training Third World Educational Administrators: Methods and Materials. Project Listing: National and International Research and Development Activities Concerned with the Training of Educational Administrators and Related Training Areas and Issues.* London: University of London, Institute of Education, 1986.

United Nations Educational, Scientific and Cultural Organization (UNESCO). *Educational Reforms: Experiences and Prospects.* Paris: UNESCO, 1979.

Vos, A. J., and Barnard, S. S. *Comparative and International Education for Student Teachers.* Durban/Pretoria: Butterworth Publishers (Pty) Ltd., 1984.

Williamson, B. *Education, Social Structure and Development: A Comparative Analysis.* London: Macmillan, 1979.

World Bank. *Education: Sector Policy Paper.* Washington, D.C.: The World Bank, April 1980.

_____. *Education in Sub-Saharan Africa: Policies for Adjustment, Revitalization, and Expansion.* Washington, D.C.: The World Bank, 1988.

_____. *World Development Report 1990.* New York: Oxford University Press, 1990.

ARTICLES, REPORTS, SEMINARS, SYMPOSIA AND WORKSHOPS

Adams, R.S. 'The Administration of Reform: Inferences Drawn from the Study of Educational Innovations'. *The Generalisation of Educational Innovations: the Administrator's Perspective,* pp. 35 – 67. Contributions to a workshop held at the International Institute for Educational Planning. Paris: 8 – 10 December 1980.

Allama Iqbal Open University. *Educational Planning and Management.* EPM 503 M.A. Volume III. *Plan Implementation and Management.* Islamabad: Allama Iqbal Open University, 1979.

_____. _____. EPM 501. Volume I. *Concepts of Educational Planning.* Islamabad, Allama Iqbal Open University, 1979.

Asian Programme of Educational Innovation for Development (APEID). *Technical Working Group Meeting on the Preparation of Key Personnel in Administrative and Supervisory Positions for Support to Innovations in the Teaching and Learning Process.* Seoul: UNESCO Regional Office for Education in Asia, 29 September – 11 October 1980.

Ayman, I. 'Problems of Training in Educational Administration'. *Bulletin of the UNESCO Regional Office for Education in Asia,* No. 15 (June 1974), 219 – 227.

Bernede, J.F. 'Towards a New Approach to the Training of Educational Administrators'. *Training Programmes in Educational Administration: Symposium on Management and Administration of Educational Services and Establishments.* Paris: UNESCO, July 1976.

_____. 'Training Educational Administrators in Central America'. *Prospects: Quarterly Review of Education,* Volume 7 No. 1 (1977), 113 – 117.

Boundy, K. 'Management and Administration of Educational Services and Establishments'. *UNESCO Symposium on the Management and Administration of Educational Services and Establishments.* Paris: UNESCO, 26 – 30 July 1976.

Cistone, P.J. 'School Boards and the Political Fact'. *Conference on the Politics of Education: Some Main Themes and Issues.* Toronto: Ontario Institute for Studies in Education, May 28 – 30, 1972..

Chinapah, V. 'Educational Planning, Administration and Management in Africa: A Regional Study of Achievements, Shortcomings and Future Challenges'. Working document for *The International Congress on Planning and Management of Educational Development.* Mexico: 26 – 30 March 1990.

Commonwealth Secretariat. *Eighth Commonwealth Education Conference Report.* Colombo, Sri Lanka: 5 – 13 August 1980.

Coombe, T. 'Integral Planning for the Staffing Function in Education'. Paper presented at *The International Conference on Education and Development: Sharing our Experiences.* London: Institute of Education, University of London, 15 – 17 March 1988.

_____. *A Consultation on Higher Education in Africa.* Report to the Ford Foundation and the Rockefeller Foundation. New York: January 1991.

Duran, G.R. 'A Conceptual Framework for the Reform of Educational Administration'. *Prospects: Quarterly Review of Education,* Vol. 7, No. 1 (1977), 65 – 72.

Elboim-Dror, R. 'The Resistance to Change of Educational Administration'. *Futures: The Journal of Forecasting and Planning,* Vol. 3, No. 3 (September 1971), 201 – 214.

Guruge, A.W.P. and Berstecher, D.G. 'Personnel Management'. *Notes, Comments ... (Child, Family, Community) Digest,* No. 9 (1984), 25 – 43.

International Institute for Educational Planning. *XXVIth Annual Training Programme in Educational Planning and Administration (190/91).* Paris: IIEP, 1990.

Ishumi, A.G.M. 'The Place of Education in the Economy'. *International Journal of Educational Development,* Vol. 3, No. 3 (1983), 337 – 349.

Kuhanga, N.A. 'The Use of Higher Education Institutions for Training and Research in Education'. *International Journal of Educational Development,* Vol. 3, No. 3 (1983), 313 – 323.

Lourie, S. 'Education and Society: the Problems of Change'. *Prospects: Quarterly Review of Education,* Vol. 4, No. 4 (Winter 1974), 541 – 553.

Lyons, R.F. 'Some Problems in Educational Administration'. *Prospects: Quarterly Review of Education* Vol. 7, No.1 (1977), 58 – 64.

Lungu, G.F. 'Some Critical Issues in the Training of Educational Administrators for Developing Countries in Africa'. *International Journal of Educational Development,* Vol. 3, No. 1 (1983), 85 – 96.

Majasan, J.A. 'Educational Administration in African Countries'. *Educational Administration Bulletin* Vol. 3, No. 1 (Autumn 1974), 26 – 31.

Mbamba, A.M. 'Report on Second Residential Course for the Training of Trainers in Educational Management'. *UNESCO/SIDA Funds-in-Trust Project for the Training of Trainers in Educational Management for Some English-Speaking African Countries (503/RAF/16).* Harare: UNESCO Regional Office for Science and Technology for Africa (ROSTA) (Nairobi), 22 February – 11 March 1988.

_____. 'Report on Sub-Regional Workshop for Trainers in Educational Management'. *UNESCO/SIDA Funds-in-Trust Project for the Training of Trainers in Educational Management for Some English- Speaking African Countries (503/RAF/16).* Arusha: UNESCO Regional Office for Science and Technology in Africa (ROSTA) (Nairobi), 23 April – 11 May 1990..

Malpica, C.N. 'Educational Administration and its Relation with Planning and Research'. *The Fundamentals of Educational Planning,* No. 66. Paris: International Institute for Educational Planning, (June 1980).

_____ and Rassekh, S. *The Generalisation of Educational Innovations: the Administrator's Perspective.* Contributions to a workshop held at the International Institute for Educational Planning, Paris: 8 – 10 December 1980.

Mellor, W.L. 'Some Problems in the Administration of Education'. *Seminar on Education and Development.* International Institute for Educational Planning. Senlis: 6 – 8 October 1980.

Miklos, E. (a) 'Educational Administration in an Era of Transition'. *Educafrica, Bulletin of the UNESCO Regional Office for Education in Africa,* Vol. 1, No. 2 (December 1974), 5 – 9.

_____. (b) *The Training of School Administrators and Supervisors.* Report prepared for the Department of Higher Education and Training of Educational Personnel of UNESCO. Edmonton: University of Alberta, May 1974.

_____. 'Educational Administration: Future Directions'. *Prospects: Quarterly Review of Education,* Vol. 7, No. 1 (1977), 96 – 103.

_____. 'Educational Administration 1959 – 1981: A Profession in Evolution'. *Educational Administration Quarterly,* Vol. 19, No. 3 (Summer 1983), 153 – 177.

Murphy, P.J. 'A New Professional Linkage for Educational Administrators in Developing Countries'. *International Journal of Educational Development,* Vol. 3, No. 2 (1983), 159 – 163.

Ogunniyi, O. 'The Training of Educational Administrators in Africa'. *Educafrica,* Vol. 1, No. 2 (December 1974), 39 – 58.

Paul, S. *Training for Public Administration and Management in Developing Countries: A Review.* World Bank Staff Working Paper No. 584, Management and Development Series, No. 11. Washington, D.C.: The World Bank, 1983.

Reilly, W. 'Management and Training for Development: the Hombe Thesis'. *Public Administration and Development,* Vol. 7 (1987), 25 – 42.

Renon, G. 'Training Administrators and Educational Administration Requirements'. *Prospects: Quarterly Review of Education,* Vol. 7, No. 1 (1977), 73 – 81.

Richardson III, H.J. 'Malawi: Between Black and White Africa'. *Africa Report* Vol. 15, No. 2 (February 1970), 18 – 21.

Singh, R.R., and Guruge, A.W.P. 'Administration of Education in the Asia Region'. *Prospects: Quarterly Review of Education,* Vol. 7, No.1 (1977), 118 – 126.

United Nations Educational, Scientific and Cultural Organization (UNESCO). *Symposium on Management and Administration of Educational Services and Establishments.* Final Report. Paris: 26 – 30 July 1976.

_____. *Functions of Educational Administration.* Training Materials in Educational Planning, Administration and Facilities. Paris: UNESCO Division of Educational Policy and Planning, EPP/TM/05, January 1987.

Walton, J. 'The Dissimilarity of Educational Administration'. *Management in Education: Reader 1, the Management of Organizations and Individuals,* pp. 14 – 19. Edited by V. Houghton, R. Mc Hugh and C. Morgan. United Kingdom: Ward Lock Educational in Association with The Open University, 1975.

Watson, P.E. 'Planner-Administrator Dissonance: A Development Dilemma in Education'. *Educational Planning,* Vol. 1, No. 2 (October 1974), 9 – 17.

Weiler, H. 'Education and Development from the Age of Innocence to the Age of Scepticism'. *Comparative Education,* Vol. 14, No. 3 (October 1978), 179 – 198.

Wilson, M.J. 'Problems of Administrative Change in Formal Education'. *Educafrica,* Vol. 1, No. 2 (1974), 11 – 24.

INTERVIEWS

FRANCE

Course Co-ordinator of the UNESCO International Institute for Educational Planning's Annual Training Programme in Educational Planning and Administration, Paris, 5/01/1988.

Director, UNESCO International Institute for Educational Planning, Paris, 10/01/1988.

GERMANY
Head of Scholarship Programmes for Developing Countries, Otto Benecke Stiftung, Bonn, 22/12/1986.

NAMIBIA
The Academy
Dean, Faculty of Economic and Management Sciences, Windhoek, 1/11/1988.
Deputy Director, Bureau of Management Consultation, Windhoek, 31/10/1988.
Director, Technikon, Windhoek, 31/10/1988.
Director, Bureau of Research, Windhoek, 31/10/1988.
Faculty Officer, Academy Accredited Campuses, Windhoek, 27/11/1988.
Head, College for Out of School Training, Windhoek, 28/10/1988.
Head, Distance Education Section, Windhoek, 1/11/1988.
Lecturer in Educational Administration, Faculty of Education, Windhoek, 31/10/1988.
Lecturer in Public Administration, Technikon, Windhoek, 31/10/1988.
Public Relations Division, Windhoek, 28/10/1988.
Secretary of the Rector, Windhoek, 31/10/1988.

Central Personnel Institution (CPI)
Director of Efficiency and Auxiliary Services, Windhoek, 16/11/1988.
Personnel Services, Windhoek, 14/10/1988.
Training and Publicity Division, Windhoek, 13/10/1988.

Department of National Education (DNE)
Director of Culture, Windhoek, 17/10/1988.
Director of Educational Auxiliary Services, Windhoek, 12/10/1988.
Director of Educational Control, Windhoek, 11 and 12/10/1988.
Head of Formal Education, Windhoek, 6 and 11/10/1988.
Head Subject Adviser, Formal Education, Windhoek, 27/10 and 4/11/1988.
Inspector, Non-Formal Education, Windhoek, 14/10/1988.
Inspector of Education (Bushmen), Windhoek, 14/10/1988.
Subject Adviser (English), Formal Education, Windhoek, 28/10/1988.
Subject Adviser, Non-Formal Education, Windhoek, 2/11/1988.
Subject Adviser (Science), Formal Education, Windhoek, 4/11/1988.

Ministry of Education and Culture (MOEC)
Chief Education Officer, Secondary Education, Windhoek, 3/08/1993.
Chief Education Planner, Windhoek, 2 and 4/08/1993.
Deputy Minister, Windhoek, 5/08/1993.
Director of Administration and Logistics, Windhoek, 4/08/1993.

ODA (UK) Sponsored Consultant and Adviser to the Planning Division, Windhoek, 2/08/1993.

Permanent Secretary, Windhoek, 3/08/1993.

Professional and Resource Development Division, National Institute for Educational Development, Windhoek, 3/08/1993.

Senior Development Adviser, Windhoek, 2/08/1993.

SIDA-sponsored Co-ordinator of Foreign Aid, Windhoek, 3/08/1993.

Under Secretary, Formal Education, Windhoek, 2 and 3/08/1993.

Office of the Prime Minister

Deputy Chief, Training Policies and Co-ordination Division, Directorate of Human Resources Management and Development, Windhoek, 6/08/1993.

Director, Training Policies and Co-ordination Division, Directorate of Human Resources Management and Development, Windhoek, 6/08/1993.

Otto Benecke Stiftung

Scholarship Director, Otto Benecke Stiftung, Windhoek, 21/11/1988.

Scholarships Programme, Otto Benecke Stiftung, Windhoek, 22/11/1988.

University of Namibia

Dean of Studies, Windhoek, 4 and 5/08/1993.

Dean of the Faculty of Education, Windhoek, 6/08/1993.

Director, Centre for Public Service Training, Windhoek, 5/08/1993.

Other

Deputy Director, Herero Directorate of Education and Culture, Windhoek, 17/10/1988.

Director, Department of Formal Education, Council of Churches in Namibia, Windhoek, 20/10/1988.

Director, Rössing Foundation, Windhoek, 18/10/1988.

Director, White Directorate of Education and Culture, Windhoek, 20/10/1988.

Lecturer, Rössing Education Centre, Windhoek, 28/10/1988.

Senior Chief Control Official (Bushmen), Central Government, Windhoek, 12/10/1988.

The University Centre for Studies in Namibia (TUCSIN), Windhoek, 17/10/1988.

UNITED KINGDOM

Administrator, Namibia Refugee Project, London, 18/07/1985.

Central and Southern Africa Department, Overseas Development Administration, London, 1/12/1986.

Chief Project Officer, Fellowship and Training Programme, Commonwealth Secretariat, London, 24/02/1987 and 7/06/1990.

David Simon, Namibian Specialist and Lecturer in Geography and Development Studies at Royal Holloway and Bedford New College, University of London, London, 10/05/1991.

Deputy Representative, United Nations High Commission for Refugees, London, 23/10/1986.

Director, Africa Educational Trust, London, 12/11/1985.

Director, International Extension College (Cambridge), London, 12/11/1985.

Director of Planning of the Namibian Ministry of Education and Culture, London, 11/09/1991.

The Namibian Minister of Education and Culture, London, 8/11/1990.

ZIMBABWE
Ministry of Education and Culture (MOEC)

Deputy Chief Education Officer, Standards Control, Harare, 7/09/1988.

Deputy Chief Education Officer, Teacher Education, Harare, 15/09/1988.

Deputy Secretary for Finance and Administration, Higher Education, Harare, 6/09/1988.

Deputy Secretary for Higher Institutions, Harare, 8/09/1988.

Deputy Secretary for Policy and Planning, Higher Education, Harare, 6/09/1988.

Minister for Primary and Secondary Education, Harare, 8/09/1988.

Secretary for Primary and Secondary Education, Harare, 8/09/1988.

University of Zimbabwe

Lecturer in Education, Faculty of Education, Harare, 13/09/1988.

Secretary of the Faculty of Education, Harare, 13/09/1988.

Other

Director of the Zimbabwe Foundation for Education with Production, Harare, 2/09/1988.

Director of the Zimbabwe Institute of Development Studies, Harare, 1/09/1988.

Director of the Zimbabwe Institute of Public Administration and Management, Harare, 5/09/1988.

INDEX

441